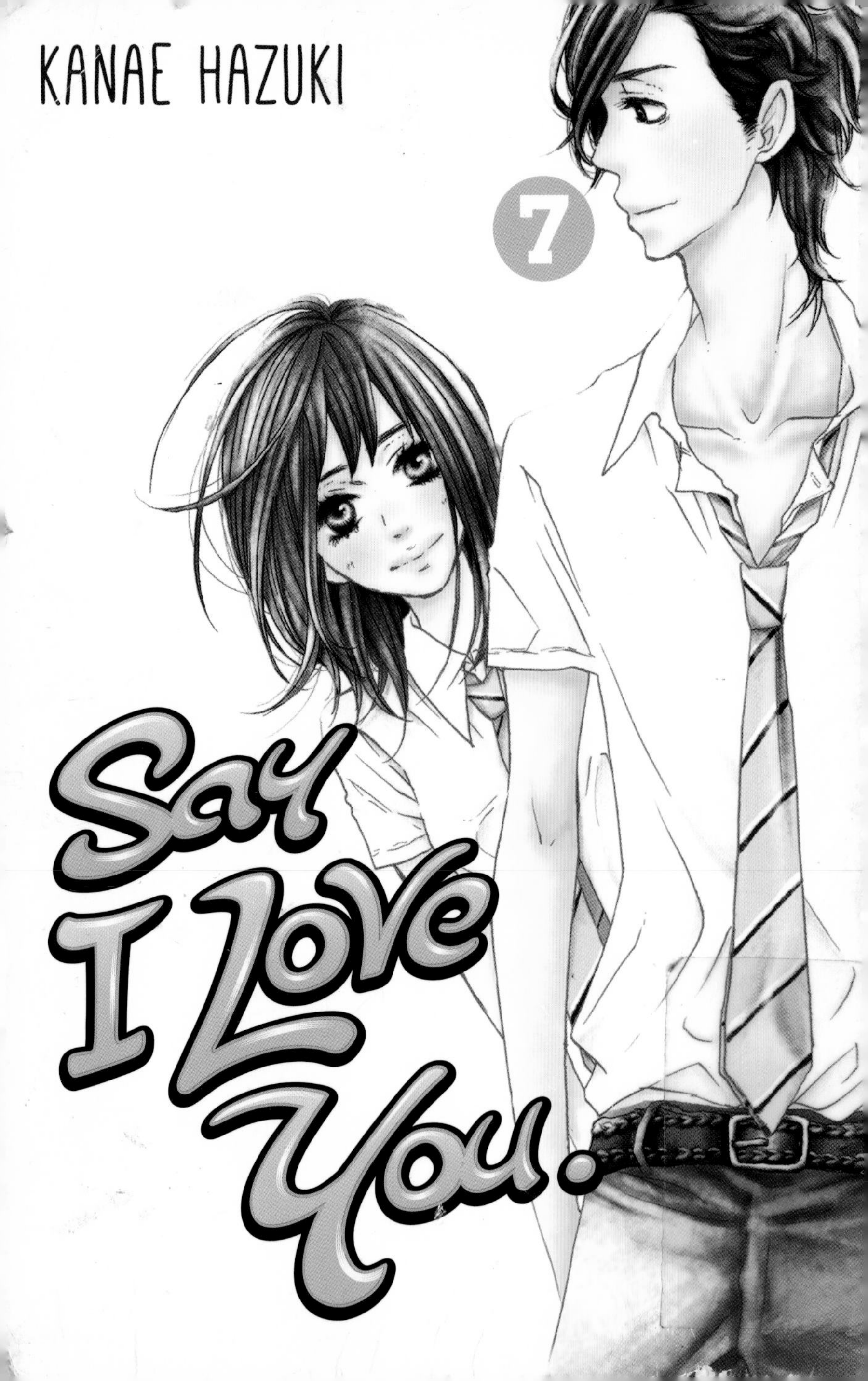
KANAE HAZUKI
7
Say I Love You.

Say I Love You.

7

by
Kanae
Hazuki

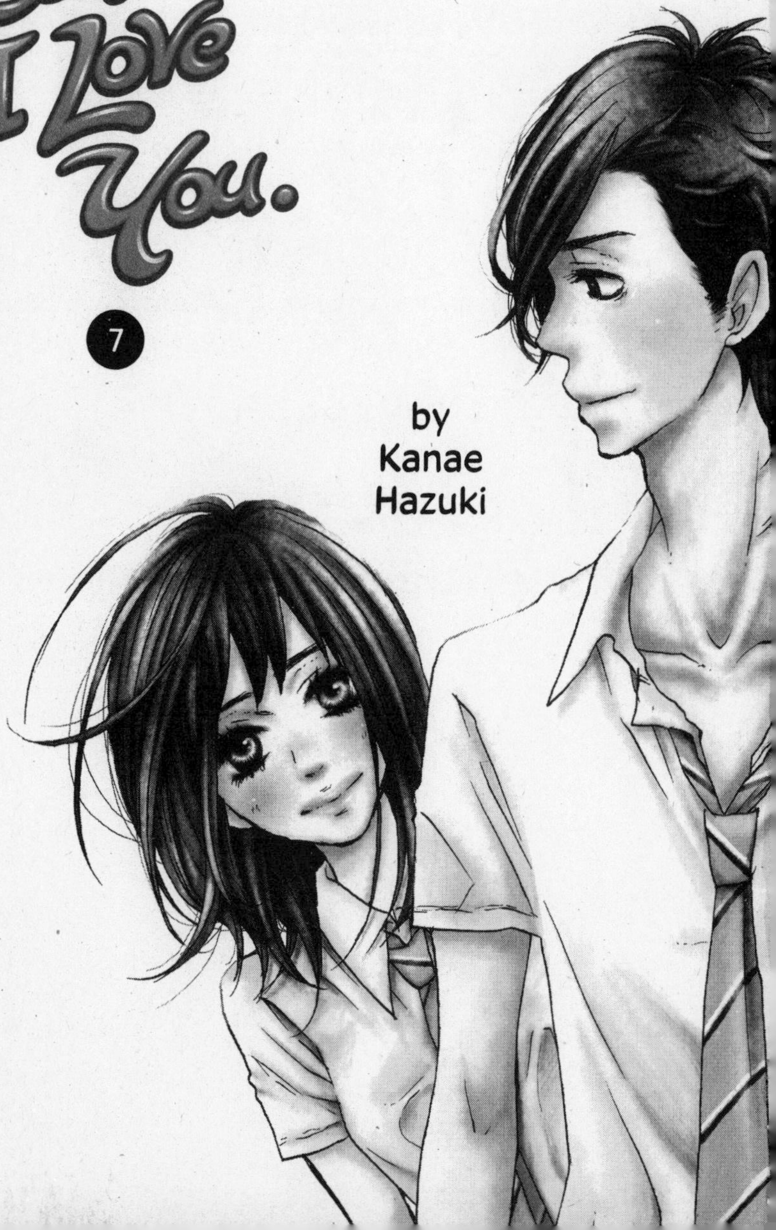

Kanae Hazuki
presents

Chapter 25

Chapter 26

Chapter 27

Chapter 28

C H A R A C T E R S

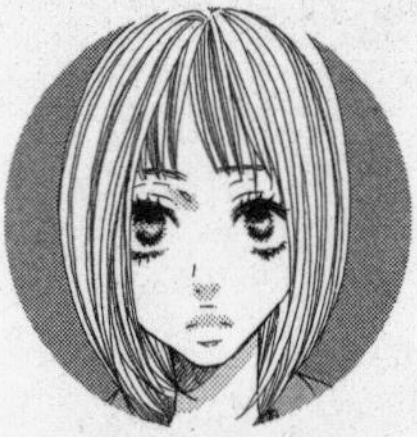

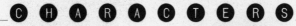

Mei Tachibana

A girl who hasn't had a single friend, let alone a boyfriend, in sixteen years, and has lived her life trusting no one. She finds herself attracted to Yamato, who, for some reason, just won't leave her alone, and they start dating.

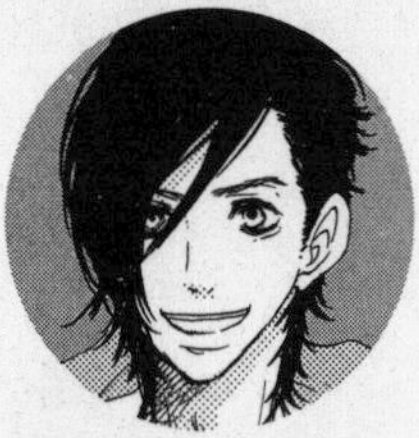

Yamato Kurosawa

The most popular boy at Mei's school. He has the love of many girls, yet for some reason, he is obsessed with Mei, the brooding weirdo girl from another class.

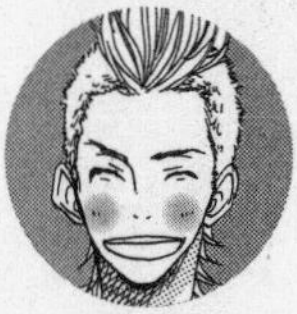

Kai

Yamato's classmate from middle school who had been the victim of bullying. For his own reasons, he started high school a year late. He likes Mei and told her so, but...?

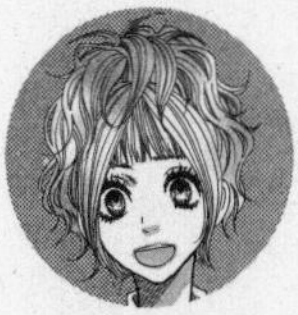

Megumi

An amateur model who has her sights set on Yamato. She transferred to his school and got him a modeling job, and the two gradually grew closer. She was plotting to pull Mei and Yamato apart, but...?

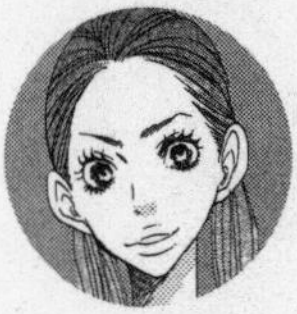

Aiko

She likes Yamato and was jealous of Mei, but now that she has seen Mei trying so hard to confront her own insecurities, she has decided to cheer her on. They were put in the same class in their second year of high school.

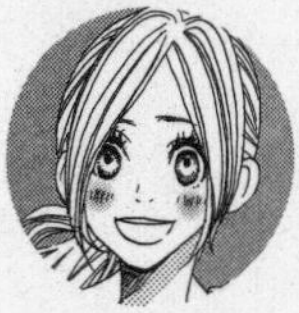

Asami

A girl who treats Mei as a real friend. She had a thing for Yamato, but now she is dating his friend Nakanishi. She and Mei were put in different classes in their second year of high school.

S T O R Y

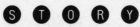

Mei Tachibana spent sixteen years without a single friend or boyfriend. One day she accidentally injured Yamato Kurosawa, the most popular boy in her school. Ironically, that made him like her, and he unilaterally decided that they were friends. He even kissed her like he meant it. Mei was gradually drawn in by Yamato's kindness and sincerity, and they started dating. Gradually, she realized that she was in love. Despite complications such as Megumi's desire for Yamato, and Kai's love of Mei, the two of them reached their first anniversary. During summer vacation, they went on an overnight trip to celebrate, and at last they had their first night alone...?!

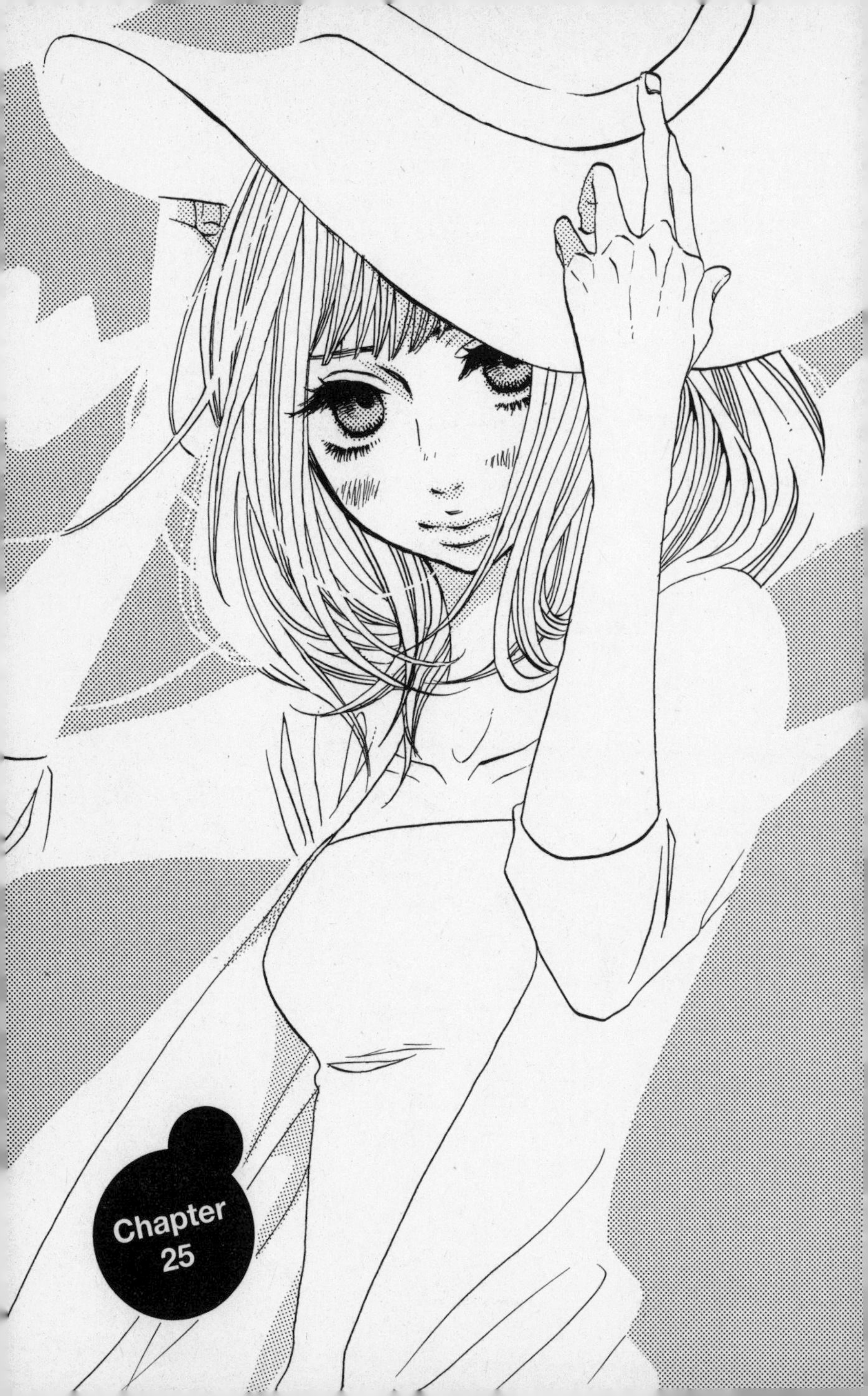
Chapter
25

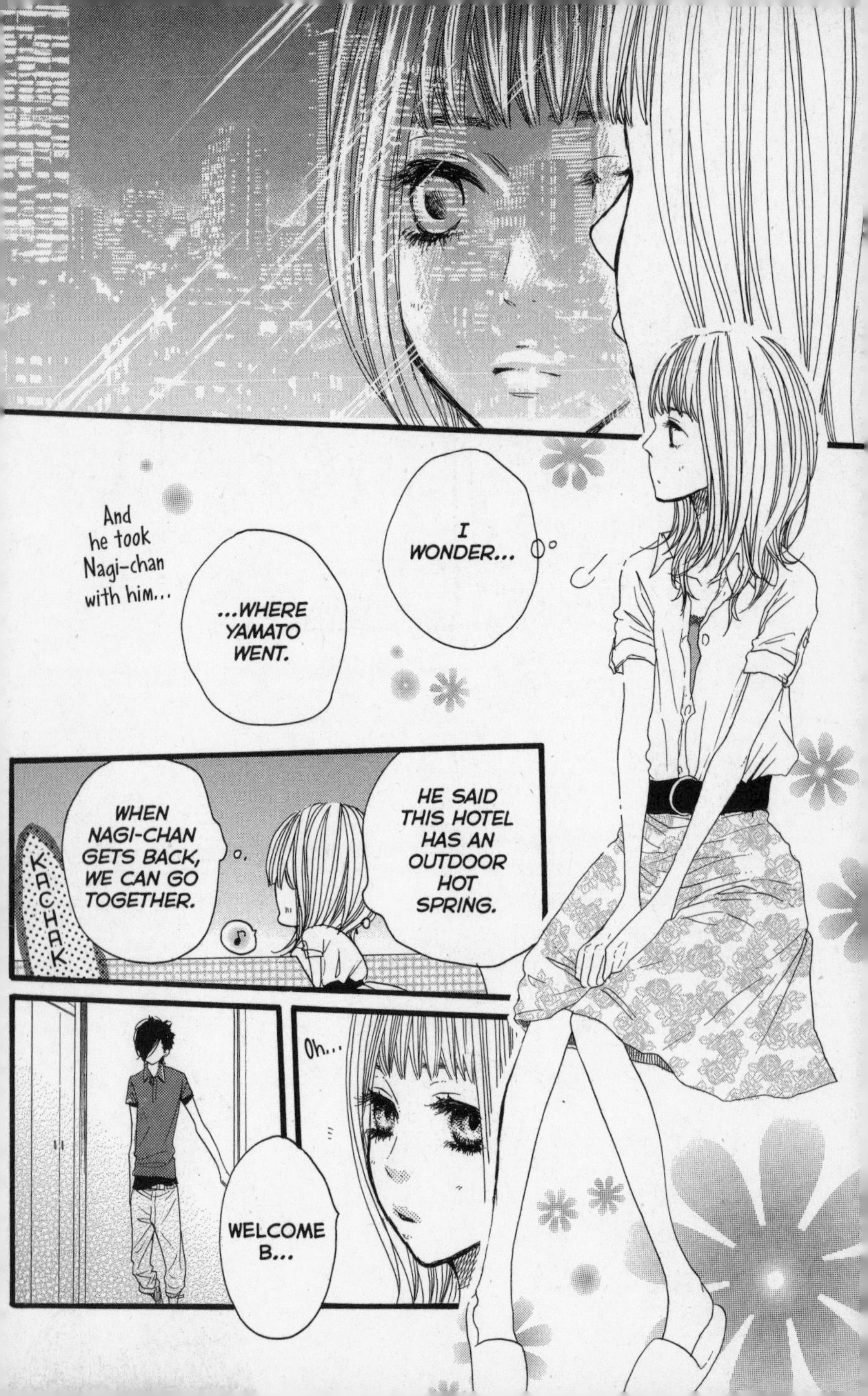
I WONDER...
...WHERE YAMATO WENT.
And he took Nagi-chan with him...
HE SAID THIS HOTEL HAS AN OUTDOOR HOT SPRING.
WHEN NAGI-CHAN GETS BACK, WE CAN GO TOGETHER.
KACHAK
Oh...
WELCOME B...

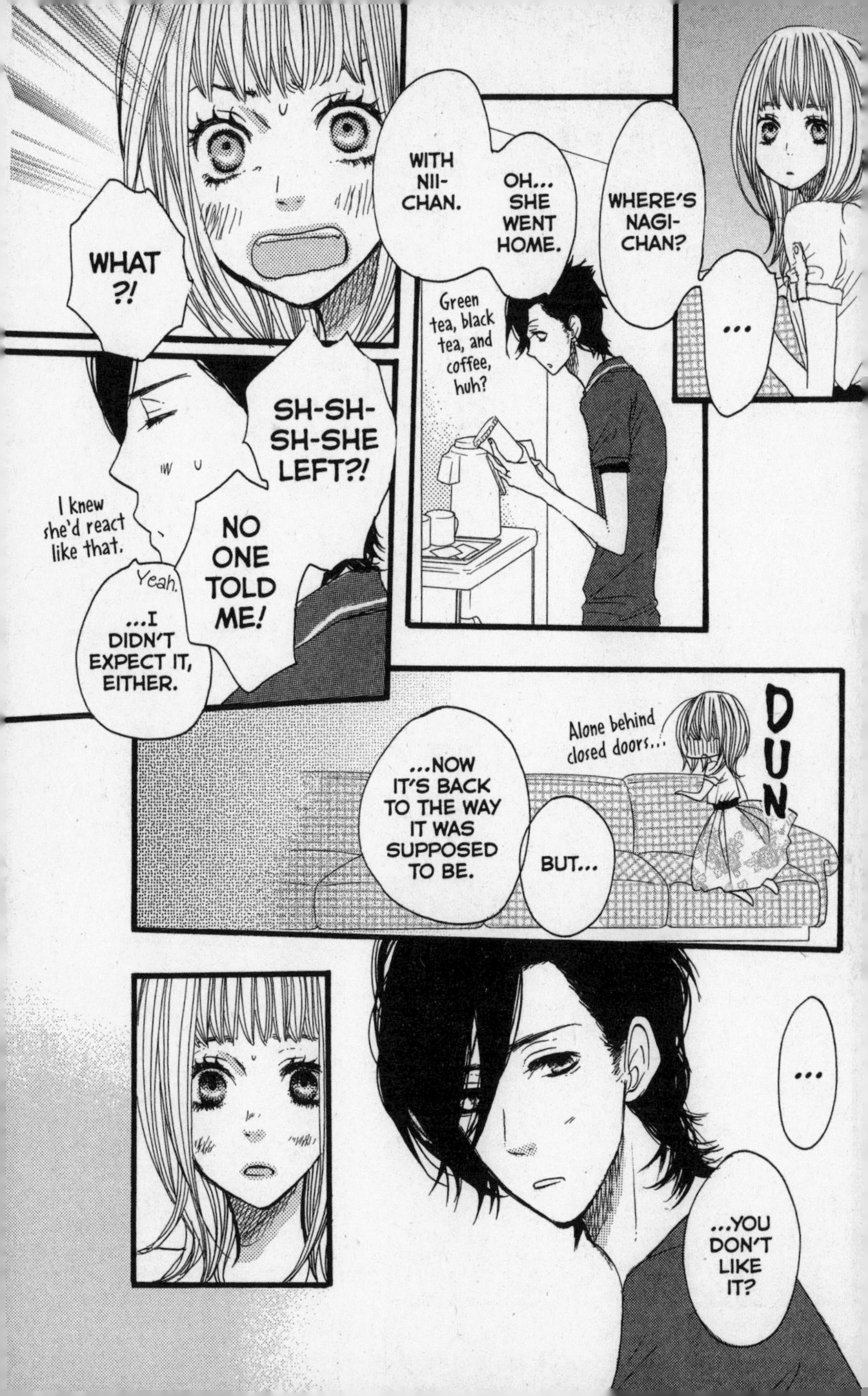
WHERE'S NAGI-CHAN?
...
OH... SHE WENT HOME.
WITH NII-CHAN.
Green tea, black tea, and coffee, huh?
WHAT ?!
SH-SH-SH-SHE LEFT?!
NO ONE TOLD ME!
I knew she'd react like that.
Yeah.
...I DIDN'T EXPECT IT, EITHER.
DUN
Alone behind closed doors...
BUT...
...NOW IT'S BACK TO THE WAY IT WAS SUPPOSED TO BE.
...
...YOU DON'T LIKE IT?

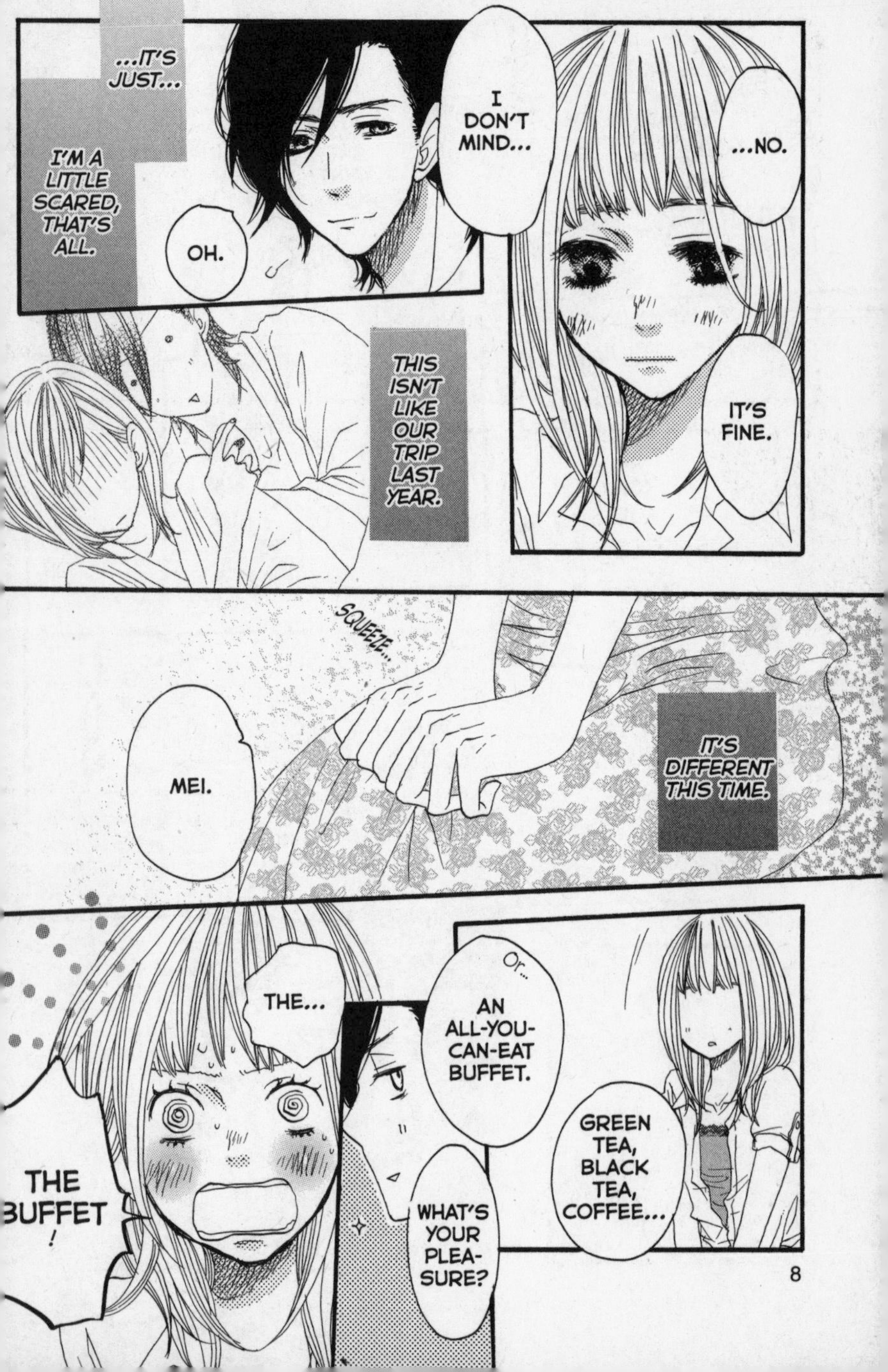
...NO.
I DON'T MIND...
IT'S FINE.
OH.
...IT'S JUST...
I'M A LITTLE SCARED, THAT'S ALL.
THIS ISN'T LIKE OUR TRIP LAST YEAR.
IT'S DIFFERENT THIS TIME.
SQUEEZE...
MEI.
GREEN TEA, BLACK TEA, COFFEE...
Or...
AN ALL-YOU-CAN-EAT BUFFET.
WHAT'S YOUR PLEA-SURE?
THE...
THE BUFFET!

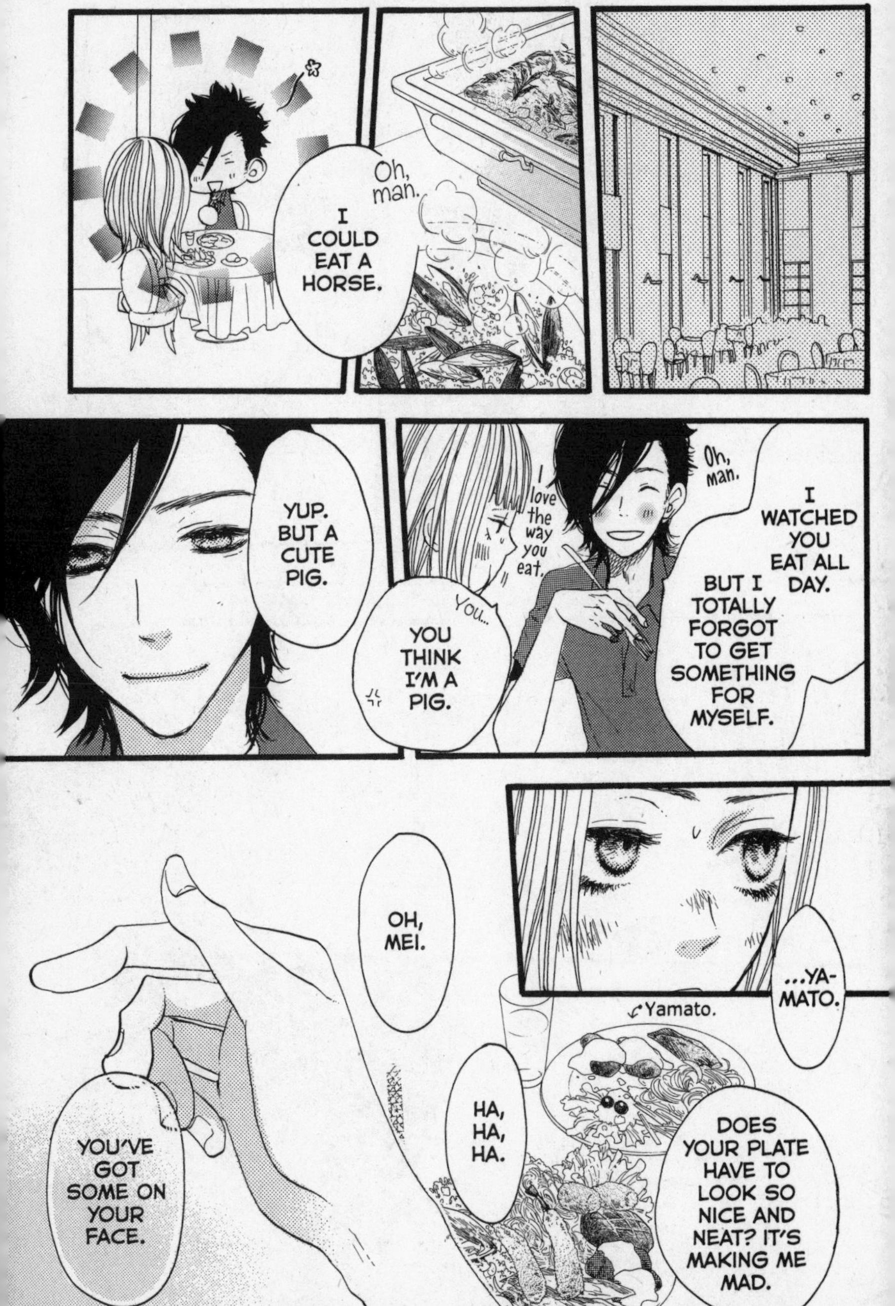
Oh, man.
I COULD EAT A HORSE.
Oh, man.
I WATCHED YOU EAT ALL DAY.
BUT I TOTALLY FORGOT TO GET SOMETHING FOR MYSELF.
I love the way you eat.
You...
YOU THINK I'M A PIG.
YUP. BUT A CUTE PIG.
...YA-MATO.
OH, MEI.
Yamato.
DOES YOUR PLATE HAVE TO LOOK SO NICE AND NEAT? IT'S MAKING ME MAD.
HA, HA, HA.
Mei.
YOU'VE GOT SOME ON YOUR FACE.

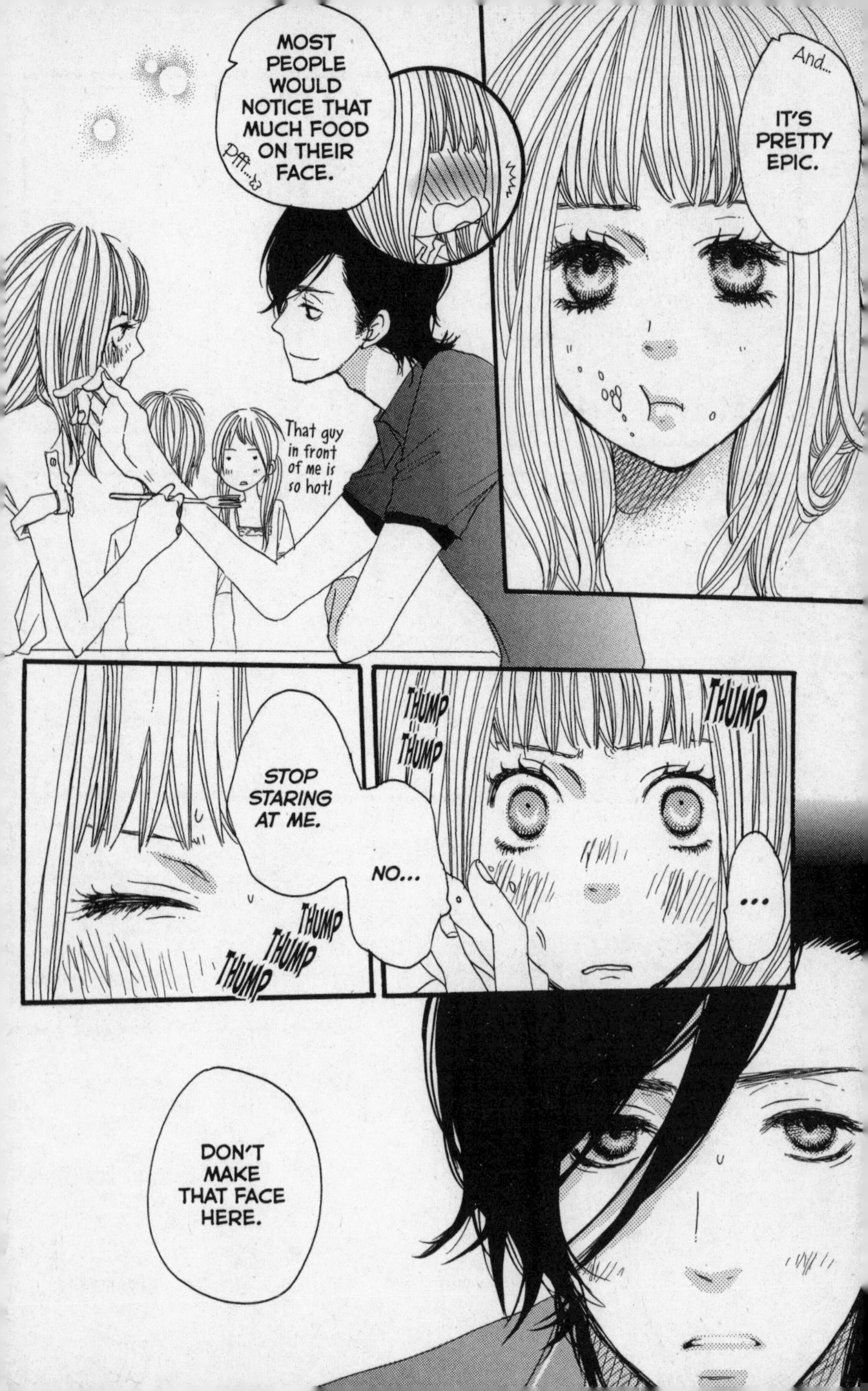
And...
IT'S PRETTY EPIC.
MOST PEOPLE WOULD NOTICE THAT MUCH FOOD ON THEIR FACE.
Pfft...
That guy in front of me is so hot!
THUMP
THUMP THUMP
...
STOP STARING AT ME.
NO...
THUMP THUMP THUMP
DON'T MAKE THAT FACE HERE.

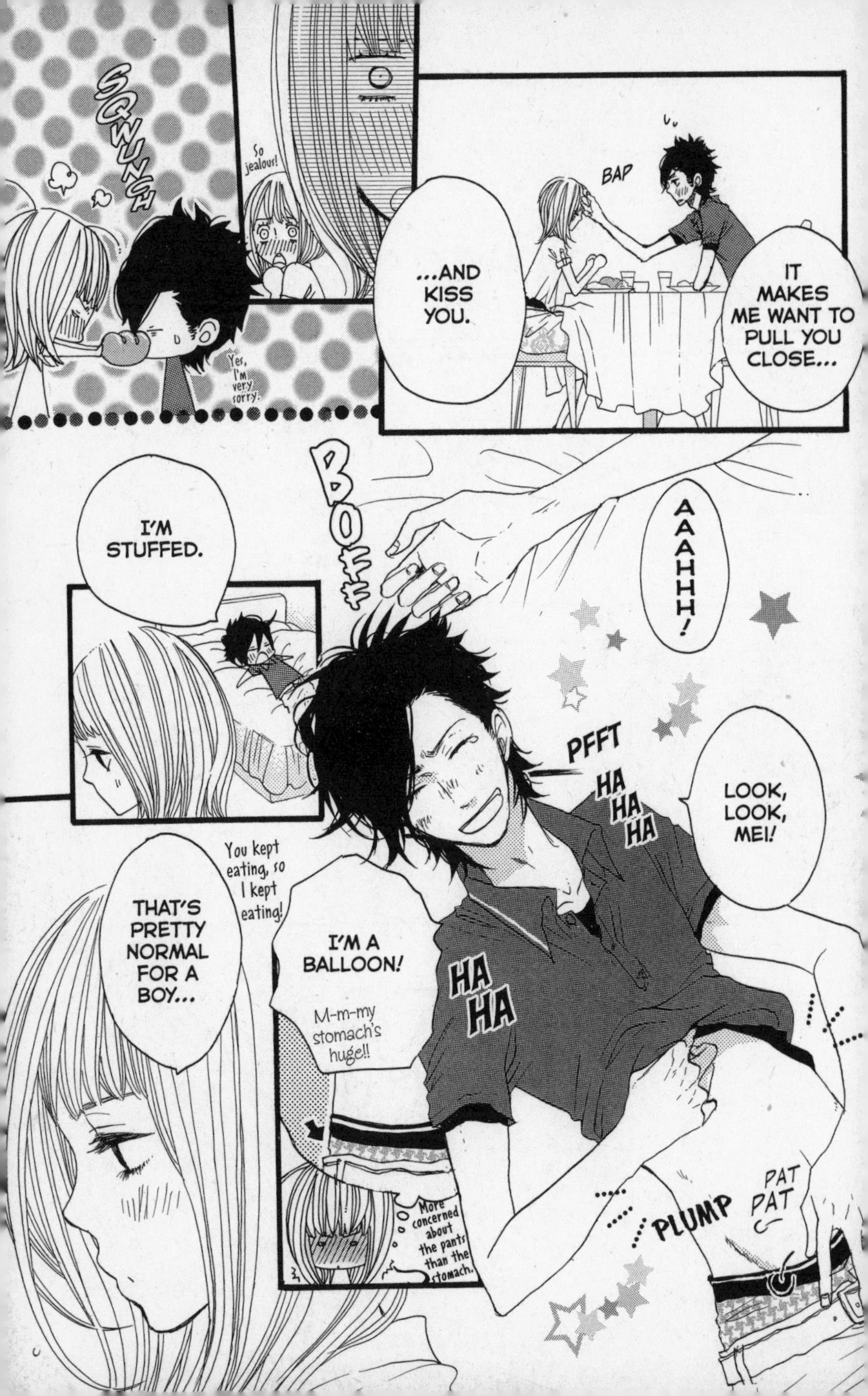
IT MAKES ME WANT TO PULL YOU CLOSE...
BAP
...AND KISS YOU.
So jealous!
SQWUNCH
Yes, I'm very sorry.
I'M STUFFED.
AAAHHH!
BOFF
LOOK, LOOK, MEI!
PFFT
HA HA HA
I'M A BALLOON!
HA HA
M-m-my stomach's huge!!
PAT PAT
PLUMP
You kept eating, so I kept eating!
THAT'S PRETTY NORMAL FOR A BOY...
More concerned about the pants than the stomach.

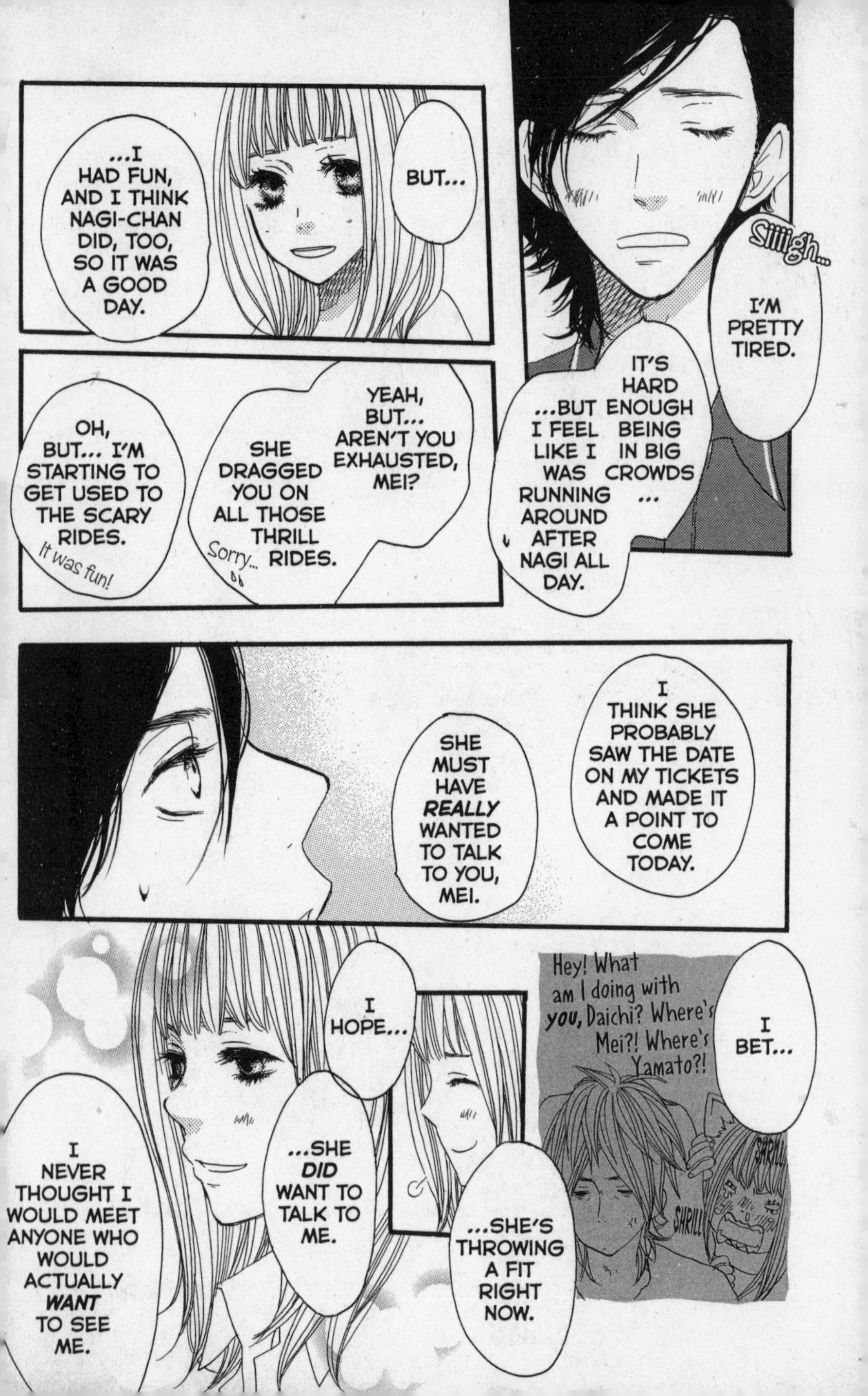
Siiiigh...
I'M PRETTY TIRED.
IT'S HARD ENOUGH BEING IN BIG CROWDS...
...BUT I FEEL LIKE I WAS RUNNING AROUND AFTER NAGI ALL DAY.
BUT...
...I HAD FUN, AND I THINK NAGI-CHAN DID, TOO, SO IT WAS A GOOD DAY.
YEAH, BUT... AREN'T YOU EXHAUSTED, MEI?
SHE DRAGGED YOU ON ALL THOSE THRILL RIDES.
Sorry...
OH, BUT... I'M STARTING TO GET USED TO THE SCARY RIDES.
It was fun!
I THINK SHE PROBABLY SAW THE DATE ON MY TICKETS AND MADE IT A POINT TO COME TODAY.
SHE MUST HAVE *REALLY* WANTED TO TALK TO YOU, MEI.
I BET...
Hey! What am I doing with **you**, Daichi? Where's Mei?! Where's Yamato?!
SHRILL
SHRILL
...SHE'S THROWING A FIT RIGHT NOW.
I HOPE...
...SHE *DID* WANT TO TALK TO ME.
I NEVER THOUGHT I WOULD MEET ANYONE WHO WOULD ACTUALLY *WANT* TO SEE ME.

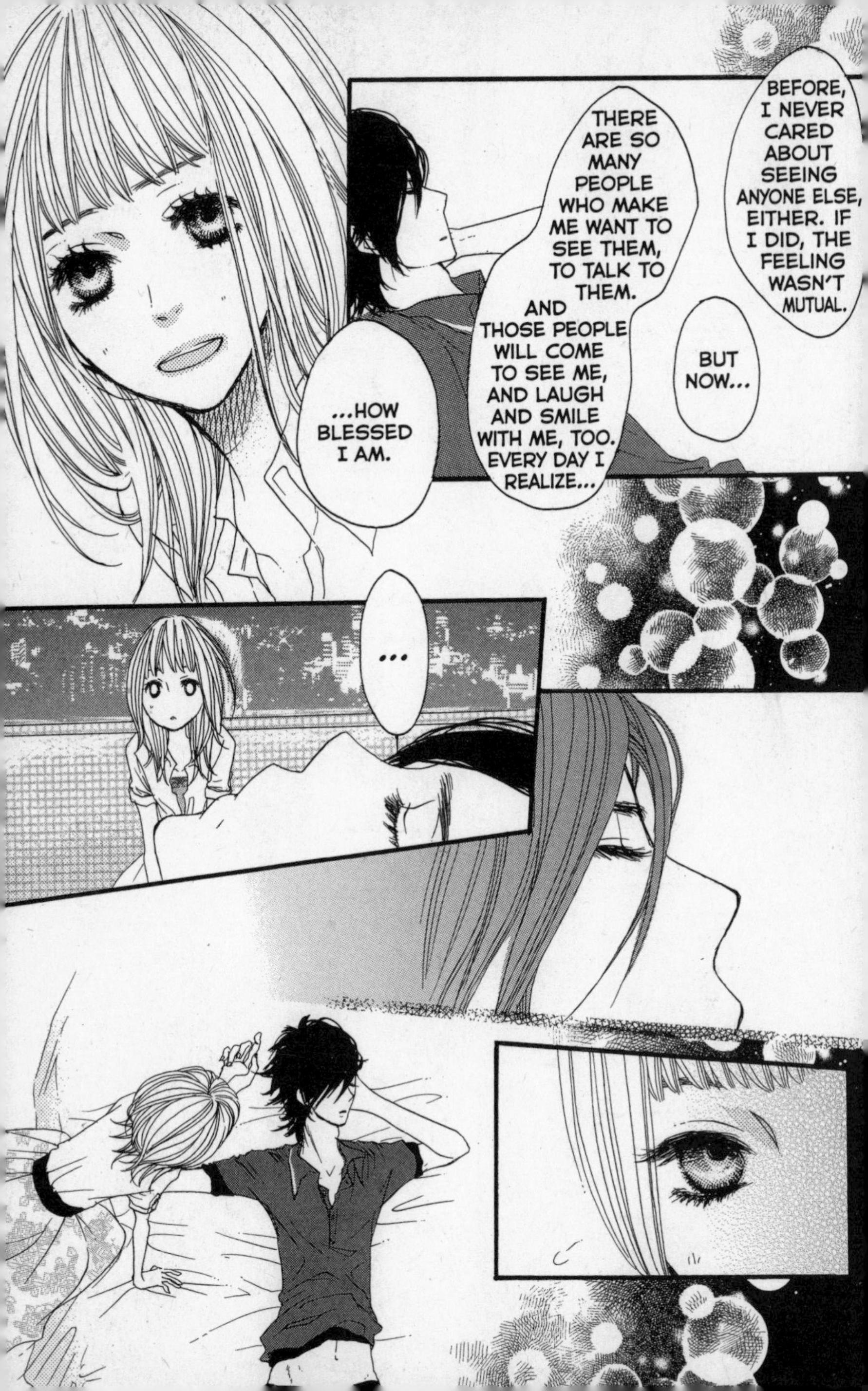
BEFORE, I NEVER CARED ABOUT SEEING ANYONE ELSE, EITHER. IF I DID, THE FEELING WASN'T MUTUAL.
BUT NOW...
THERE ARE SO MANY PEOPLE WHO MAKE ME WANT TO SEE THEM, TO TALK TO THEM.
AND THOSE PEOPLE WILL COME TO SEE ME, AND LAUGH AND SMILE WITH ME, TOO. EVERY DAY I REALIZE...
...HOW BLESSED I AM.
...

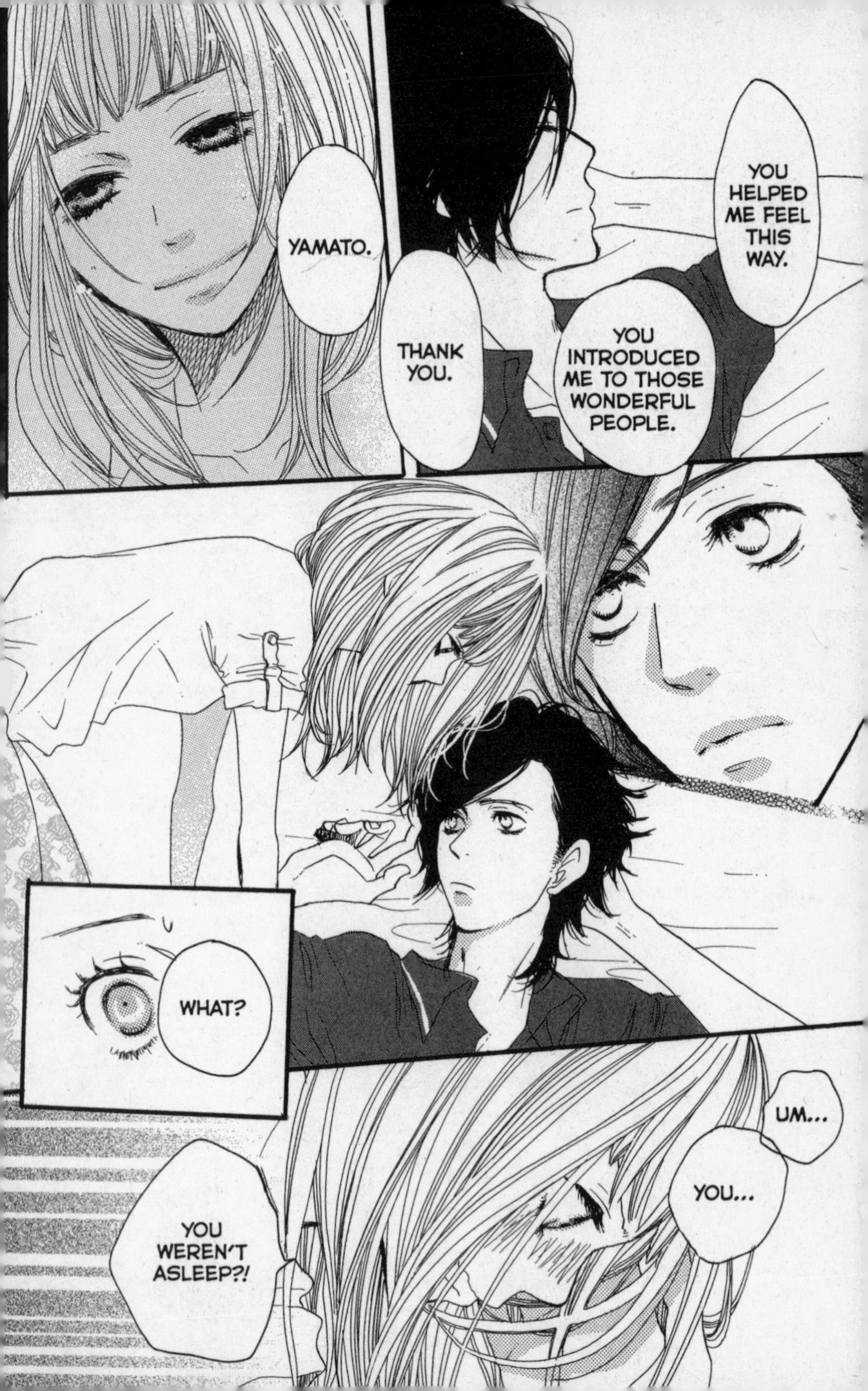
YOU HELPED ME FEEL THIS WAY.
YOU INTRODUCED ME TO THOSE WONDERFUL PEOPLE.
THANK YOU.
YAMATO.
WHAT?
UM...
YOU...
YOU WEREN'T ASLEEP?!

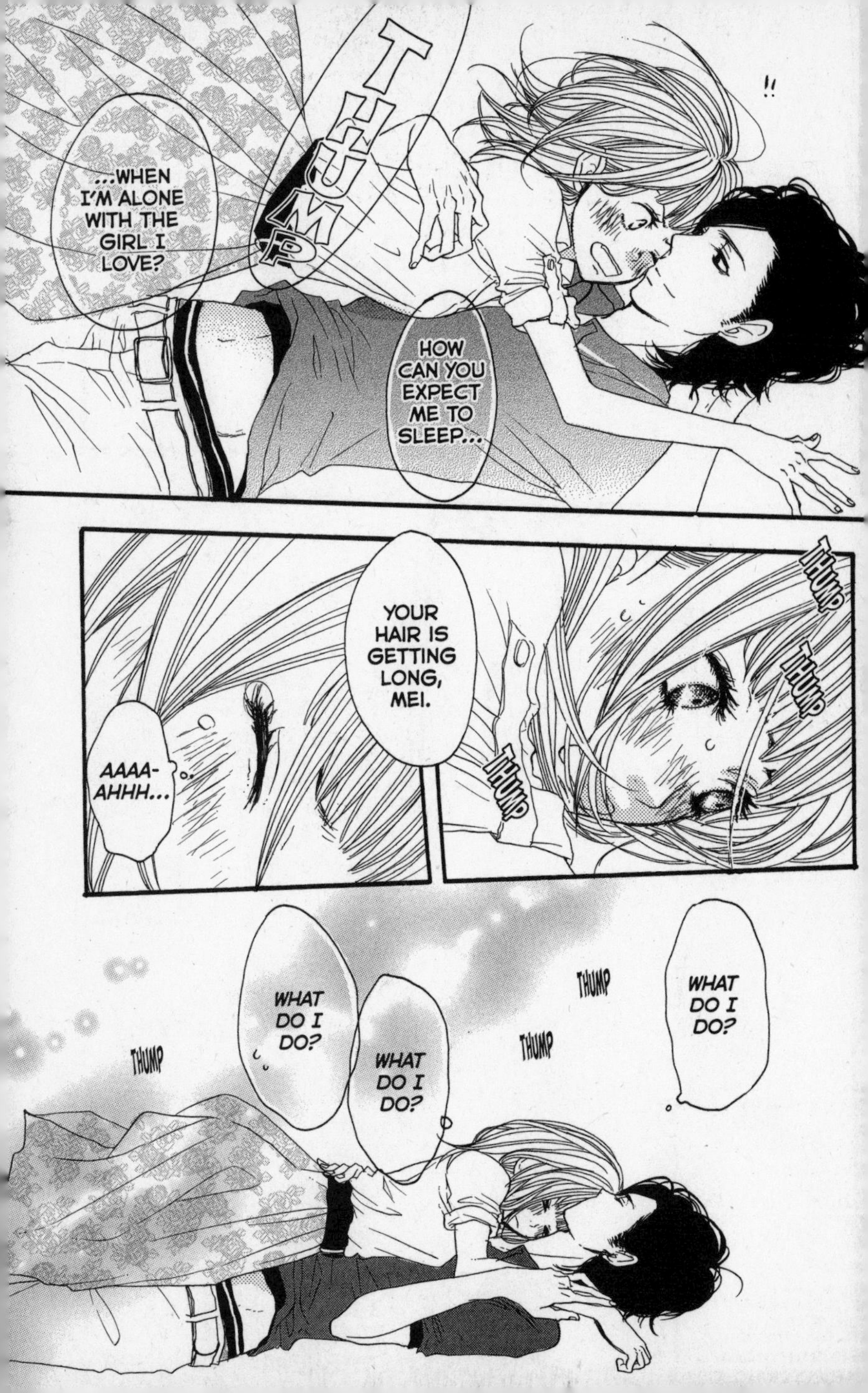
!!
THUMP
HOW CAN YOU EXPECT ME TO SLEEP...
...WHEN I'M ALONE WITH THE GIRL I LOVE?
THUMP
THUMP
THUMP
YOUR HAIR IS GETTING LONG, MEI.
AAAA-AHHH...
WHAT DO I DO?
THUMP
THUMP
WHAT DO I DO?
WHAT DO I DO?
THUMP

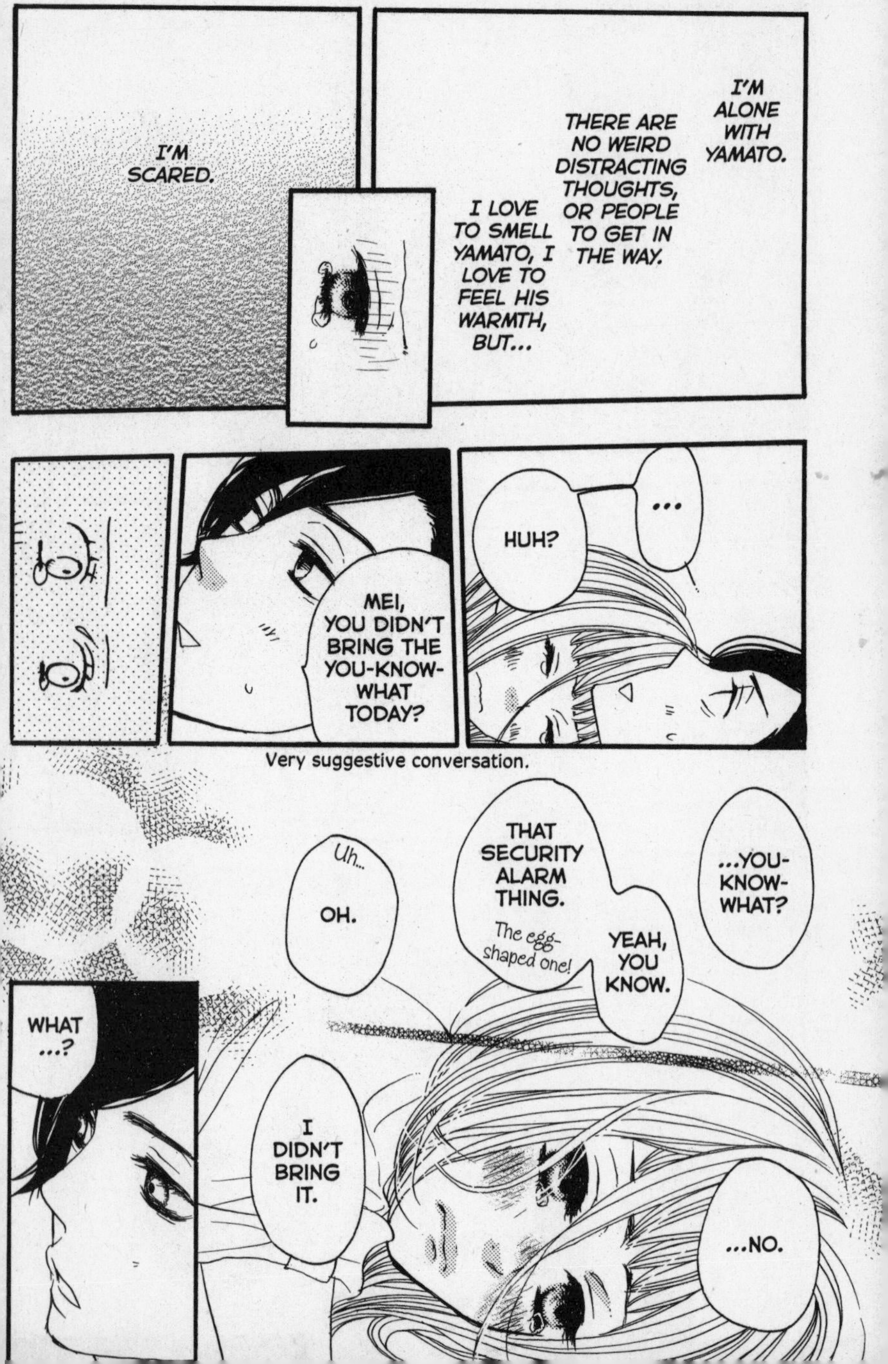
I'M ALONE WITH YAMATO.
THERE ARE NO WEIRD DISTRACTING THOUGHTS, OR PEOPLE TO GET IN THE WAY.
I LOVE TO SMELL YAMATO, I LOVE TO FEEL HIS WARMTH, BUT...
I'M SCARED.
...
HUH?
MEI, YOU DIDN'T BRING THE YOU-KNOW-WHAT TODAY?
Very suggestive conversation.
...YOU-KNOW-WHAT?
THAT SECURITY ALARM THING.
The egg-shaped one!
YEAH, YOU KNOW.
Uh...
OH.
...NO.
I DIDN'T BRING IT.
WHAT...?

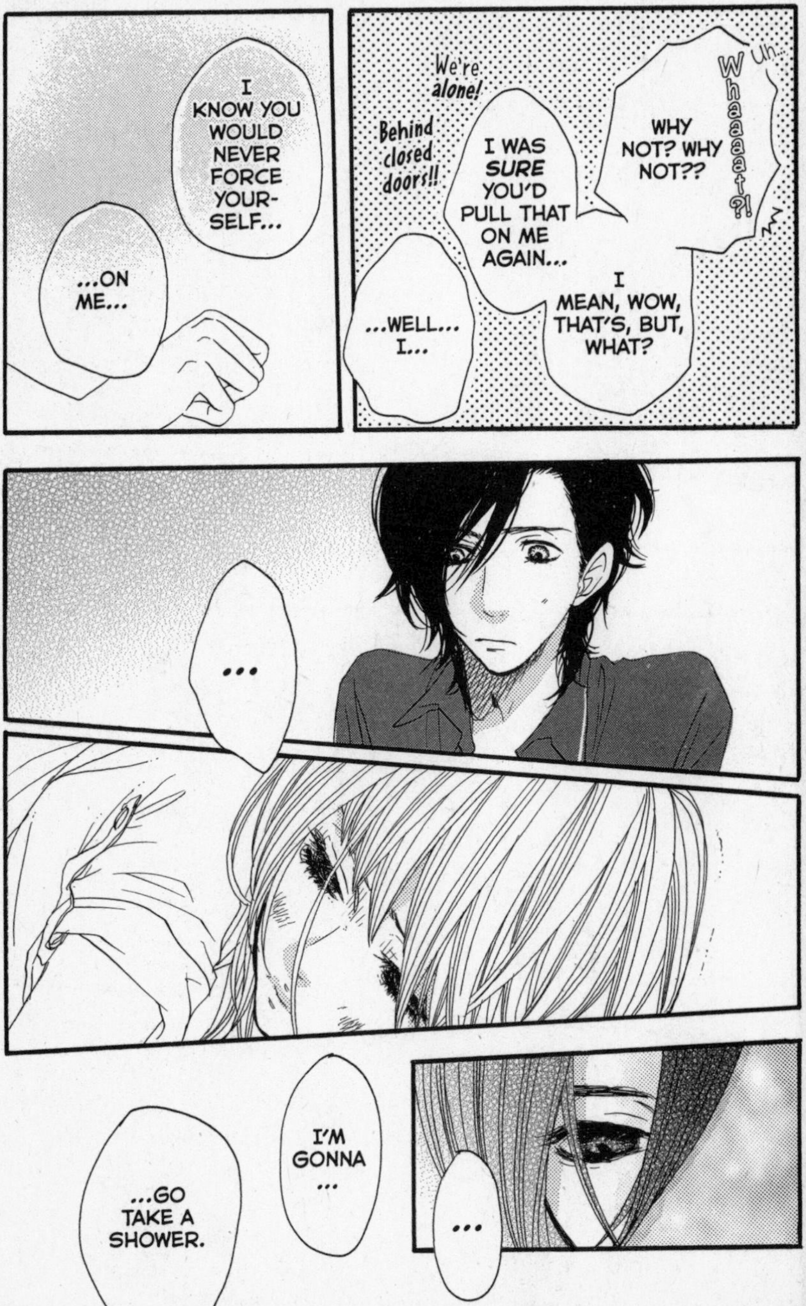
Uh...
Whaaaat?!
WHY NOT? WHY NOT??
I MEAN, WOW, THAT'S, BUT, WHAT?
We're alone!
Behind closed doors!!
I WAS SURE YOU'D PULL THAT ON ME AGAIN...
...WELL... I...
I KNOW YOU WOULD NEVER FORCE YOURSELF...
...ON ME...
...
...
I'M GONNA...
...GO TAKE A SHOWER.

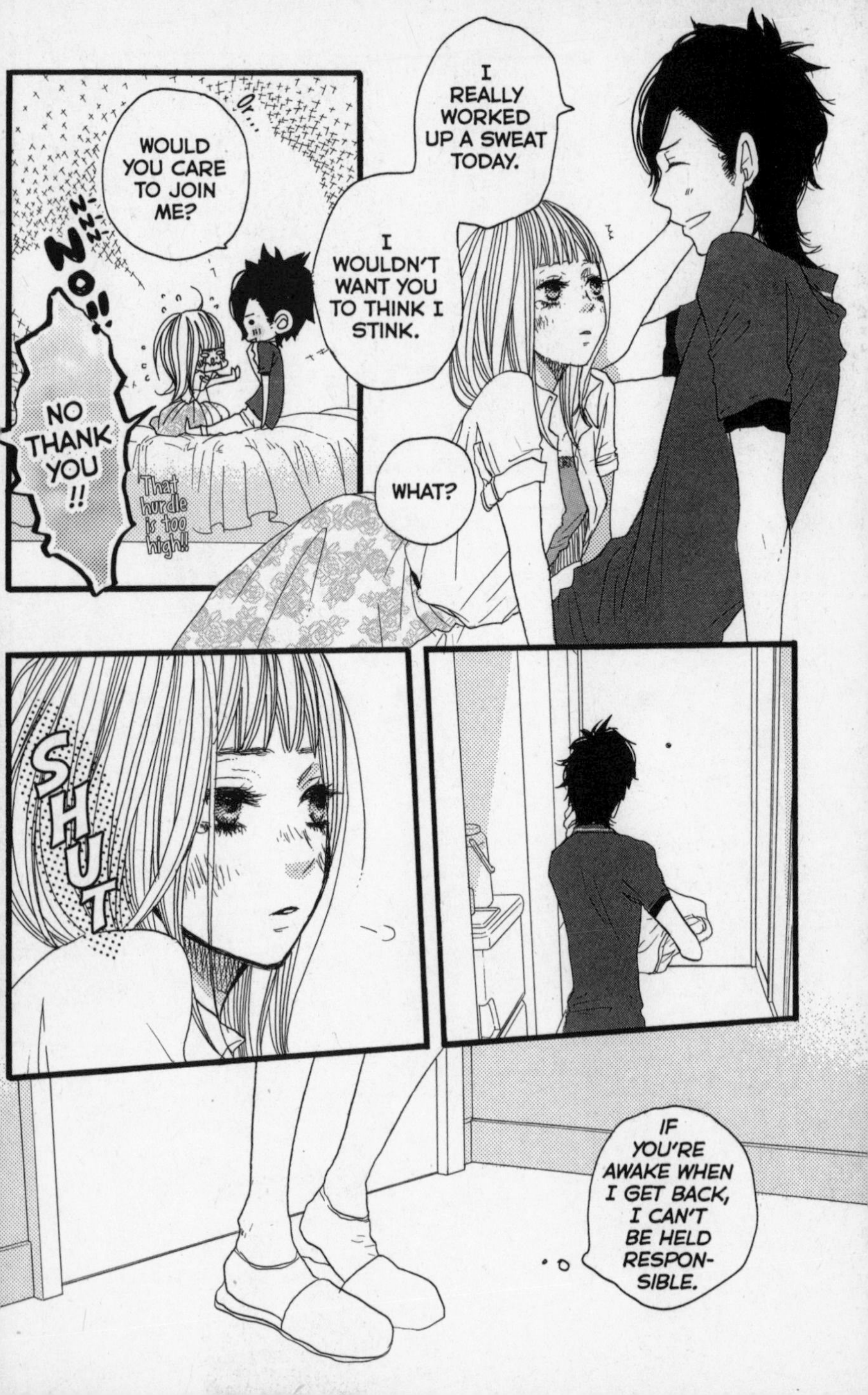
I REALLY WORKED UP A SWEAT TODAY.
I WOULDN'T WANT YOU TO THINK I STINK.
WHAT?
Or...
WOULD YOU CARE TO JOIN ME?
NNNO!!
NO THANK YOU!!
That hurdle is too high!!
SHUT
IF YOU'RE AWAKE WHEN I GET BACK, I CAN'T BE HELD RESPONSIBLE.

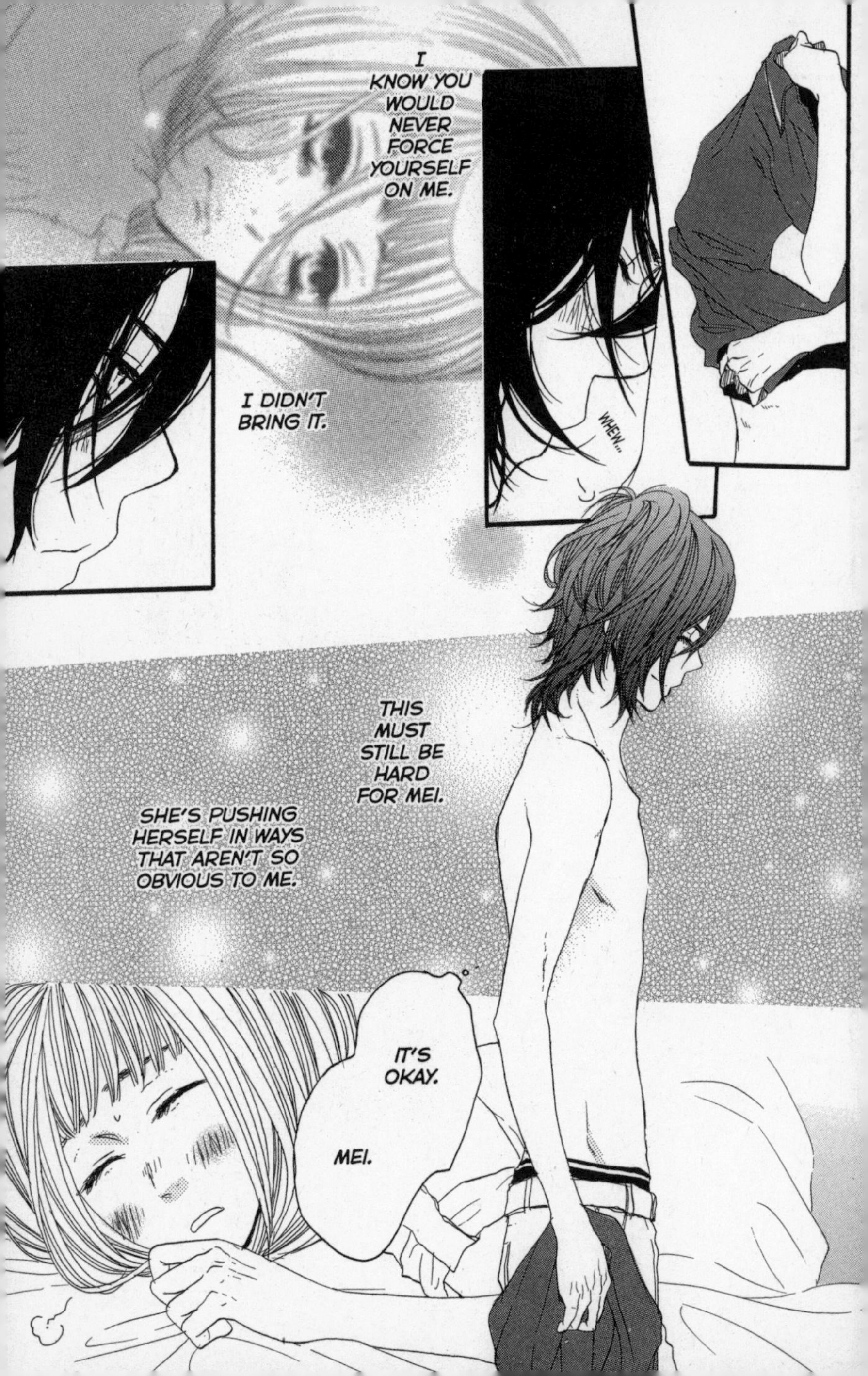

WHEW...
I KNOW YOU WOULD NEVER FORCE YOURSELF ON ME.
I DIDN'T BRING IT.
THIS MUST STILL BE HARD FOR MEI.
SHE'S PUSHING HERSELF IN WAYS THAT AREN'T SO OBVIOUS TO ME.
IT'S OKAY.
MEI.

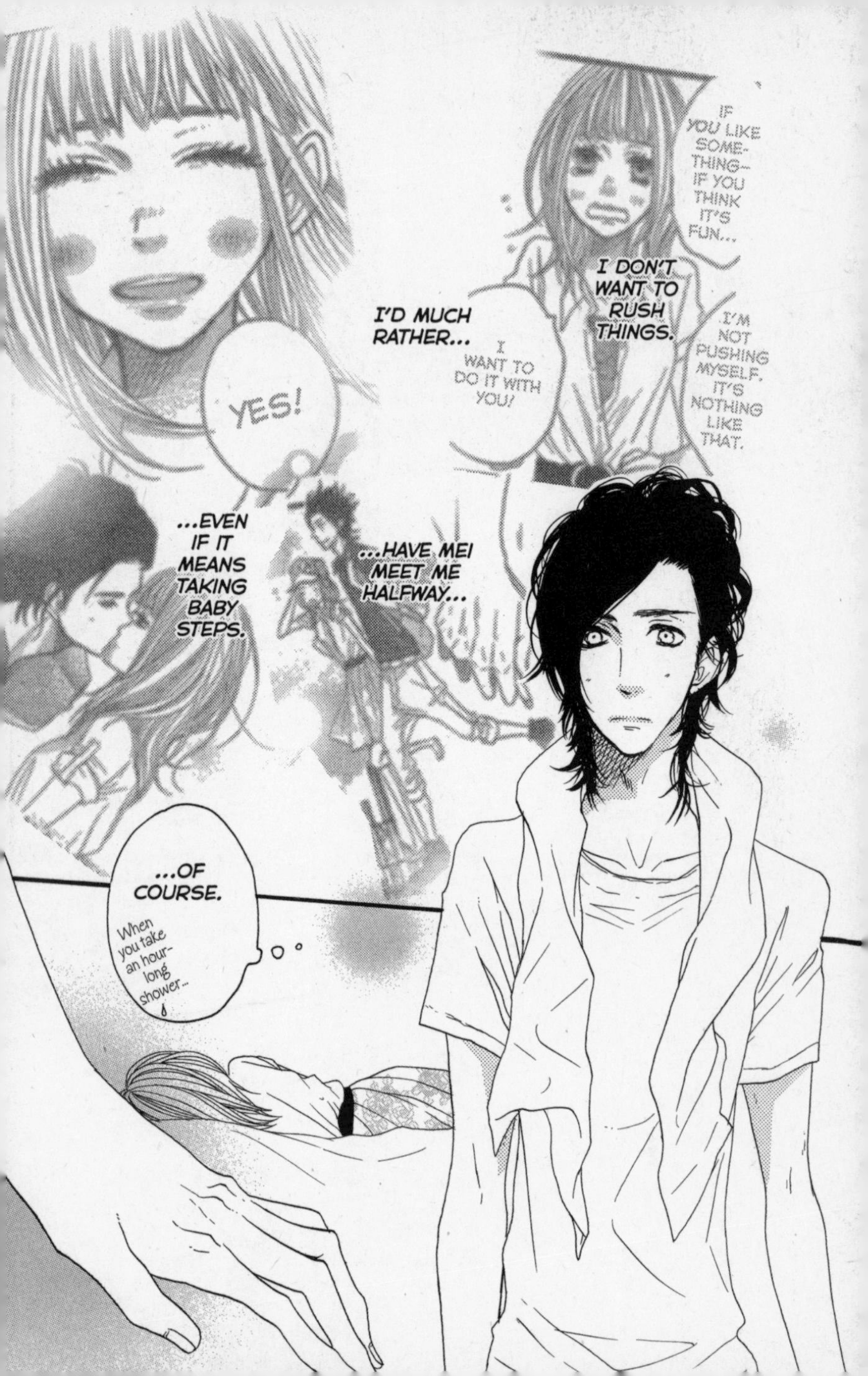
IF YOU LIKE SOME-THING— IF YOU THINK IT'S FUN...
I'M NOT PUSHING MYSELF. IT'S NOTHING LIKE THAT.
I DON'T WANT TO RUSH THINGS.
I WANT TO DO IT WITH YOU!
I'D MUCH RATHER...
YES!
...HAVE MEI MEET ME HALFWAY...
...EVEN IF IT MEANS TAKING BABY STEPS.
...OF COURSE.
When you take an hour-long shower...

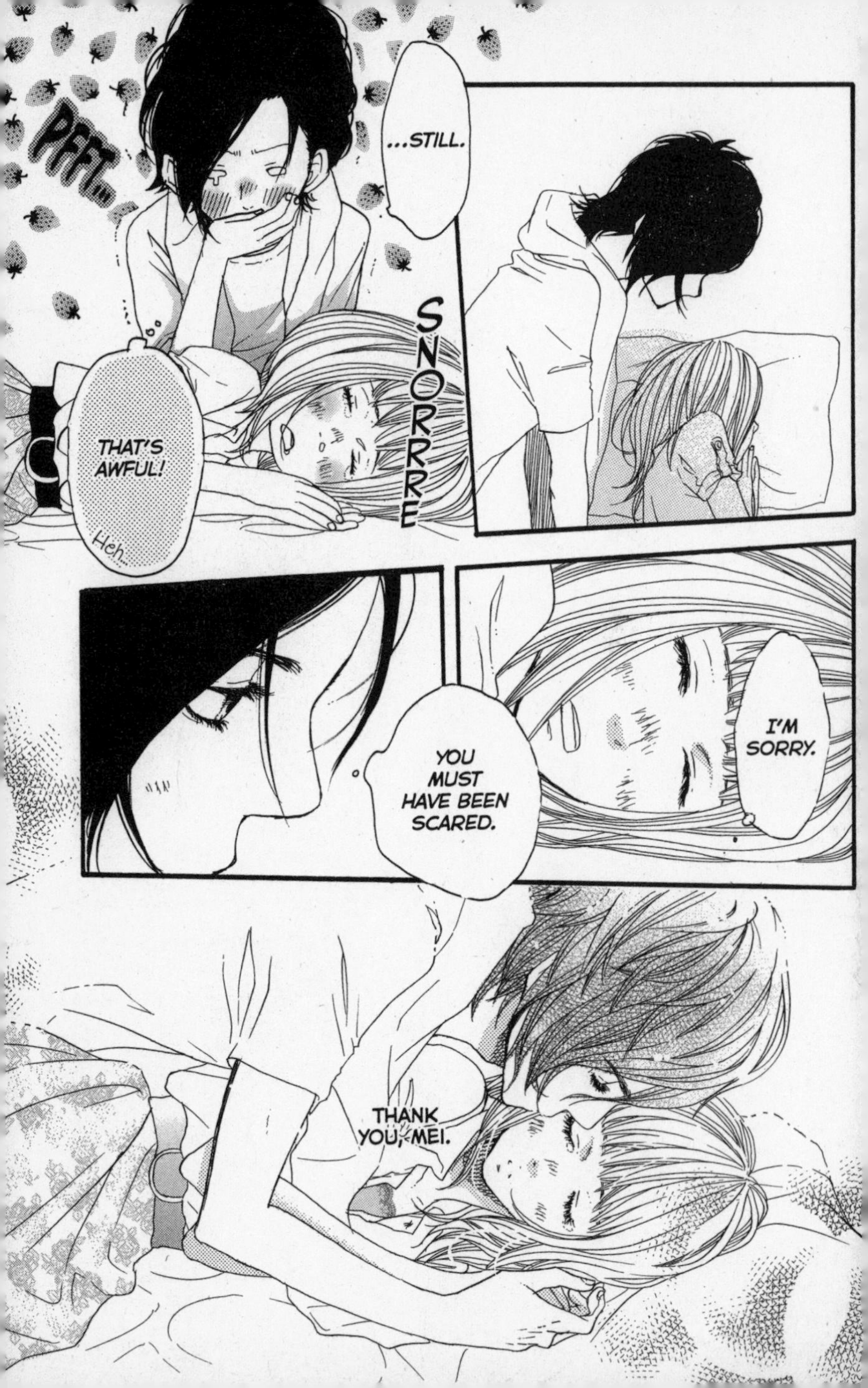
...STILL.
PFFT...
SNORRRE
THAT'S AWFUL!
Heh...
I'M SORRY.
YOU MUST HAVE BEEN SCARED.
THANK YOU, MEI.

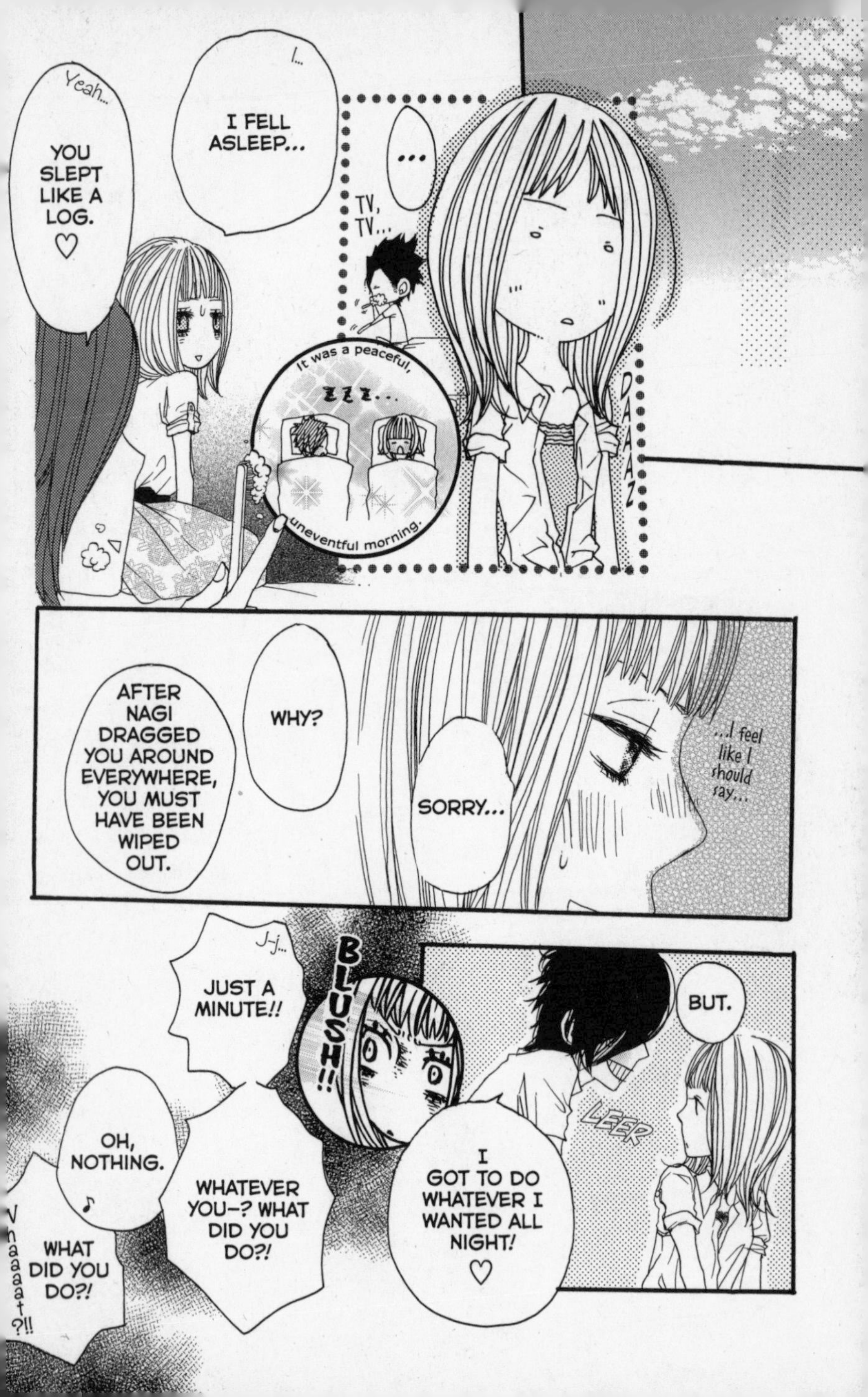
...
TV, TV...
It was a peaceful, ZZZ... uneventful morning.
DAAAZ
I...
I FELL ASLEEP...
Yeah...
YOU SLEPT LIKE A LOG. ♡
...I feel like I should say...
SORRY...
WHY?
AFTER NAGI DRAGGED YOU AROUND EVERYWHERE, YOU MUST HAVE BEEN WIPED OUT.
BUT.
LEER
I GOT TO DO WHATEVER I WANTED ALL NIGHT! ♡
BLUSH!!
J-j...
JUST A MINUTE!!
WHATEVER YOU-? WHAT DID YOU DO?!
OH, NOTHING. ♪
WHAT DID YOU DO?!
Vnaaaat?!!

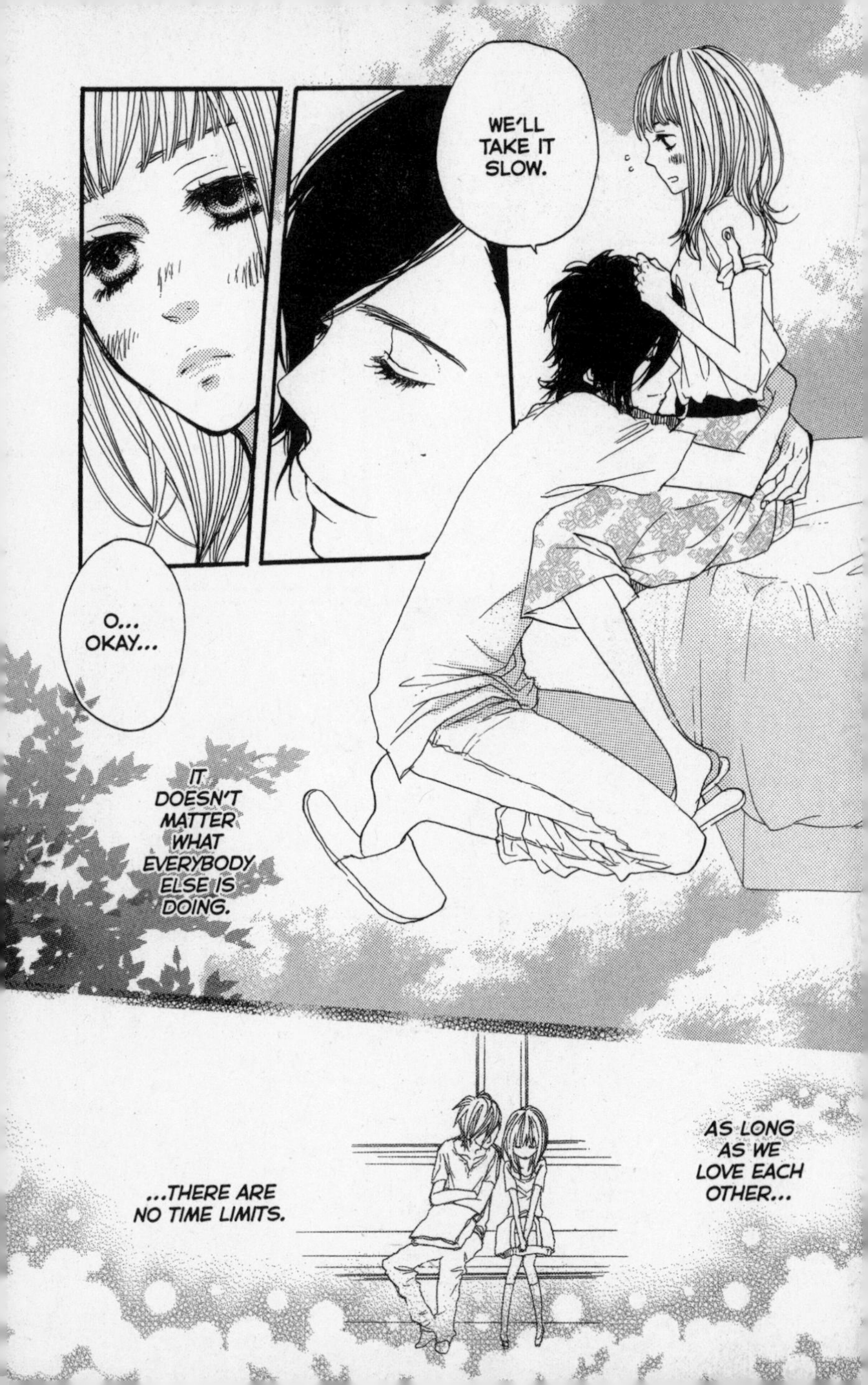
WE'LL TAKE IT SLOW.
O... OKAY...
IT DOESN'T MATTER WHAT EVERYBODY ELSE IS DOING.
AS LONG AS WE LOVE EACH OTHER...
...THERE ARE NO TIME LIMITS.

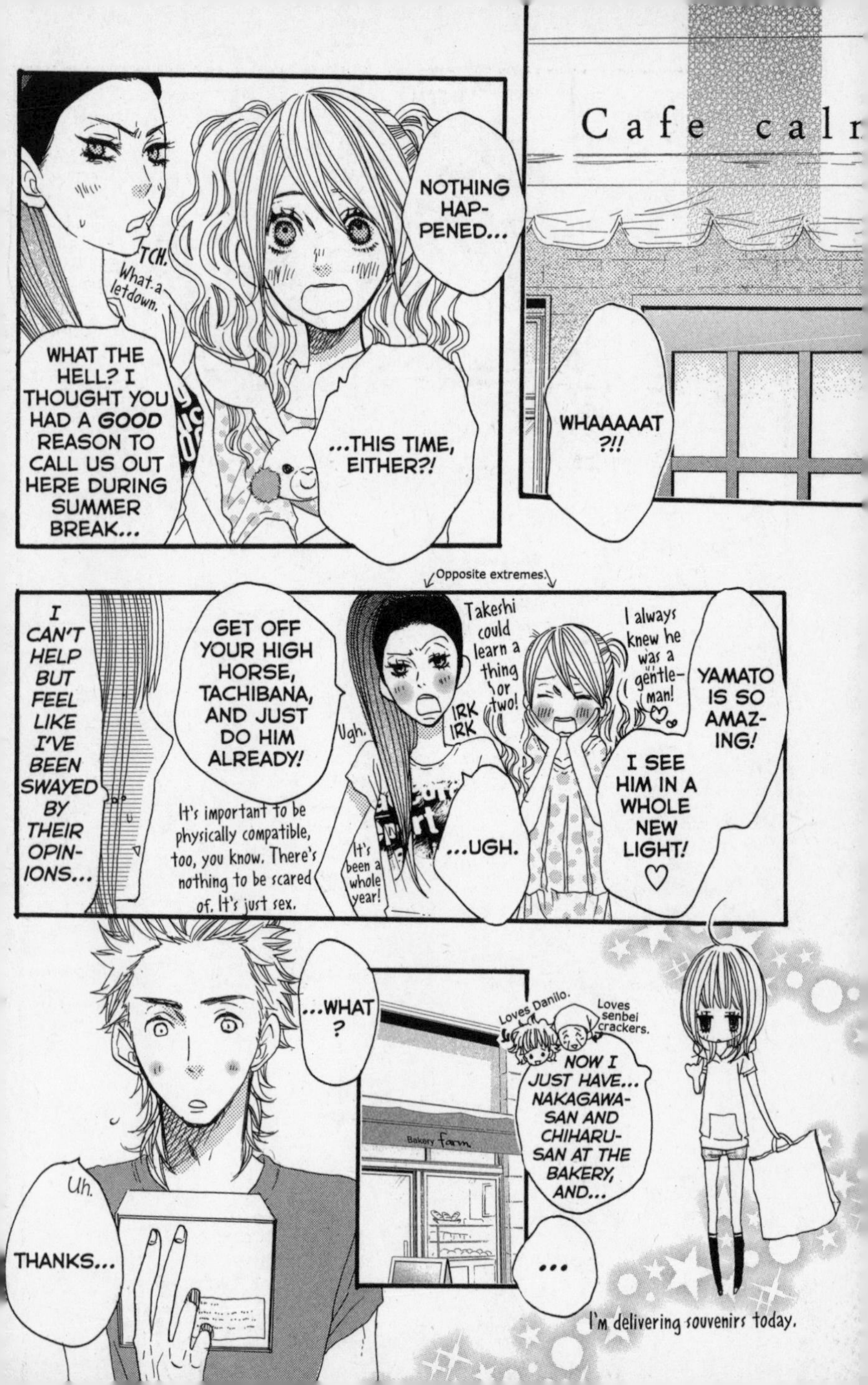
Cafe cal
WHAAAAAT ?!!
NOTHING HAPPENED...
...THIS TIME, EITHER?!
TCH. What a letdown.
WHAT THE HELL? I THOUGHT YOU HAD A GOOD REASON TO CALL US OUT HERE DURING SUMMER BREAK...
Opposite extremes.
YAMATO IS SO AMAZING!
I always knew he was a gentleman! ♡
I SEE HIM IN A WHOLE NEW LIGHT! ♡
Takeshi could learn a thing or two!
IRK IRK
GET OFF YOUR HIGH HORSE, TACHIBANA, AND JUST DO HIM ALREADY!
Ugh.
...UGH.
It's been a whole year!
It's important to be physically compatible, too, you know. There's nothing to be scared of. It's just sex.
I CAN'T HELP BUT FEEL LIKE I'VE BEEN SWAYED BY THEIR OPINIONS...
I'm delivering souvenirs today.
Loves senbei crackers.
Loves Danilo.
NOW I JUST HAVE... NAKAGAWA-SAN AND CHIHARU-SAN AT THE BAKERY, AND...
...
Bakery farm
...WHAT ?
Uh.
THANKS...

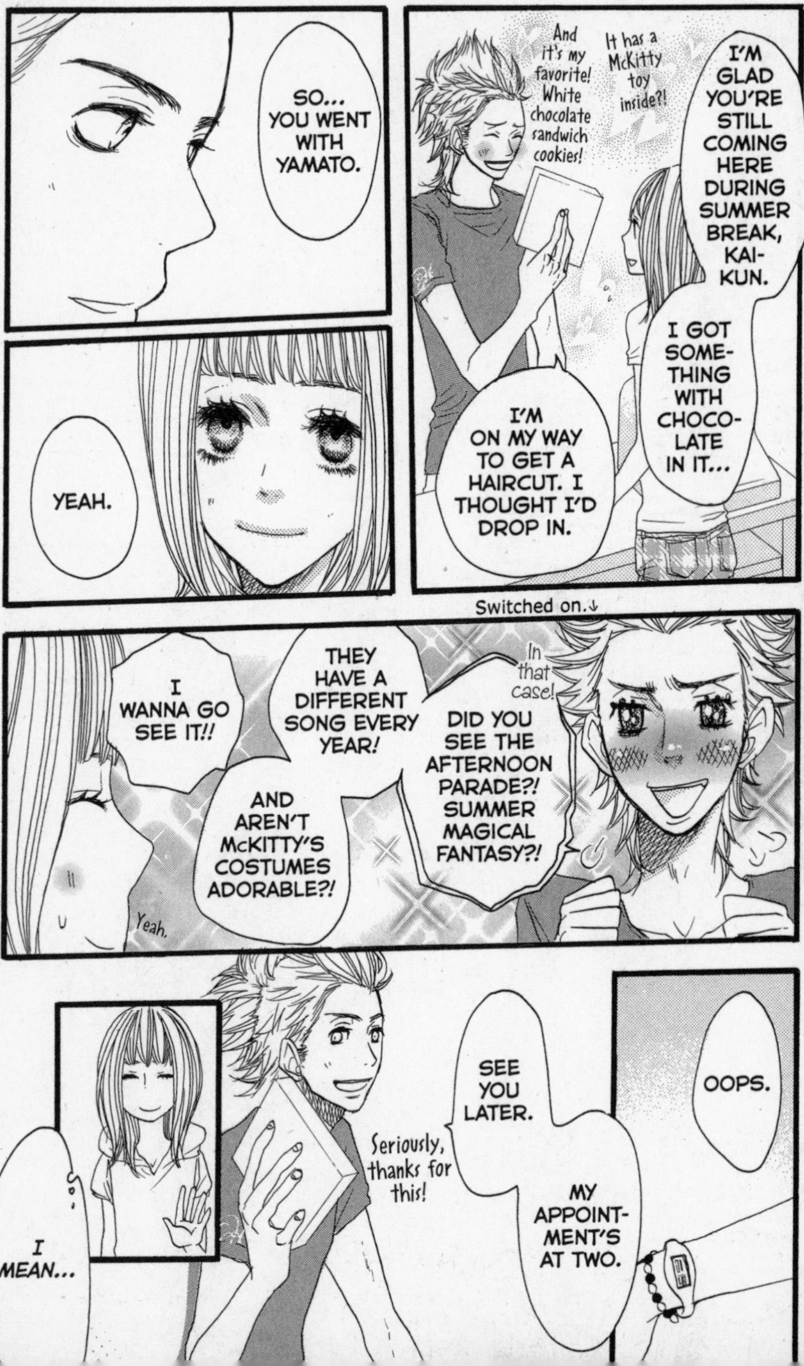
I'M GLAD YOU'RE STILL COMING HERE DURING SUMMER BREAK, KAI-KUN.
I GOT SOME-THING WITH CHOCO-LATE IN IT...
It has a McKitty toy inside?!
And it's my favorite! White chocolate sandwich cookies!
I'M ON MY WAY TO GET A HAIRCUT. I THOUGHT I'D DROP IN.
SO... YOU WENT WITH YAMATO.
YEAH.
Switched on.↓
In that case!
DID YOU SEE THE AFTERNOON PARADE?! SUMMER MAGICAL FANTASY?!
THEY HAVE A DIFFERENT SONG EVERY YEAR!
AND AREN'T McKITTY'S COSTUMES ADORABLE?!
I WANNA GO SEE IT!!
Yeah.
OOPS.
MY APPOINT-MENT'S AT TWO.
SEE YOU LATER.
Seriously, thanks for this!
I MEAN...

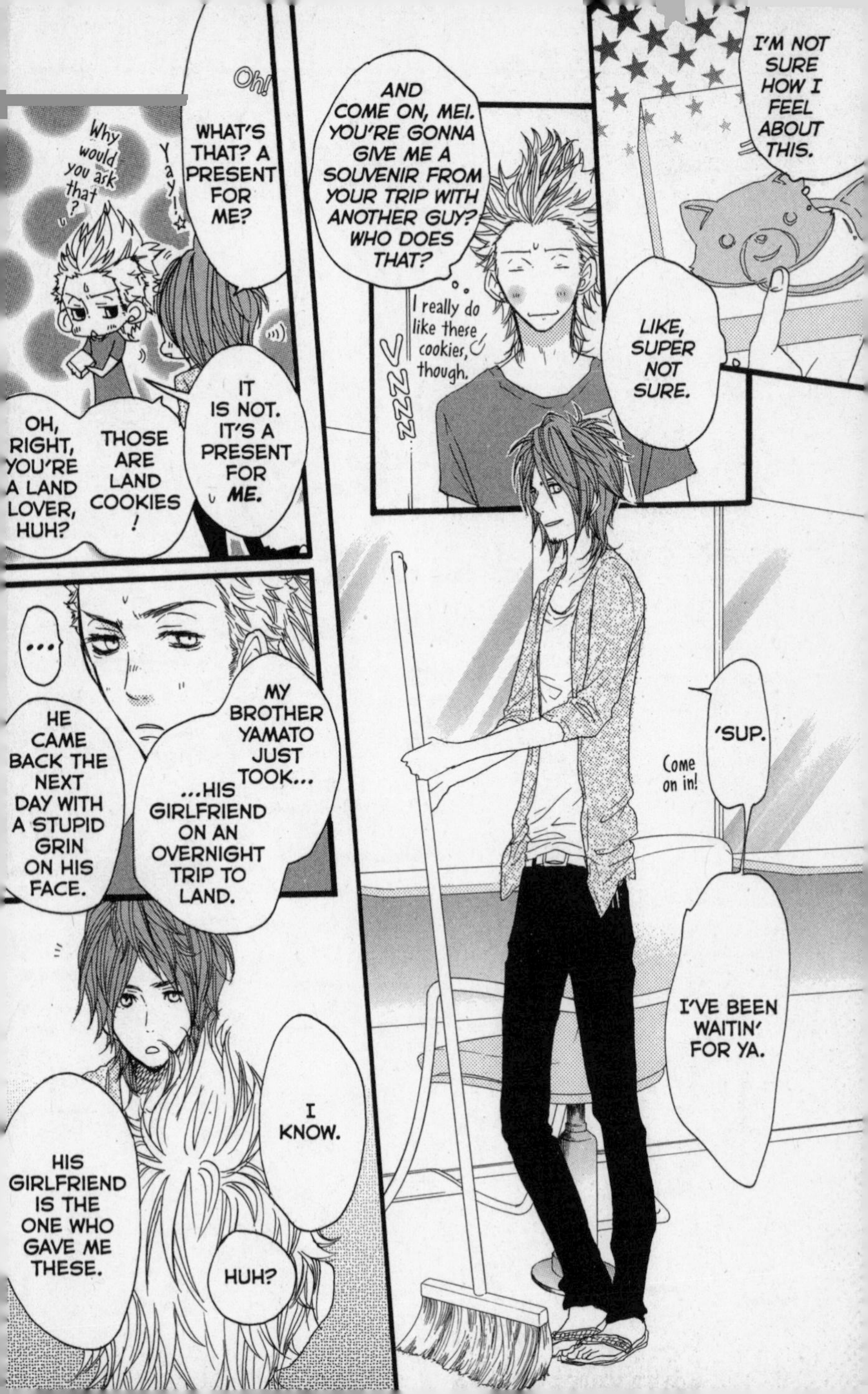
I'M NOT SURE HOW I FEEL ABOUT THIS.
LIKE, SUPER NOT SURE.
AND COME ON, MEI. YOU'RE GONNA GIVE ME A SOUVENIR FROM YOUR TRIP WITH ANOTHER GUY? WHO DOES THAT?
VNNN
I really do like these cookies, though.
'SUP.
Come on in!
I'VE BEEN WAITIN' FOR YA.
Oh!
WHAT'S THAT? A PRESENT FOR ME?
Yay!☆
Why would you ask that?
IT IS NOT. IT'S A PRESENT FOR *ME.*
THOSE ARE LAND COOKIES!
OH, RIGHT, YOU'RE A LAND LOVER, HUH?
...
MY BROTHER YAMATO JUST TOOK...
...HIS GIRLFRIEND ON AN OVERNIGHT TRIP TO LAND.
HE CAME BACK THE NEXT DAY WITH A STUPID GRIN ON HIS FACE.
I KNOW.
HIS GIRLFRIEND IS THE ONE WHO GAVE ME THESE.
HUH?

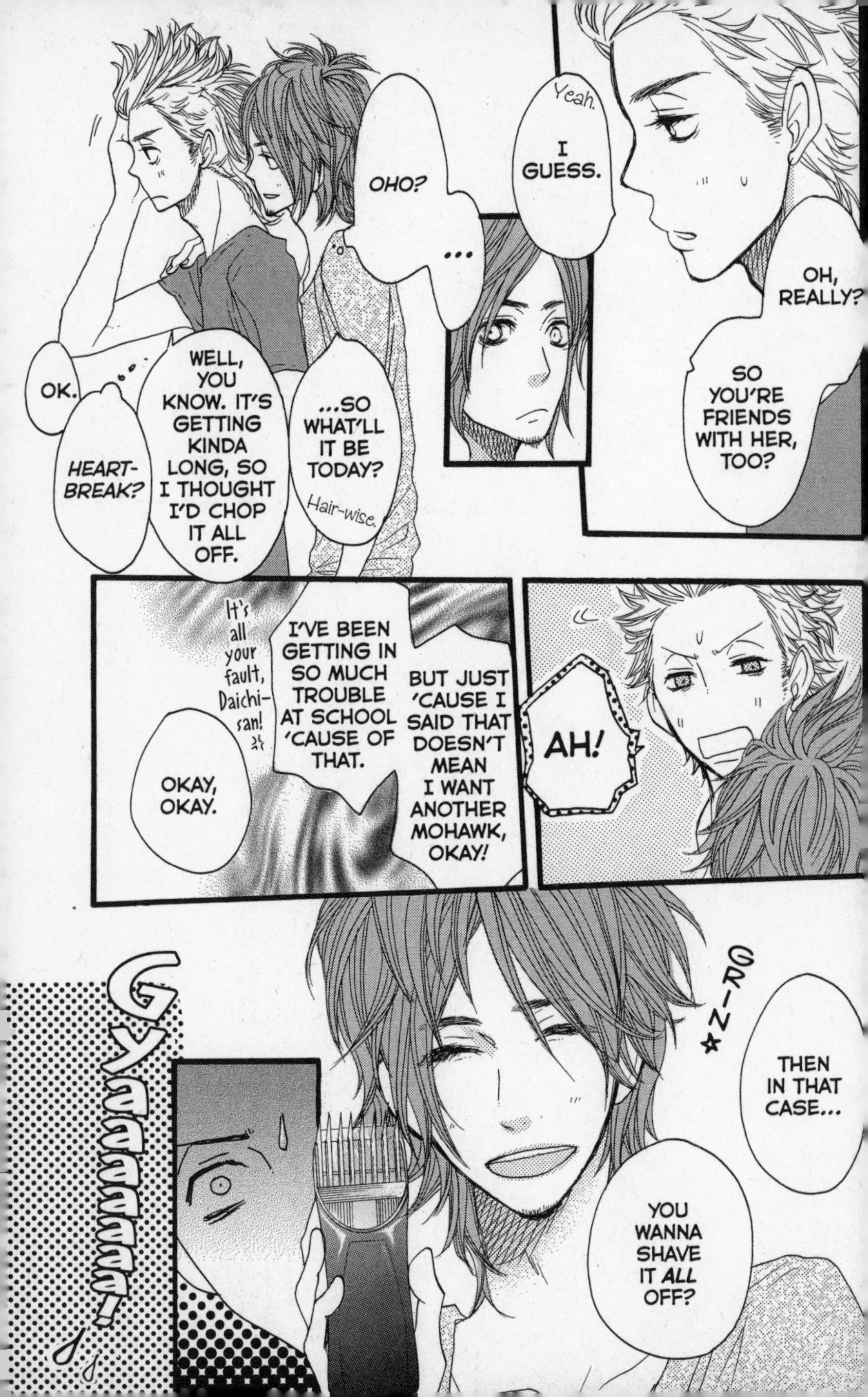
Yeah.
I GUESS.
OH, REALLY?
SO YOU'RE FRIENDS WITH HER, TOO?
...
OHO?
...SO WHAT'LL IT BE TODAY?
Hair-wise.
WELL, YOU KNOW. IT'S GETTING KINDA LONG, SO I THOUGHT I'D CHOP IT ALL OFF.
OK.
HEART-BREAK?
AH!
BUT JUST 'CAUSE I SAID THAT DOESN'T MEAN I WANT ANOTHER MOHAWK, OKAY!
I'VE BEEN GETTING IN SO MUCH TROUBLE AT SCHOOL 'CAUSE OF THAT.
It's all your fault, Daichi-san!
OKAY, OKAY.
GRIN☆
THEN IN THAT CASE...
YOU WANNA SHAVE IT ALL OFF?
GYAAAAAAAAA!

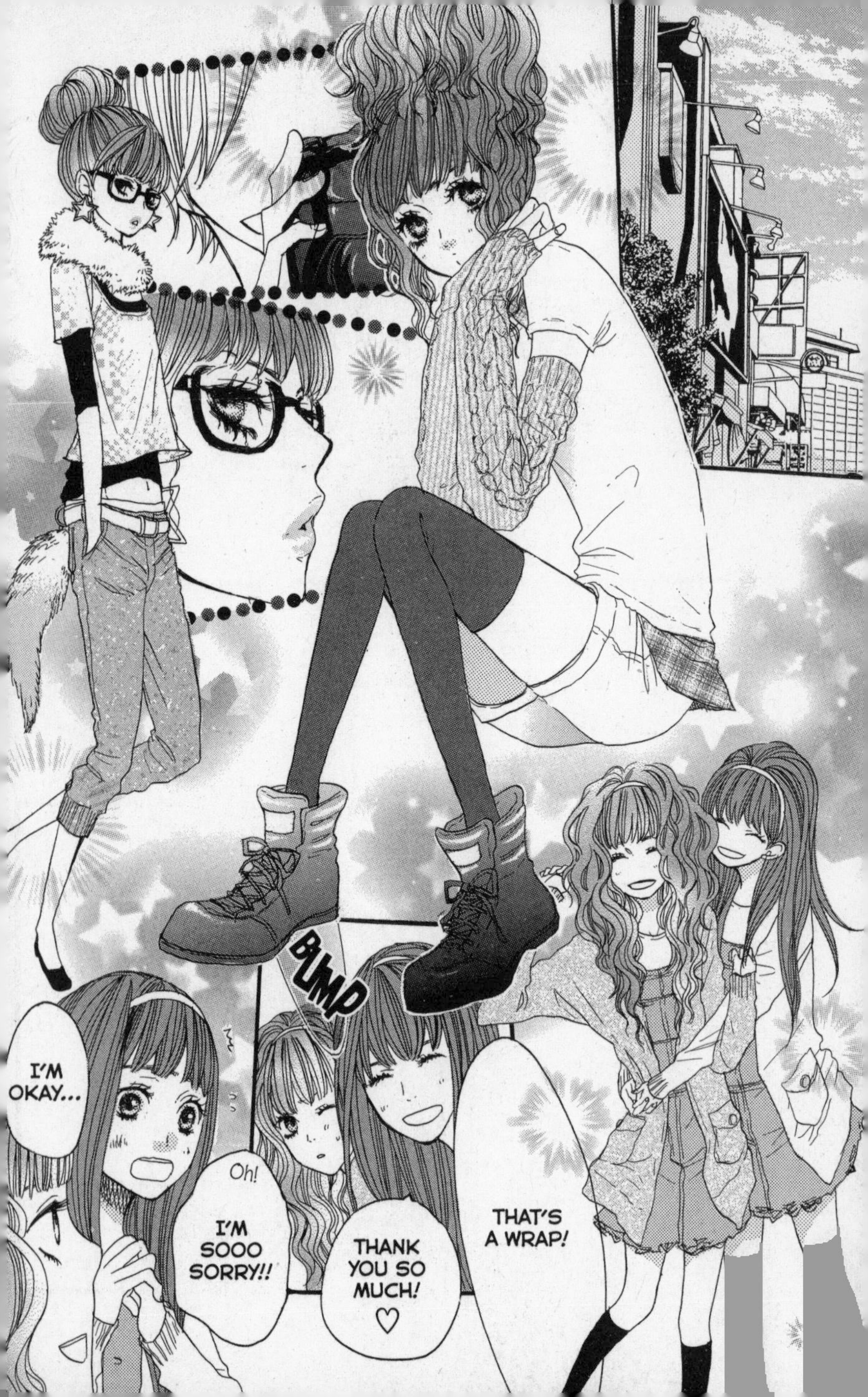
BUMP
THAT'S A WRAP!
THANK YOU SO MUCH! ♡
Oh!
I'M SOOO SORRY!!
I'M OKAY...

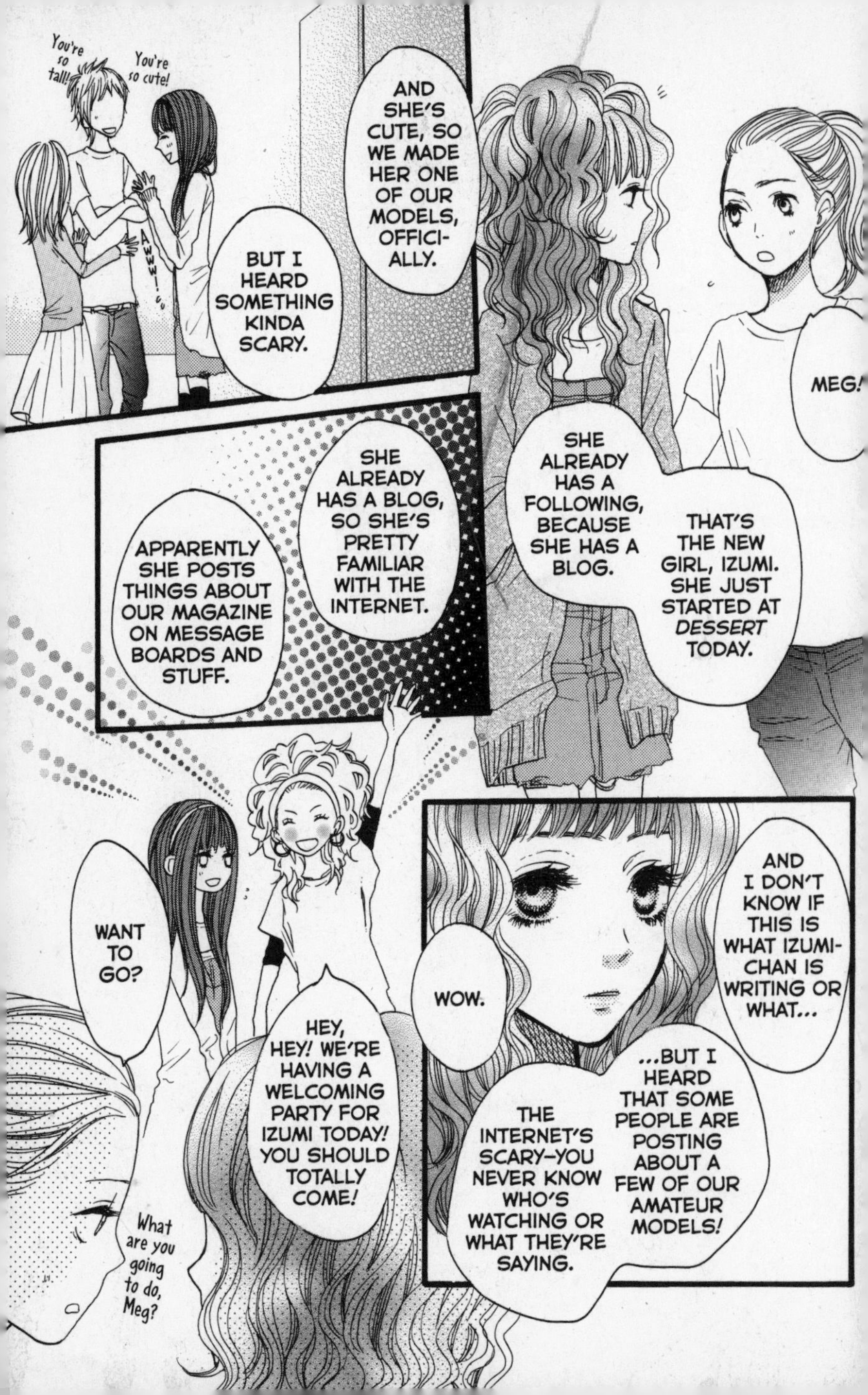
MEG!
THAT'S THE NEW GIRL, IZUMI. SHE JUST STARTED AT *DESSERT* TODAY.
SHE ALREADY HAS A FOLLOWING, BECAUSE SHE HAS A BLOG.
AND SHE'S CUTE, SO WE MADE HER ONE OF OUR MODELS, OFFICIALLY.
BUT I HEARD SOMETHING KINDA SCARY.
You're so cute!
You're so tall!
Awww!
SHE ALREADY HAS A BLOG, SO SHE'S PRETTY FAMILIAR WITH THE INTERNET.
APPARENTLY SHE POSTS THINGS ABOUT OUR MAGAZINE ON MESSAGE BOARDS AND STUFF.
AND I DON'T KNOW IF THIS IS WHAT IZUMI-CHAN IS WRITING OR WHAT...
...BUT I HEARD THAT SOME PEOPLE ARE POSTING ABOUT A FEW OF OUR AMATEUR MODELS!
THE INTERNET'S SCARY—YOU NEVER KNOW WHO'S WATCHING OR WHAT THEY'RE SAYING.
WOW.
HEY, HEY! WE'RE HAVING A WELCOMING PARTY FOR IZUMI TODAY! YOU SHOULD TOTALLY COME!
WANT TO GO?
What are you going to do, Meg?

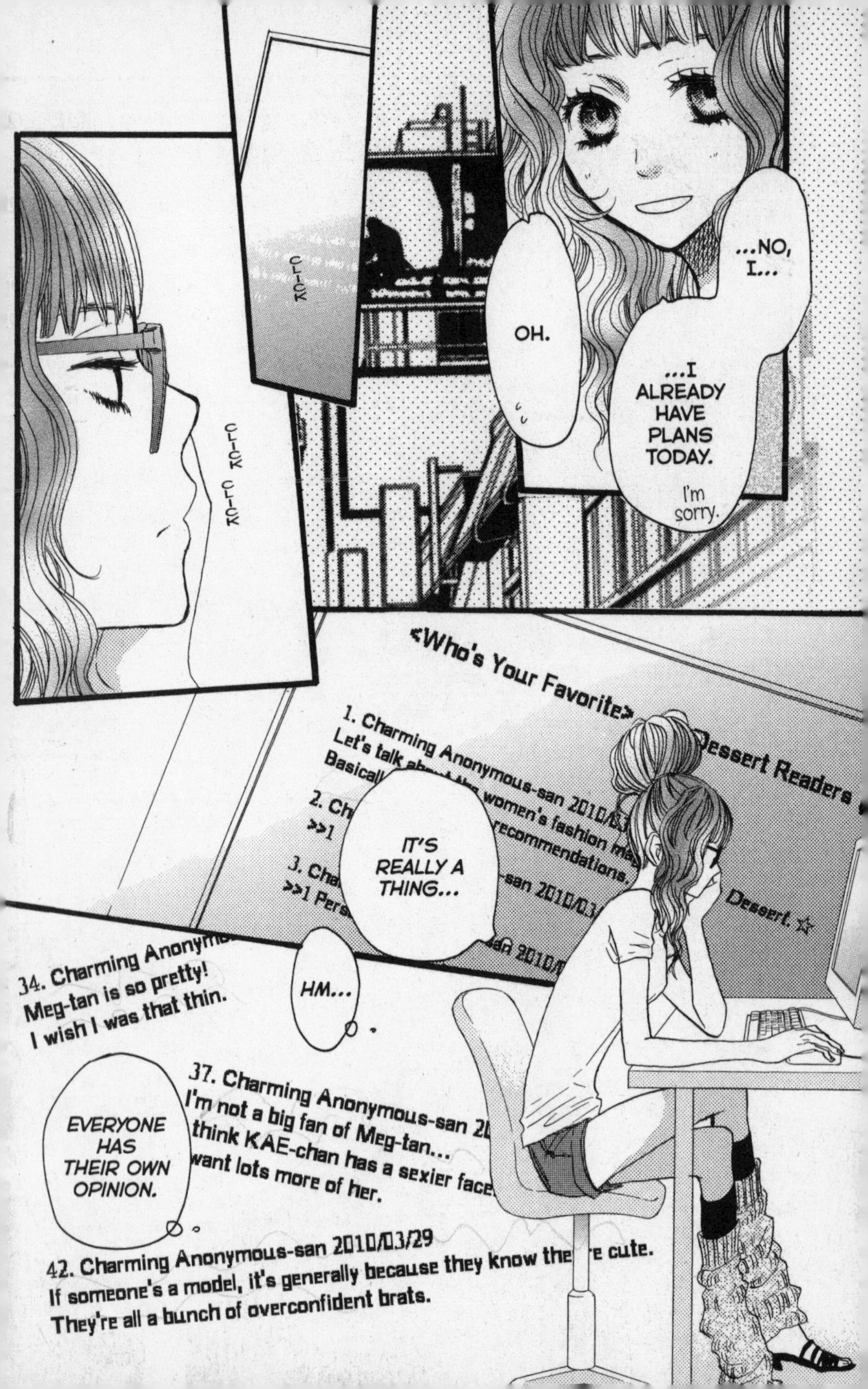

...NO, I...
OH.
...I ALREADY HAVE PLANS TODAY.
I'm sorry.
CLICK
CLICK CLICK
<Who's Your Favorite> Dessert Readers
1. Charming Anonymous-san 2010/0
Let's talk ab women's fashion ma
Basicall recommendations.
2. Ch
>>1
3. Cha -san 2010/03
>>1 Pers Dessert. ☆
IT'S REALLY A THING...
HM...
34. Charming Anonym
Meg-tan is so pretty!
I wish I was that thin.
37. Charming Anonymous-san 20
I'm not a big fan of Meg-tan...
think KAE-chan has a sexier face
want lots more of her.
EVERYONE HAS THEIR OWN OPINION.
42. Charming Anonymous-san 2010/03/29
If someone's a model, it's generally because they know the re cute.
They're all a bunch of overconfident brats.

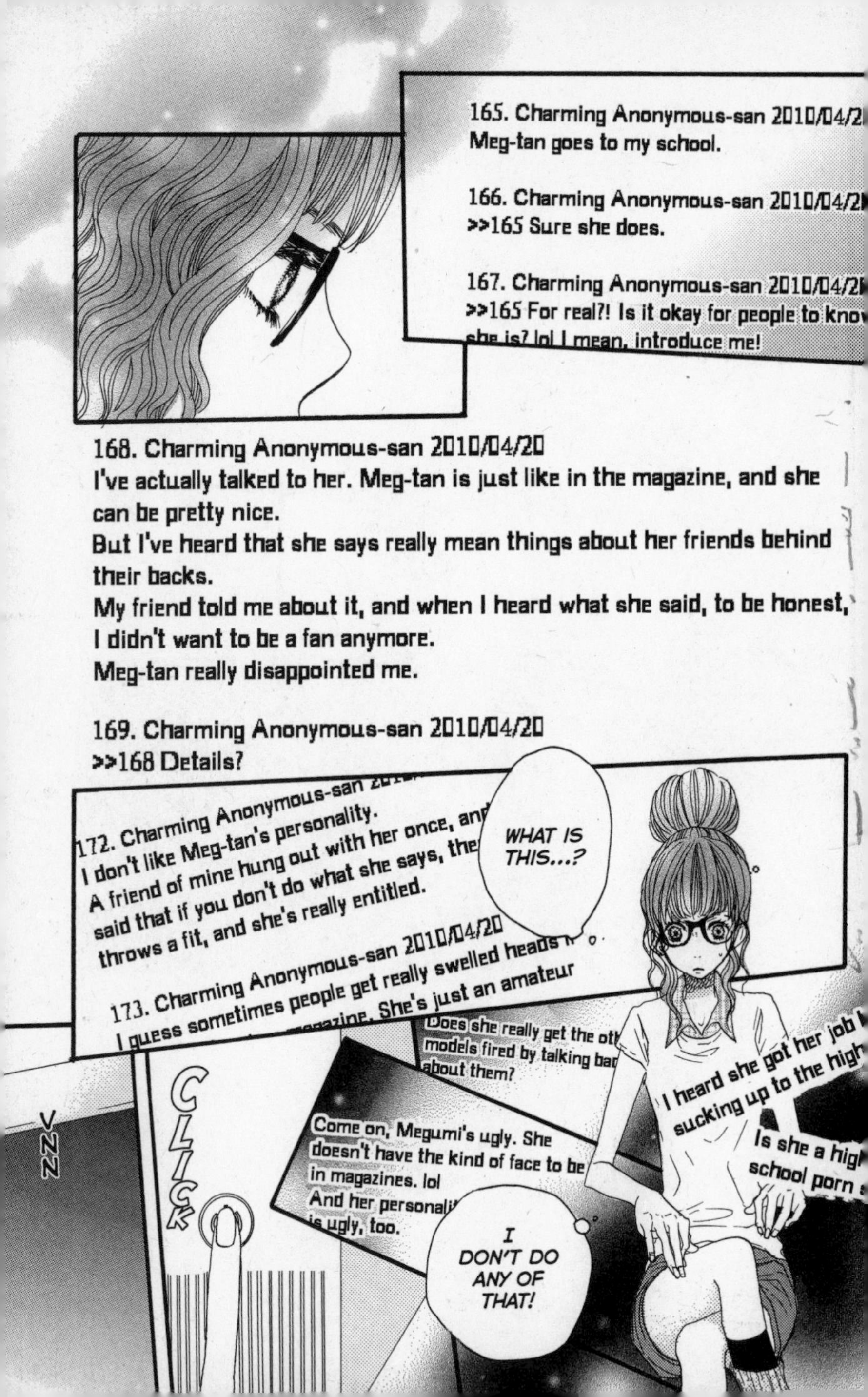
165. Charming Anonymous-san 2010/04/2
Meg-tan goes to my school.
166. Charming Anonymous-san 2010/04/2
>>165 Sure she does.
167. Charming Anonymous-san 2010/04/2
>>165 For real?! Is it okay for people to kno
she is? lol I mean, introduce me!
168. Charming Anonymous-san 2010/04/20
I've actually talked to her. Meg-tan is just like in the magazine, and she can be pretty nice.
But I've heard that she says really mean things about her friends behind their backs.
My friend told me about it, and when I heard what she said, to be honest, I didn't want to be a fan anymore.
Meg-tan really disappointed me.
169. Charming Anonymous-san 2010/04/20
>>168 Details?
WHAT IS THIS...?
172. Charming Anonymous-san
I don't like Meg-tan's personality.
A friend of mine hung out with her once, an
said that if you don't do what she says, the
throws a fit, and she's really entitled.
173. Charming Anonymous-san 2010/04/20
I guess sometimes people get really swelled heads
magazine. She's just an amateur
I heard she got her job
sucking up to the high
Is she a hig
school porn
Does she really get the ot
models fired by talking ba
about them?
Come on, Megumi's ugly. She doesn't have the kind of face to be in magazines. lol
And her personali
is ugly, too.
I DON'T DO ANY OF THAT!
CLICK

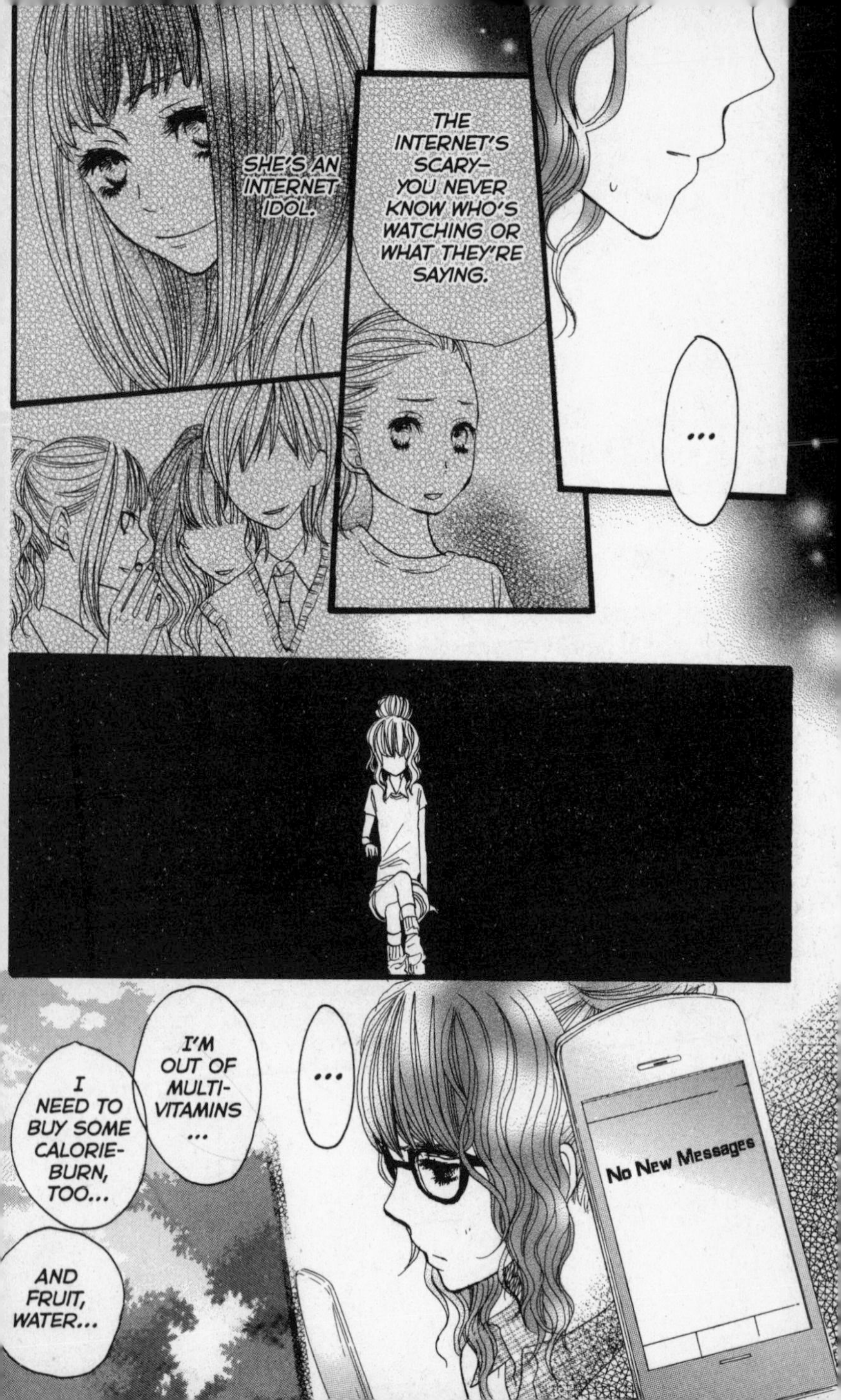
...
THE INTERNET'S SCARY— YOU NEVER KNOW WHO'S WATCHING OR WHAT THEY'RE SAYING.
SHE'S AN INTERNET IDOL.
No New Messages
...
I'M OUT OF MULTI-VITAMINS...
I NEED TO BUY SOME CALORIE-BURN, TOO...
AND FRUIT, WATER...

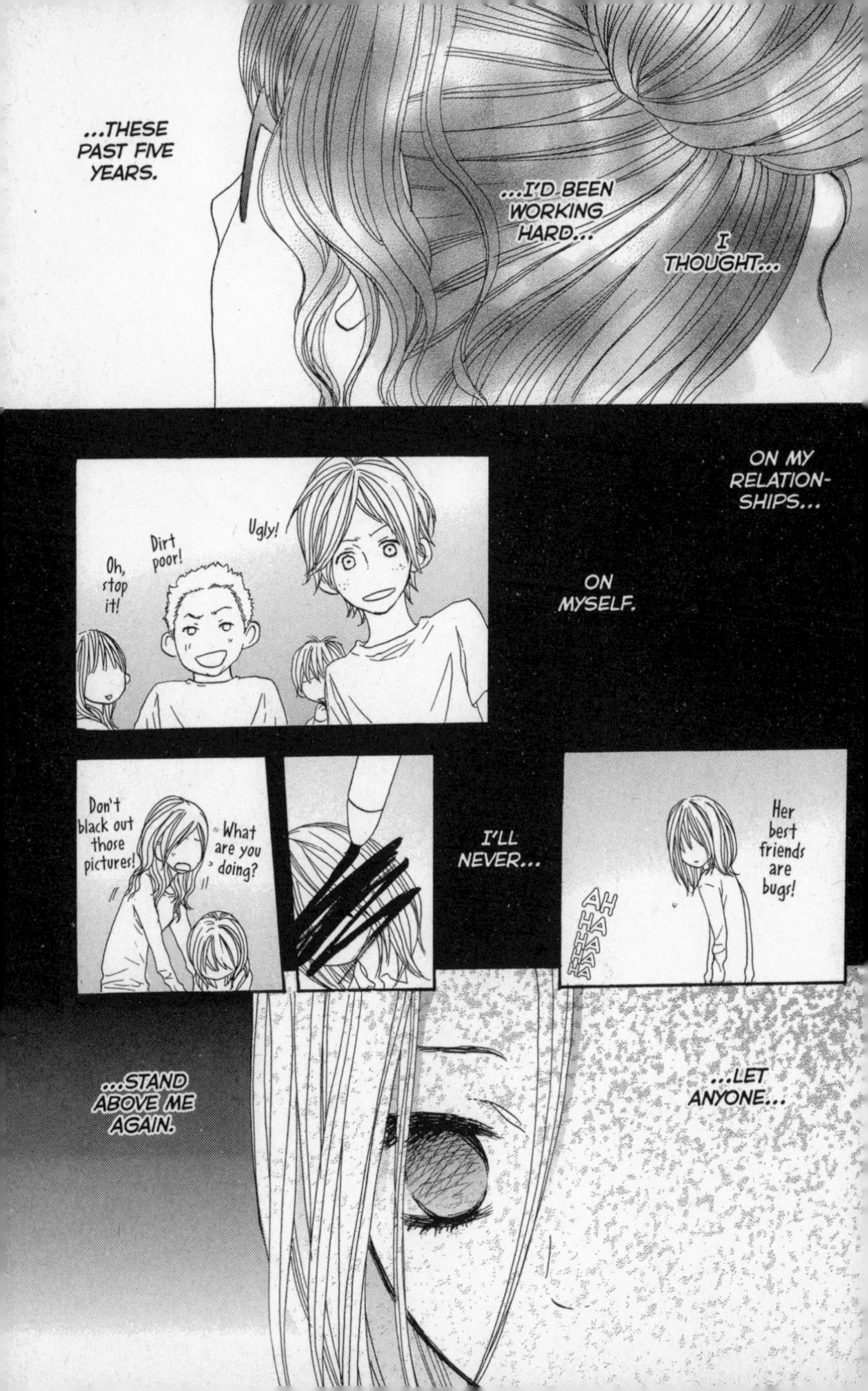
I THOUGHT...
...I'D BEEN WORKING HARD...
...THESE PAST FIVE YEARS.
ON MY RELATIONSHIPS...
ON MYSELF.
Ugly!
Dirt poor!
Oh, stop it!
Her best friends are bugs!
AHAHAHAHA
I'LL NEVER...
What are you doing?
Don't black out those pictures!
...LET ANYONE...
...STAND ABOVE ME AGAIN.

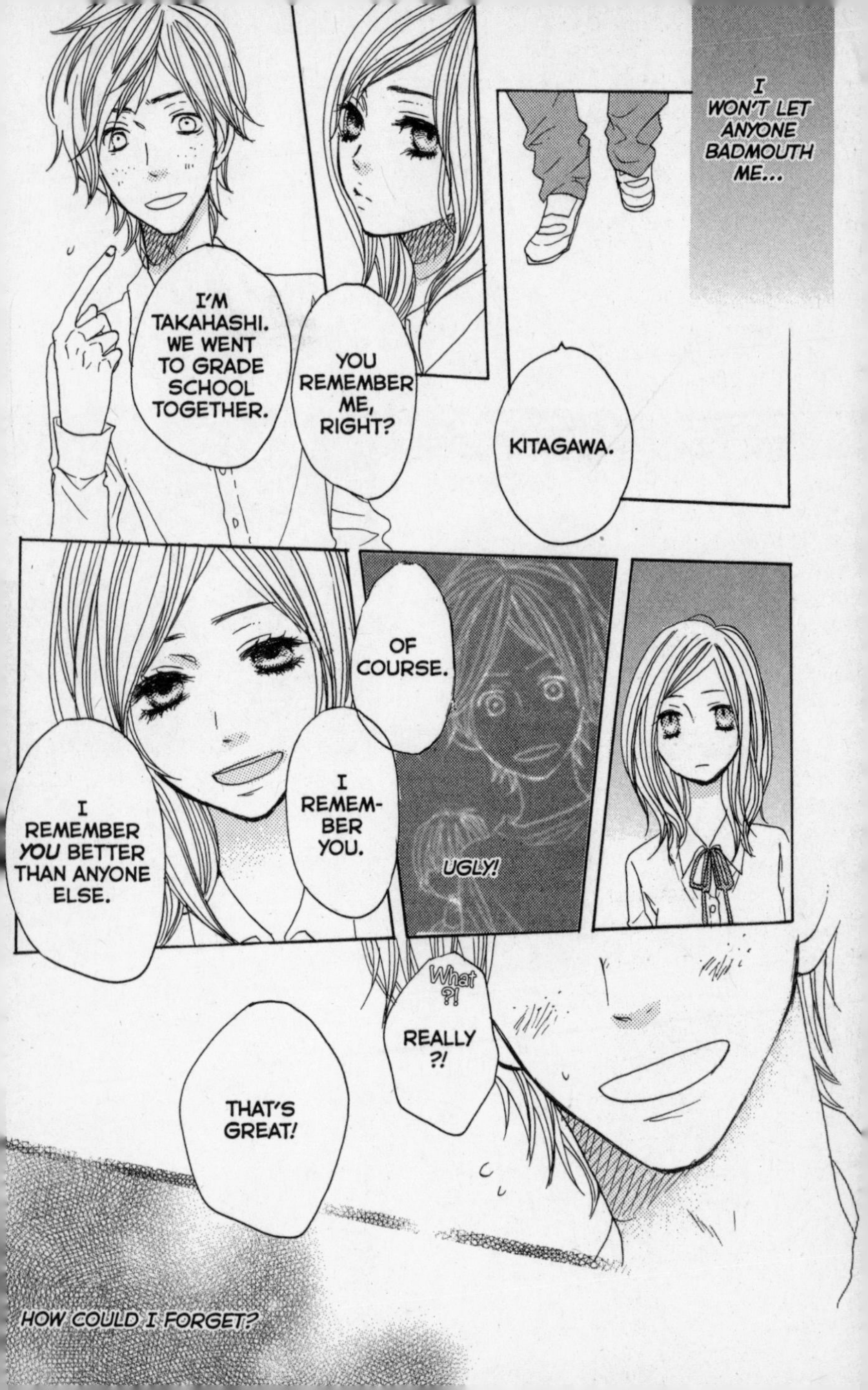
I WON'T LET ANYONE BADMOUTH ME...
KITAGAWA.
I'M TAKAHASHI. WE WENT TO GRADE SCHOOL TOGETHER.
YOU REMEMBER ME, RIGHT?
UGLY!
OF COURSE.
I REMEMBER YOU.
I REMEMBER *YOU* BETTER THAN ANYONE ELSE.
What?!
REALLY?!
THAT'S GREAT!
HOW COULD I FORGET?

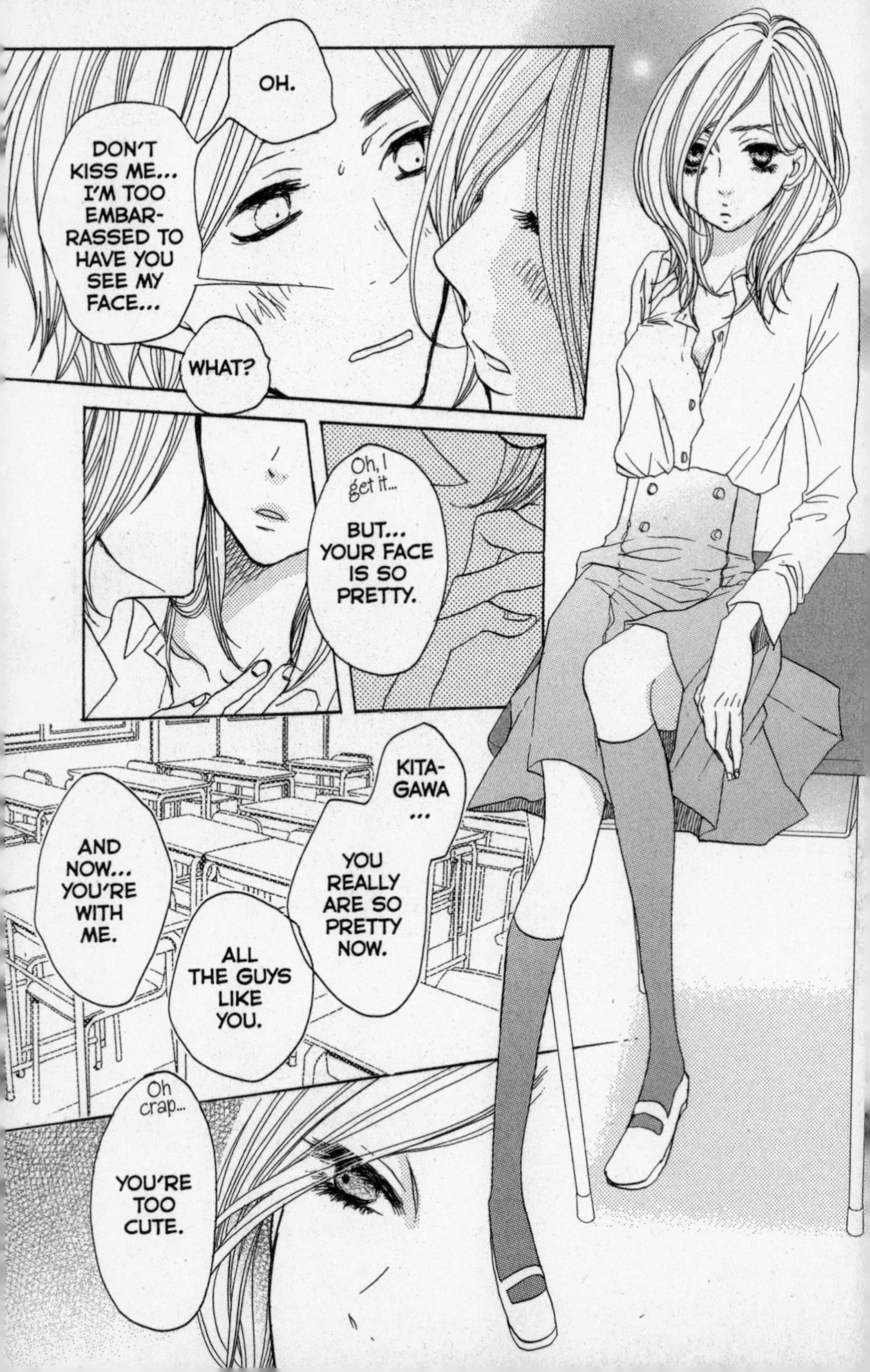
OH.
DON'T KISS ME... I'M TOO EMBAR-RASSED TO HAVE YOU SEE MY FACE...
WHAT?
Oh, I get it...
BUT... YOUR FACE IS SO PRETTY.
KITA-GAWA...
YOU REALLY ARE SO PRETTY NOW.
ALL THE GUYS LIKE YOU.
AND NOW... YOU'RE WITH ME.
Oh crap...
YOU'RE TOO CUTE.

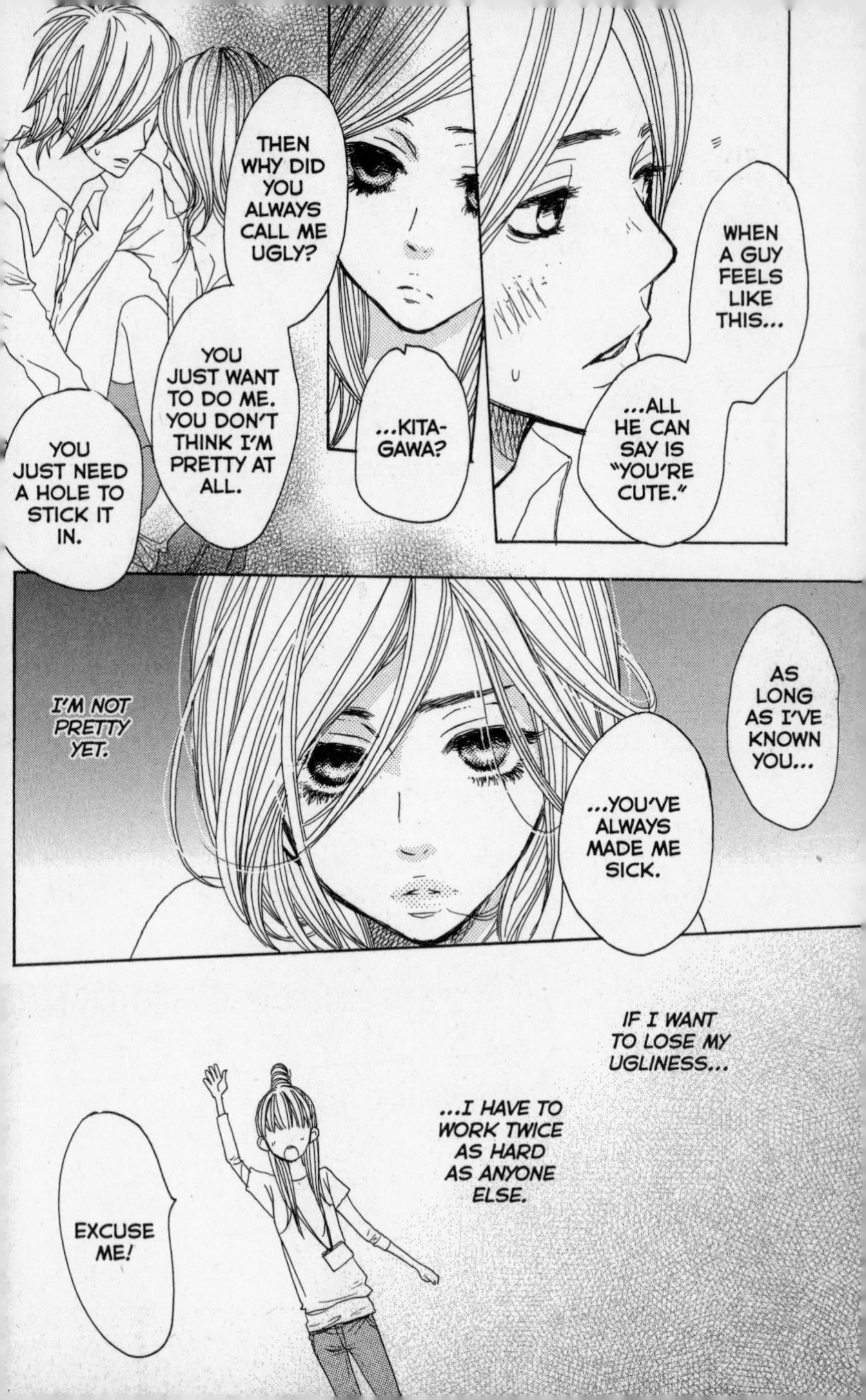
WHEN A GUY FEELS LIKE THIS...
...ALL HE CAN SAY IS "YOU'RE CUTE."
...KITA-GAWA?
THEN WHY DID YOU ALWAYS CALL ME UGLY?
YOU JUST WANT TO DO ME. YOU DON'T THINK I'M PRETTY AT ALL.
YOU JUST NEED A HOLE TO STICK IT IN.
AS LONG AS I'VE KNOWN YOU...
...YOU'VE ALWAYS MADE ME SICK.
I'M NOT PRETTY YET.
IF I WANT TO LOSE MY UGLINESS...
...I HAVE TO WORK TWICE AS HARD AS ANYONE ELSE.
EXCUSE ME!

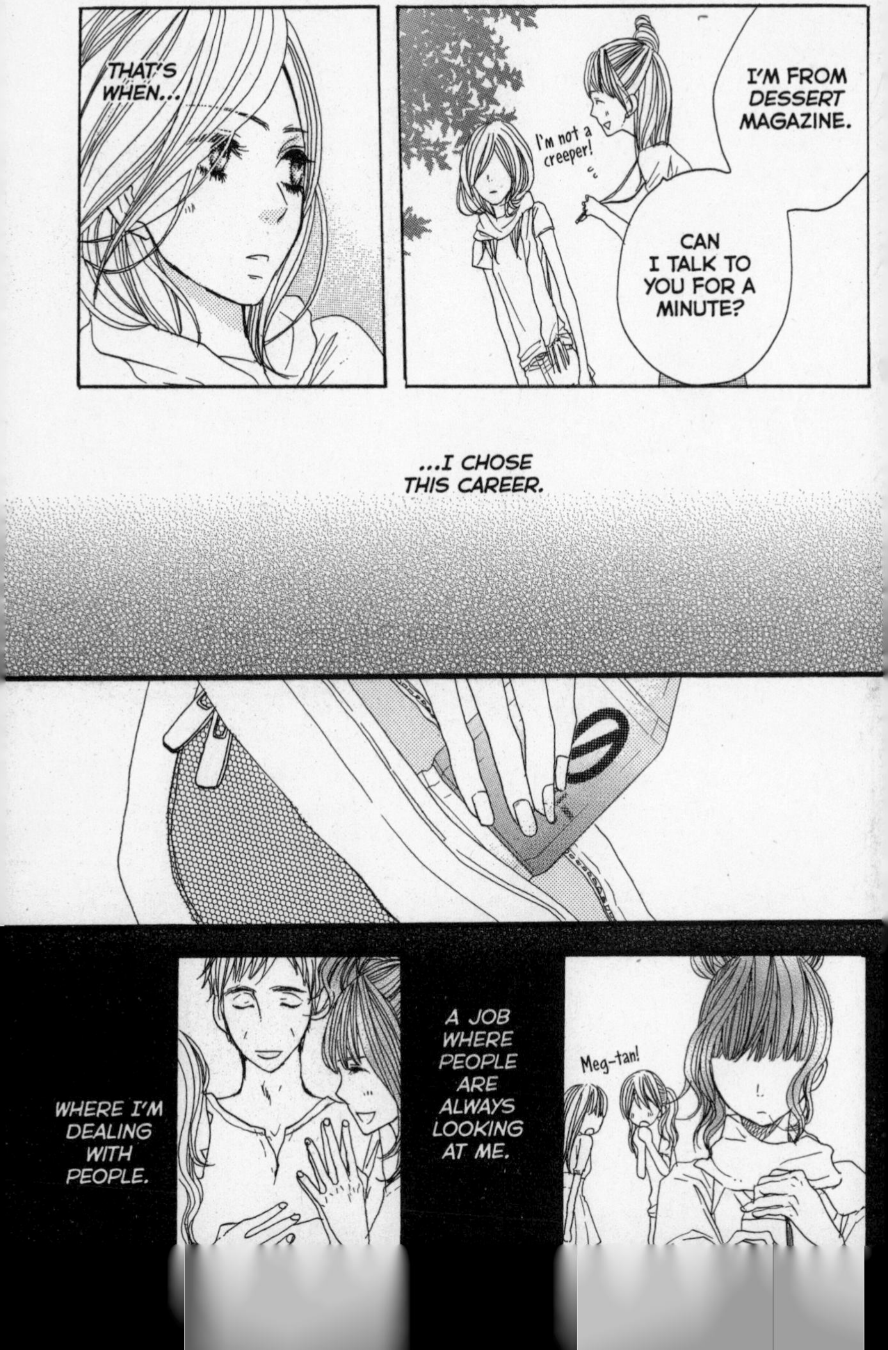
I'M FROM DESSERT MAGAZINE.
CAN I TALK TO YOU FOR A MINUTE?
I'm not a creeper!
THAT'S WHEN...
...I CHOSE THIS CAREER.
Meg-tan!
A JOB WHERE PEOPLE ARE ALWAYS LOOKING AT ME.
WHERE I'M DEALING WITH PEOPLE.

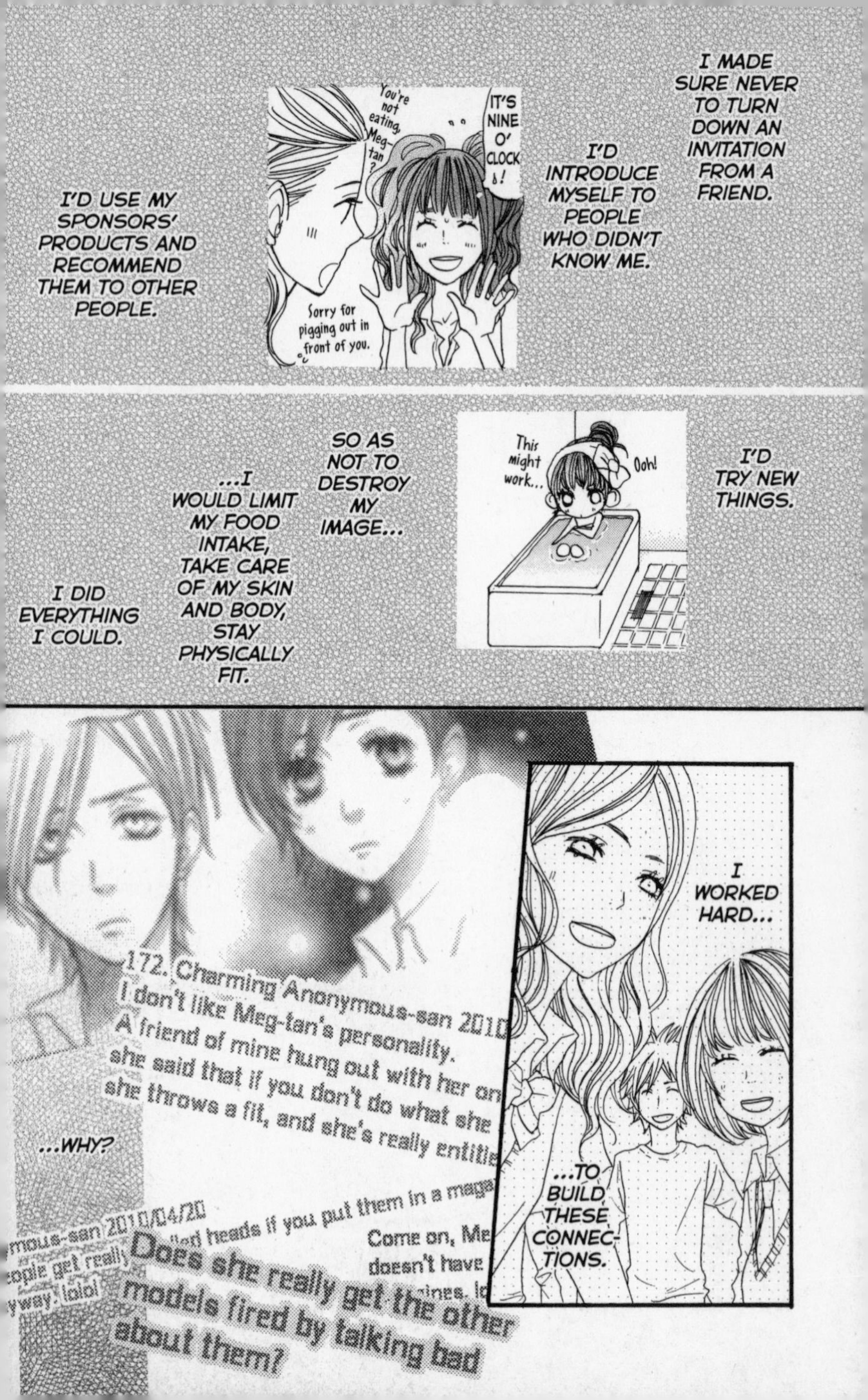

I MADE SURE NEVER TO TURN DOWN AN INVITATION FROM A FRIEND.
I'D INTRODUCE MYSELF TO PEOPLE WHO DIDN'T KNOW ME.
IT'S NINE O' CLOCK ♪!
You're not eating, Meg-tan?
Sorry for pigging out in front of you.
I'D USE MY SPONSORS' PRODUCTS AND RECOMMEND THEM TO OTHER PEOPLE.
I'D TRY NEW THINGS.
Ooh!
This might work...
SO AS NOT TO DESTROY MY IMAGE...
...I WOULD LIMIT MY FOOD INTAKE, TAKE CARE OF MY SKIN AND BODY, STAY PHYSICALLY FIT.
I DID EVERYTHING I COULD.
I WORKED HARD...
...TO BUILD THESE CONNECTIONS.
172. Charming Anonymous-san 2010
I don't like Meg-tan's personality.
A friend of mine hung out with her on
she said that if you don't do what she
she throws a fit, and she's really entitle
...WHY?
heads if you put them in a maga
mous-san 2010/04/20
Come on, Me
doesn't have
Does she really get the other models fired by talking bad about them?

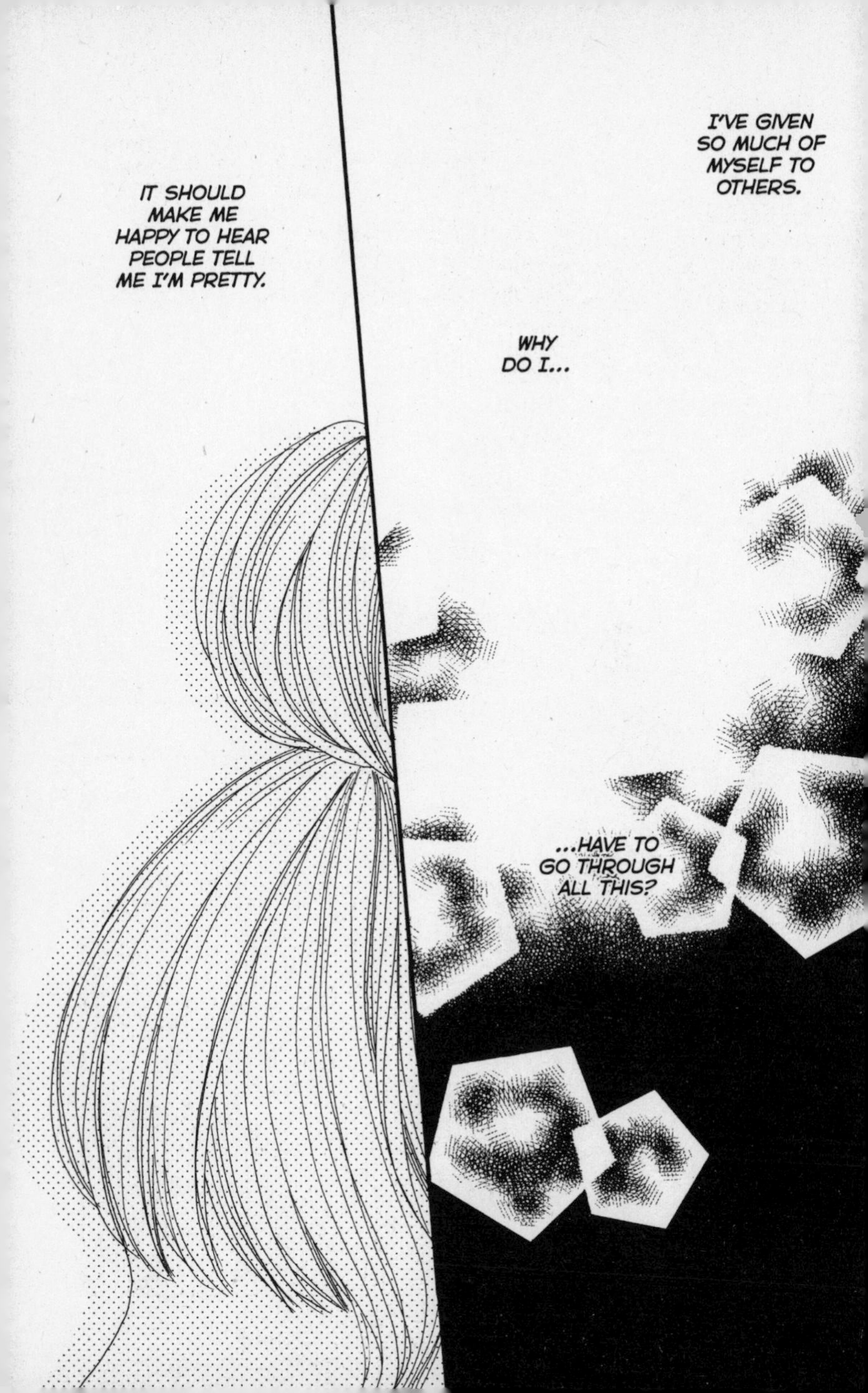
I'VE GIVEN SO MUCH OF MYSELF TO OTHERS.
WHY DO I...
...HAVE TO GO THROUGH ALL THIS?
IT SHOULD MAKE ME HAPPY TO HEAR PEOPLE TELL ME I'M PRETTY.

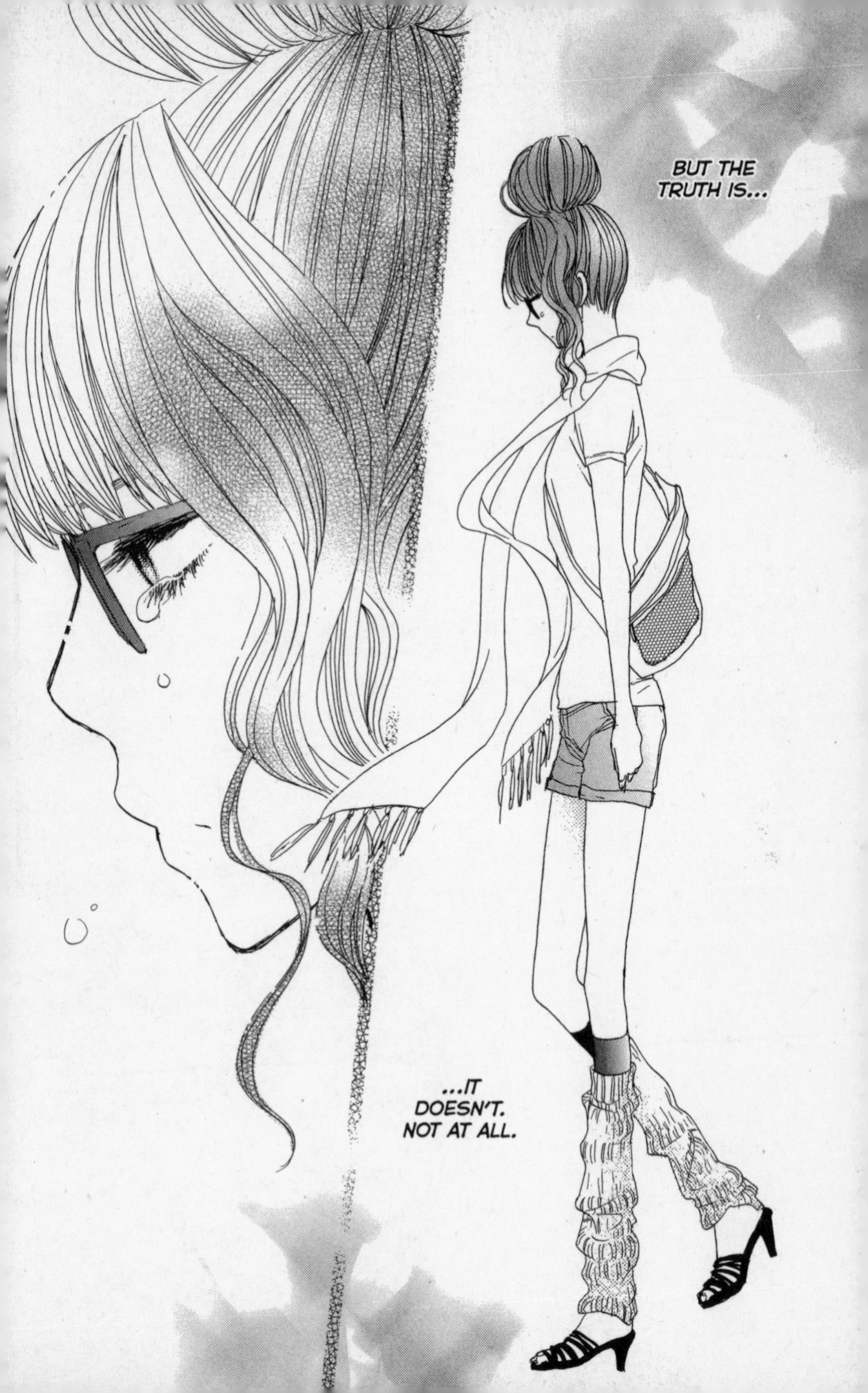
BUT THE TRUTH IS...
...IT DOESN'T. NOT AT ALL.

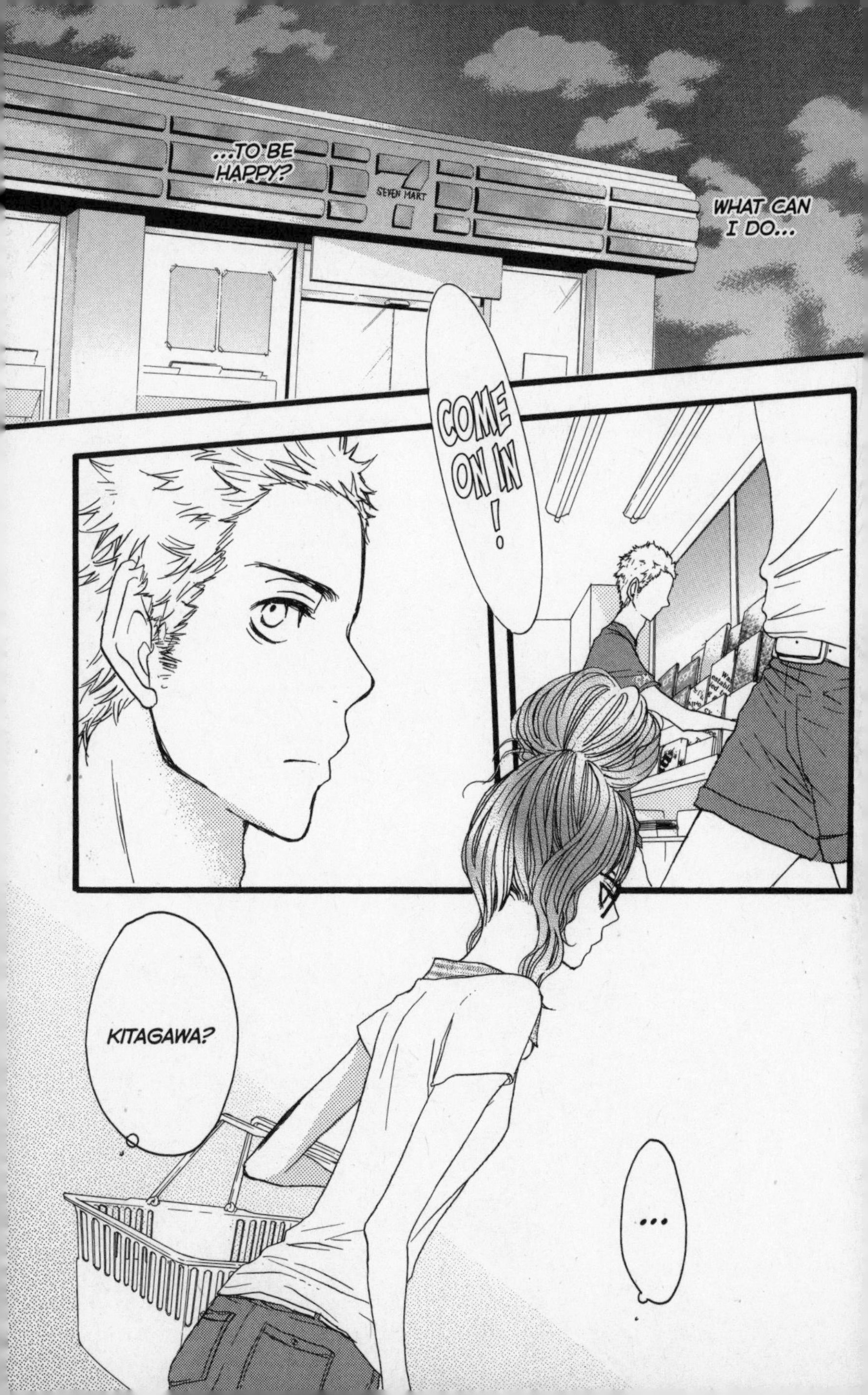
WHAT CAN I DO...
...TO BE HAPPY?
SEVEN MART
COME ON IN!
KITAGAWA?
...

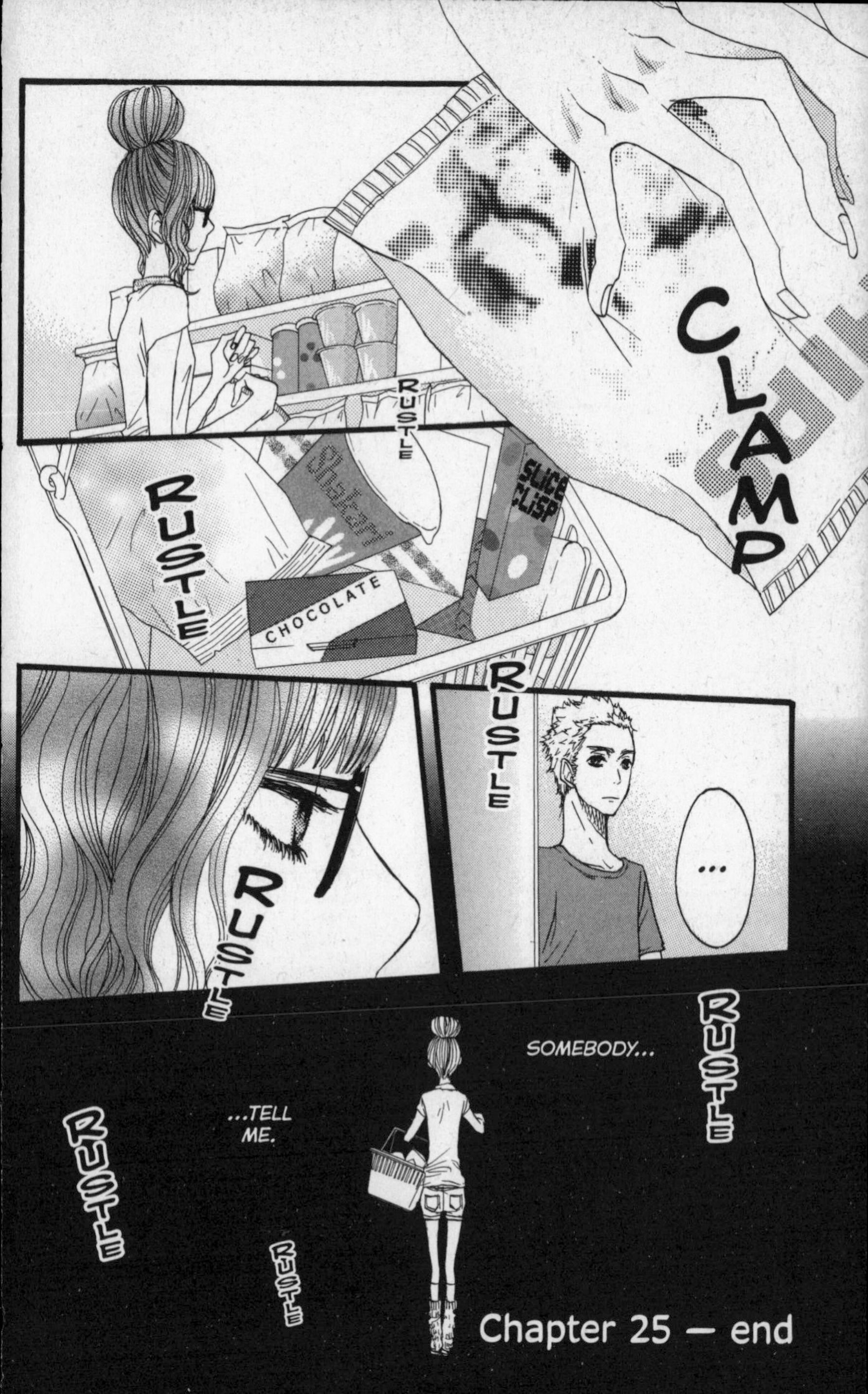
CLAMP
RUSTLE
RUSTLE
SLICE CLISP
CHOCOLATE
RUSTLE
...
RUSTLE
RUSTLE
SOMEBODY...
...TELL ME.
RUSTLE
RUSTLE
Chapter 25 — end

Say "I love you".

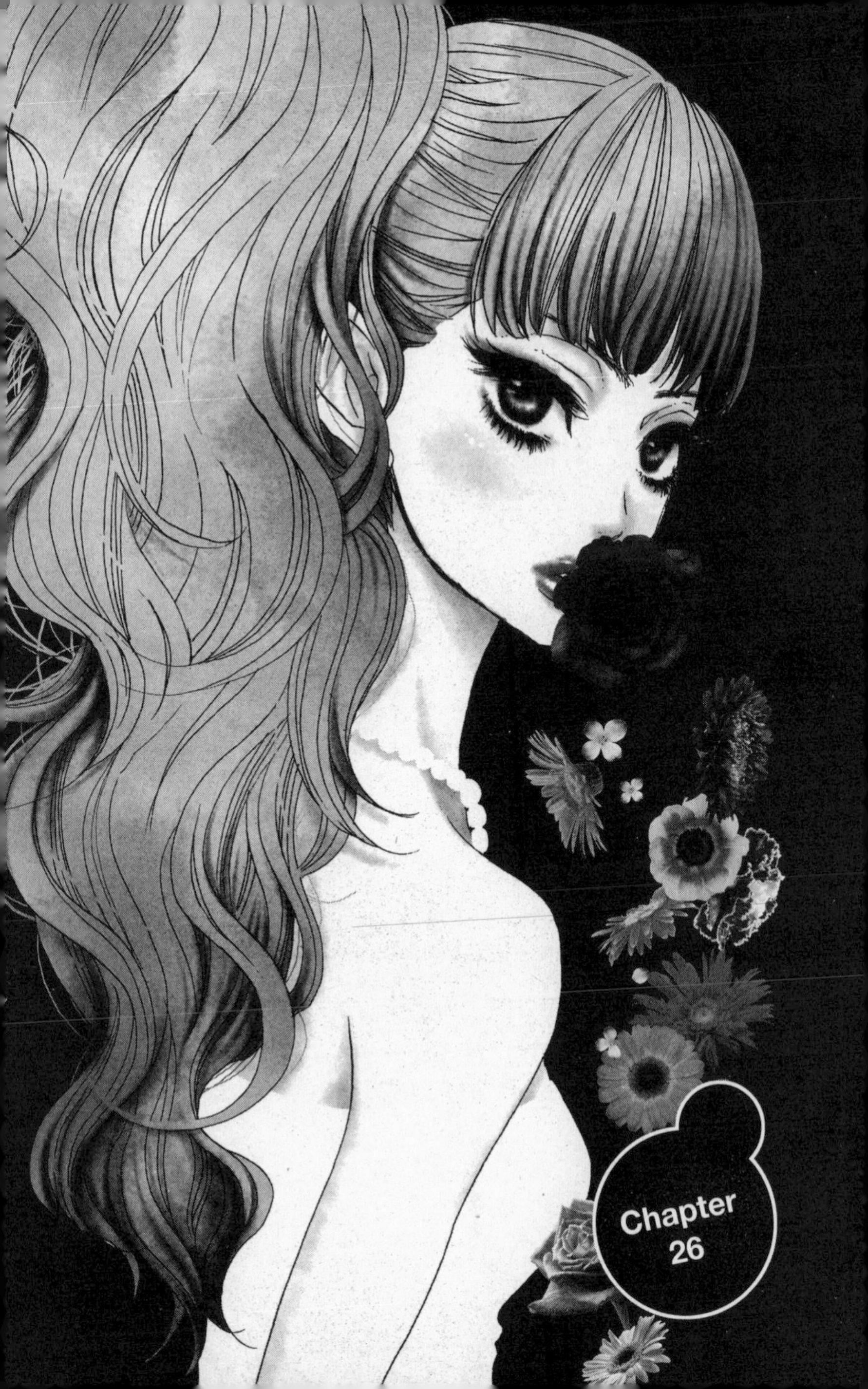
Chapter
26

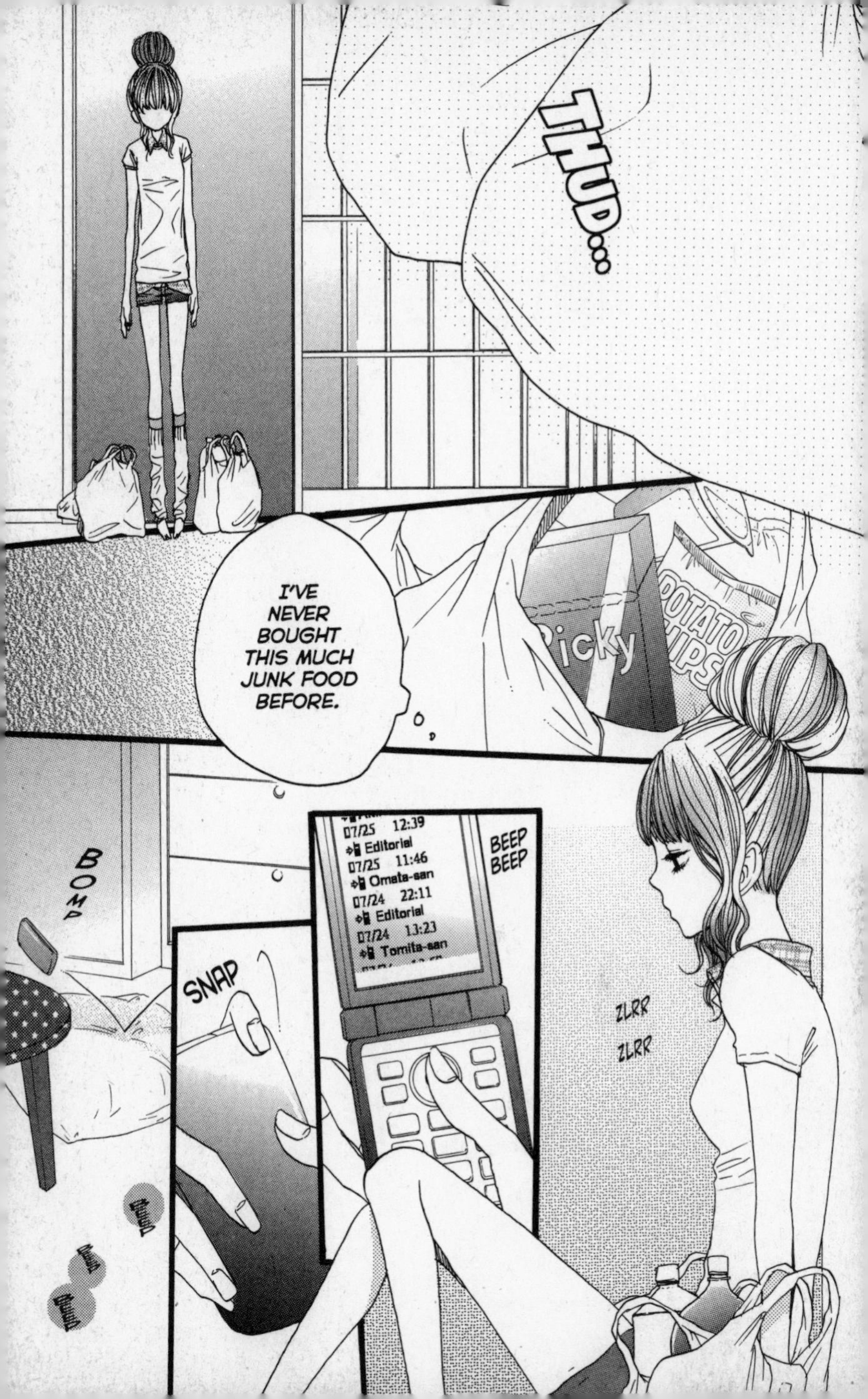
THUD...
I'VE NEVER BOUGHT THIS MUCH JUNK FOOD BEFORE.
Picky
POTATO CHIPS
BEEP BEEP
07/25 12:39
Editorial
07/25 11:46
Omata-san
07/24 22:11
Editorial
07/24 13:23
Tomita-san
ZLRR
ZLRR
SNAP
BOMP

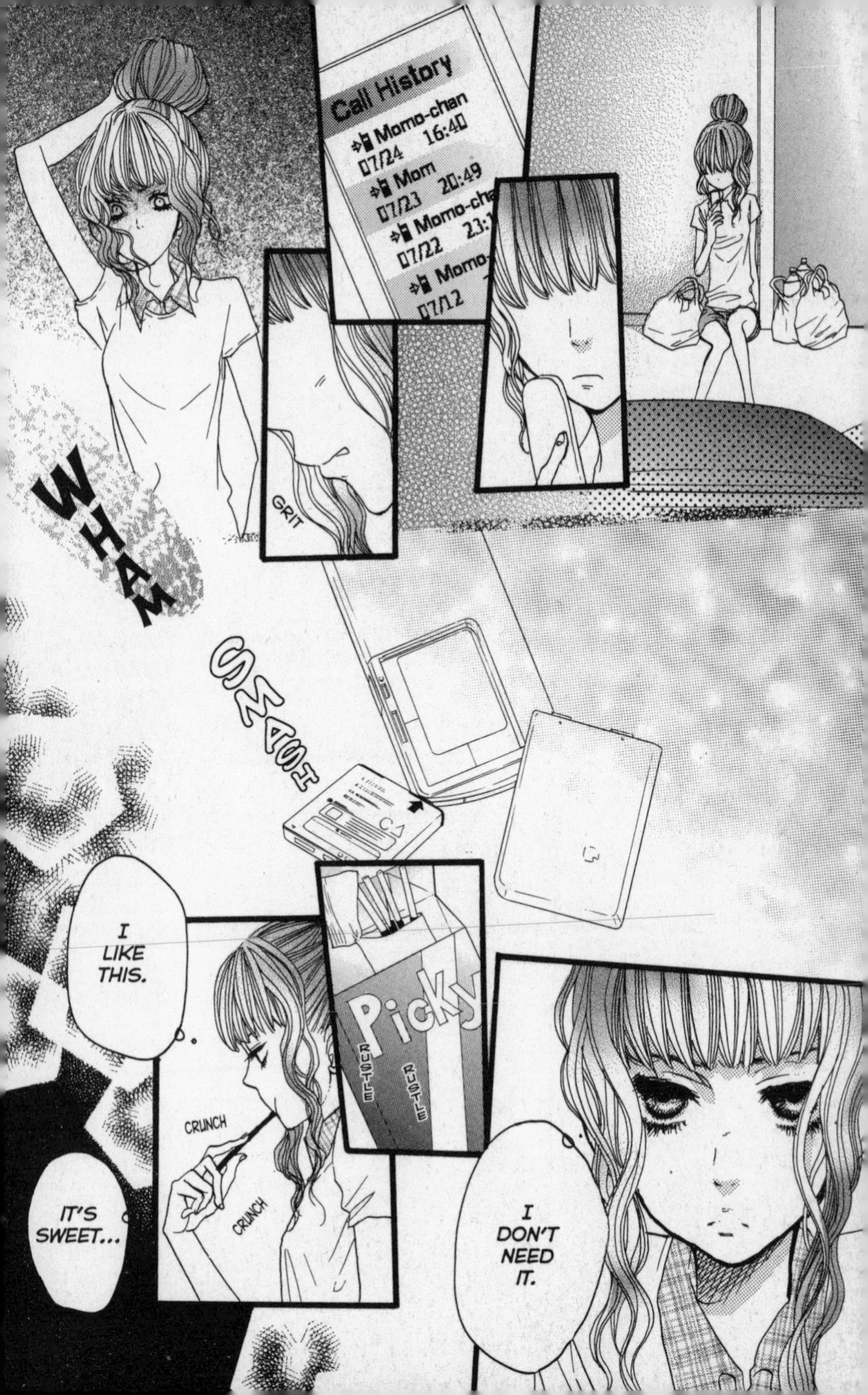
Call History
Momo-chan
07/24 16:40
Mom
07/23 20:49
GRIT
WHAM
SMASH
I DON'T NEED IT.
Picky
RUSTLE
RUSTLE
I LIKE THIS.
CRUNCH
CRUNCH
IT'S SWEET...

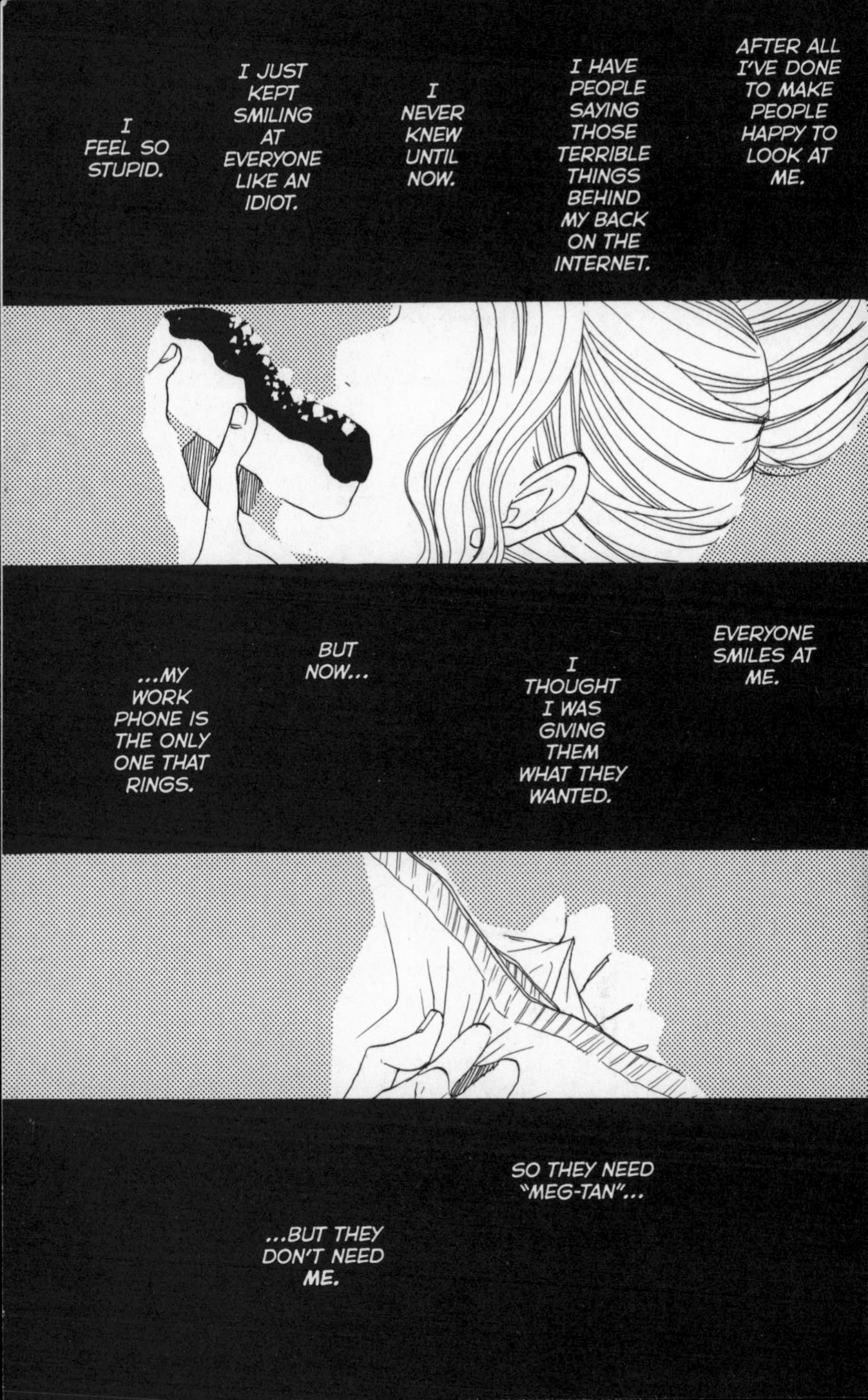

AFTER ALL I'VE DONE TO MAKE PEOPLE HAPPY TO LOOK AT ME.
I HAVE PEOPLE SAYING THOSE TERRIBLE THINGS BEHIND MY BACK ON THE INTERNET.
I NEVER KNEW UNTIL NOW.
I JUST KEPT SMILING AT EVERYONE LIKE AN IDIOT.
I FEEL SO STUPID.
EVERYONE SMILES AT ME.
I THOUGHT I WAS GIVING THEM WHAT THEY WANTED.
BUT NOW...
...MY WORK PHONE IS THE ONLY ONE THAT RINGS.
SO THEY NEED "MEG-TAN"...
...BUT THEY DON'T NEED ME.

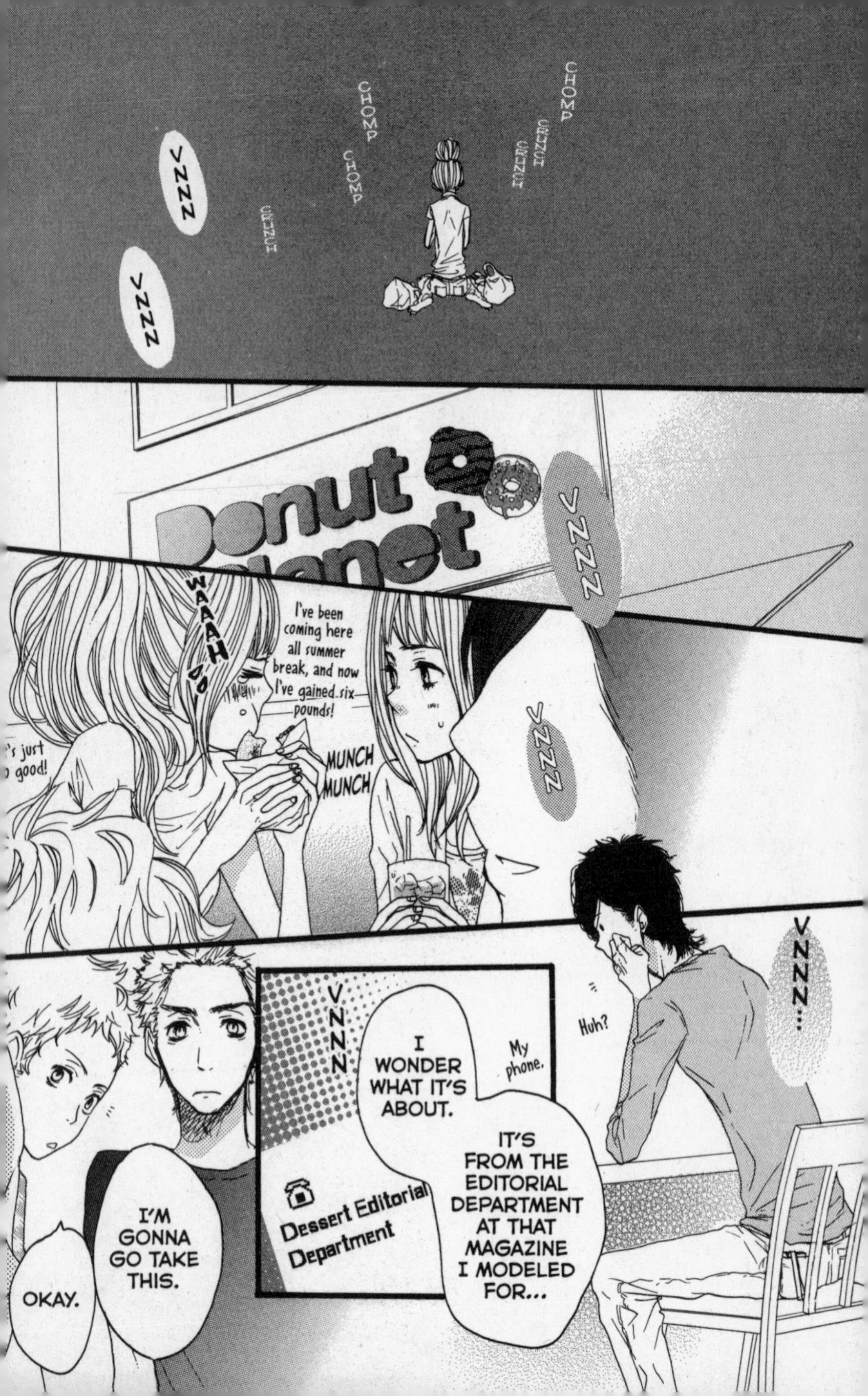
CHOMP
CRUNCH
CRUNCH
CHOMP
CHOMP
CRUNCH
VNNN
VNNN
Donut Planet
VNNN
VNNN
I've been coming here all summer break, and now I've gained six pounds!
WAAAAH
MUNCH MUNCH
's just
good!
VNNN...
Huh?
My phone.
VNNN
I WONDER WHAT IT'S ABOUT.
IT'S FROM THE EDITORIAL DEPARTMENT AT THAT MAGAZINE I MODELED FOR...
Dessert Editorial Department
I'M GONNA GO TAKE THIS.
OKAY.

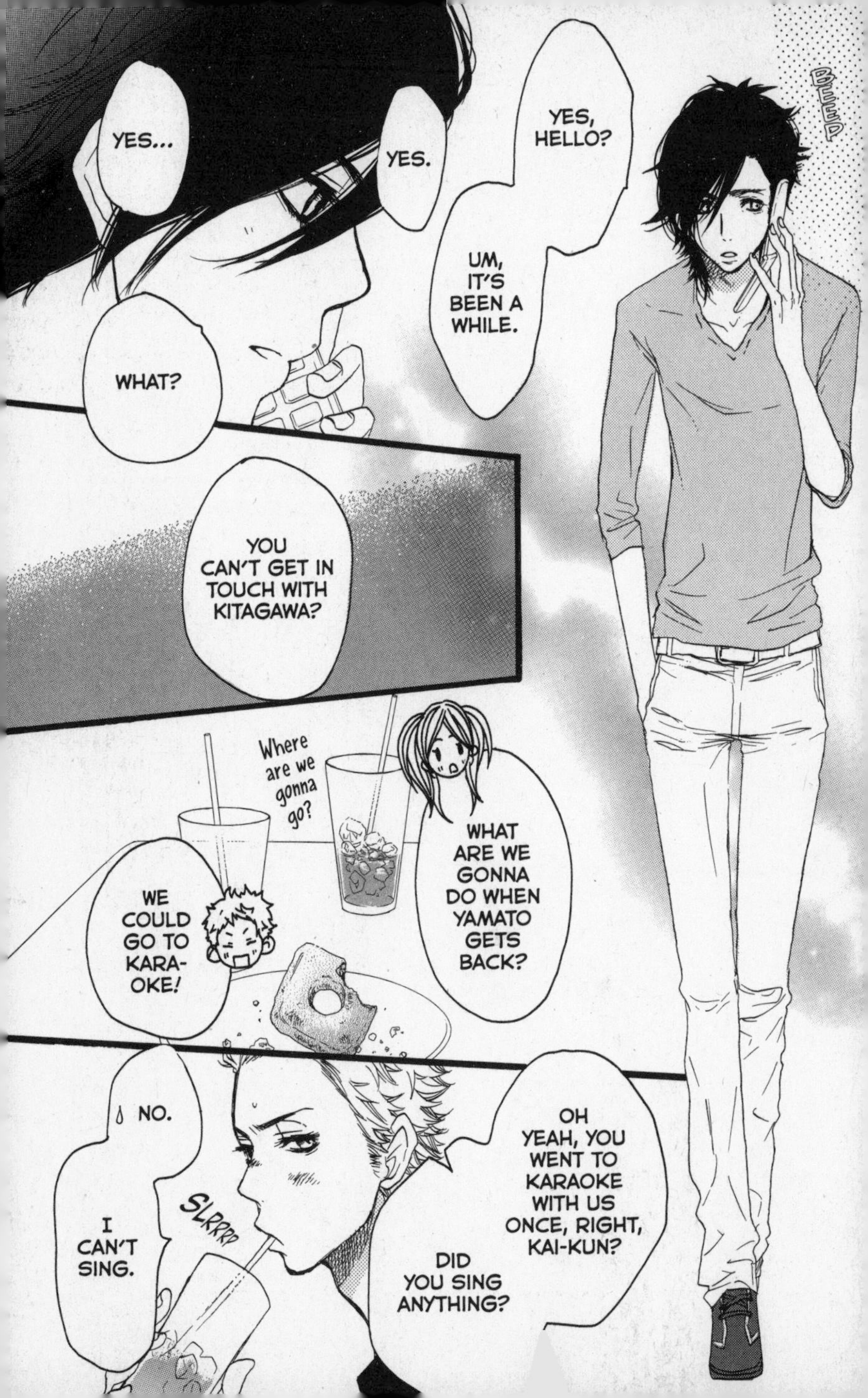
BEEP
YES, HELLO?
UM, IT'S BEEN A WHILE.
YES.
YES...
WHAT?
YOU CAN'T GET IN TOUCH WITH KITAGAWA?
WHAT ARE WE GONNA DO WHEN YAMATO GETS BACK?
Where are we gonna go?
WE COULD GO TO KARA-OKE!
OH YEAH, YOU WENT TO KARAOKE WITH US ONCE, RIGHT, KAI-KUN?
DID YOU SING ANYTHING?
NO.
SLRRRP
I CAN'T SING.

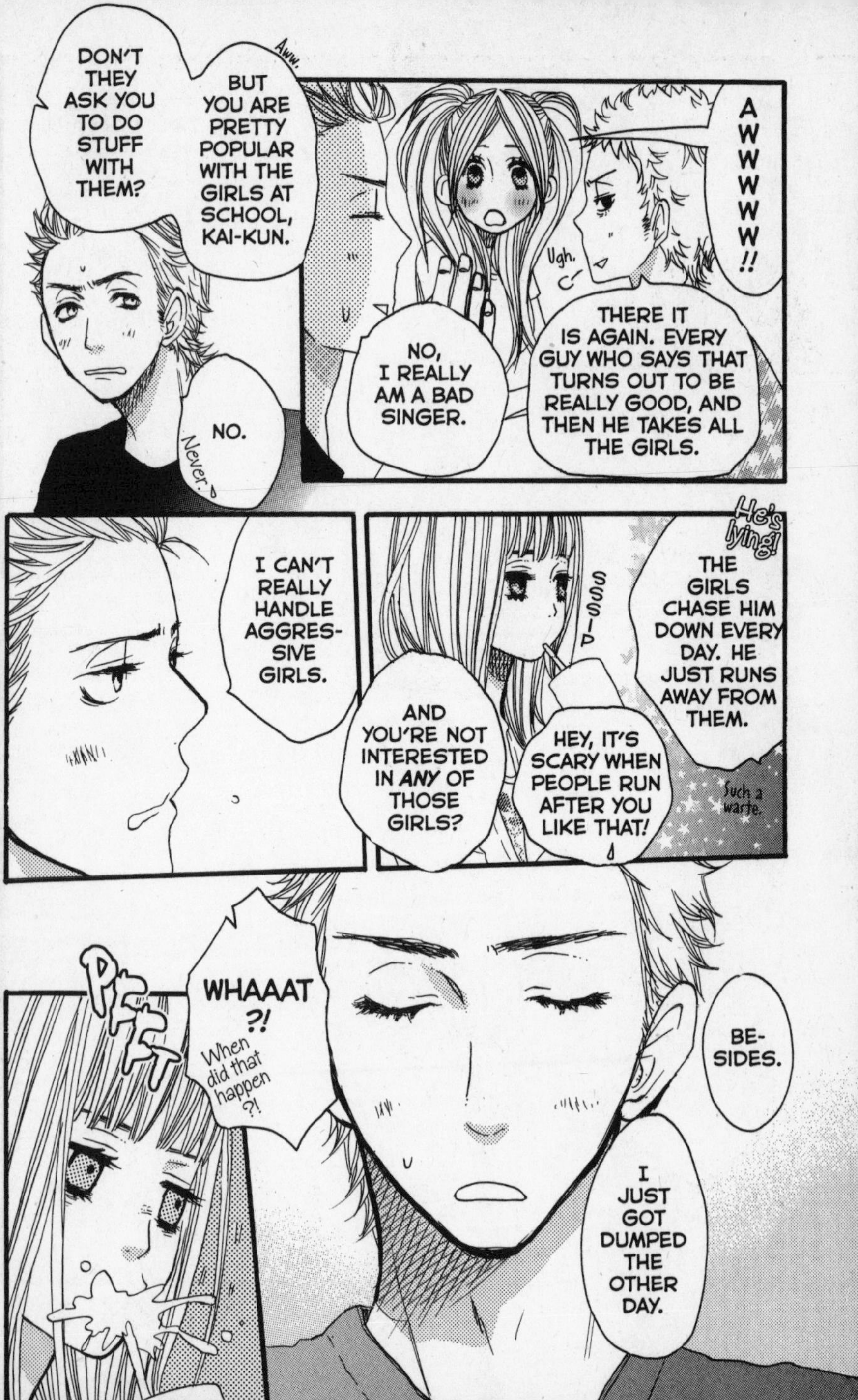
AWWWWWW!!
Ugh.
THERE IT IS AGAIN. EVERY GUY WHO SAYS THAT TURNS OUT TO BE REALLY GOOD, AND THEN HE TAKES ALL THE GIRLS.
NO, I REALLY AM A BAD SINGER.
Aww.
BUT YOU ARE PRETTY POPULAR WITH THE GIRLS AT SCHOOL, KAI-KUN.
DON'T THEY ASK YOU TO DO STUFF WITH THEM?
NO.
Never.
He's lying!
THE GIRLS CHASE HIM DOWN EVERY DAY. HE JUST RUNS AWAY FROM THEM.
SSSIP
HEY, IT'S SCARY WHEN PEOPLE RUN AFTER YOU LIKE THAT!
Such a waste.
AND YOU'RE NOT INTERESTED IN *ANY* OF THOSE GIRLS?
I CAN'T REALLY HANDLE AGGRES-SIVE GIRLS.
BE-SIDES.
I JUST GOT DUMPED THE OTHER DAY.
WHAAAT?!
When did that happen?!
PFFT

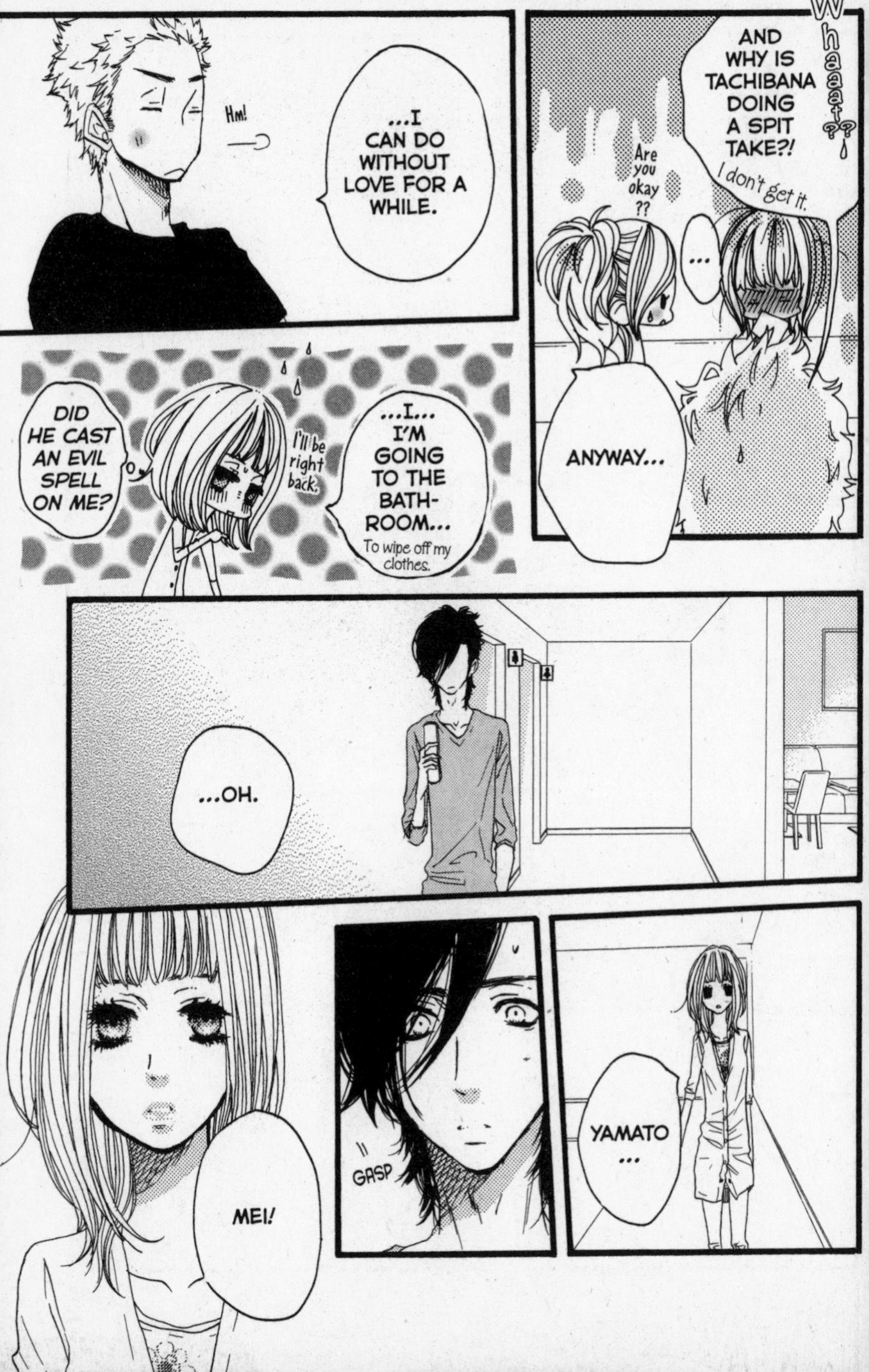
Whaaat??
AND WHY IS TACHIBANA DOING A SPIT TAKE?!
I don't get it.
Are you okay ??
...
ANYWAY...
Hm!
...I CAN DO WITHOUT LOVE FOR A WHILE.
...I... I'M GOING TO THE BATHROOM...
To wipe off my clothes.
I'll be right back.
DID HE CAST AN EVIL SPELL ON ME?
...OH.
YAMATO ...
GASP
MEI!

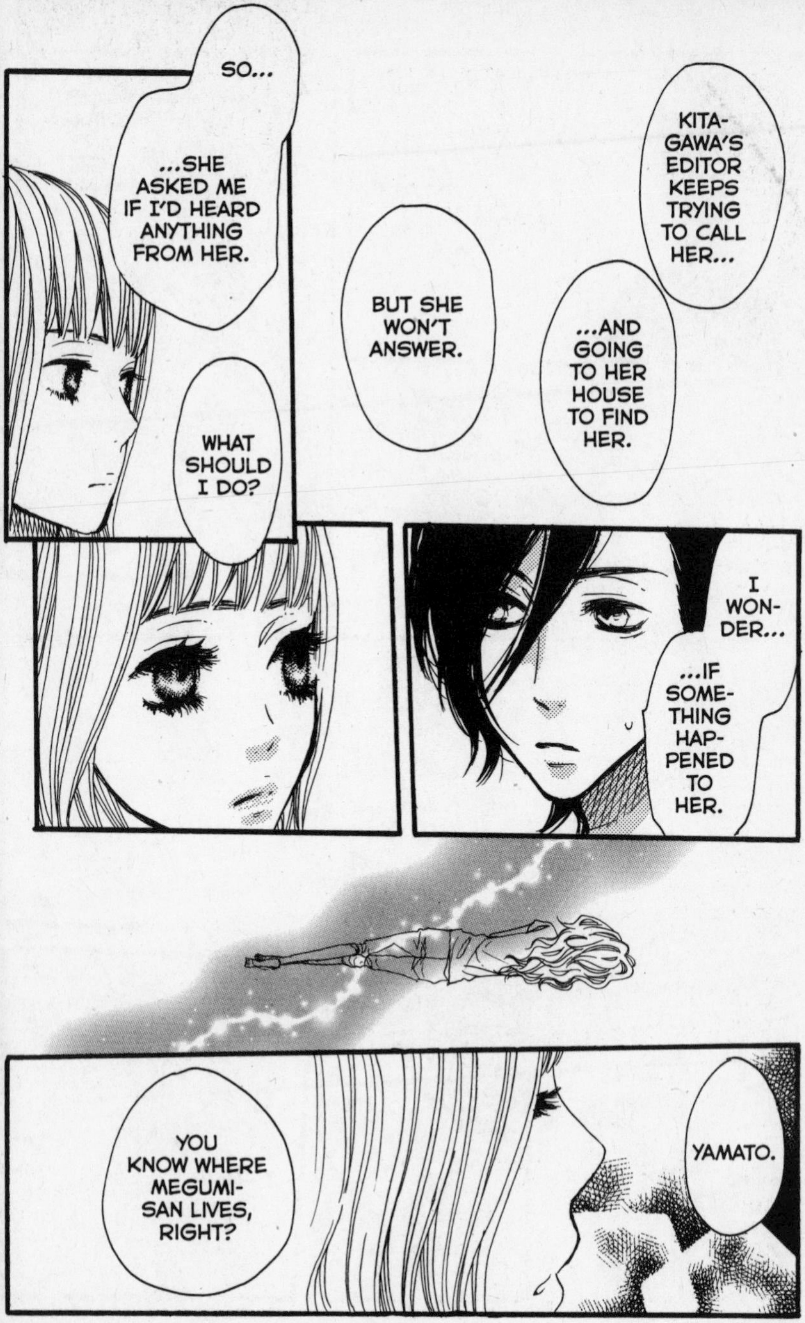
KITA-GAWA'S EDITOR KEEPS TRYING TO CALL HER...
...AND GOING TO HER HOUSE TO FIND HER.
BUT SHE WON'T ANSWER.
SO...
...SHE ASKED ME IF I'D HEARD ANYTHING FROM HER.
WHAT SHOULD I DO?
I WON-DER...
...IF SOME-THING HAP-PENED TO HER.
YAMATO.
YOU KNOW WHERE MEGUMI-SAN LIVES, RIGHT?

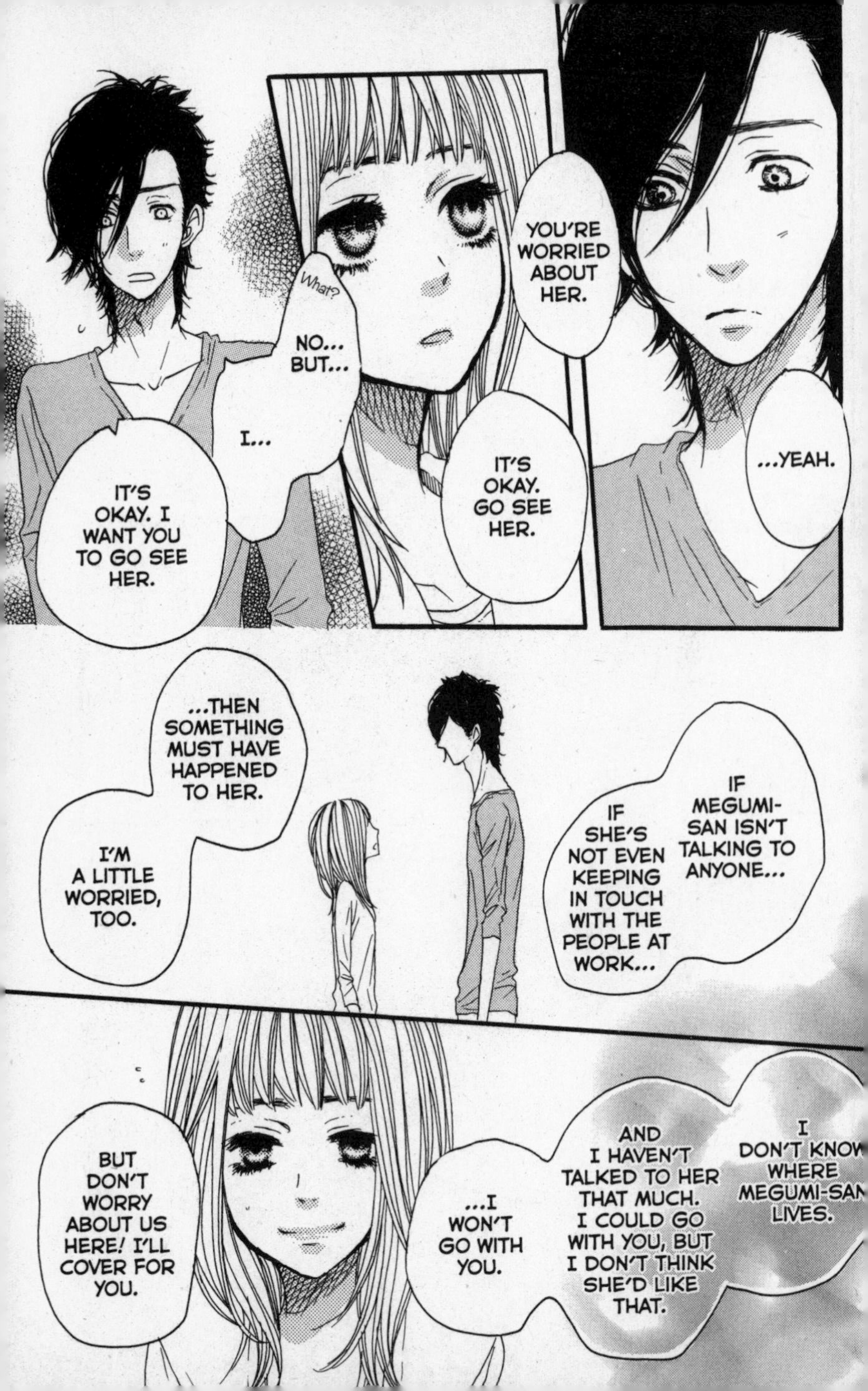
YOU'RE WORRIED ABOUT HER.
...YEAH.
IT'S OKAY. GO SEE HER.
What?
NO... BUT...
I...
IT'S OKAY. I WANT YOU TO GO SEE HER.
IF MEGUMI-SAN ISN'T TALKING TO ANYONE...
IF SHE'S NOT EVEN KEEPING IN TOUCH WITH THE PEOPLE AT WORK...
...THEN SOMETHING MUST HAVE HAPPENED TO HER.
I'M A LITTLE WORRIED, TOO.
I DON'T KNOW WHERE MEGUMI-SAN LIVES.
AND I HAVEN'T TALKED TO HER THAT MUCH. I COULD GO WITH YOU, BUT I DON'T THINK SHE'D LIKE THAT.
...I WON'T GO WITH YOU.
BUT DON'T WORRY ABOUT US HERE! I'LL COVER FOR YOU.

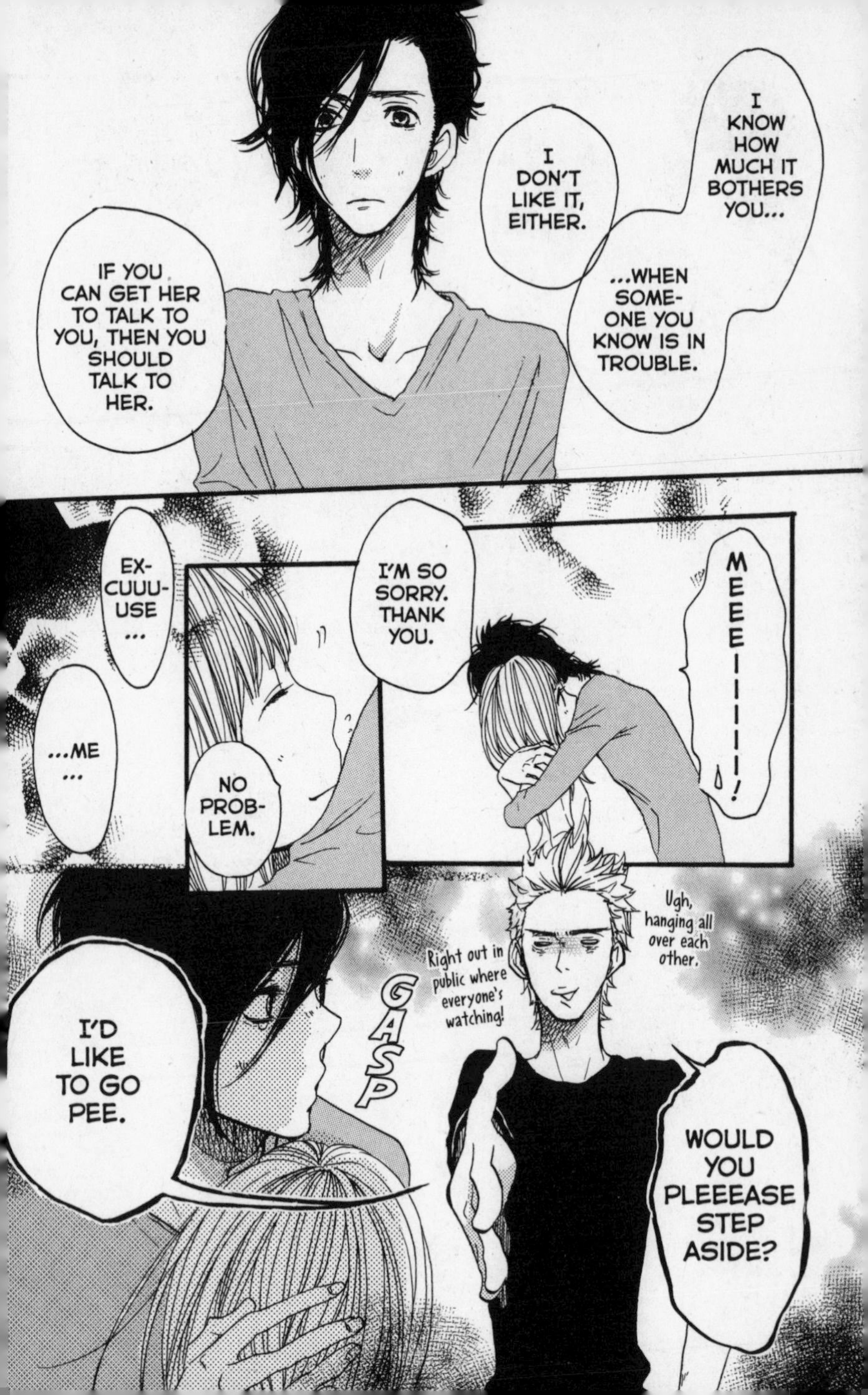
I KNOW HOW MUCH IT BOTHERS YOU...
...WHEN SOME-ONE YOU KNOW IS IN TROUBLE.
I DON'T LIKE IT, EITHER.
IF YOU CAN GET HER TO TALK TO YOU, THEN YOU SHOULD TALK TO HER.
MEEE!!!!!!
I'M SO SORRY. THANK YOU.
NO PROB-LEM.
Ugh, hanging all over each other.
Right out in public where everyone's watching!
EX-CUUU-USE...
...ME...
WOULD YOU PLEEEASE STEP ASIDE?
GASP
I'D LIKE TO GO PEE.

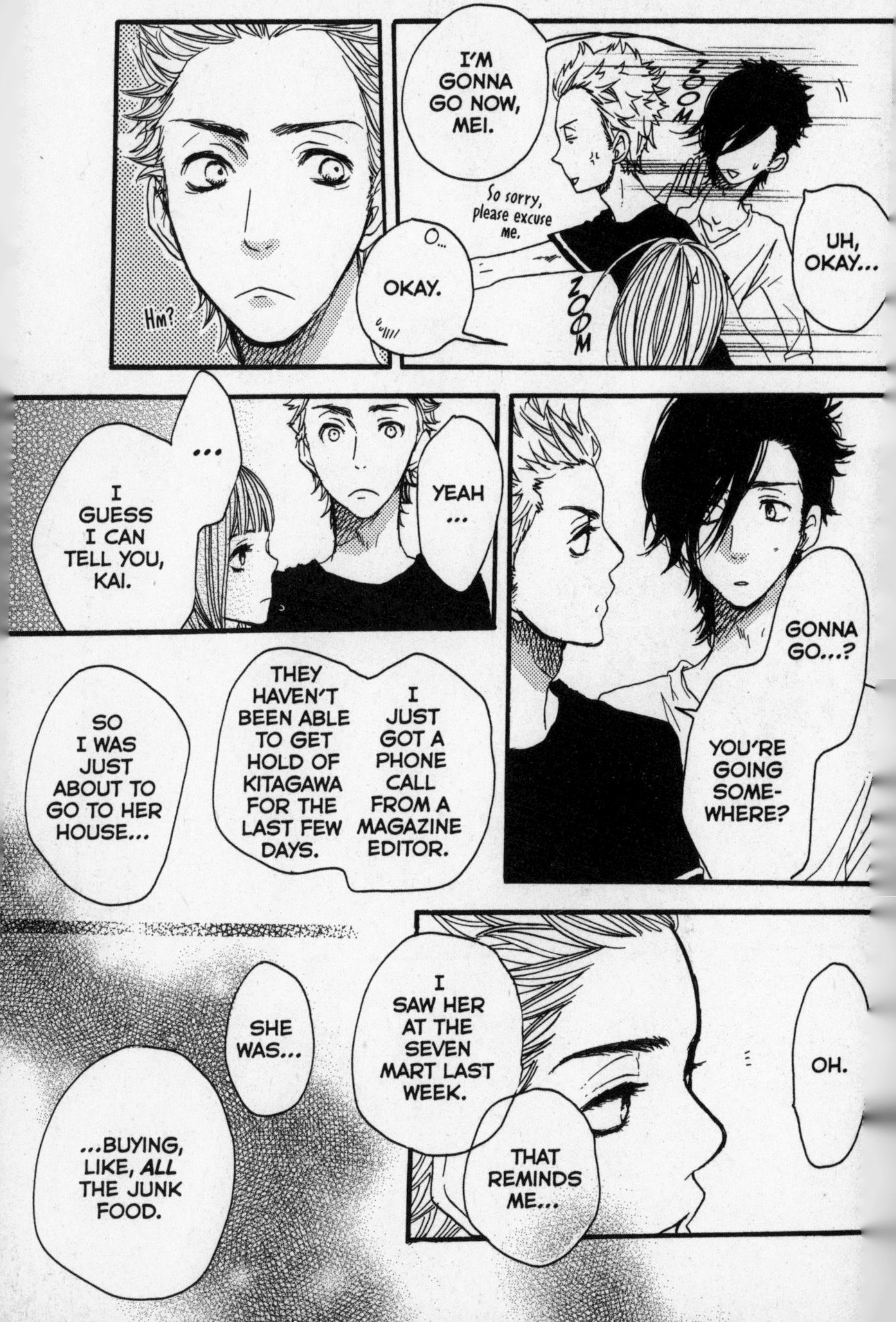
I'M GONNA GO NOW, MEI.
So sorry, please excuse me.
ZOOM
ZOOM
UH, OKAY...
O... OKAY.
Hm?
GONNA GO...?
YOU'RE GOING SOMEWHERE?
YEAH...
...
I GUESS I CAN TELL YOU, KAI.
I JUST GOT A PHONE CALL FROM A MAGAZINE EDITOR.
THEY HAVEN'T BEEN ABLE TO GET HOLD OF KITAGAWA FOR THE LAST FEW DAYS.
SO I WAS JUST ABOUT TO GO TO HER HOUSE...
OH.
THAT REMINDS ME...
I SAW HER AT THE SEVEN MART LAST WEEK.
SHE WAS...
...BUYING, LIKE, *ALL* THE JUNK FOOD.

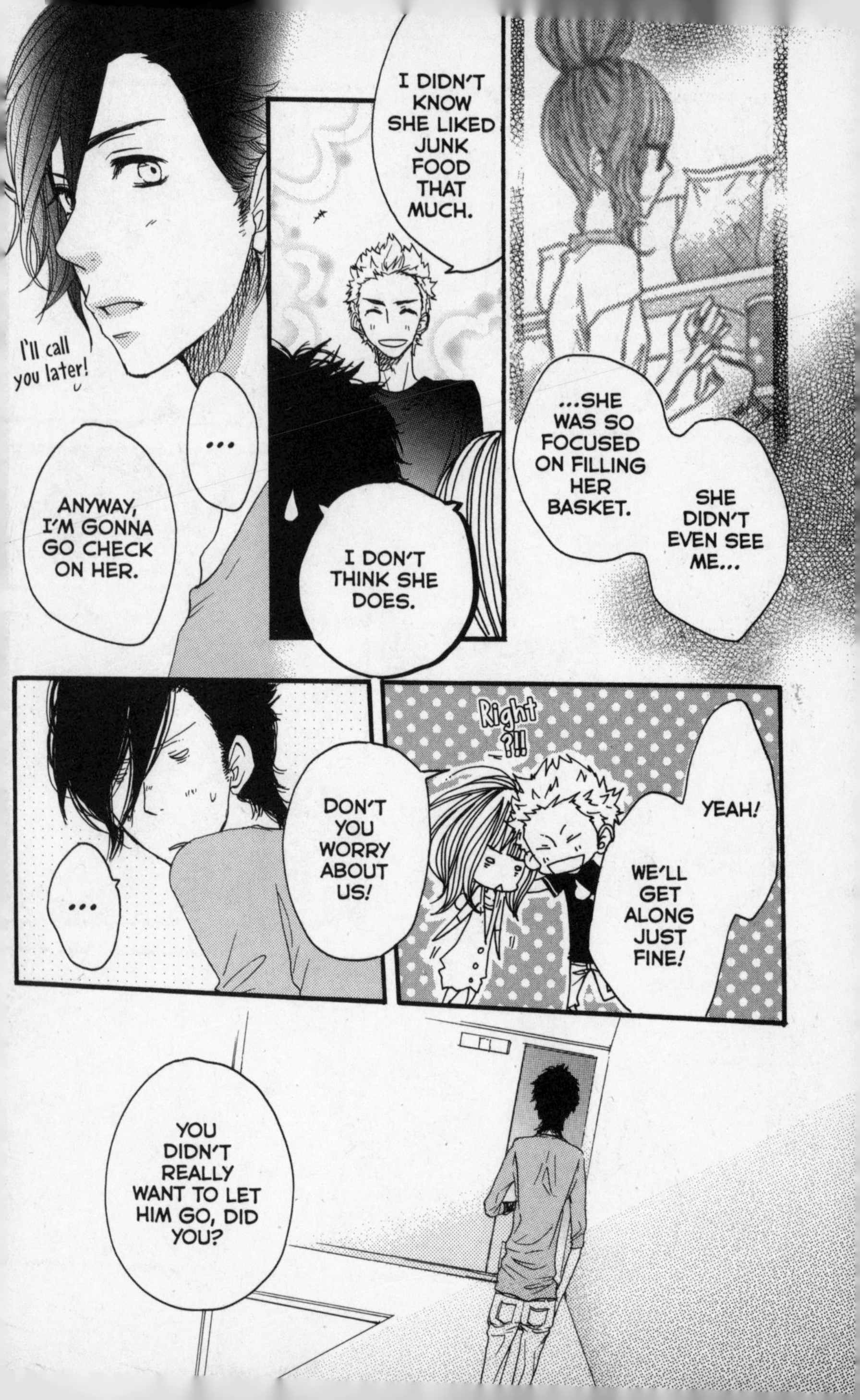
...SHE WAS SO FOCUSED ON FILLING HER BASKET.
SHE DIDN'T EVEN SEE ME...
I DIDN'T KNOW SHE LIKED JUNK FOOD THAT MUCH.
I DON'T THINK SHE DOES.
...
ANYWAY, I'M GONNA GO CHECK ON HER.
I'll call you later!
YEAH!
WE'LL GET ALONG JUST FINE!
Right ?!!
DON'T YOU WORRY ABOUT US!
...
YOU DIDN'T REALLY WANT TO LET HIM GO, DID YOU?

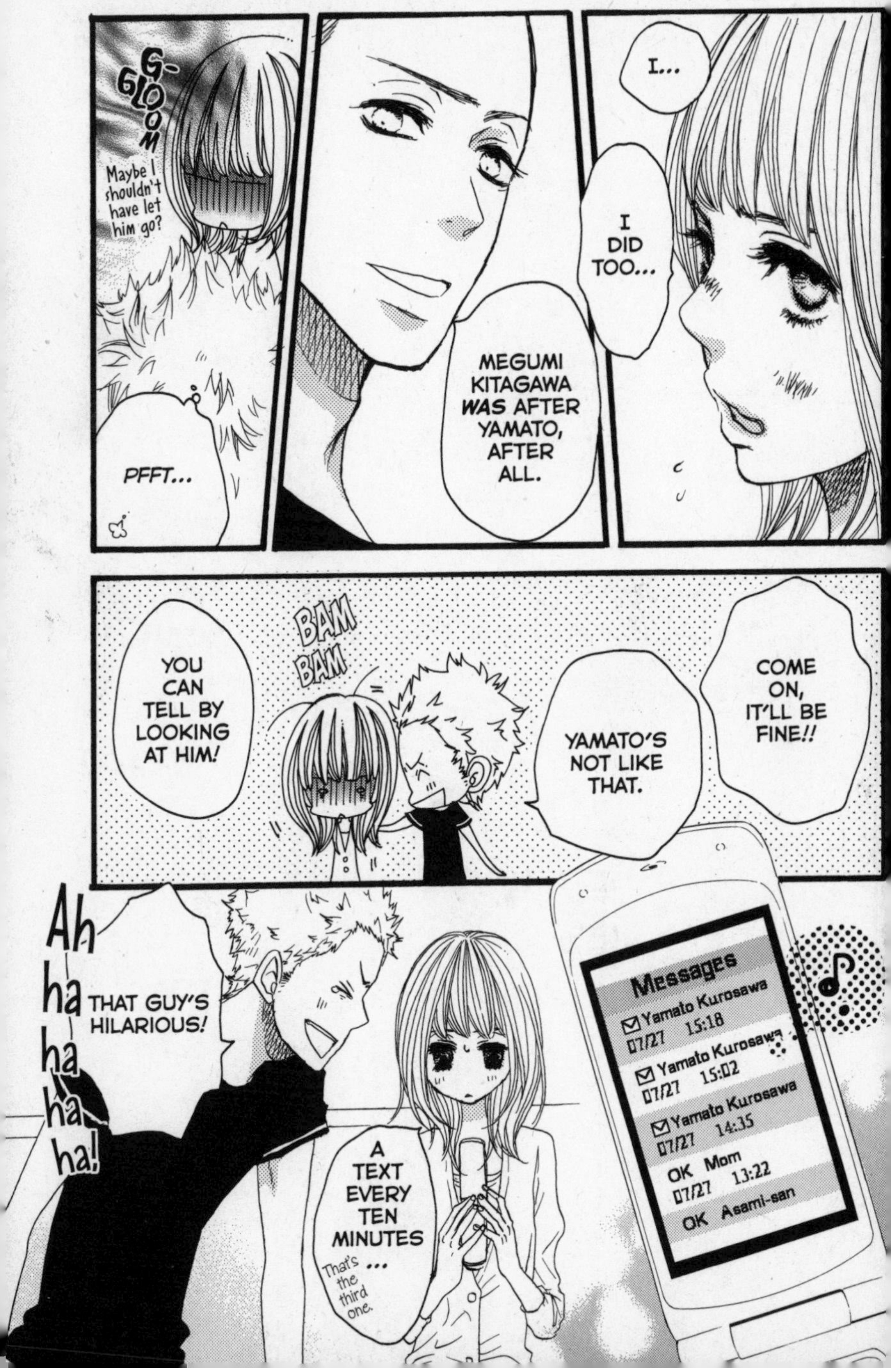
I...
I DID TOO...
MEGUMI KITAGAWA WAS AFTER YAMATO, AFTER ALL.
G-GLOOM
Maybe I shouldn't have let him go?
PFFT...
COME ON, IT'LL BE FINE!!
YAMATO'S NOT LIKE THAT.
BAM BAM
YOU CAN TELL BY LOOKING AT HIM!
Messages
Yamato Kurosawa
07/27 15:18
Yamato Kurosawa
07/27 15:02
Yamato Kurosawa
07/27 14:35
OK Mom
07/27 13:22
OK Asami-san
A TEXT EVERY TEN MINUTES...
That's the third one.
THAT GUY'S HILARIOUS!
Ah ha ha ha ha!

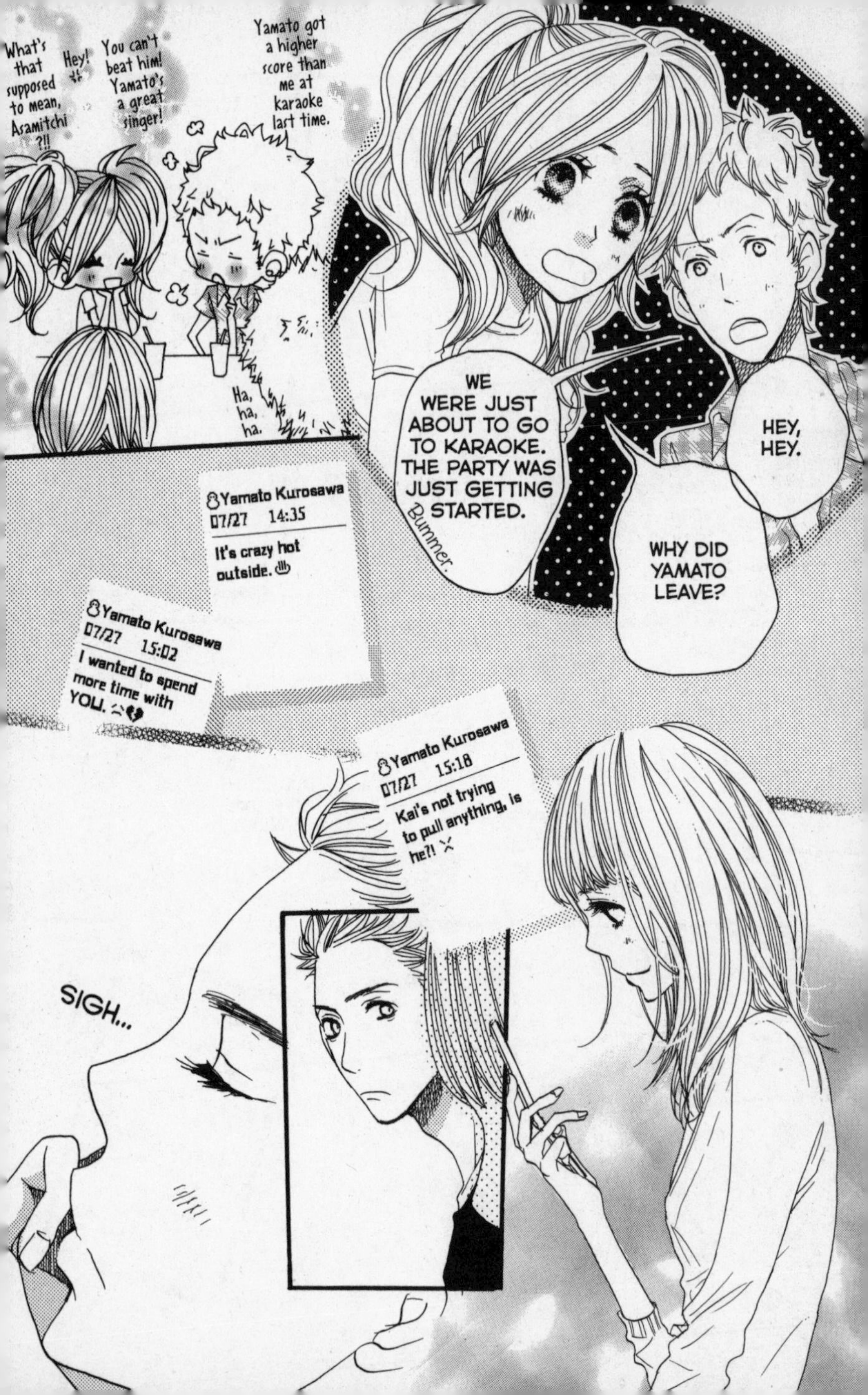
HEY, HEY.
WE WERE JUST ABOUT TO GO TO KARAOKE. THE PARTY WAS JUST GETTING STARTED.
Bummer.
WHY DID YAMATO LEAVE?
Yamato got a higher score than me at karaoke last time.
You can't beat him! Yamato's a great singer!
Hey!
What's that supposed to mean, Asamitchi?!!
Ha, ha, ha.
Yamato Kurosawa
07/27 14:35
It's crazy hot outside.
Yamato Kurosawa
07/27 15:02
I wanted to spend more time with YOU.
Yamato Kurosawa
07/27 15:18
Kai's not trying to pull anything, is he?!
SIGH...

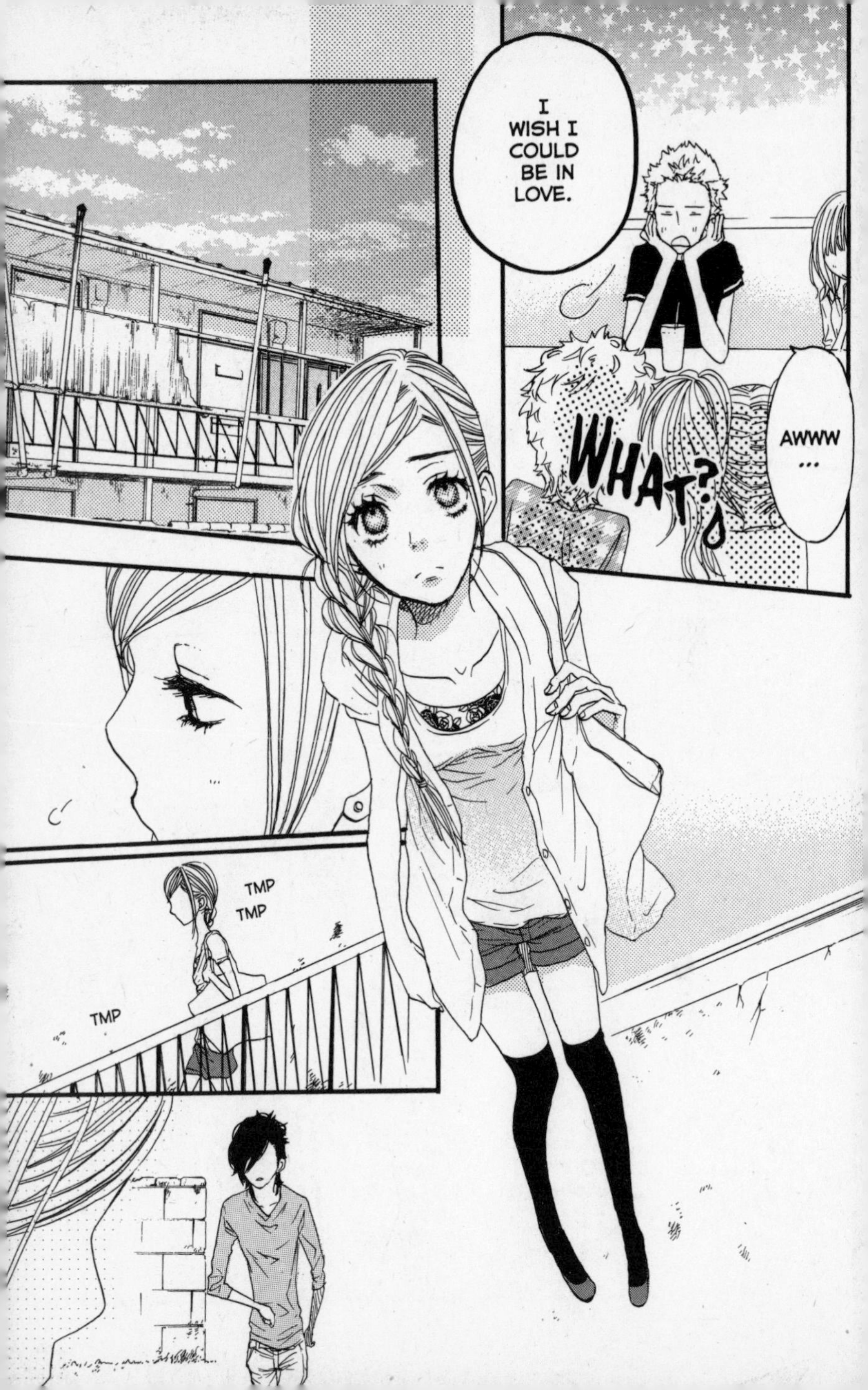
I WISH I COULD BE IN LOVE.
WHAT?
AWWW ...
...
TMP TMP
TMP

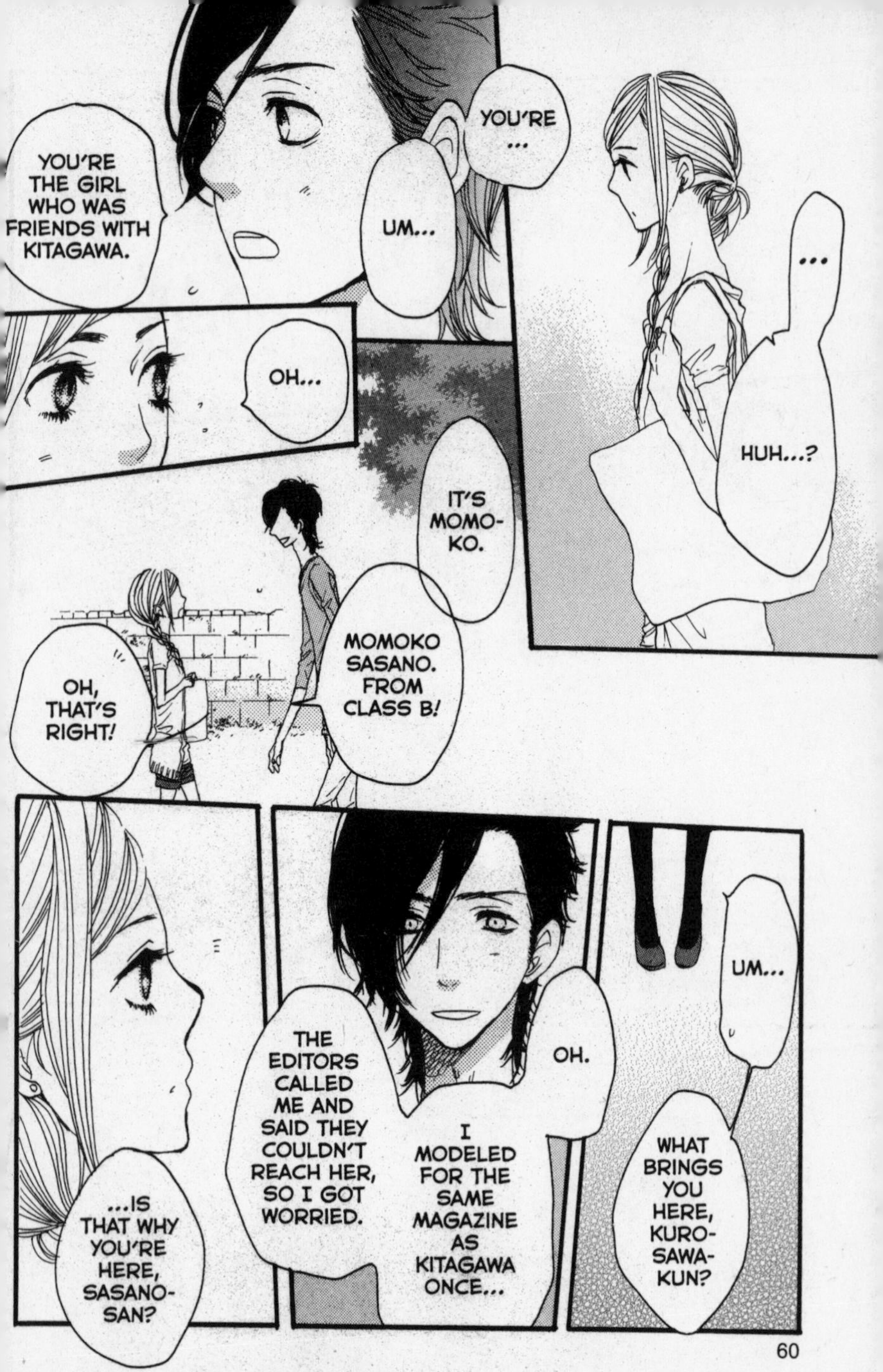
...
HUH...?
YOU'RE ...
UM...
YOU'RE THE GIRL WHO WAS FRIENDS WITH KITAGAWA.
OH...
IT'S MOMOKO.
MOMOKO SASANO. FROM CLASS B!
OH, THAT'S RIGHT!
UM...
WHAT BRINGS YOU HERE, KURO-SAWA-KUN?
OH.
I MODELED FOR THE SAME MAGAZINE AS KITAGAWA ONCE...
THE EDITORS CALLED ME AND SAID THEY COULDN'T REACH HER, SO I GOT WORRIED.
...IS THAT WHY YOU'RE HERE, SASANO-SAN?

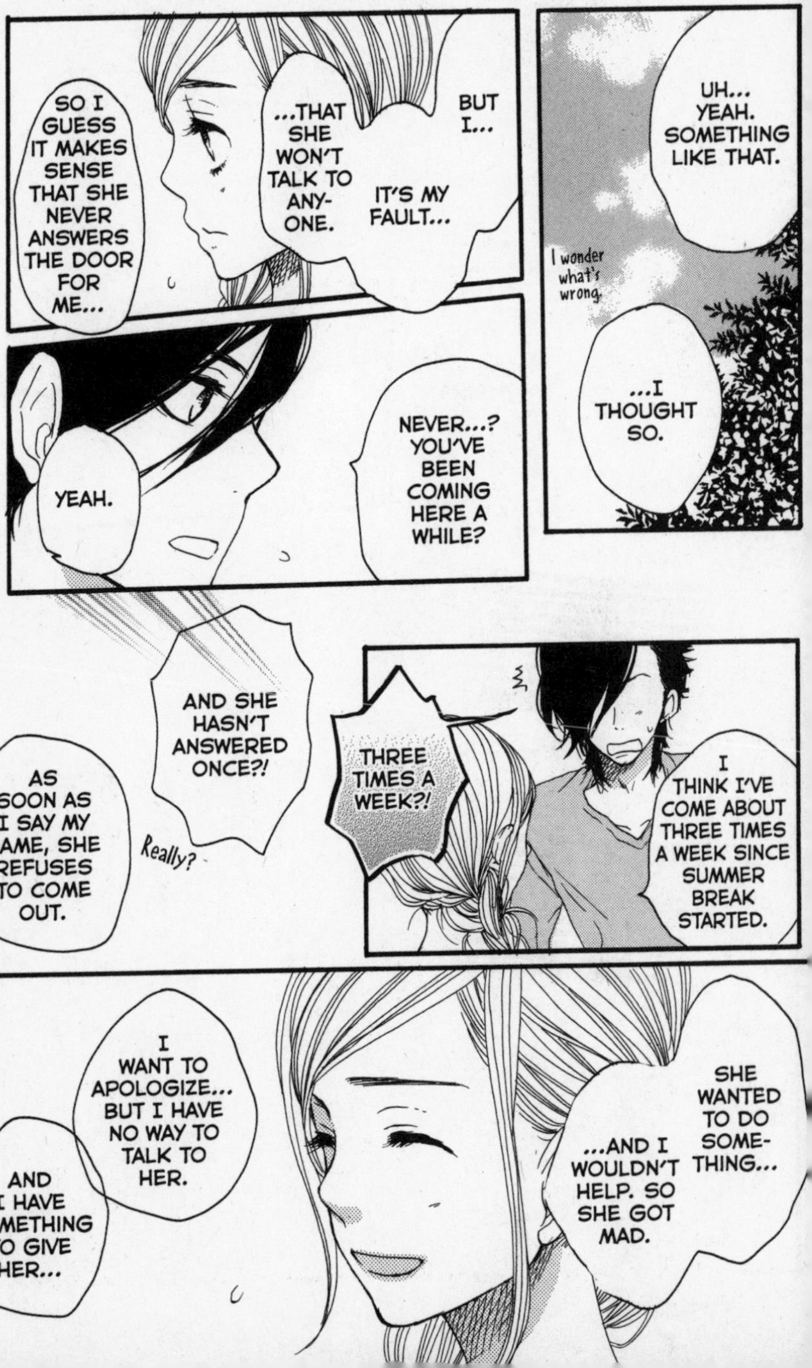
UH... YEAH. SOMETHING LIKE THAT.
I wonder what's wrong.
...I THOUGHT SO.
BUT I...
IT'S MY FAULT...
...THAT SHE WON'T TALK TO ANY-ONE.
SO I GUESS IT MAKES SENSE THAT SHE NEVER ANSWERS THE DOOR FOR ME...
NEVER...? YOU'VE BEEN COMING HERE A WHILE?
YEAH.
I THINK I'VE COME ABOUT THREE TIMES A WEEK SINCE SUMMER BREAK STARTED.
THREE TIMES A WEEK?!
AND SHE HASN'T ANSWERED ONCE?!
Really?
AS SOON AS I SAY MY NAME, SHE REFUSES TO COME OUT.
SHE WANTED TO DO SOME-THING...
...AND I WOULDN'T HELP. SO SHE GOT MAD.
I WANT TO APOLOGIZE... BUT I HAVE NO WAY TO TALK TO HER.
AND I HAVE SOMETHING TO GIVE HER...

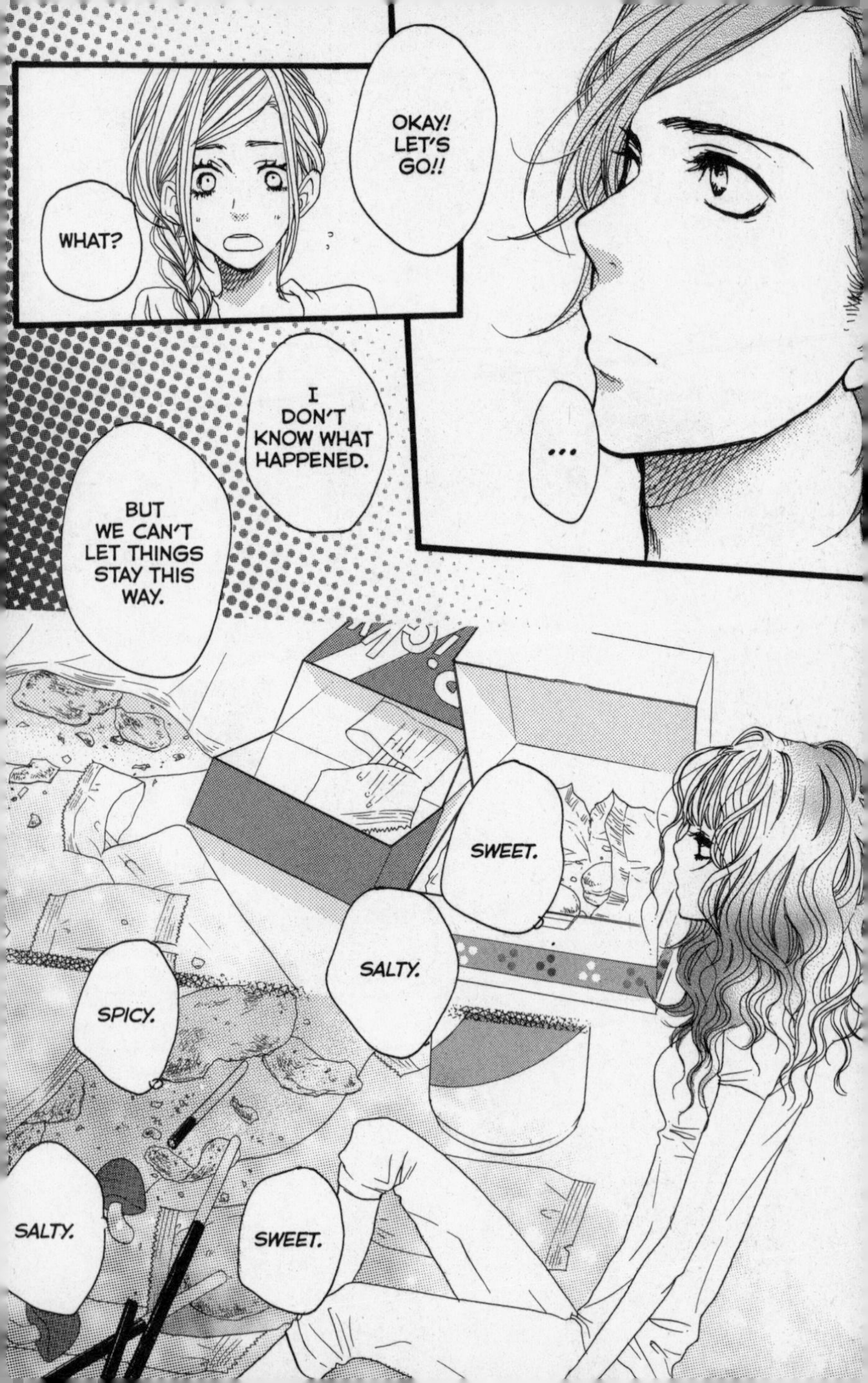
OKAY! LET'S GO!!
WHAT?
...
I DON'T KNOW WHAT HAPPENED.
BUT WE CAN'T LET THINGS STAY THIS WAY.
SWEET.
SALTY.
SPICY.
SWEET.
SALTY.

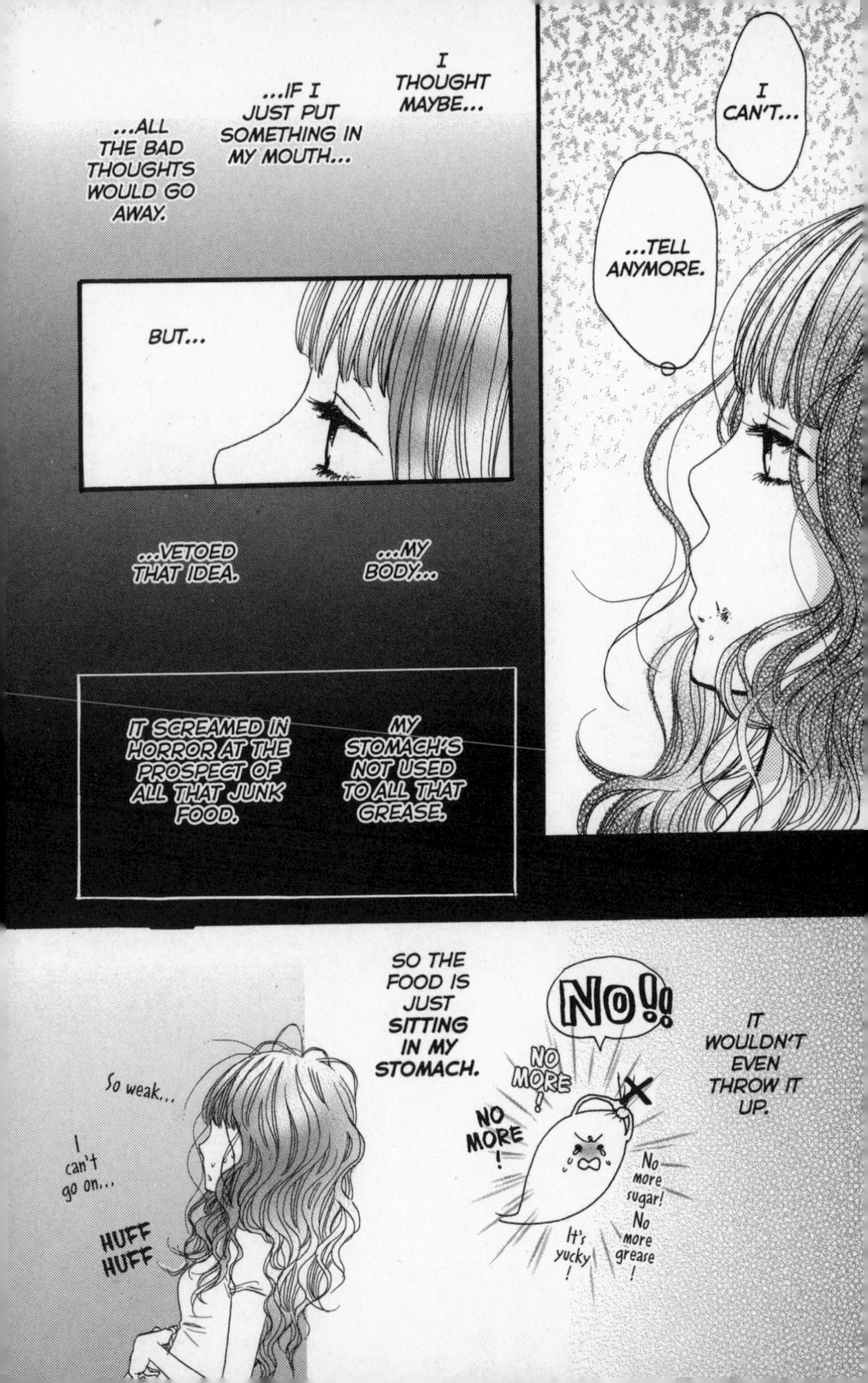
I CAN'T...
...TELL ANYMORE.
I THOUGHT MAYBE...
...IF I JUST PUT SOMETHING IN MY MOUTH...
...ALL THE BAD THOUGHTS WOULD GO AWAY.
BUT...
...MY BODY...
...VETOED THAT IDEA.
MY STOMACH'S NOT USED TO ALL THAT GREASE.
IT SCREAMED IN HORROR AT THE PROSPECT OF ALL THAT JUNK FOOD.
IT WOULDN'T EVEN THROW IT UP.
NO!!
NO MORE!
NO MORE!
No more sugar!
No more grease!
It's yucky!
SO THE FOOD IS JUST SITTING IN MY STOMACH.
So weak...
I can't go on...
HUFF HUFF

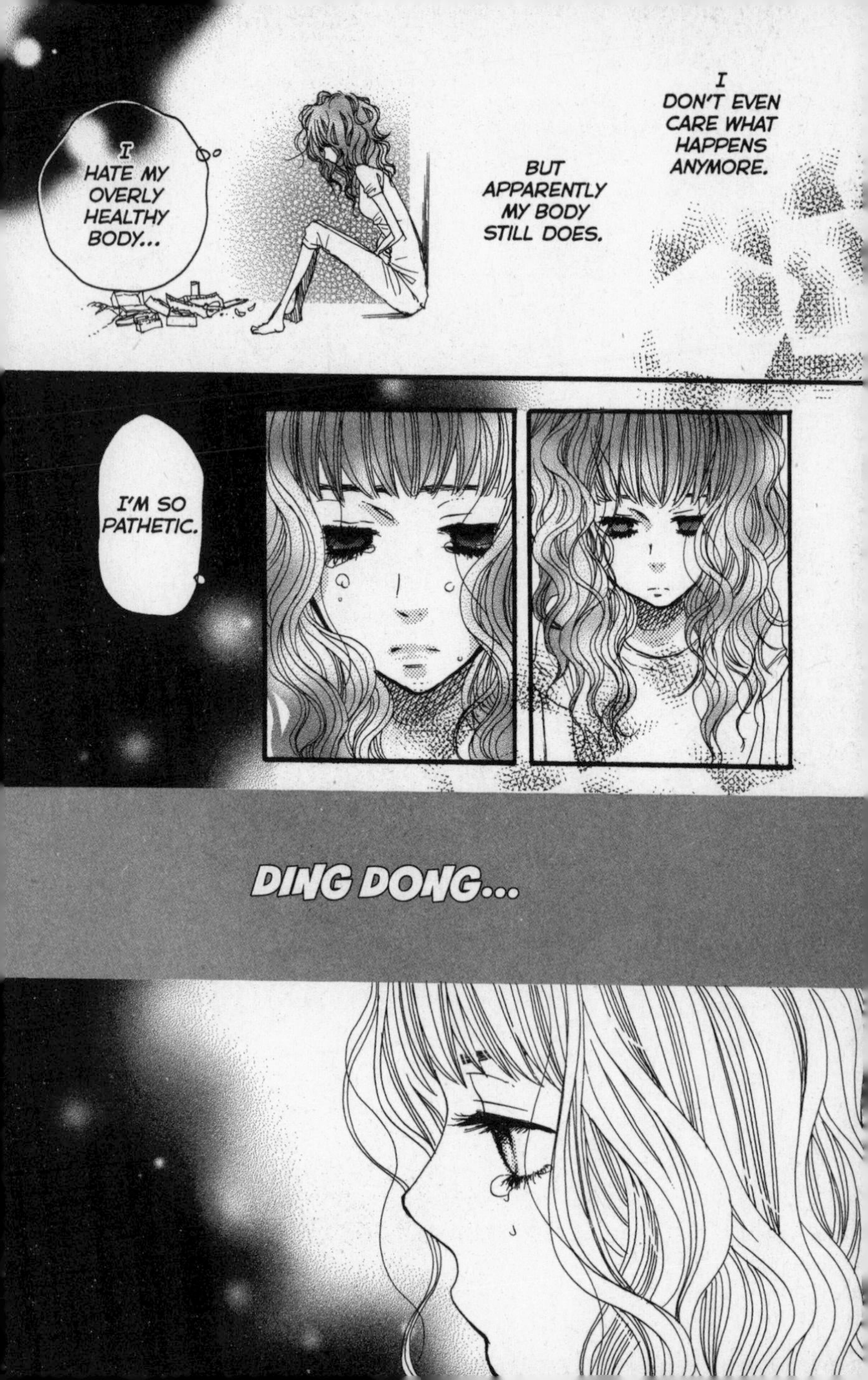
I DON'T EVEN CARE WHAT HAPPENS ANYMORE.
BUT APPARENTLY MY BODY STILL DOES.
I HATE MY OVERLY HEALTHY BODY...
I'M SO PATHETIC.
DING DONG...

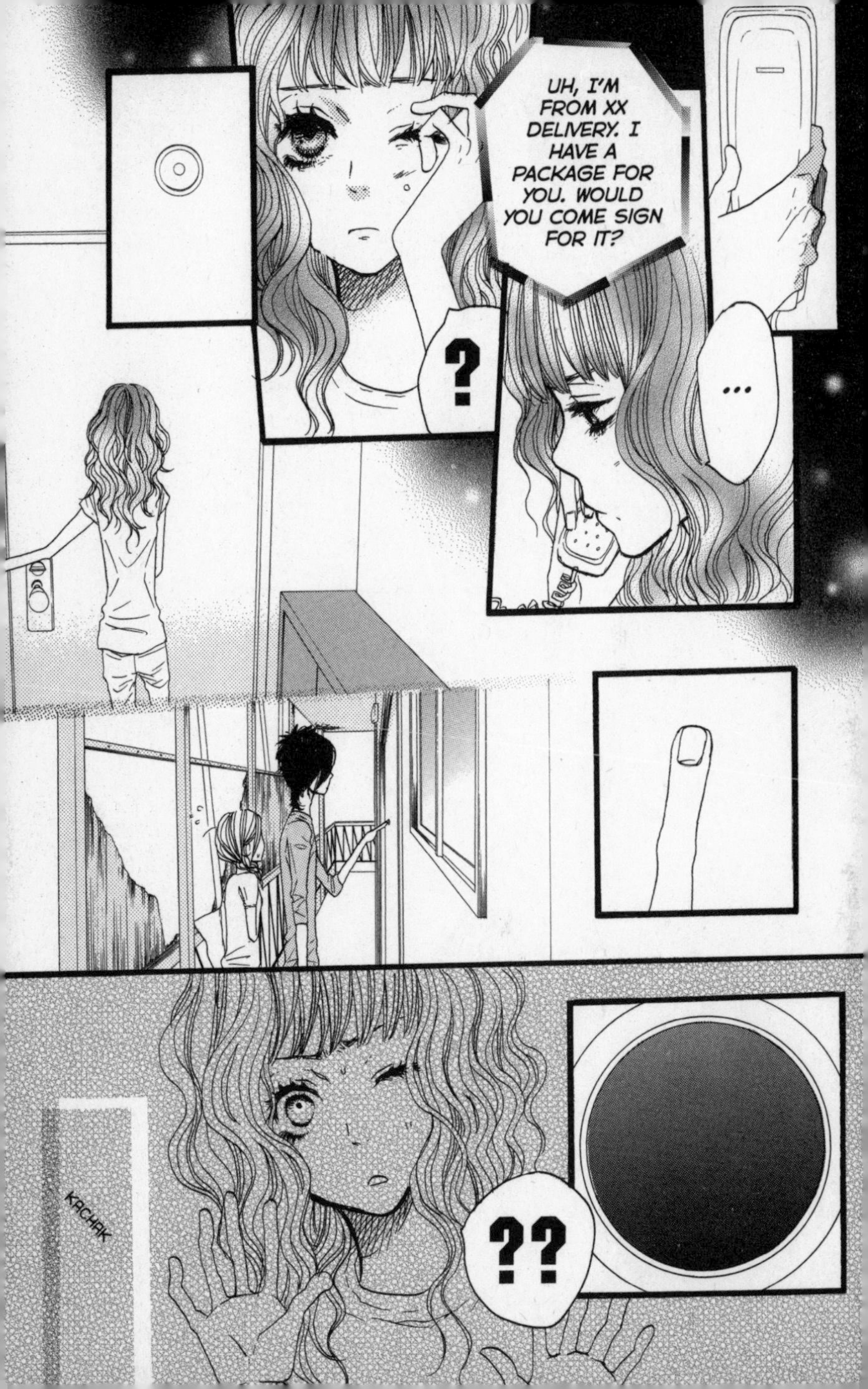
UH, I'M FROM XX DELIVERY. I HAVE A PACKAGE FOR YOU. WOULD YOU COME SIGN FOR IT?
?
...
??
KACHAK

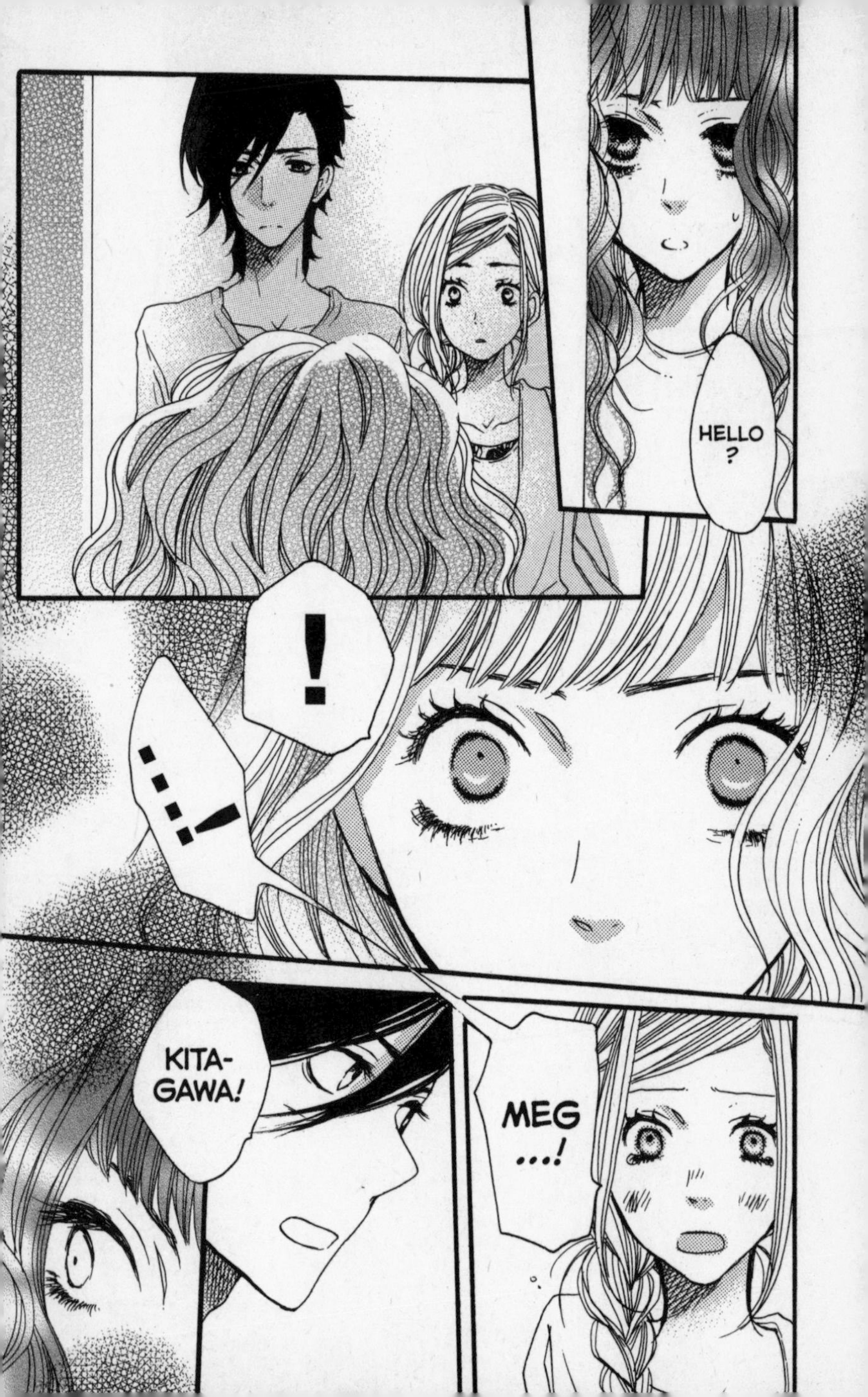
HELLO ?
!
...!
MEG ...!
KITA-GAWA!

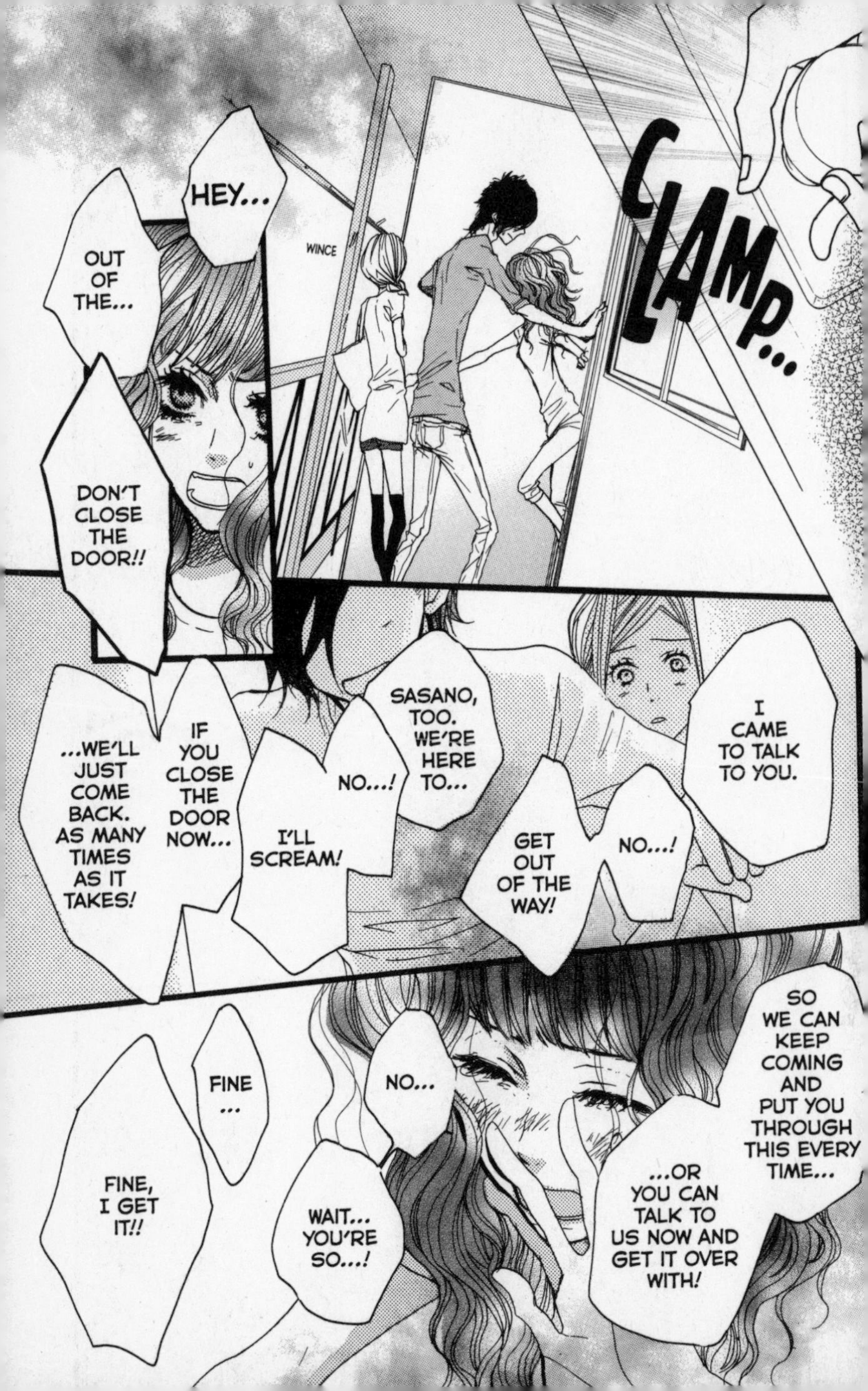
CLAMP...
WINCE
HEY...
OUT OF THE...
DON'T CLOSE THE DOOR!!
I CAME TO TALK TO YOU.
NO...!
GET OUT OF THE WAY!
SASANO, TOO. WE'RE HERE TO...
NO...!
I'LL SCREAM!
IF YOU CLOSE THE DOOR NOW...
...WE'LL JUST COME BACK. AS MANY TIMES AS IT TAKES!
SO WE CAN KEEP COMING AND PUT YOU THROUGH THIS EVERY TIME...
...OR YOU CAN TALK TO US NOW AND GET IT OVER WITH!
NO...
WAIT... YOU'RE SO...!
FINE...
FINE, I GET IT!!

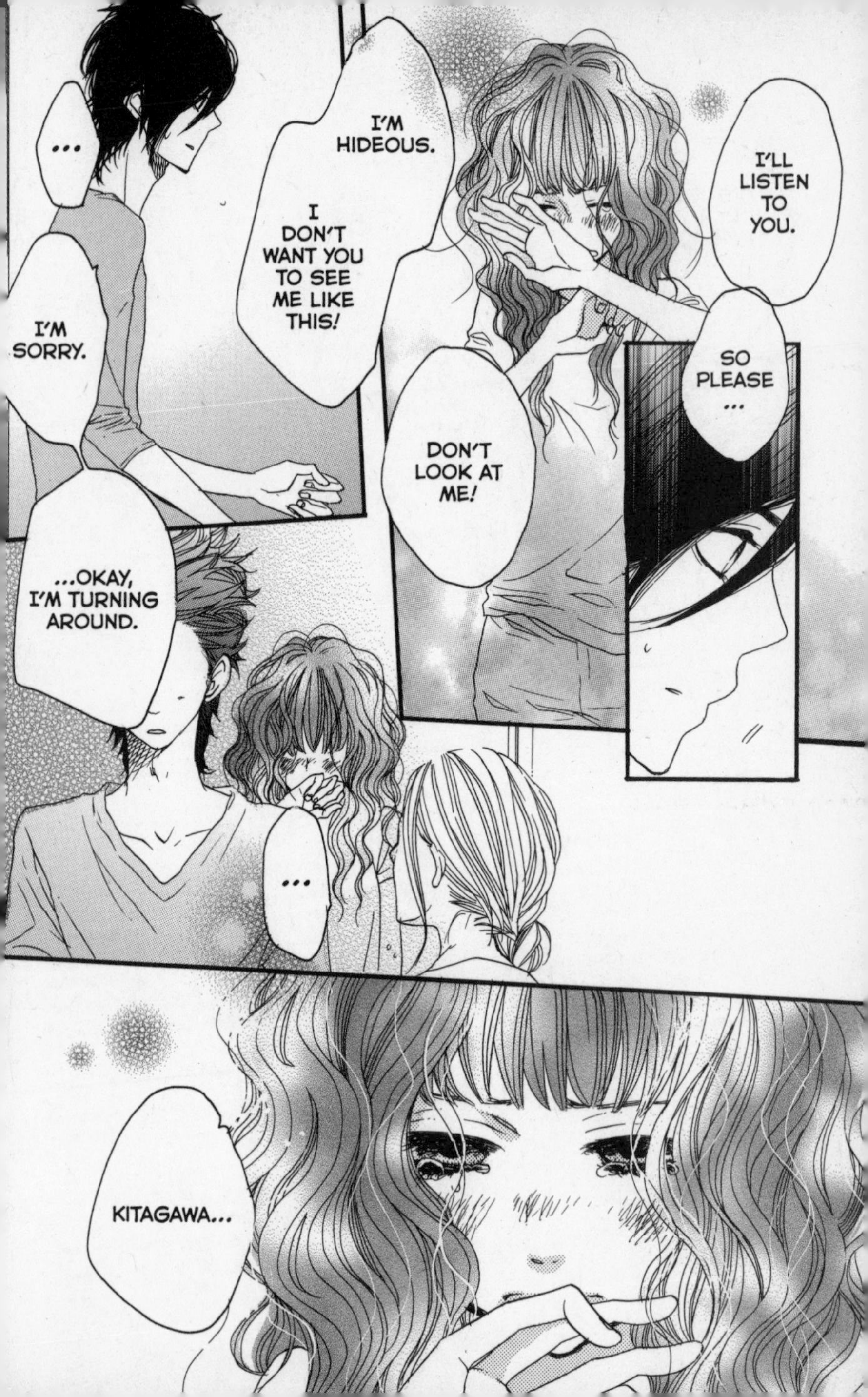
I'LL LISTEN TO YOU.
SO PLEASE ...
I'M HIDEOUS.
I DON'T WANT YOU TO SEE ME LIKE THIS!
DON'T LOOK AT ME!
...
I'M SORRY.
...OKAY, I'M TURNING AROUND.
...
KITAGAWA...

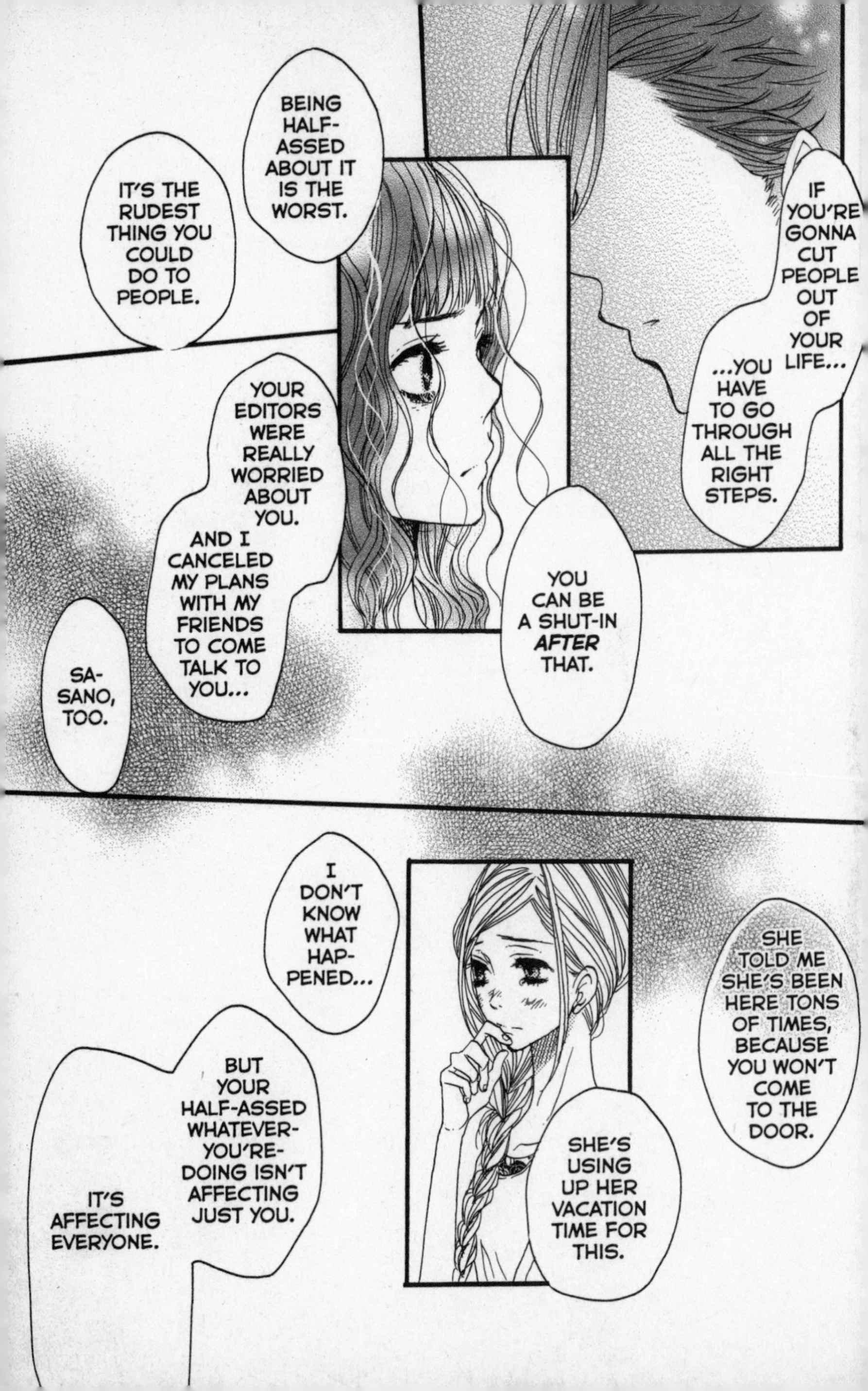
IF YOU'RE GONNA CUT PEOPLE OUT OF YOUR LIFE...
...YOU HAVE TO GO THROUGH ALL THE RIGHT STEPS.
BEING HALF-ASSED ABOUT IT IS THE WORST.
IT'S THE RUDEST THING YOU COULD DO TO PEOPLE.
YOU CAN BE A SHUT-IN *AFTER* THAT.
YOUR EDITORS WERE REALLY WORRIED ABOUT YOU.
AND I CANCELED MY PLANS WITH MY FRIENDS TO COME TALK TO YOU...
SA-SANO, TOO.
SHE TOLD ME SHE'S BEEN HERE TONS OF TIMES, BECAUSE YOU WON'T COME TO THE DOOR.
SHE'S USING UP HER VACATION TIME FOR THIS.
I DON'T KNOW WHAT HAP-PENED...
BUT YOUR HALF-ASSED WHATEVER-YOU'RE-DOING ISN'T AFFECTING JUST YOU.
IT'S AFFECTING EVERYONE.

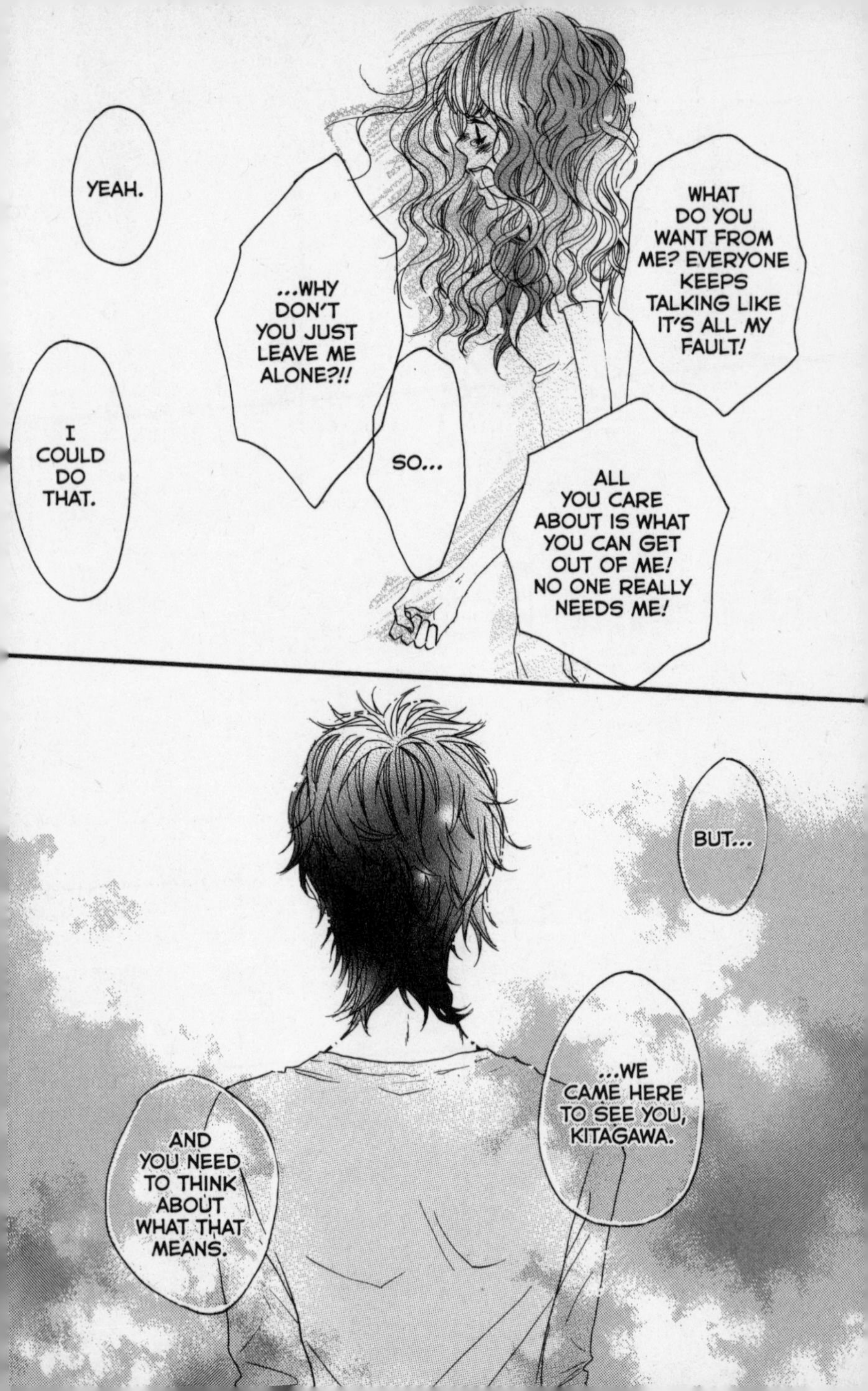
WHAT DO YOU WANT FROM ME? EVERYONE KEEPS TALKING LIKE IT'S ALL MY FAULT!
ALL YOU CARE ABOUT IS WHAT YOU CAN GET OUT OF ME! NO ONE REALLY NEEDS ME!
SO...
...WHY DON'T YOU JUST LEAVE ME ALONE?!!
YEAH.
I COULD DO THAT.
BUT...
...WE CAME HERE TO SEE YOU, KITAGAWA.
AND YOU NEED TO THINK ABOUT WHAT THAT MEANS.

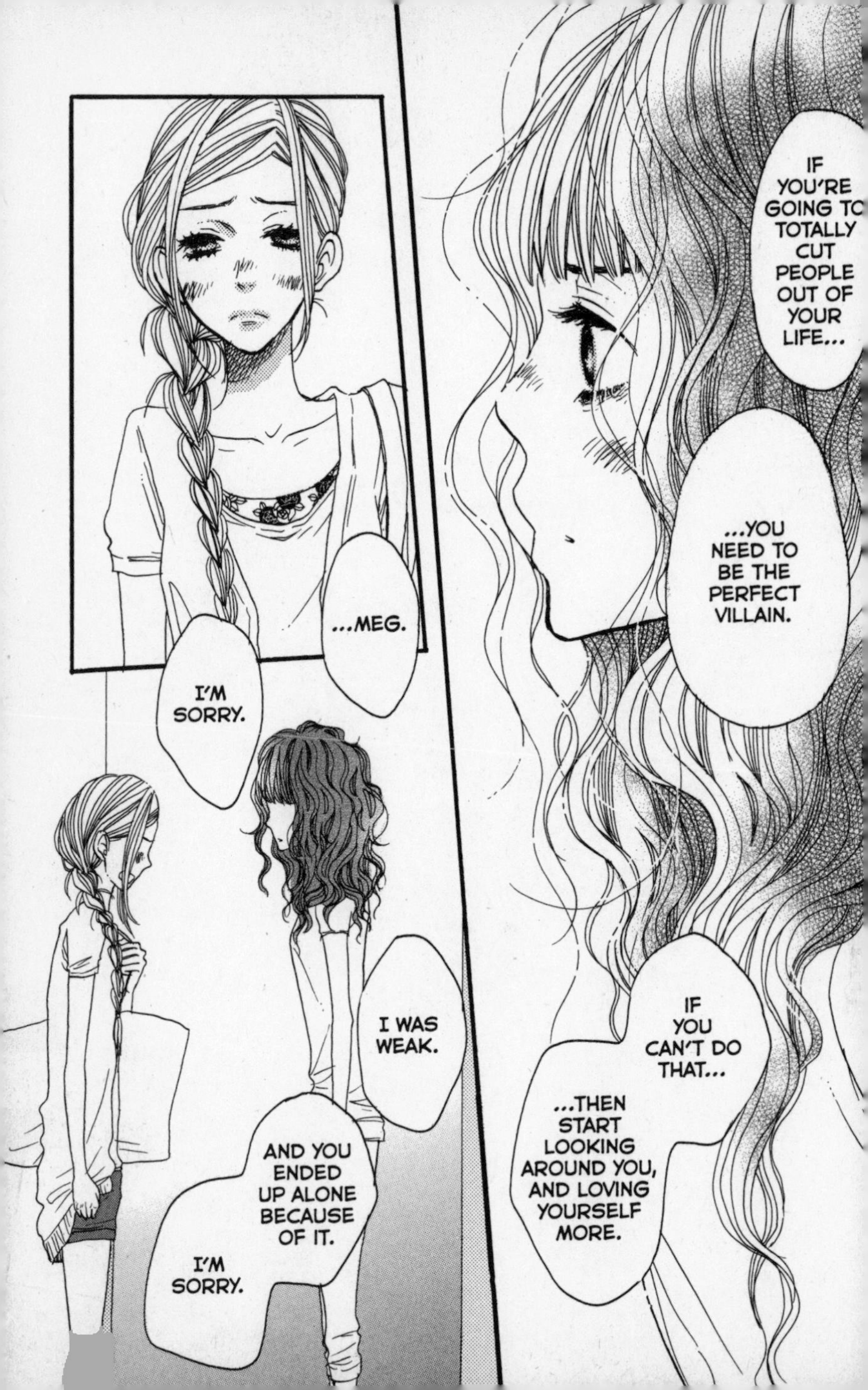
IF YOU'RE GOING TO TOTALLY CUT PEOPLE OUT OF YOUR LIFE...
...YOU NEED TO BE THE PERFECT VILLAIN.
IF YOU CAN'T DO THAT...
...THEN START LOOKING AROUND YOU, AND LOVING YOURSELF MORE.
...MEG.
I'M SORRY.
I WAS WEAK.
AND YOU ENDED UP ALONE BECAUSE OF IT.
I'M SORRY.

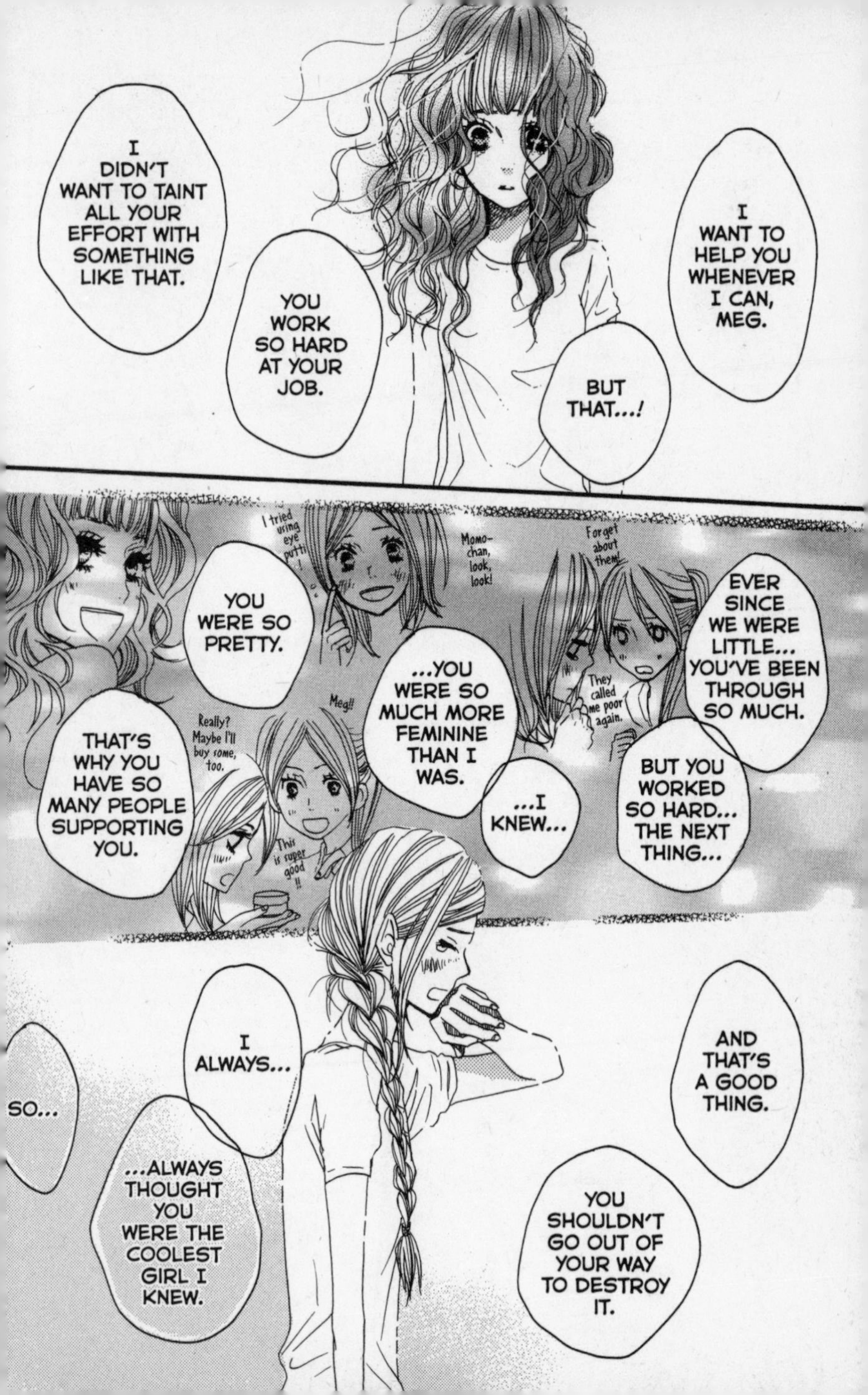
I WANT TO HELP YOU WHENEVER I CAN, MEG.
BUT THAT...!
YOU WORK SO HARD AT YOUR JOB.
I DIDN'T WANT TO TAINT ALL YOUR EFFORT WITH SOMETHING LIKE THAT.
EVER SINCE WE WERE LITTLE... YOU'VE BEEN THROUGH SO MUCH.
Forget about them!
They called me poor again.
BUT YOU WORKED SO HARD... THE NEXT THING...
...I KNEW...
Momo-chan, look, look!
I tried using eye putti!
...YOU WERE SO MUCH MORE FEMININE THAN I WAS.
YOU WERE SO PRETTY.
Meg!!
This is super good!!
Really? Maybe I'll buy some, too.
THAT'S WHY YOU HAVE SO MANY PEOPLE SUPPORTING YOU.
AND THAT'S A GOOD THING.
YOU SHOULDN'T GO OUT OF YOUR WAY TO DESTROY IT.
I ALWAYS...
...ALWAYS THOUGHT YOU WERE THE COOLEST GIRL I KNEW.
SO...

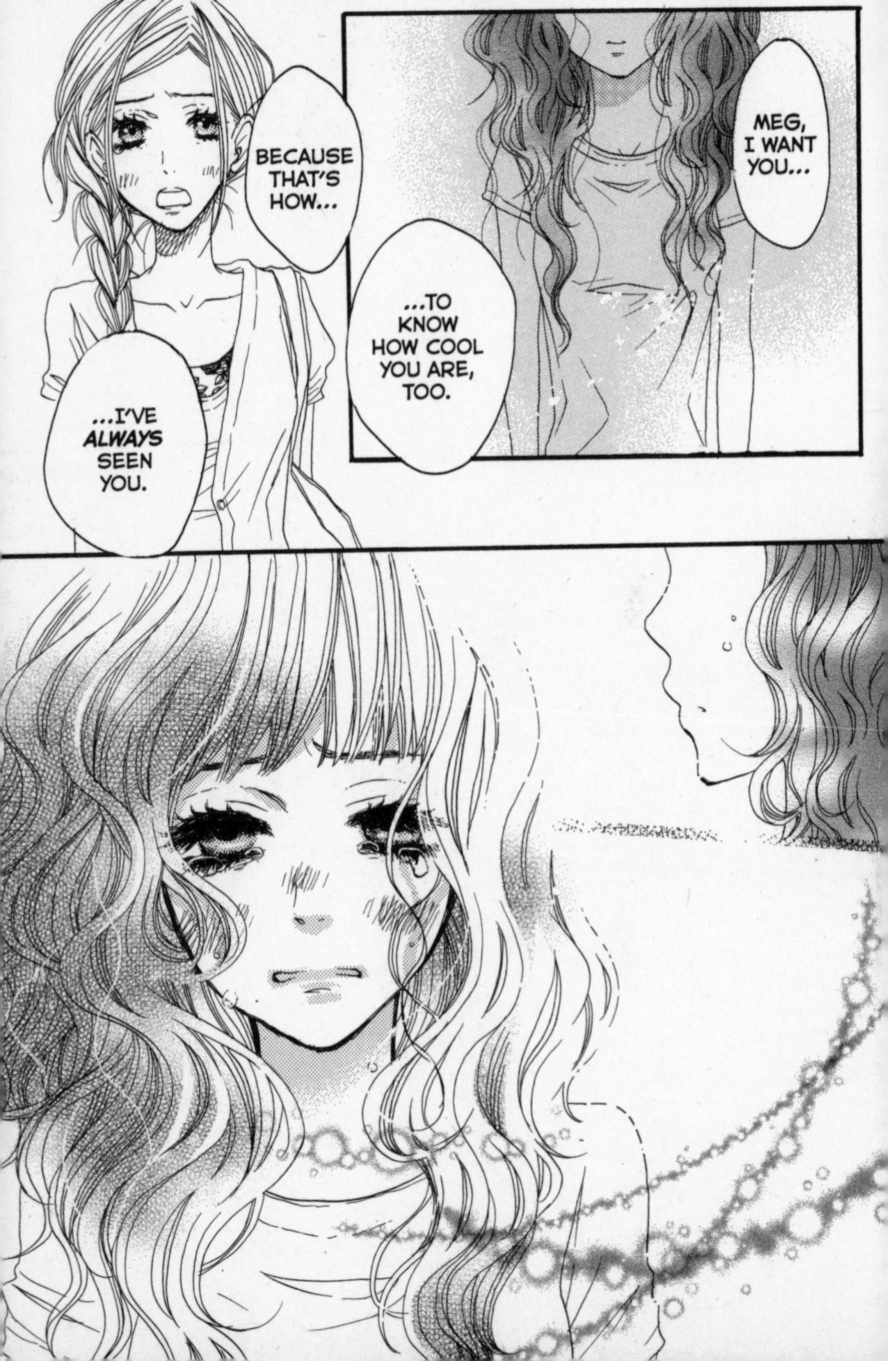
MEG, I WANT YOU...
...TO KNOW HOW COOL YOU ARE, TOO.
BECAUSE THAT'S HOW...
...I'VE *ALWAYS* SEEN YOU.

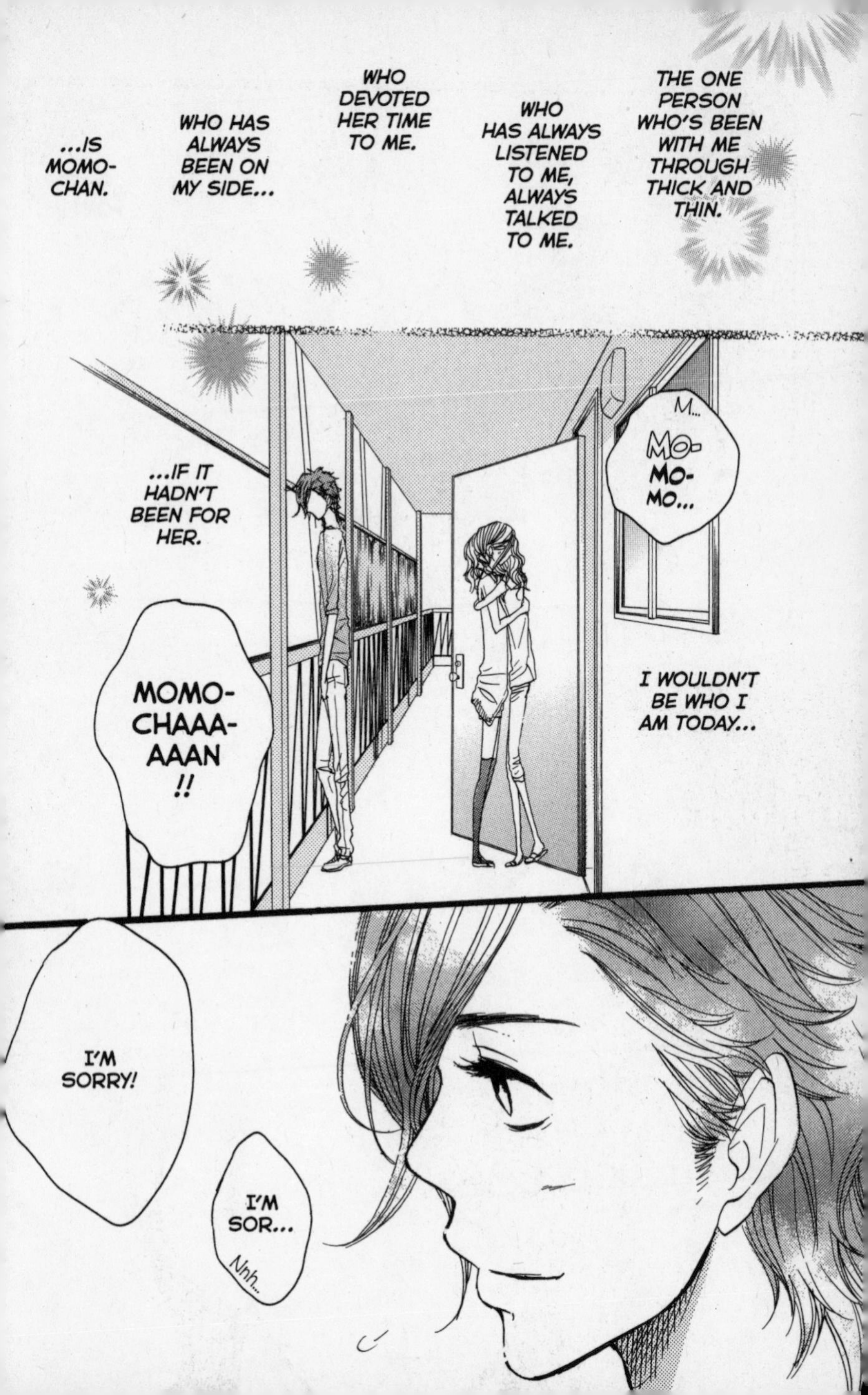
THE ONE PERSON WHO'S BEEN WITH ME THROUGH THICK AND THIN.
WHO HAS ALWAYS LISTENED TO ME, ALWAYS TALKED TO ME.
WHO DEVOTED HER TIME TO ME.
WHO HAS ALWAYS BEEN ON MY SIDE...
...IS MOMO-CHAN.
I WOULDN'T BE WHO I AM TODAY...
M... MO-MO-MO...
...IF IT HADN'T BEEN FOR HER.
MOMO-CHAAAA-AAAN!!
I'M SORRY!
I'M SOR...
Nnh...

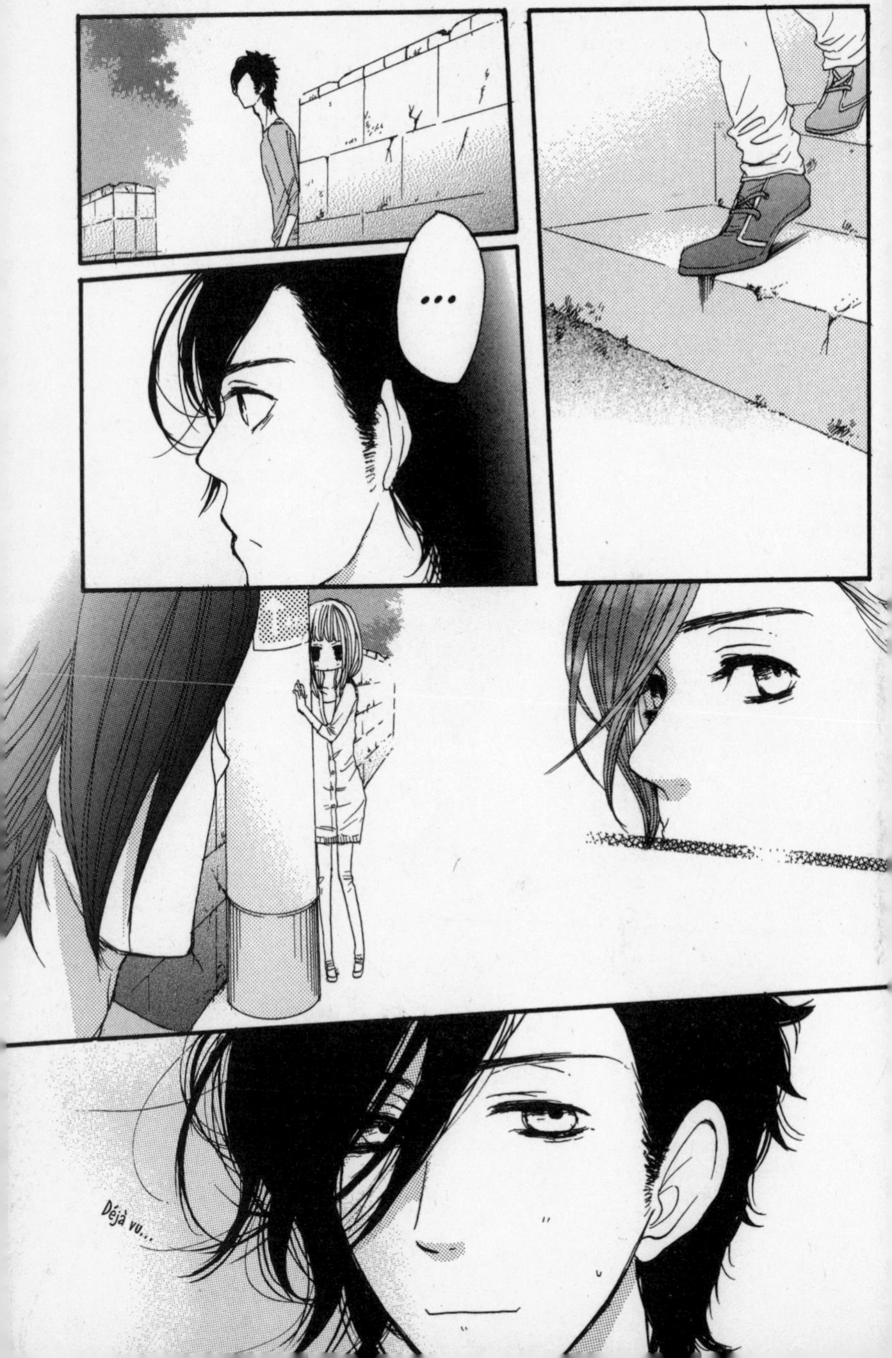
...
Déjà vu...

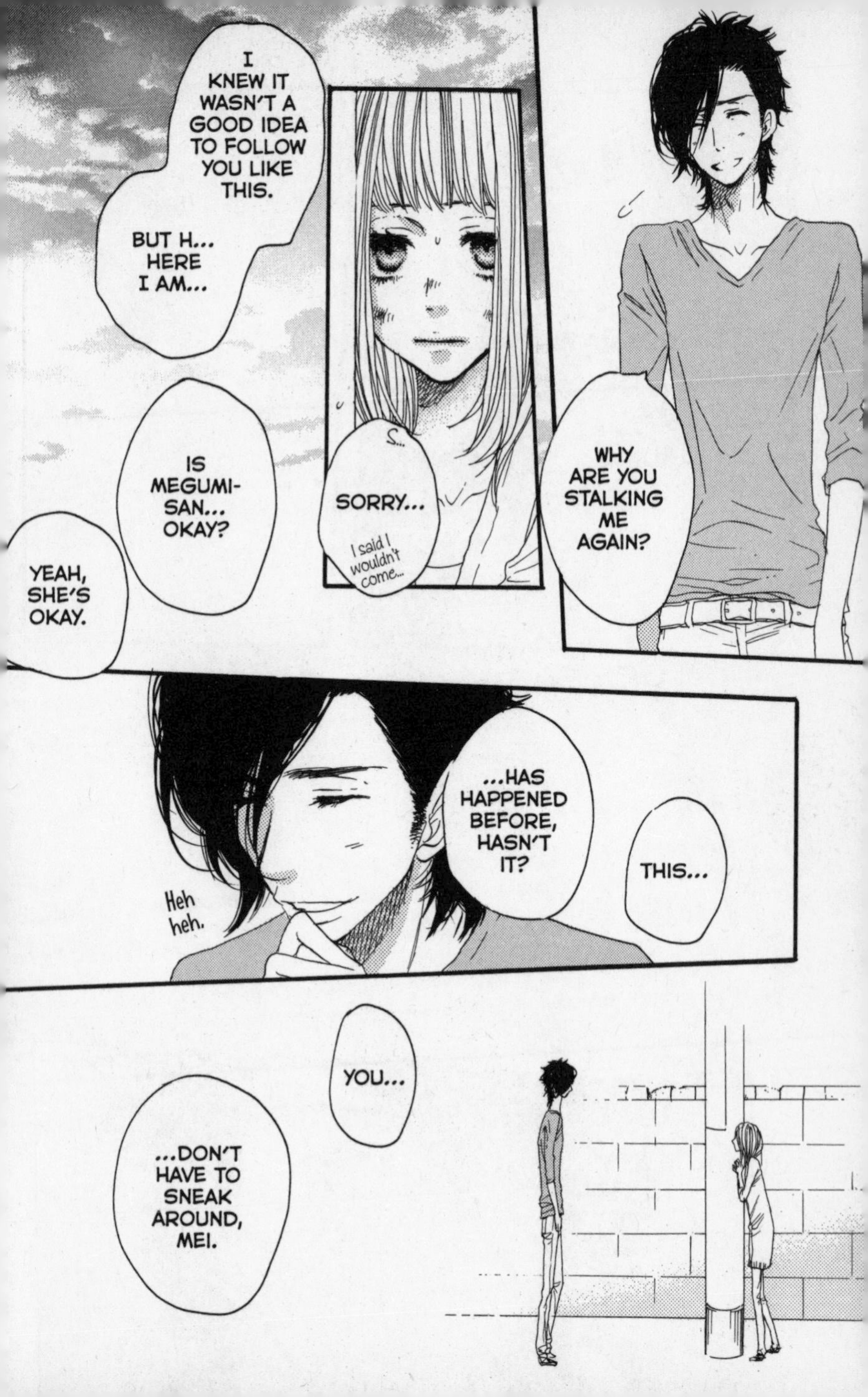
WHY ARE YOU STALKING ME AGAIN?
S...
SORRY...
I said I wouldn't come...
I KNEW IT WASN'T A GOOD IDEA TO FOLLOW YOU LIKE THIS.
BUT H... HERE I AM...
IS MEGUMI-SAN... OKAY?
YEAH, SHE'S OKAY.
THIS...
...HAS HAPPENED BEFORE, HASN'T IT?
Heh heh.
YOU...
...DON'T HAVE TO SNEAK AROUND, MEI.

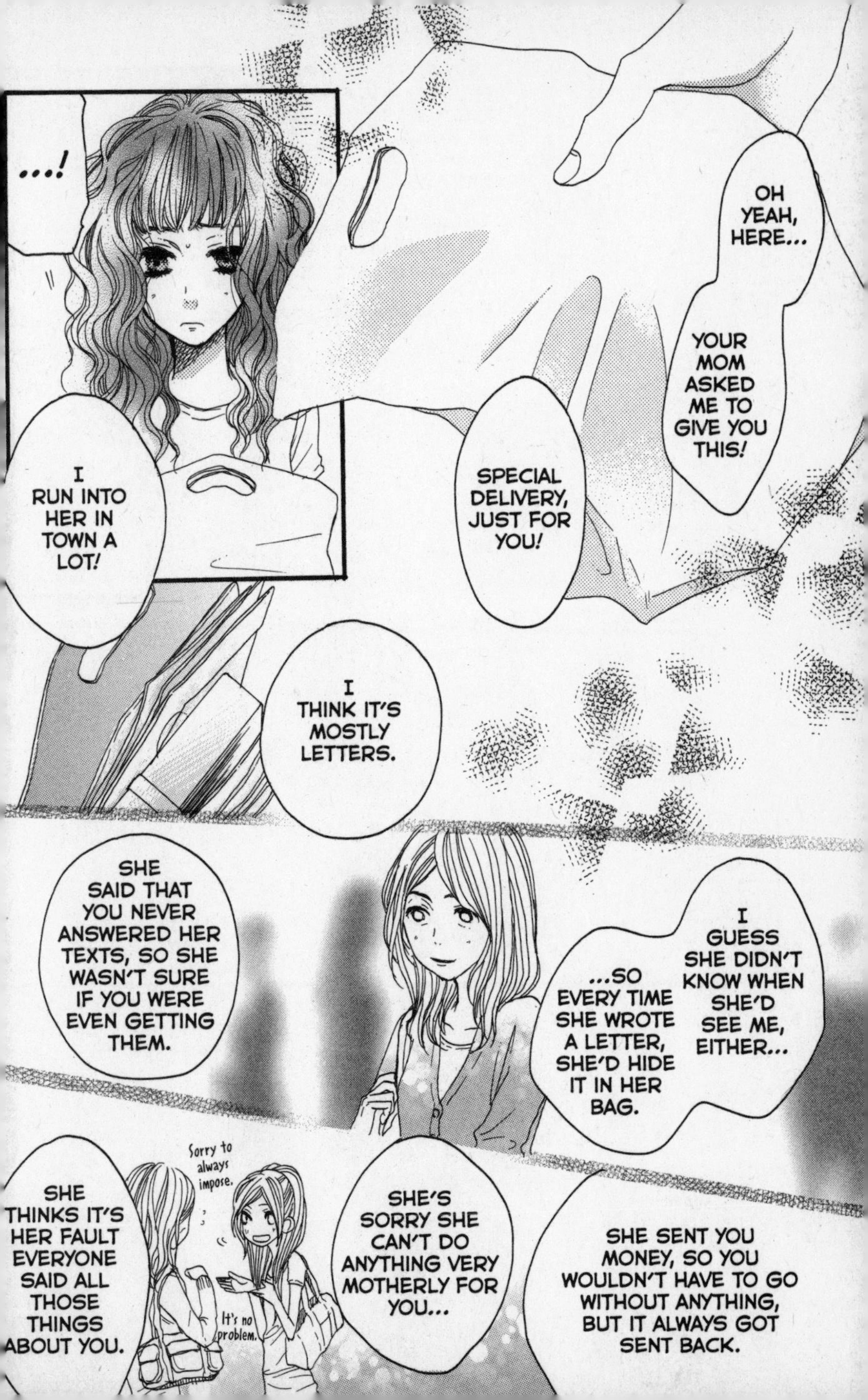
OH YEAH, HERE...
YOUR MOM ASKED ME TO GIVE YOU THIS!
SPECIAL DELIVERY, JUST FOR YOU!
...!
I RUN INTO HER IN TOWN A LOT!
I THINK IT'S MOSTLY LETTERS.
I GUESS SHE DIDN'T KNOW WHEN SHE'D SEE ME, EITHER...
...SO EVERY TIME SHE WROTE A LETTER, SHE'D HIDE IT IN HER BAG.
SHE SAID THAT YOU NEVER ANSWERED HER TEXTS, SO SHE WASN'T SURE IF YOU WERE EVEN GETTING THEM.
SHE SENT YOU MONEY, SO YOU WOULDN'T HAVE TO GO WITHOUT ANYTHING, BUT IT ALWAYS GOT SENT BACK.
SHE'S SORRY SHE CAN'T DO ANYTHING VERY MOTHERLY FOR YOU...
Sorry to always impose.
It's no problem.
SHE THINKS IT'S HER FAULT EVERYONE SAID ALL THOSE THINGS ABOUT YOU.

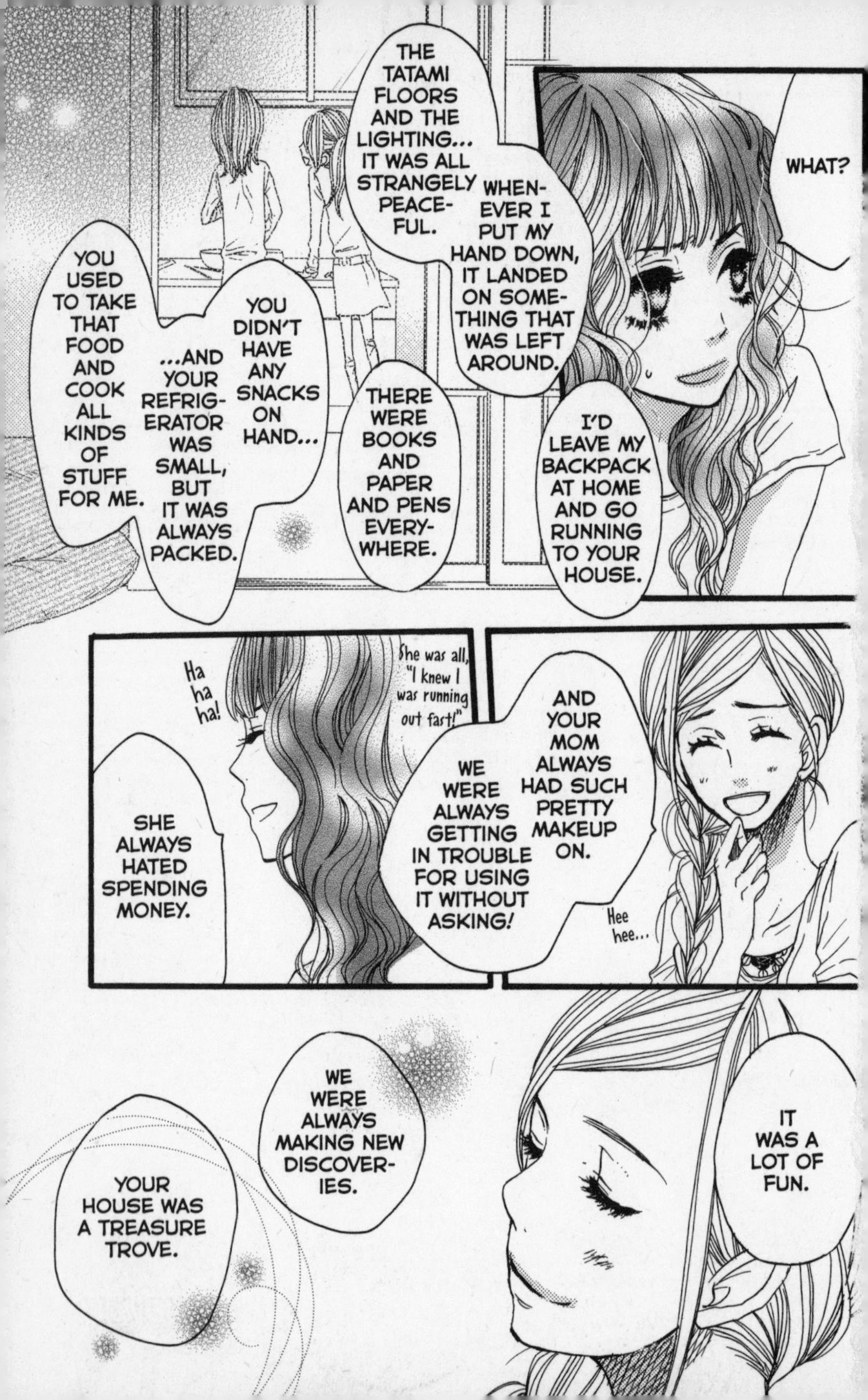
WHAT?
I'D LEAVE MY BACKPACK AT HOME AND GO RUNNING TO YOUR HOUSE.
THE TATAMI FLOORS AND THE LIGHTING... IT WAS ALL STRANGELY PEACE-FUL.
WHEN-EVER I PUT MY HAND DOWN, IT LANDED ON SOME-THING THAT WAS LEFT AROUND.
THERE WERE BOOKS AND PAPER AND PENS EVERY-WHERE.
YOU DIDN'T HAVE ANY SNACKS ON HAND...
...AND YOUR REFRIG-ERATOR WAS SMALL, BUT IT WAS ALWAYS PACKED.
YOU USED TO TAKE THAT FOOD AND COOK ALL KINDS OF STUFF FOR ME.
AND YOUR MOM ALWAYS HAD SUCH PRETTY MAKEUP ON.
WE WERE ALWAYS GETTING IN TROUBLE FOR USING IT WITHOUT ASKING!
Hee hee...
Ha ha ha!
SHE ALWAYS HATED SPENDING MONEY.
She was all, "I knew I was running out fast!"
IT WAS A LOT OF FUN.
WE WERE ALWAYS MAKING NEW DISCOVER-IES.
YOUR HOUSE WAS A TREASURE TROVE.

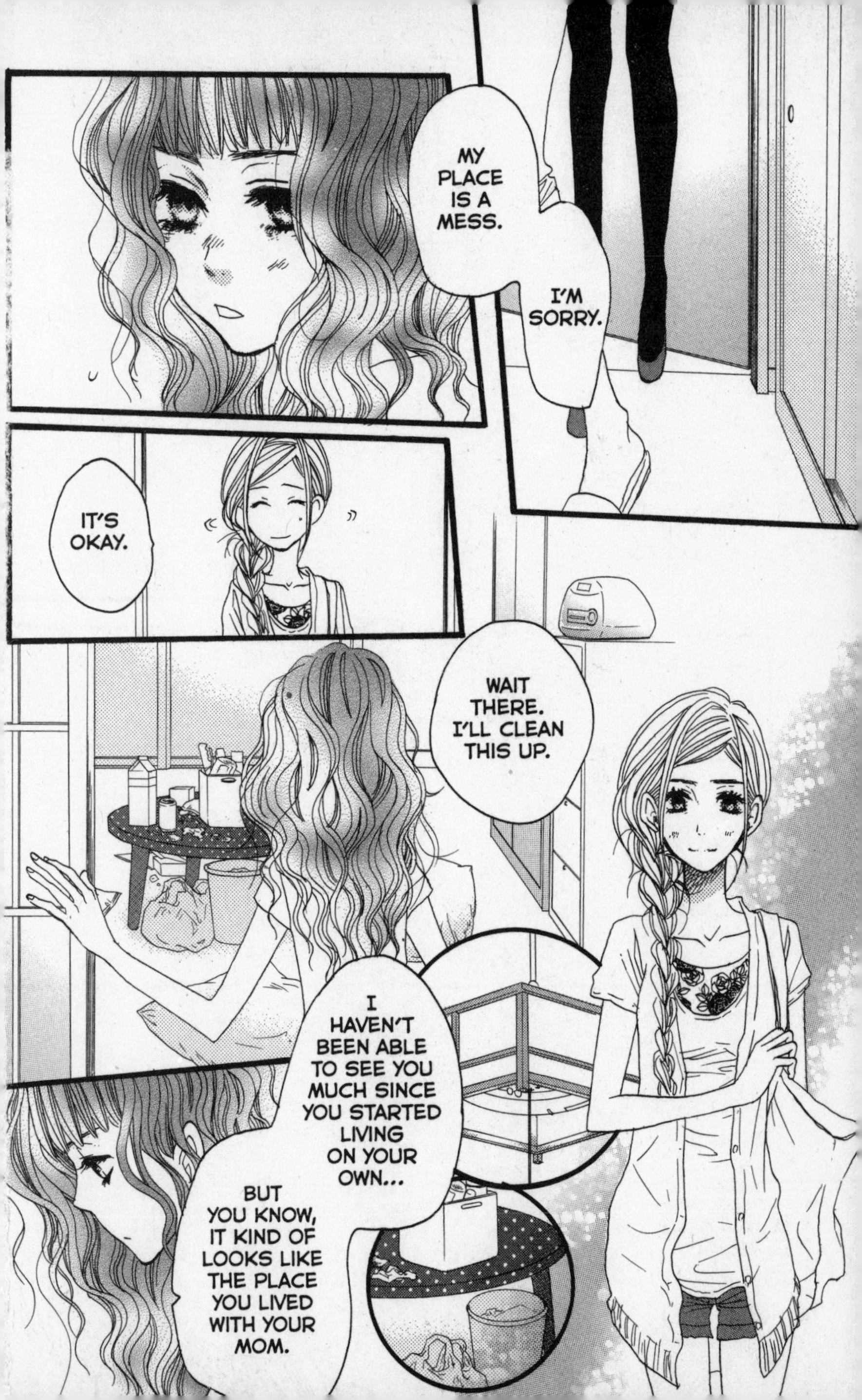
MY PLACE IS A MESS.
I'M SORRY.
IT'S OKAY.
WAIT THERE. I'LL CLEAN THIS UP.
I HAVEN'T BEEN ABLE TO SEE YOU MUCH SINCE YOU STARTED LIVING ON YOUR OWN...
BUT YOU KNOW, IT KIND OF LOOKS LIKE THE PLACE YOU LIVED WITH YOUR MOM.

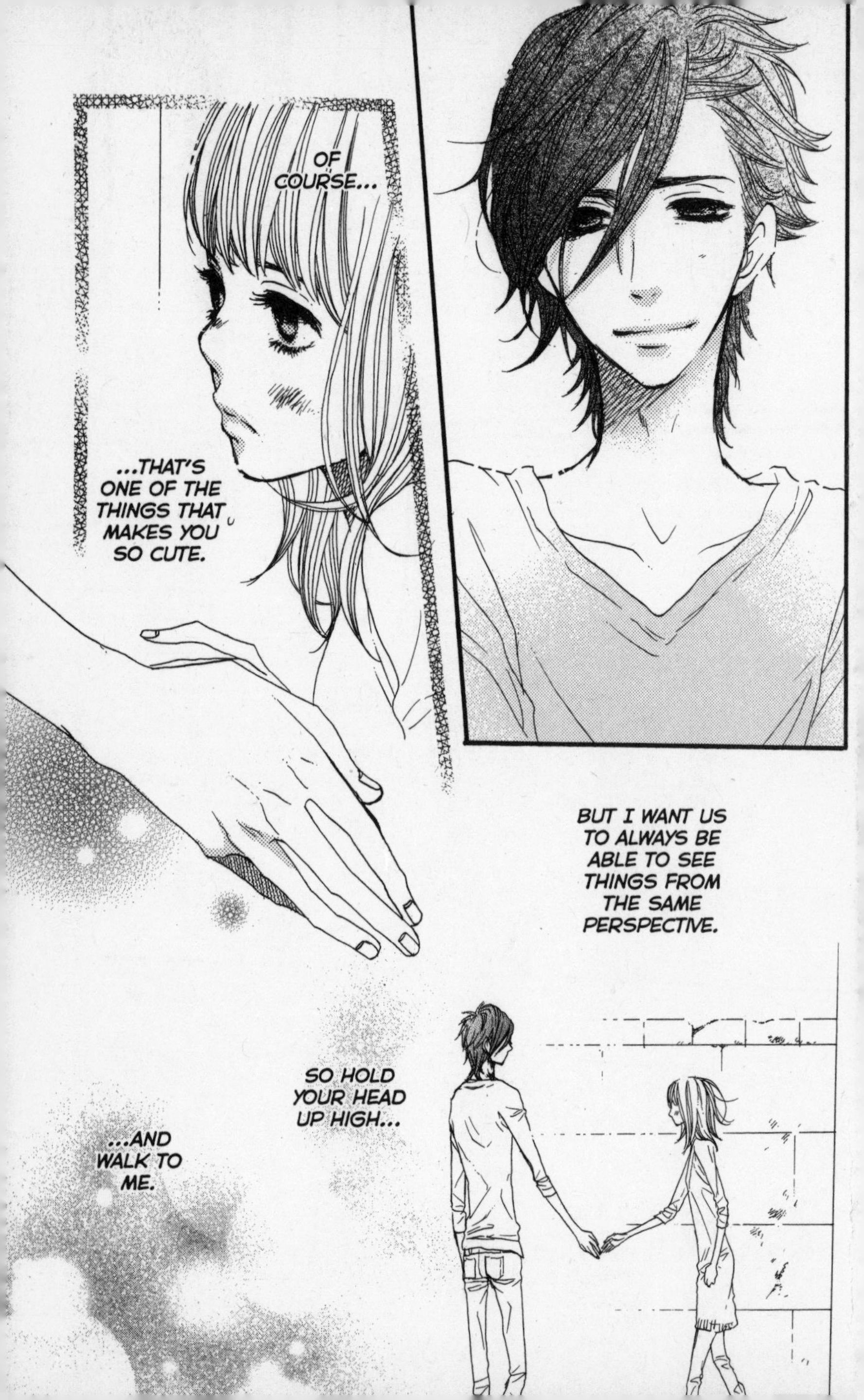
OF COURSE...
...THAT'S ONE OF THE THINGS THAT MAKES YOU SO CUTE.
BUT I WANT US TO ALWAYS BE ABLE TO SEE THINGS FROM THE SAME PERSPECTIVE.
SO HOLD YOUR HEAD UP HIGH...
...AND WALK TO ME.

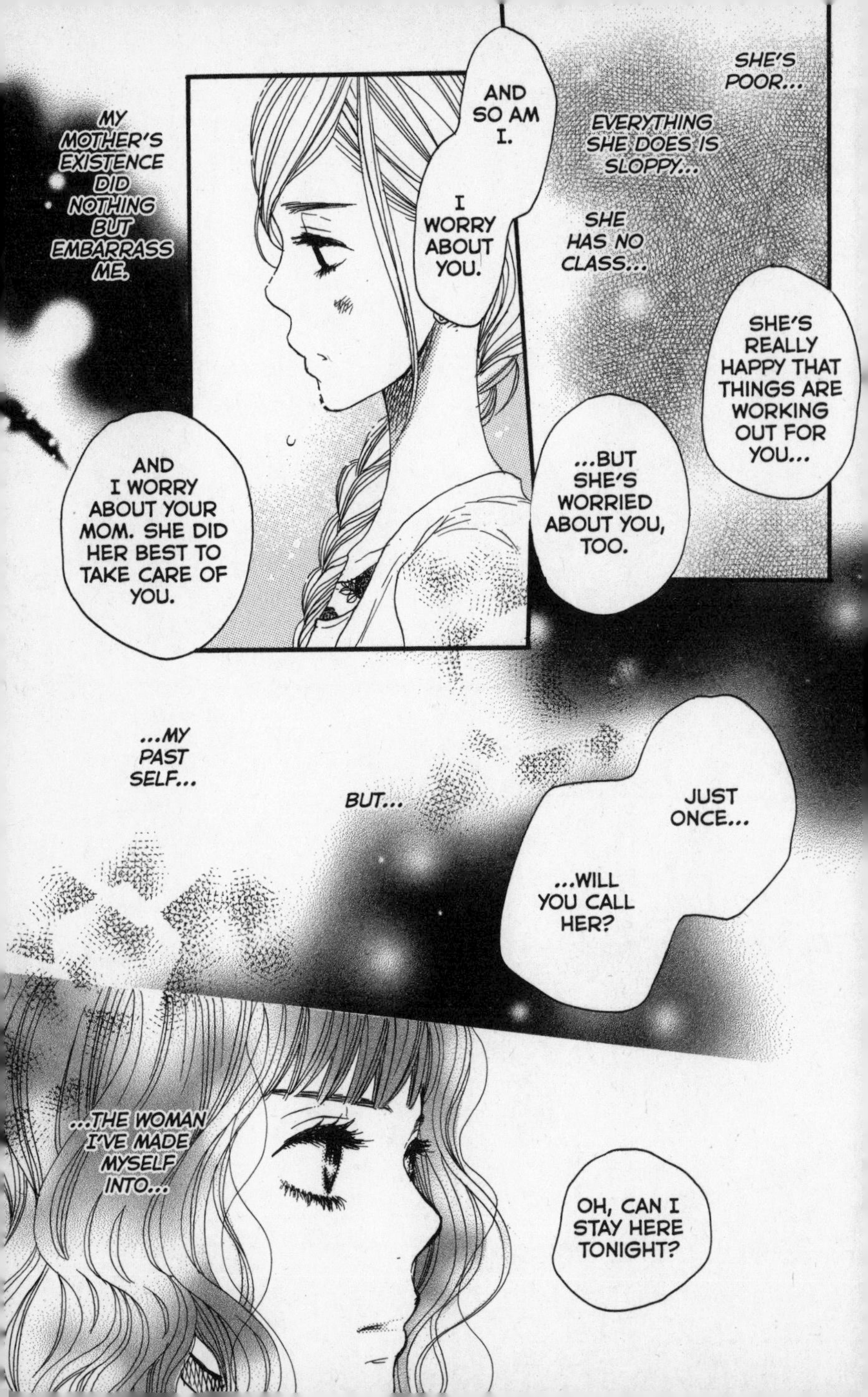
SHE'S POOR...
EVERYTHING SHE DOES IS SLOPPY...
SHE HAS NO CLASS...
SHE'S REALLY HAPPY THAT THINGS ARE WORKING OUT FOR YOU...
...BUT SHE'S WORRIED ABOUT YOU, TOO.
AND SO AM I.
I WORRY ABOUT YOU.
MY MOTHER'S EXISTENCE DID NOTHING BUT EMBARRASS ME.
AND I WORRY ABOUT YOUR MOM. SHE DID HER BEST TO TAKE CARE OF YOU.
JUST ONCE...
...WILL YOU CALL HER?
BUT...
...MY PAST SELF...
OH, CAN I STAY HERE TONIGHT?
...THE WOMAN I'VE MADE MYSELF INTO...

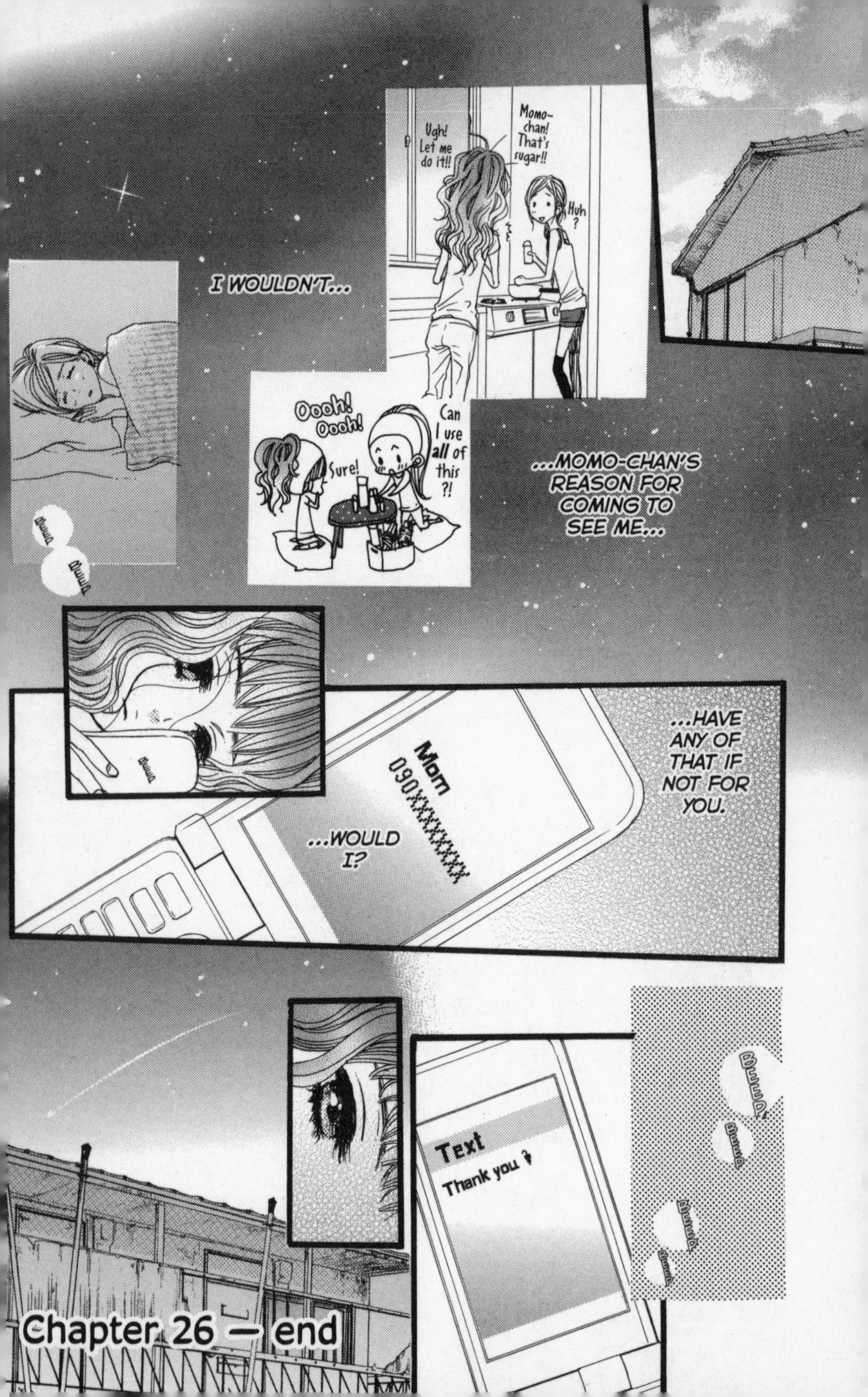
Momo-chan! That's sugar!!
Ugh! Let me do it!!
Huh?
I WOULDN'T...
Can I use all of this?!
Oooh! Oooh!
Sure!
...MOMO-CHAN'S REASON FOR COMING TO SEE ME...
...HAVE ANY OF THAT IF NOT FOR YOU.
Mom
090XXXXXXXX
...WOULD I?
Text
Thank you
Chapter 26 — end

Megumi Kitagawa

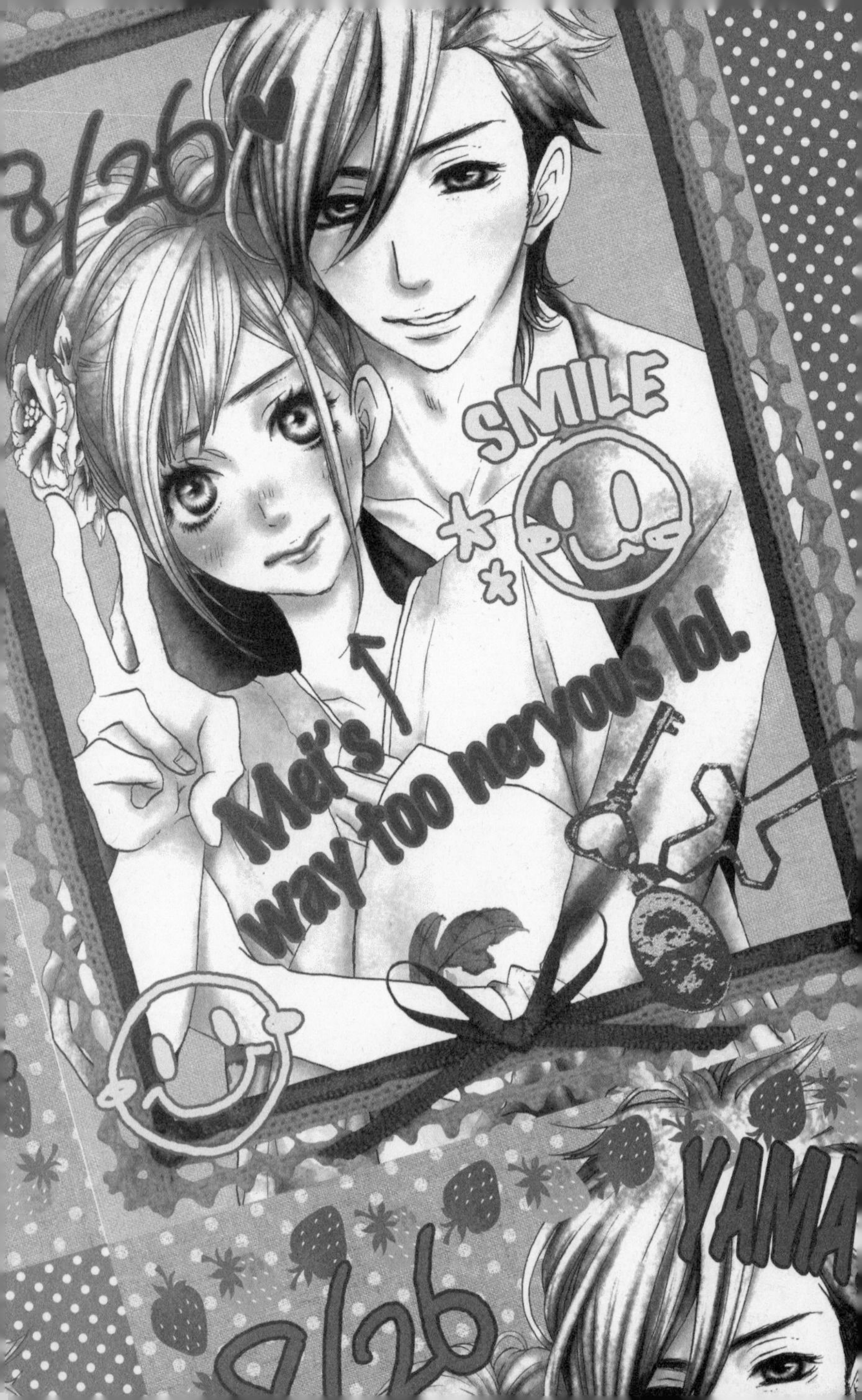

8/26
SMILE
Mei's way too nervous lol.
YAMA
9/26

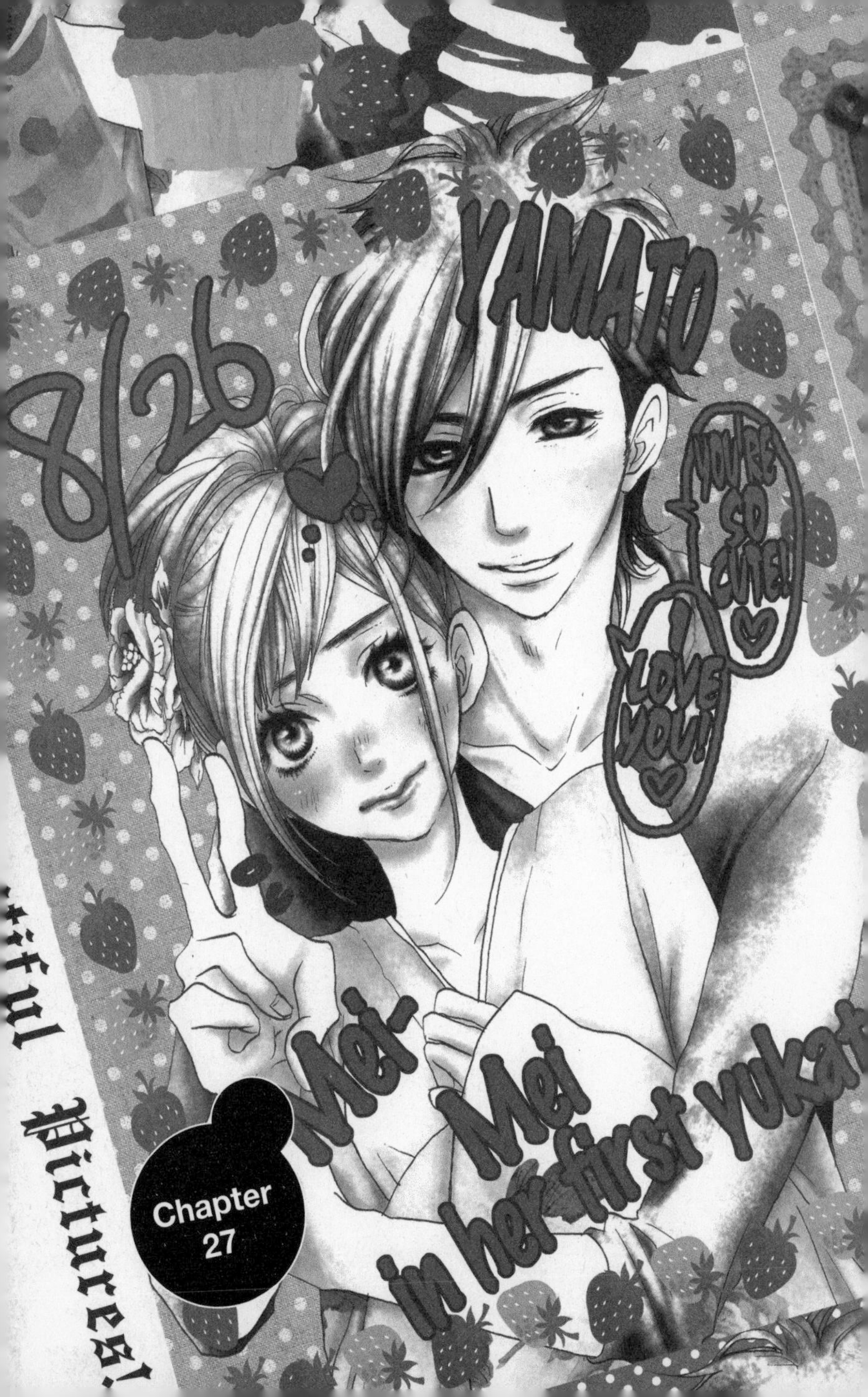
Chapter 27
Mei-Mei in her first yukat
8/26
YAMATO
YOU'RE SO CUTE!
I LOVE YOU!
iful Pictures!

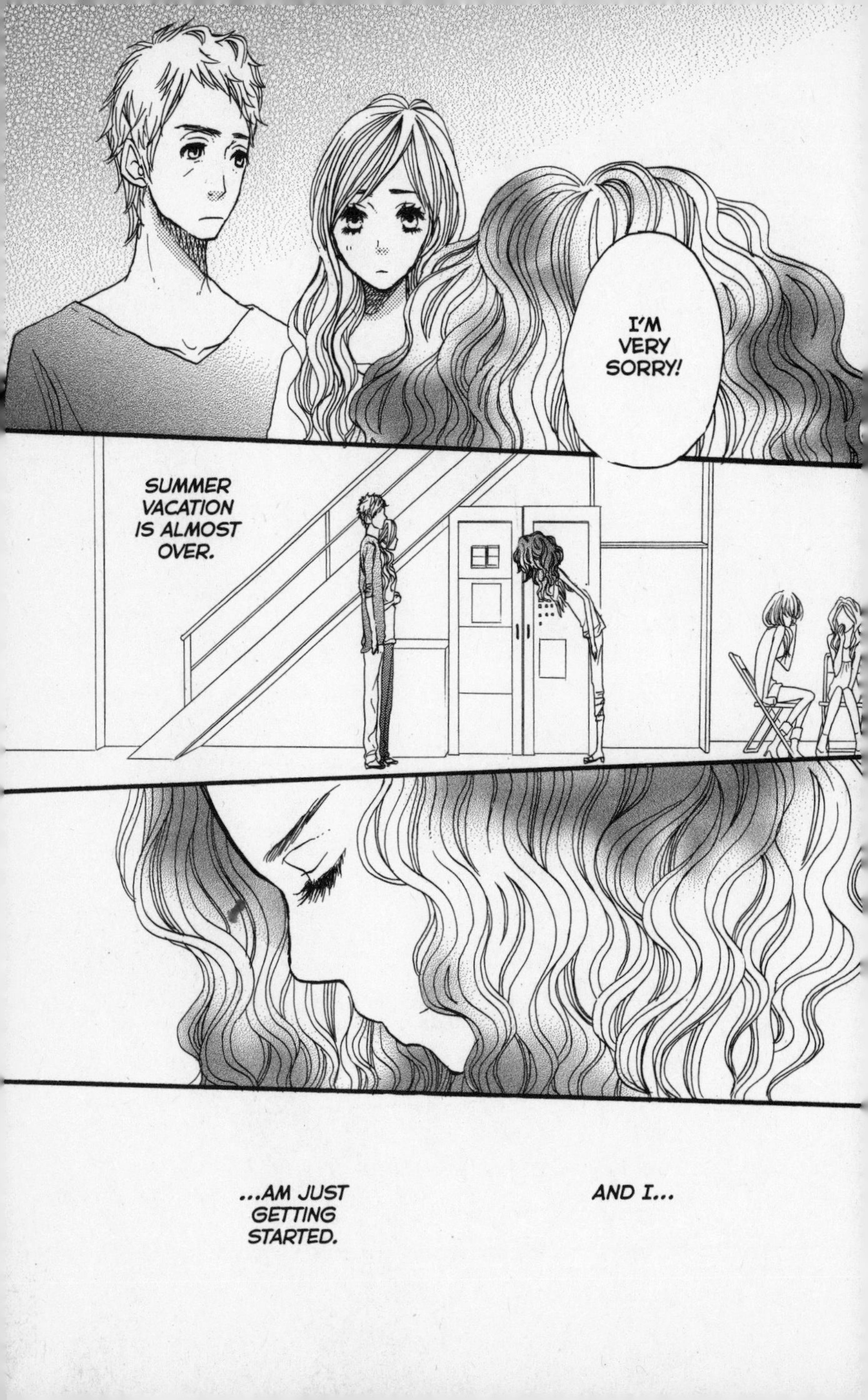
I'M VERY SORRY!
SUMMER VACATION IS ALMOST OVER.
AND I...
...AM JUST GETTING STARTED.

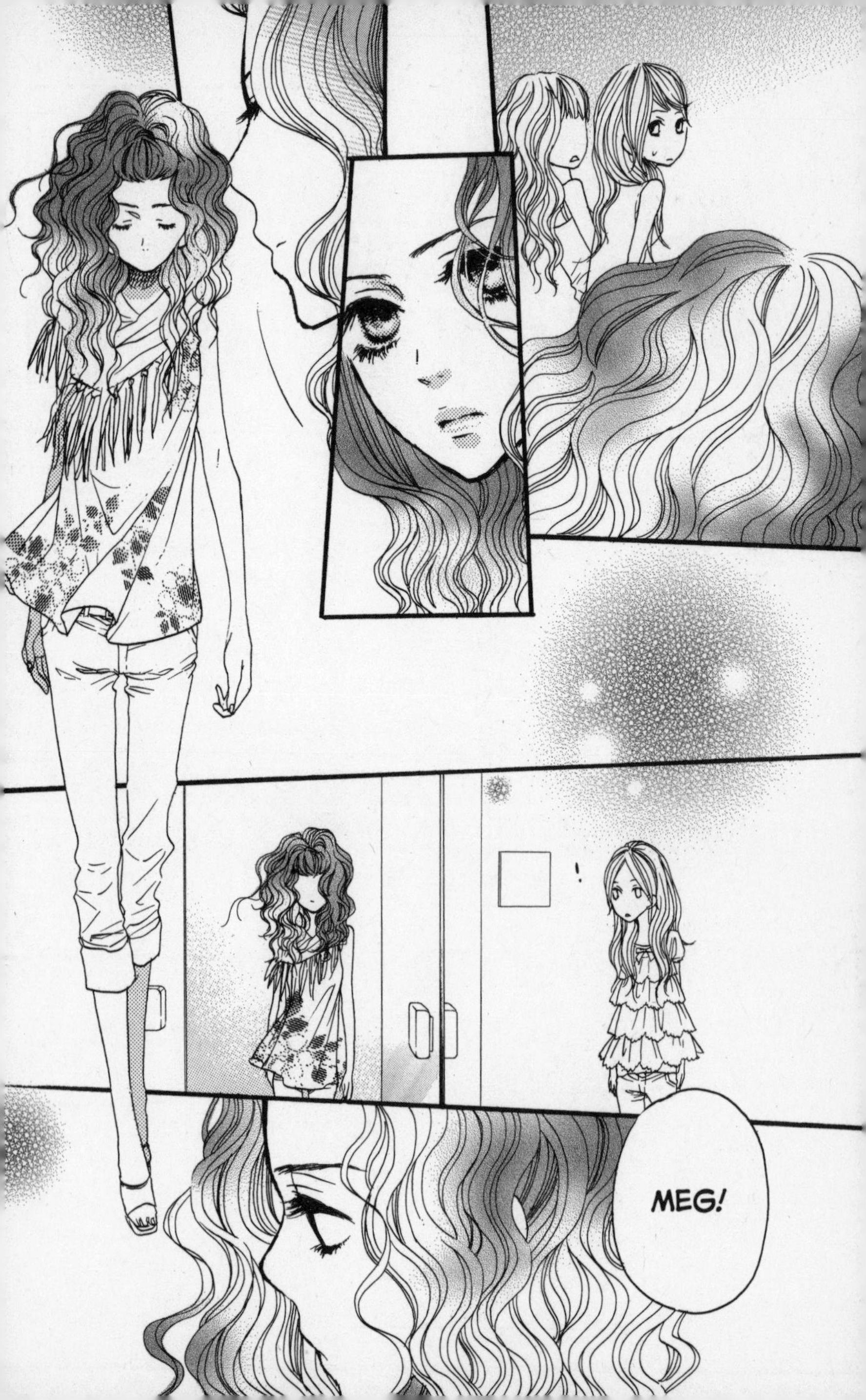
!
MEG!

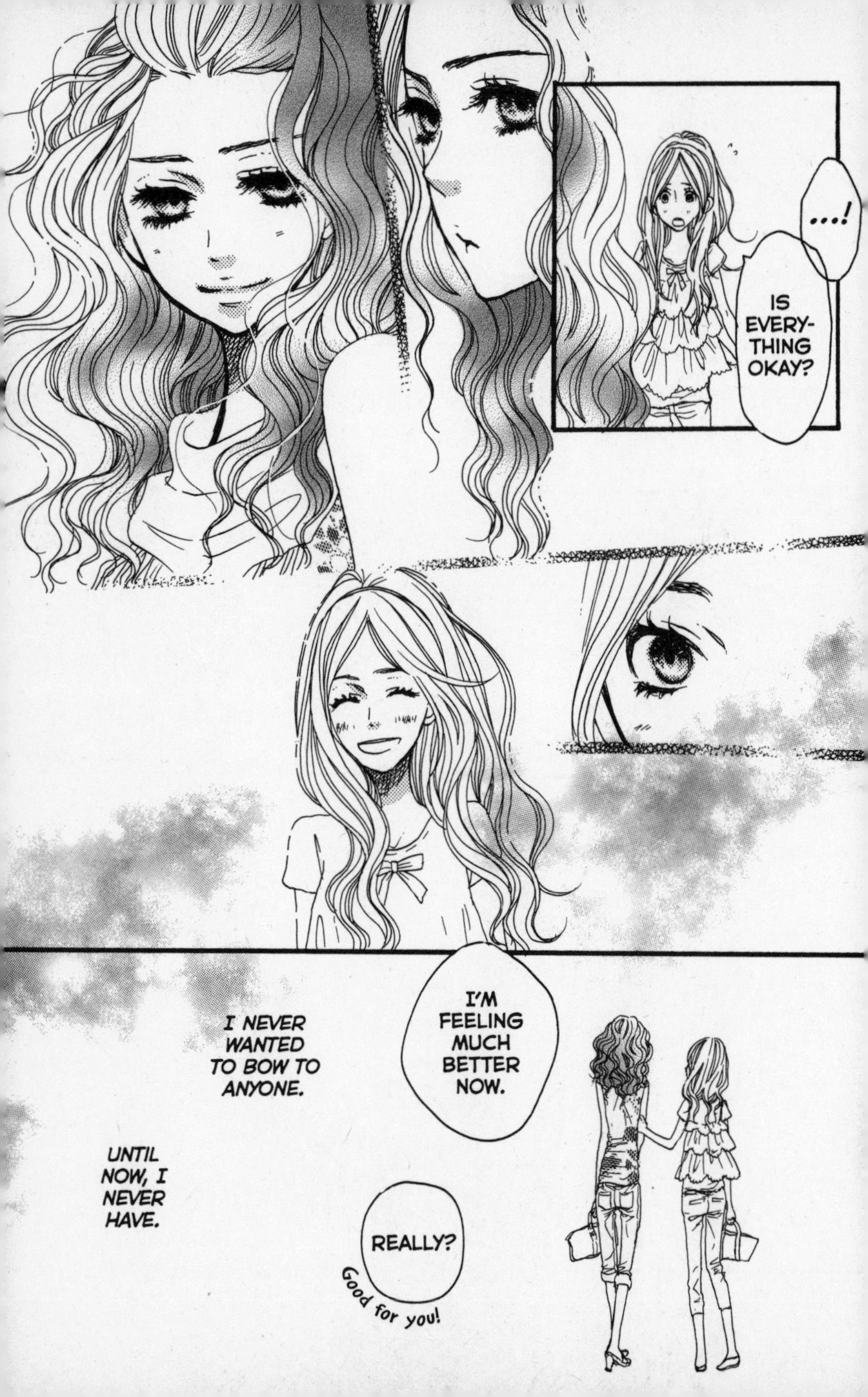
...!
IS EVERYTHING OKAY?
I'M FEELING MUCH BETTER NOW.
I NEVER WANTED TO BOW TO ANYONE.
REALLY?
Good for you!
UNTIL NOW, I NEVER HAVE.

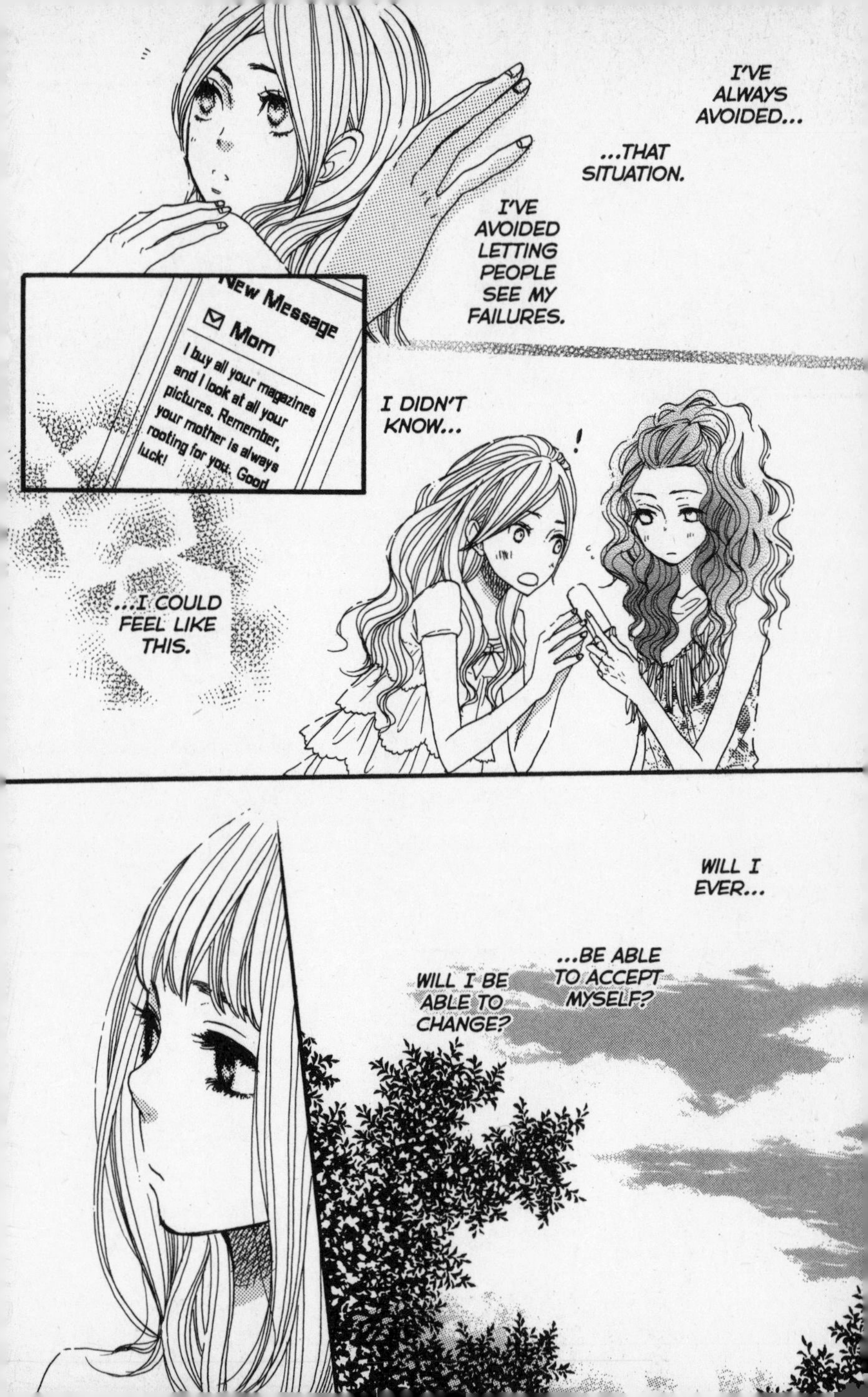
I'VE ALWAYS AVOIDED...
...THAT SITUATION.
I'VE AVOIDED LETTING PEOPLE SEE MY FAILURES.
New Message
Mom
I buy all your magazines and I look at all your pictures. Remember, your mother is always rooting for you. Good luck!
I DIDN'T KNOW...
...I COULD FEEL LIKE THIS.
WILL I EVER...
...BE ABLE TO ACCEPT MYSELF?
WILL I BE ABLE TO CHANGE?

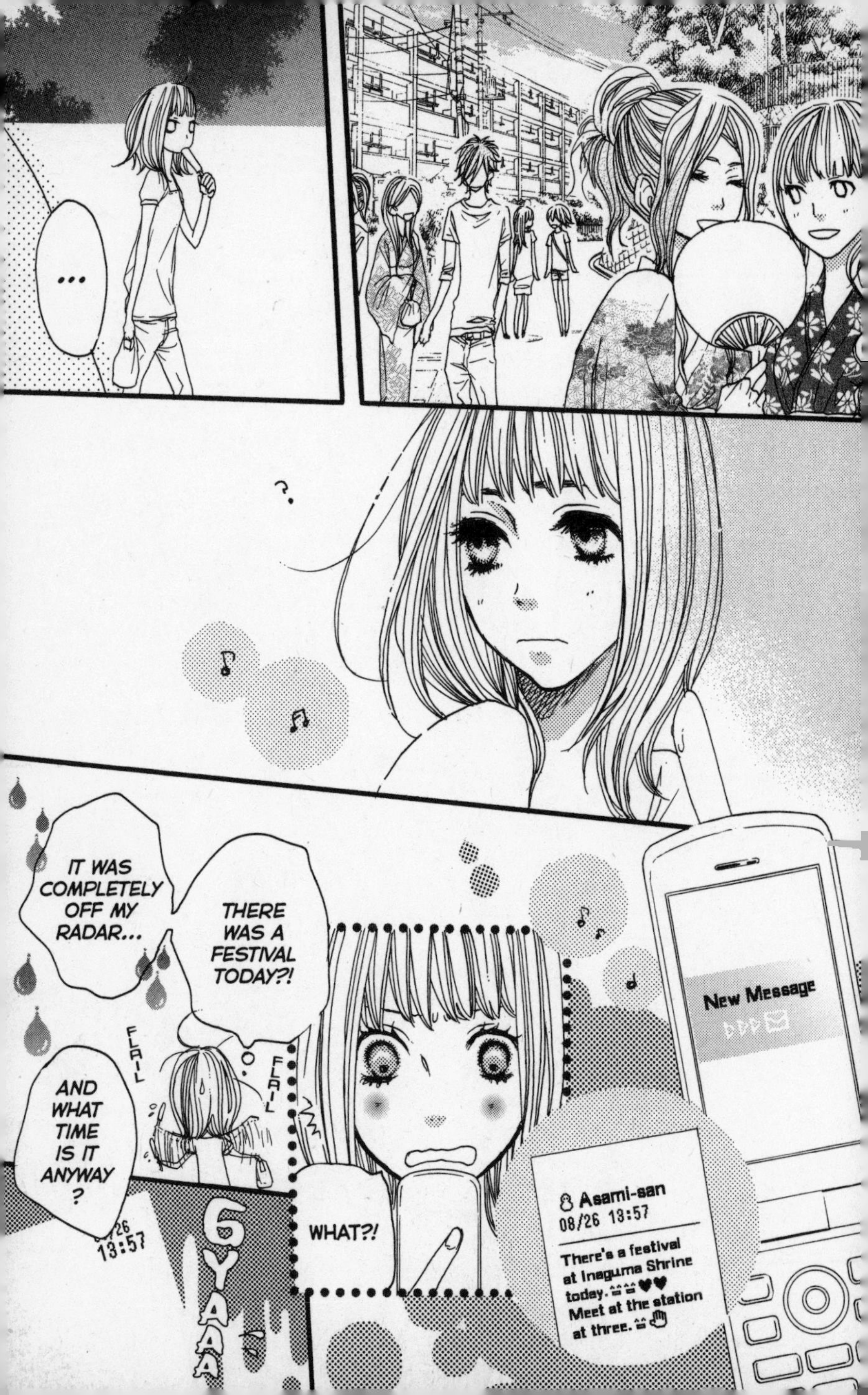
...
New Message
Asami-san
08/26 13:57
There's a festival at Inaguma Shrine today.
Meet at the station at three.
WHAT?!
THERE WAS A FESTIVAL TODAY?!
IT WAS COMPLETELY OFF MY RADAR...
FLAIL
FLAIL
AND WHAT TIME IS IT ANYWAY?
13:57
GYAAA

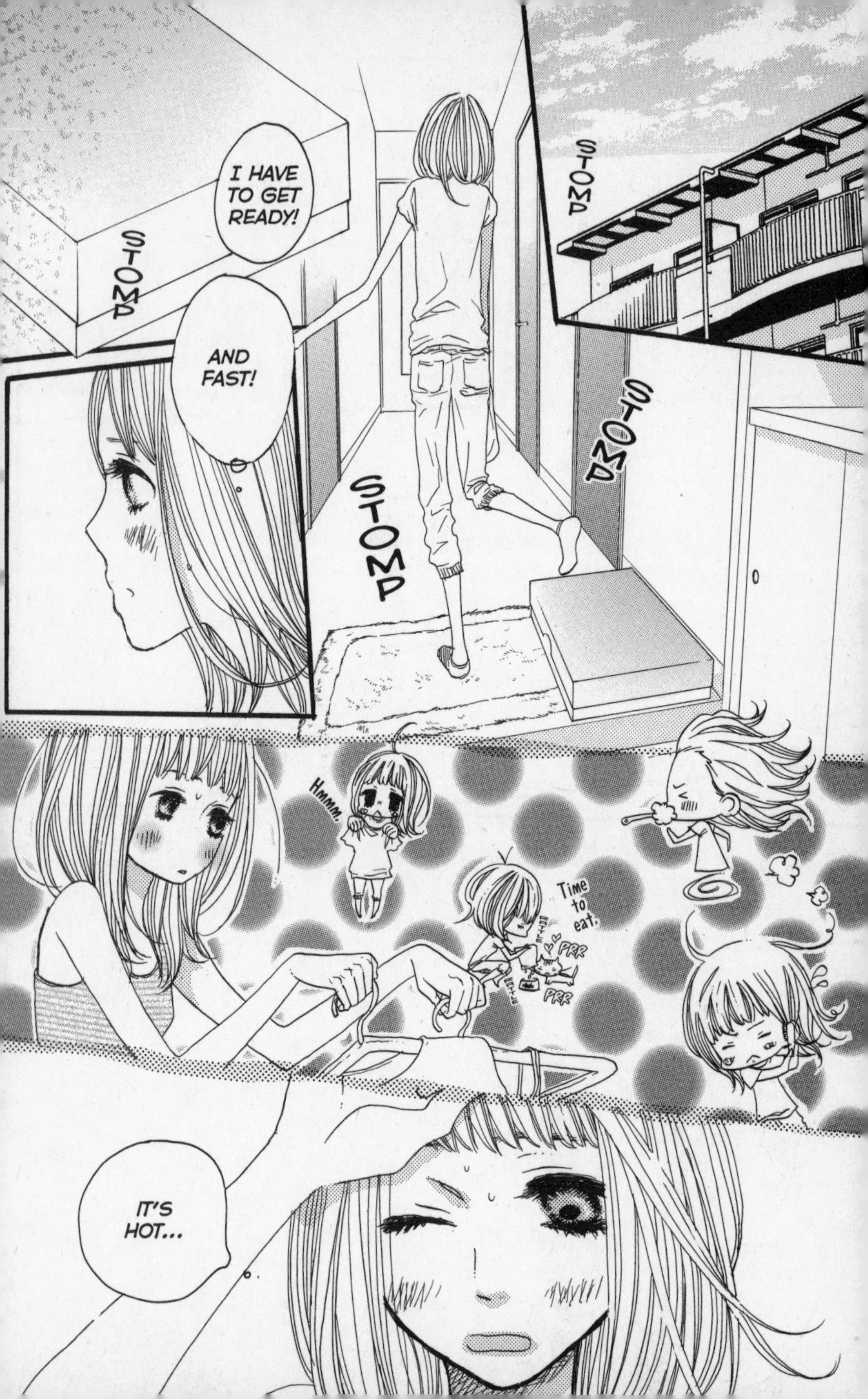
STOMP
I HAVE TO GET READY!
AND FAST!
STOMP
STOMP
STOMP
Time to eat.
PRR
PRR
Hmmm.
IT'S HOT...

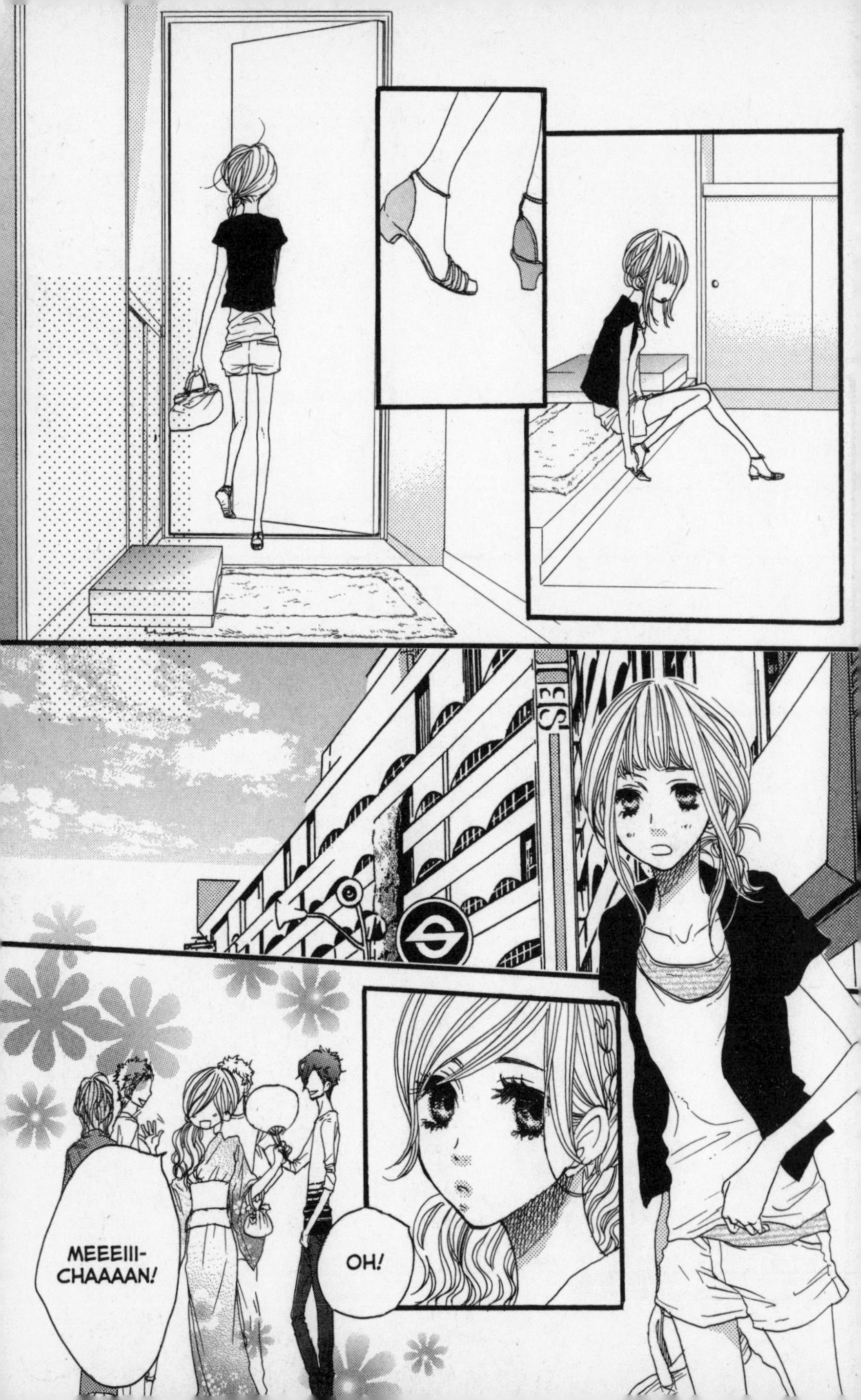
OH!
MEEEIII-CHAAAAN!

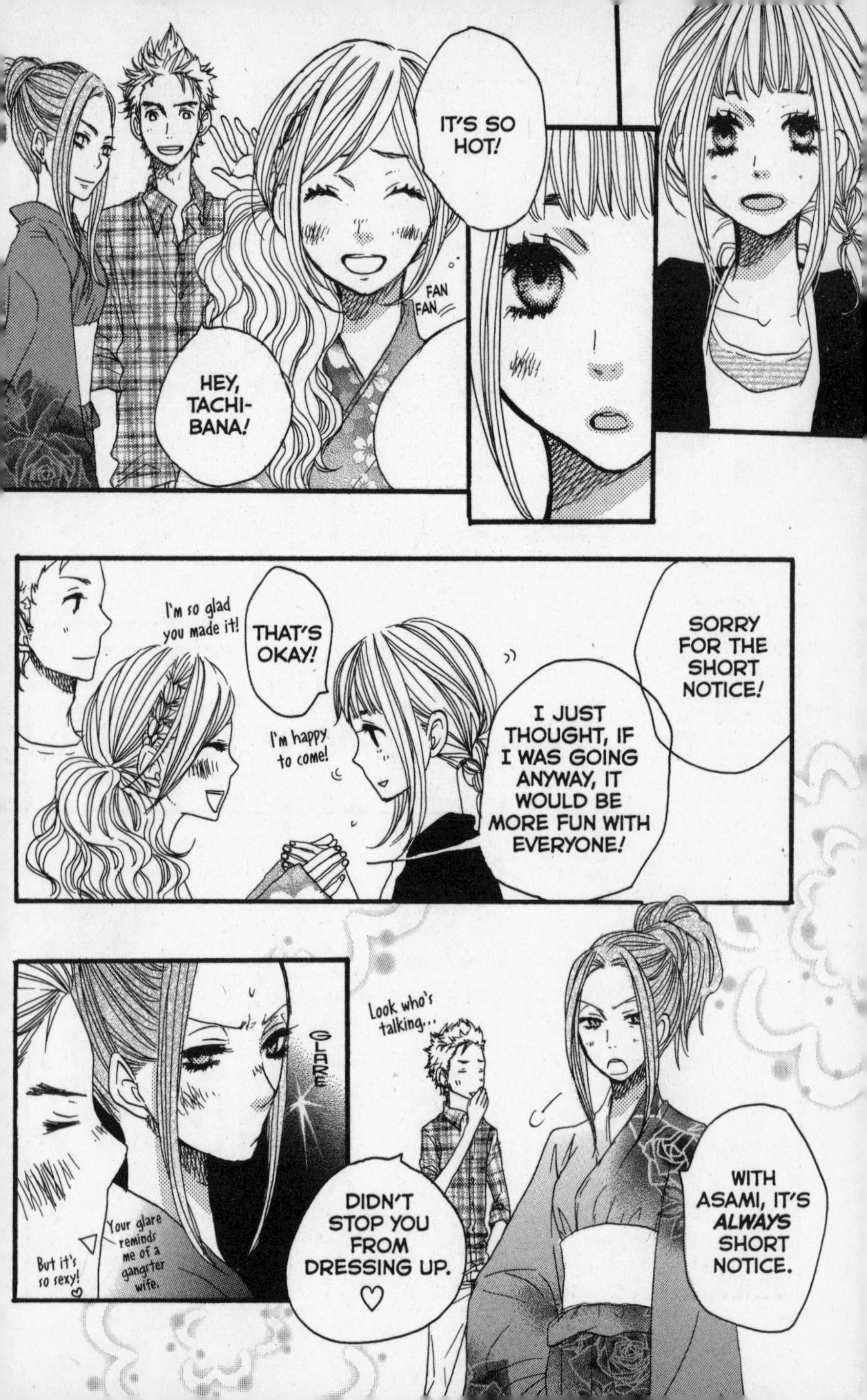
IT'S SO HOT!
FAN FAN
HEY, TACHIBANA!
SORRY FOR THE SHORT NOTICE!
I JUST THOUGHT, IF I WAS GOING ANYWAY, IT WOULD BE MORE FUN WITH EVERYONE!
THAT'S OKAY!
I'm so glad you made it!
I'm happy to come!
WITH ASAMI, IT'S *ALWAYS* SHORT NOTICE.
Look who's talking...
DIDN'T STOP YOU FROM DRESSING UP. ♡
GLARE
Your glare reminds me of a gangster wife.
But it's so sexy! ♡

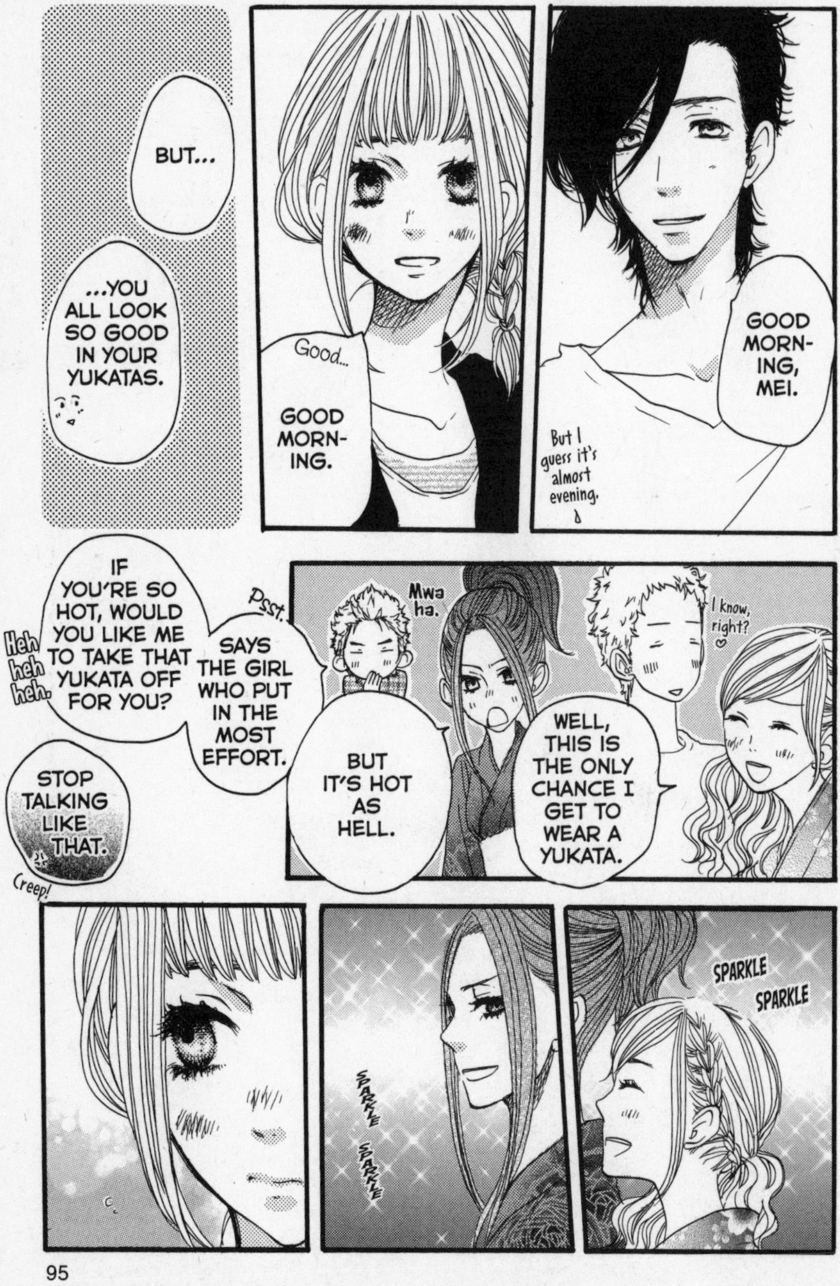
GOOD MORNING, MEI.
But I guess it's almost evening.
Good...
GOOD MORNING.
BUT...
...YOU ALL LOOK SO GOOD IN YOUR YUKATAS.
I know, right?
WELL, THIS IS THE ONLY CHANCE I GET TO WEAR A YUKATA.
Mwa ha.
BUT IT'S HOT AS HELL.
Psst.
SAYS THE GIRL WHO PUT IN THE MOST EFFORT.
IF YOU'RE SO HOT, WOULD YOU LIKE ME TO TAKE THAT YUKATA OFF FOR YOU?
Heh heh heh.
STOP TALKING LIKE THAT.
Creep!
SPARKLE SPARKLE
SPARKLE SPARKLE

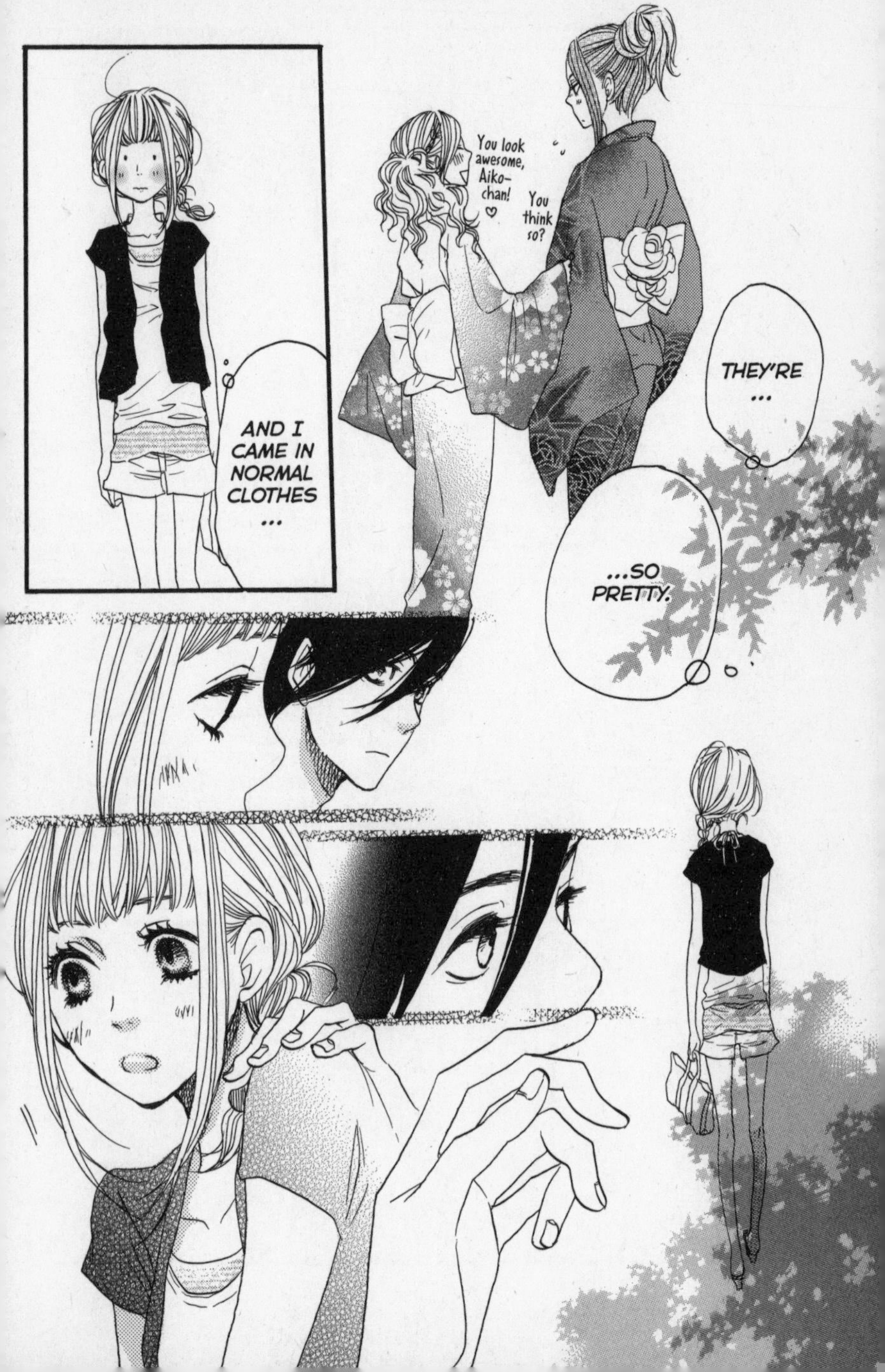
You look awesome, Aiko-chan! ♡
You think so?
THEY'RE ...
...SO PRETTY.
AND I CAME IN NORMAL CLOTHES ...

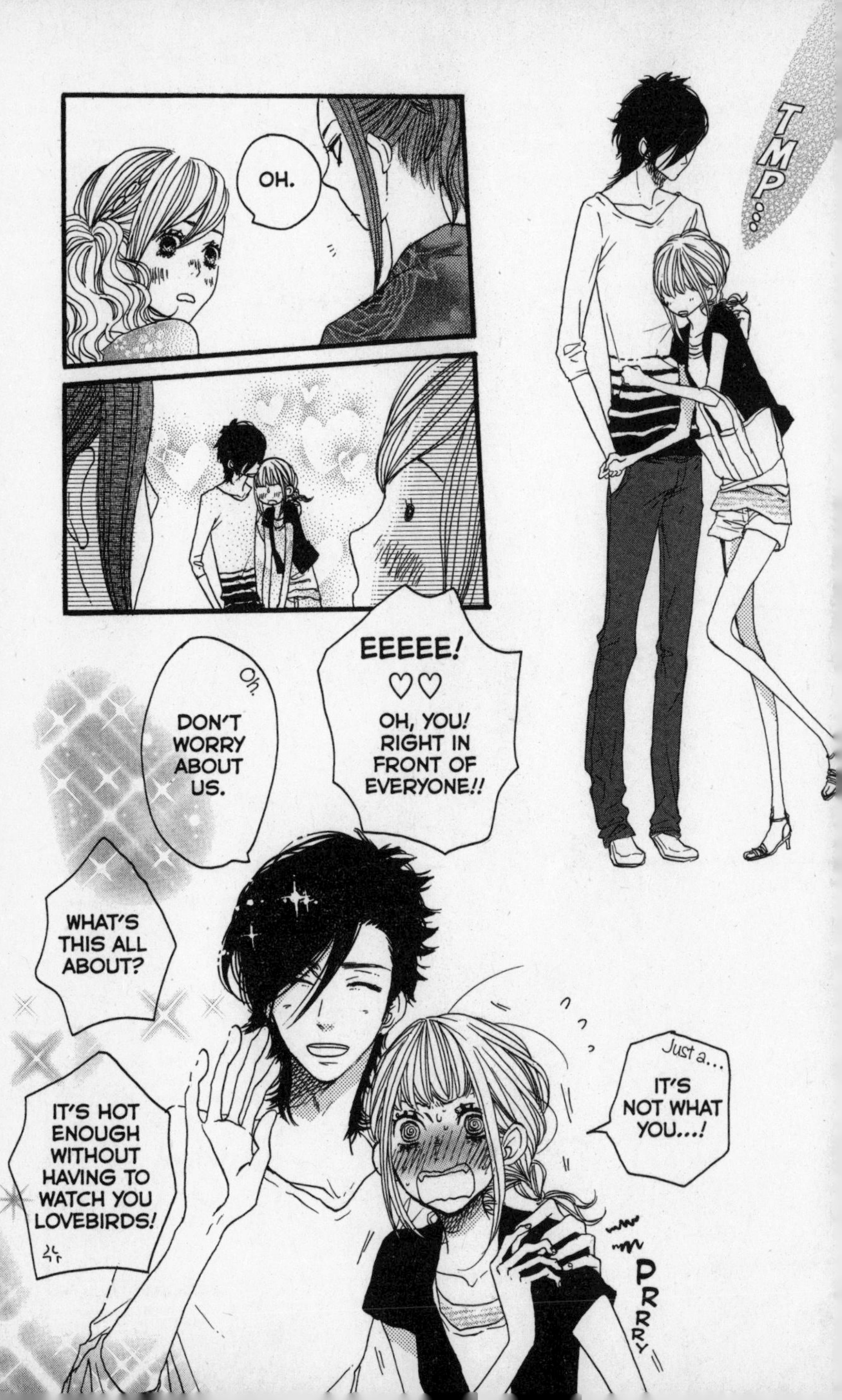
TMP...
OH.
EEEEE! ♡♡
OH, YOU! RIGHT IN FRONT OF EVERYONE!!
Oh.
DON'T WORRY ABOUT US.
Just a...
IT'S NOT WHAT YOU...!
PRRRY
WHAT'S THIS ALL ABOUT?
IT'S HOT ENOUGH WITHOUT HAVING TO WATCH YOU LOVEBIRDS!

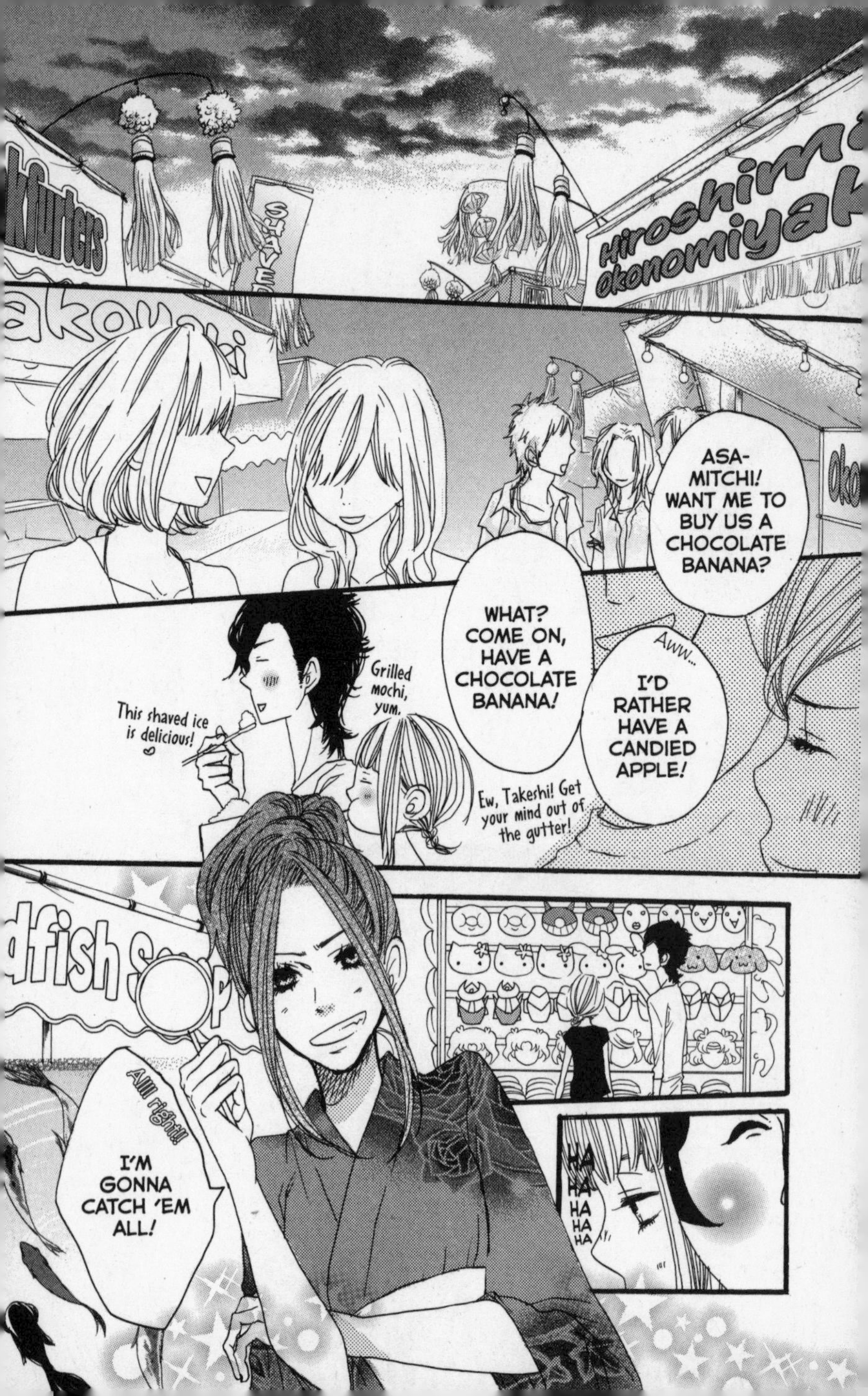

Hiroshim
okonomiyak
SHAVE
kfurters
ASA-MITCHI! WANT ME TO BUY US A CHOCOLATE BANANA?
Aww...
I'D RATHER HAVE A CANDIED APPLE!
WHAT? COME ON, HAVE A CHOCOLATE BANANA!
Grilled mochi, yum.
Ew, Takeshi! Get your mind out of the gutter!
This shaved ice is delicious!
HA HA HA HA HA HA
Allll right!!
I'M GONNA CATCH 'EM ALL!
dfish

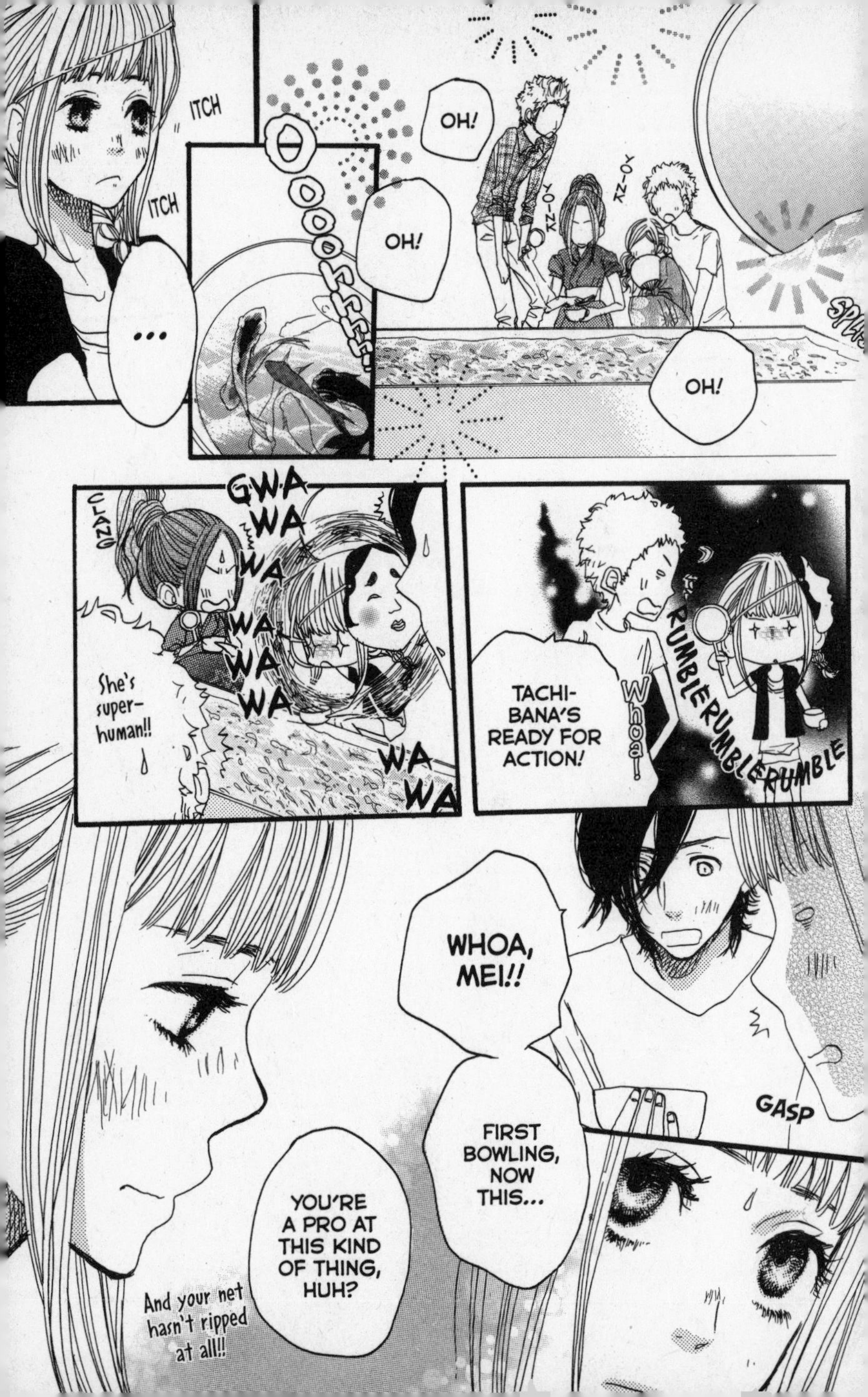

OH!
YOINK
YOINK
SPLA
OH!
OOOOOHHHH!
OH!
ITCH
ITCH
...
RUMBLE RUMBLE RUMBLE
Whoa!
TACHIBANA'S READY FOR ACTION!
CLANG
GWA WA WA WA WA WA WA WA WA
She's superhuman!!
WHOA, MEI!!
GASP
FIRST BOWLING, NOW THIS...
YOU'RE A PRO AT THIS KIND OF THING, HUH?
And your net hasn't ripped at all!!

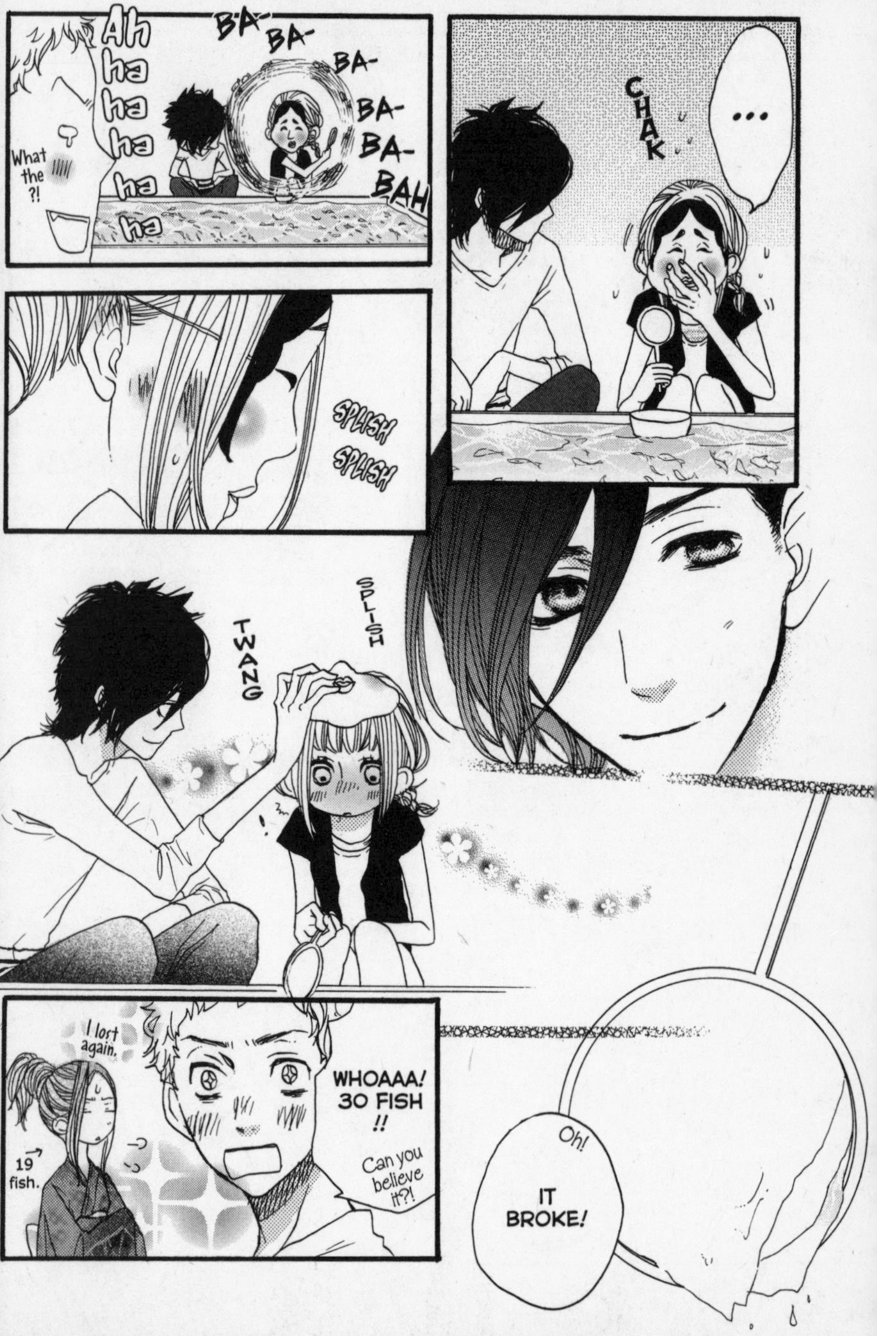
CHAK
...
BA-BA-BA-BA-BA-BAH
Ah ha ha ha ha ha
What the ?!
SPLISH SPLISH
SPLISH
TWANG
Oh!
IT BROKE!
WHOAAA! 30 FISH !!
Can you believe it?!
I lost again.
19 fish.

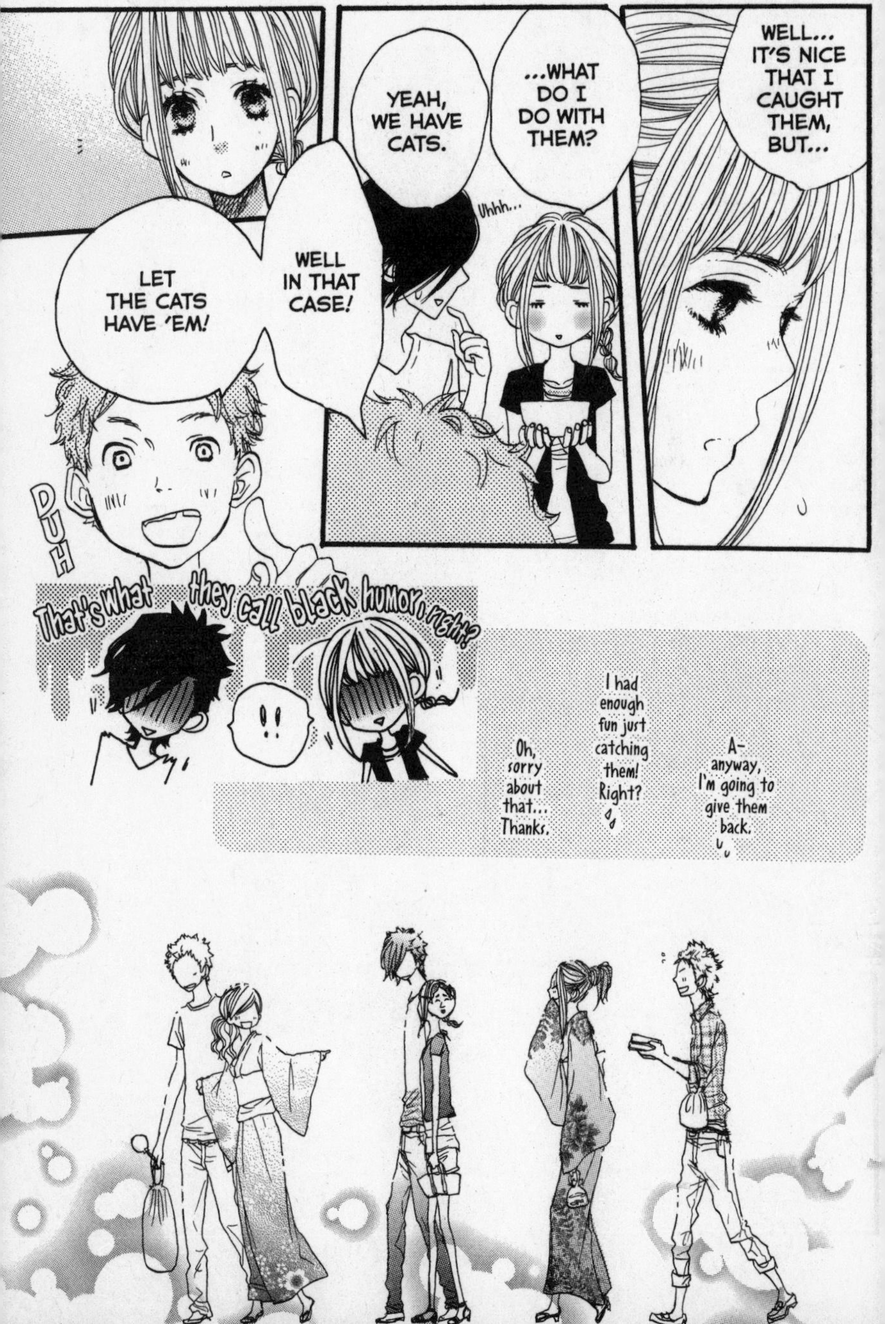
WELL... IT'S NICE THAT I CAUGHT THEM, BUT...
...WHAT DO I DO WITH THEM?
YEAH, WE HAVE CATS.
Uhhh...
WELL IN THAT CASE!
LET THE CATS HAVE 'EM!
DUH
That's what they call black humor, right?
!!
A- anyway, I'm going to give them back.
I had enough fun just catching them! Right?
Oh, sorry about that... Thanks.

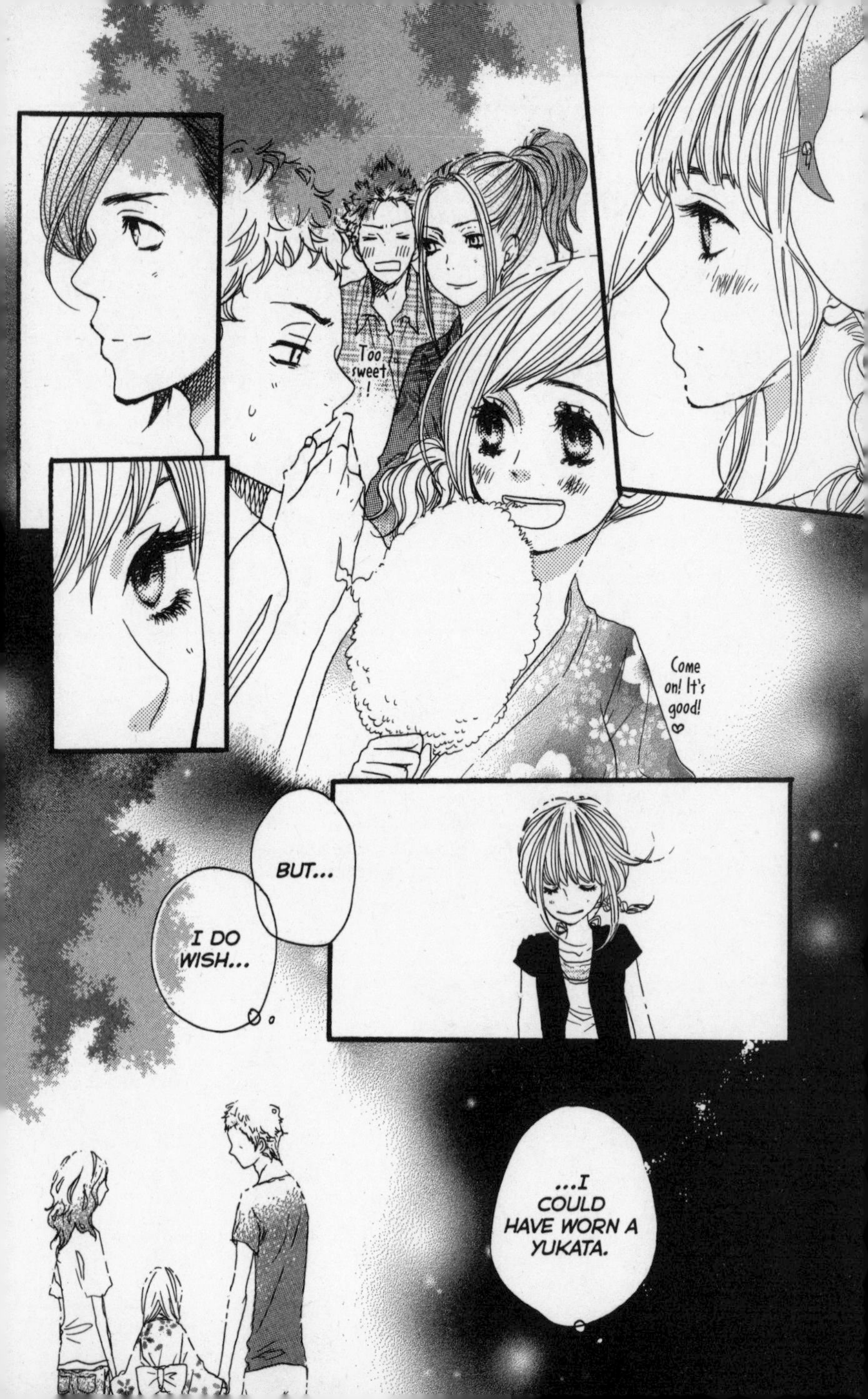
Come on! It's good!
Too sweet!
BUT...
I DO WISH...
...I COULD HAVE WORN A YUKATA.

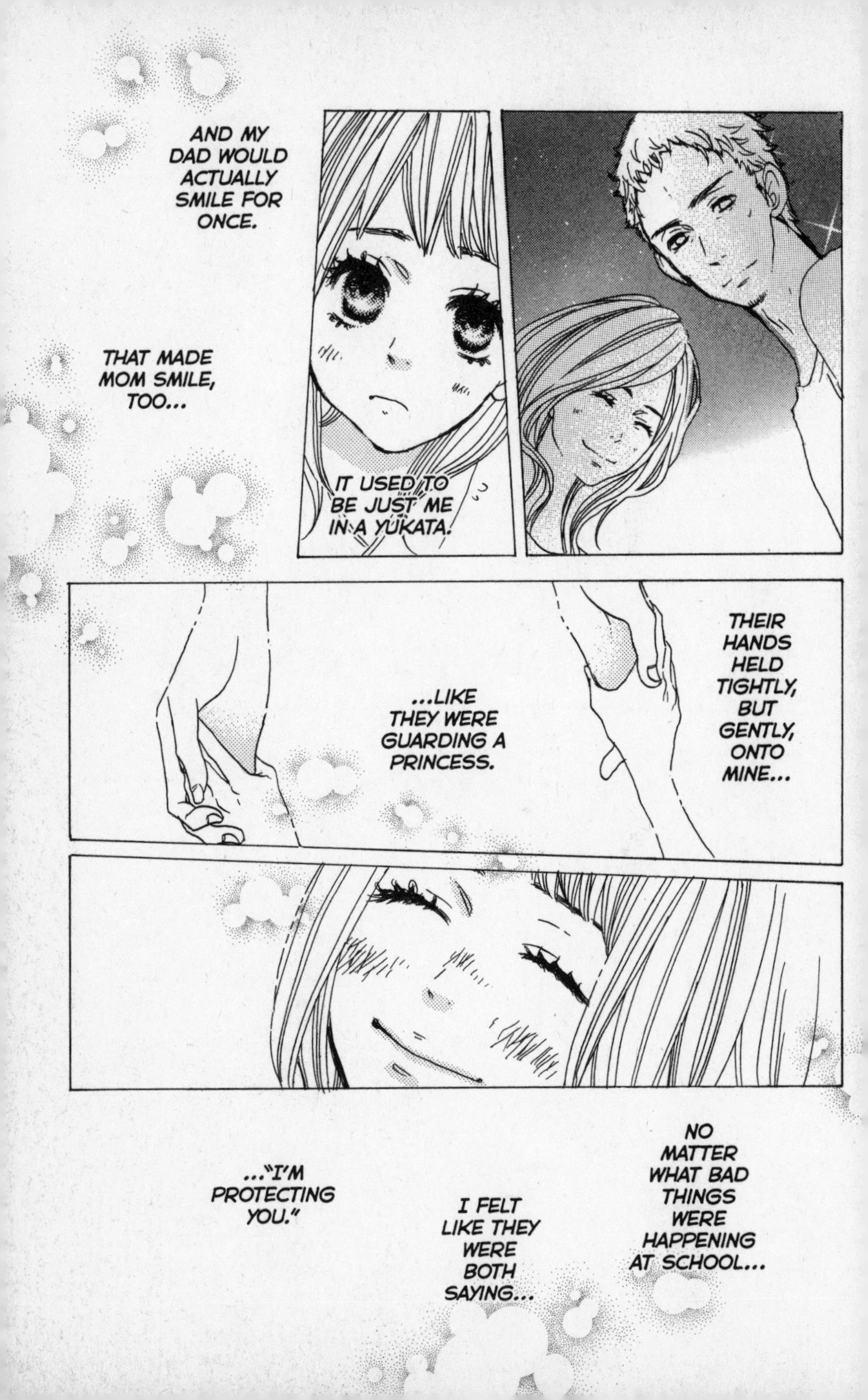
IT USED TO BE JUST ME IN A YUKATA.
AND MY DAD WOULD ACTUALLY SMILE FOR ONCE.
THAT MADE MOM SMILE, TOO...
THEIR HANDS HELD TIGHTLY, BUT GENTLY, ONTO MINE...
...LIKE THEY WERE GUARDING A PRINCESS.
NO MATTER WHAT BAD THINGS WERE HAPPENING AT SCHOOL...
I FELT LIKE THEY WERE BOTH SAYING...
..."I'M PROTECTING YOU."

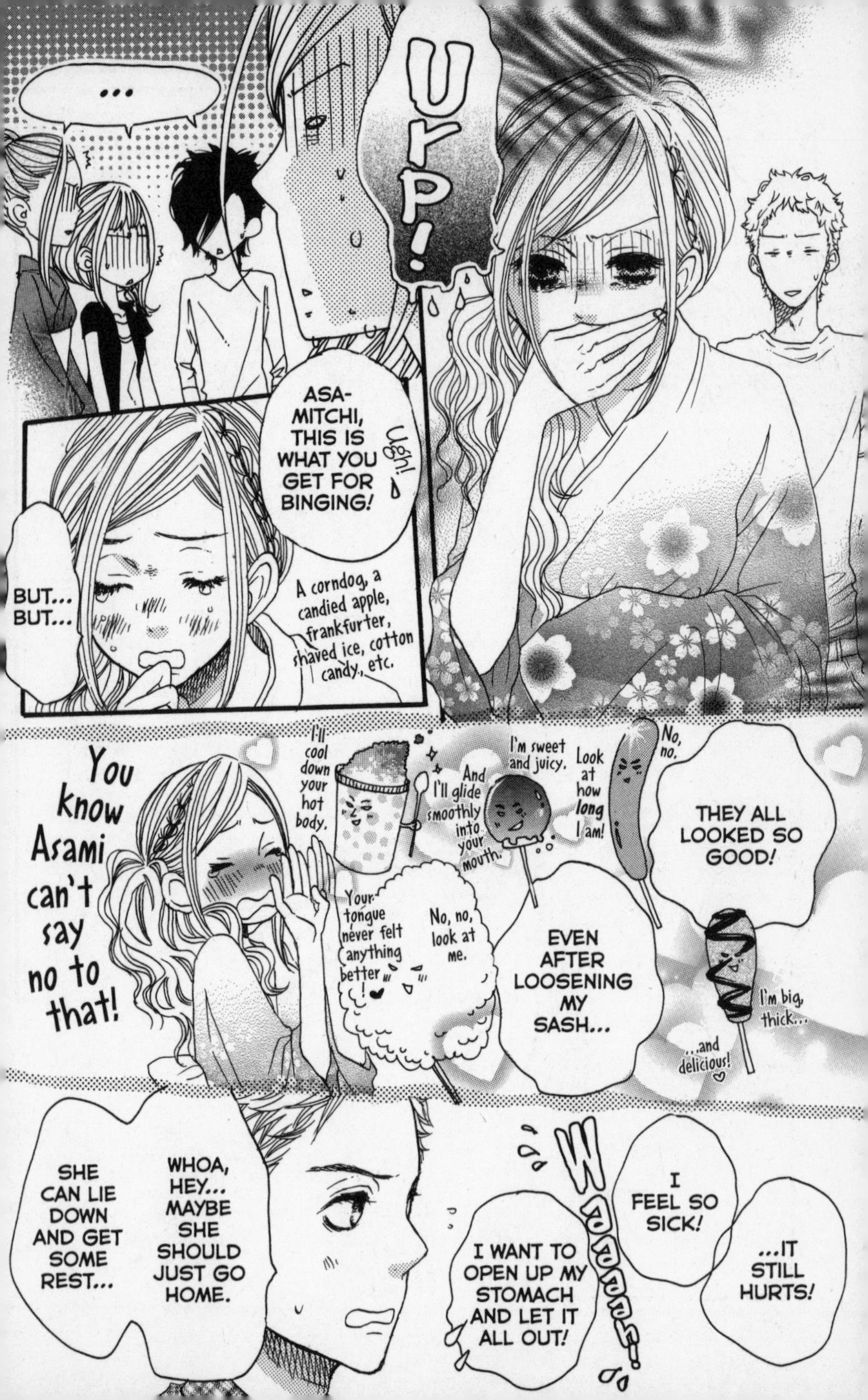
URP!
...
ASA-MITCHI, THIS IS WHAT YOU GET FOR BINGING!
Ugh!
BUT... BUT...
A corndog, a candied apple, frankfurter, shaved ice, cotton candy, etc.
THEY ALL LOOKED SO GOOD!
No, no.
Look at how long I am!
I'm sweet and juicy.
And I'll glide smoothly into your mouth.
I'll cool down your hot body.
I'm big, thick...
...and delicious!
EVEN AFTER LOOSENING MY SASH...
No, no, look at me.
Your tongue never felt anything better!
You know Asami can't say no to that!
...IT STILL HURTS!
I FEEL SO SICK!
I WANT TO OPEN UP MY STOMACH AND LET IT ALL OUT!
WHOA, HEY... MAYBE SHE SHOULD JUST GO HOME.
SHE CAN LIE DOWN AND GET SOME REST...

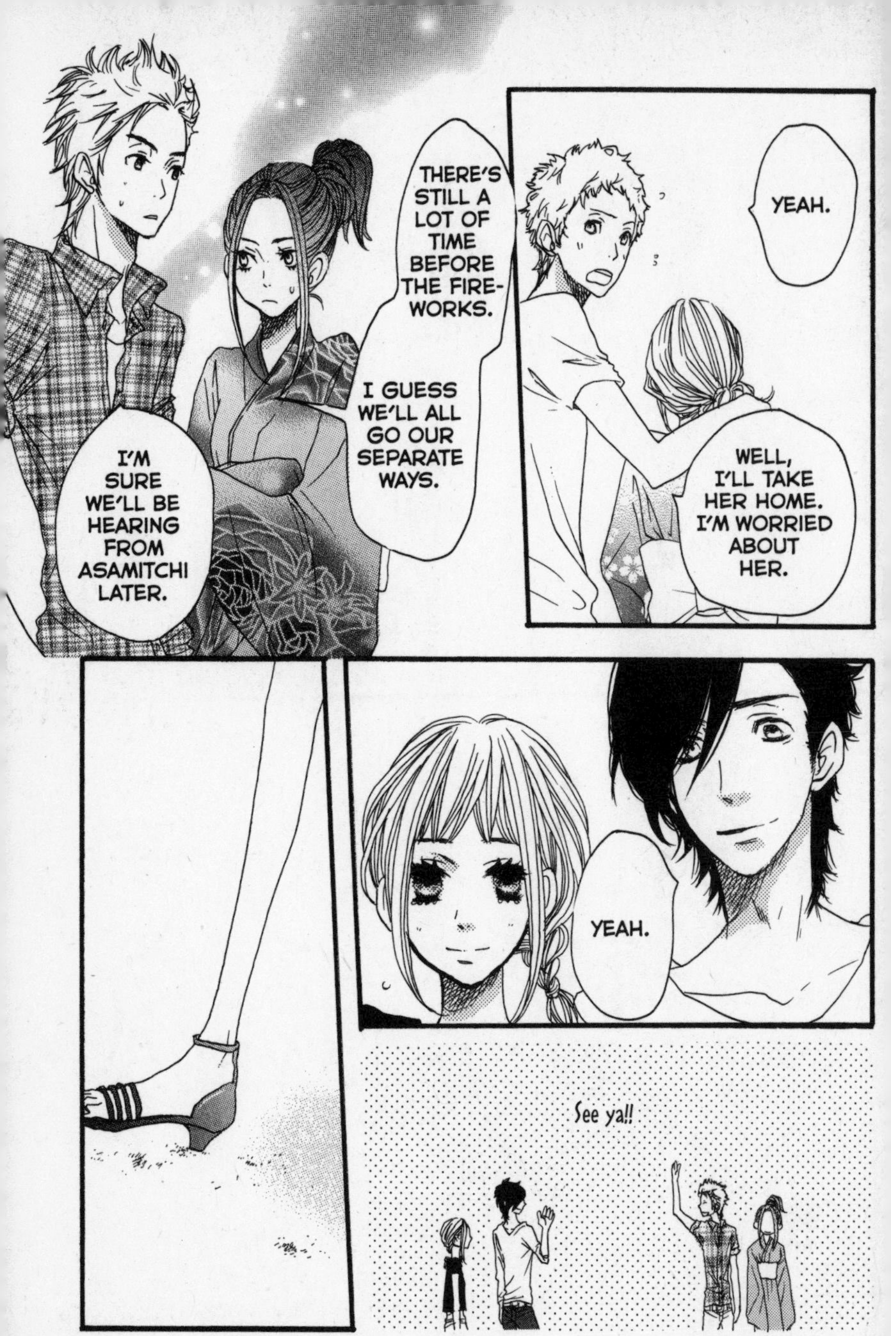
YEAH.
WELL, I'LL TAKE HER HOME. I'M WORRIED ABOUT HER.
THERE'S STILL A LOT OF TIME BEFORE THE FIRE-WORKS.
I GUESS WE'LL ALL GO OUR SEPARATE WAYS.
I'M SURE WE'LL BE HEARING FROM ASAMITCHI LATER.
YEAH.
See ya!!

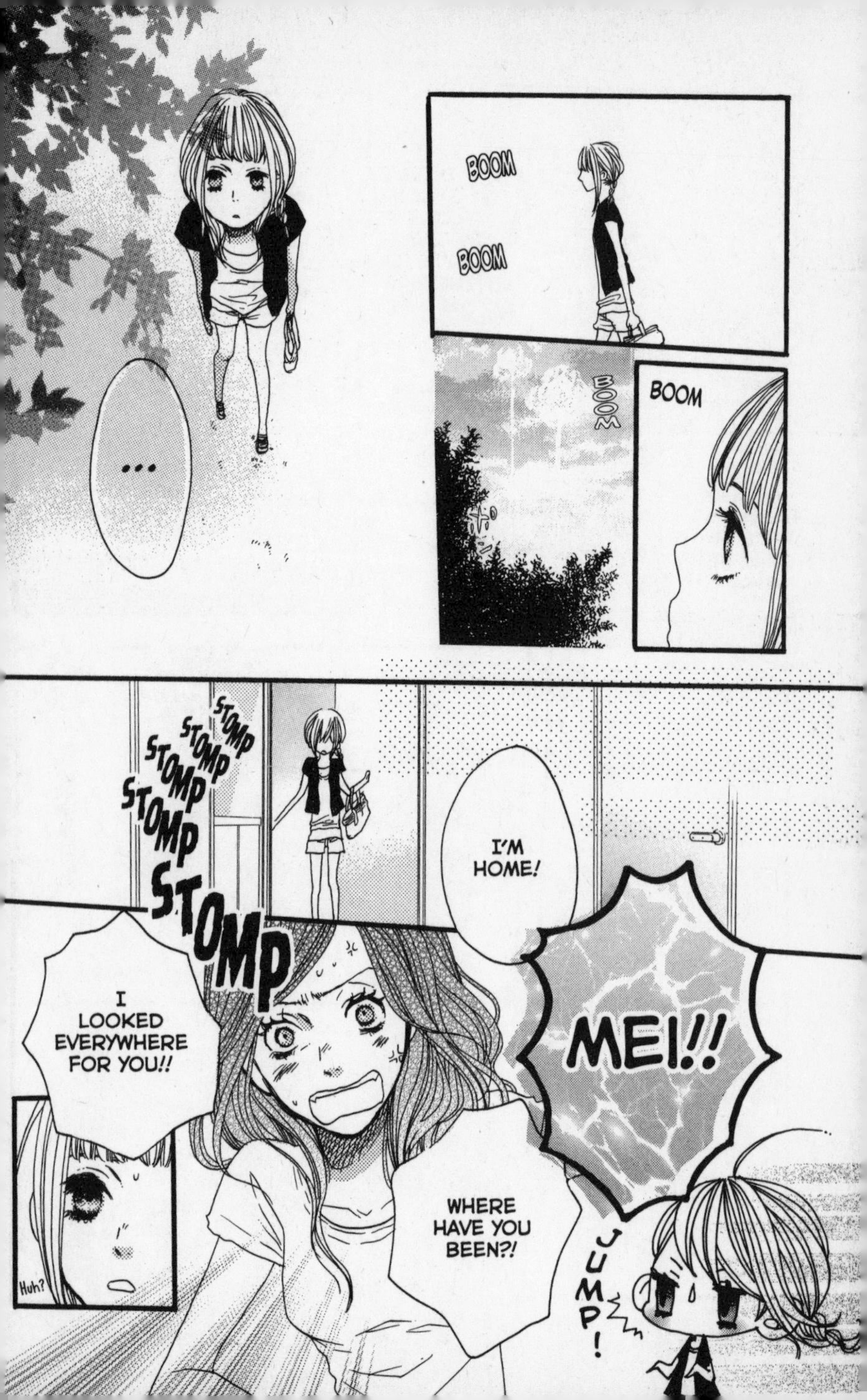
BOOM
BOOM
BOOM
BOOM
...
I'M HOME!
STOMP STOMP STOMP STOMP STOMP STOMP
MEI!!
WHERE HAVE YOU BEEN?!
I LOOKED EVERYWHERE FOR YOU!!
JUMP!
Huh?

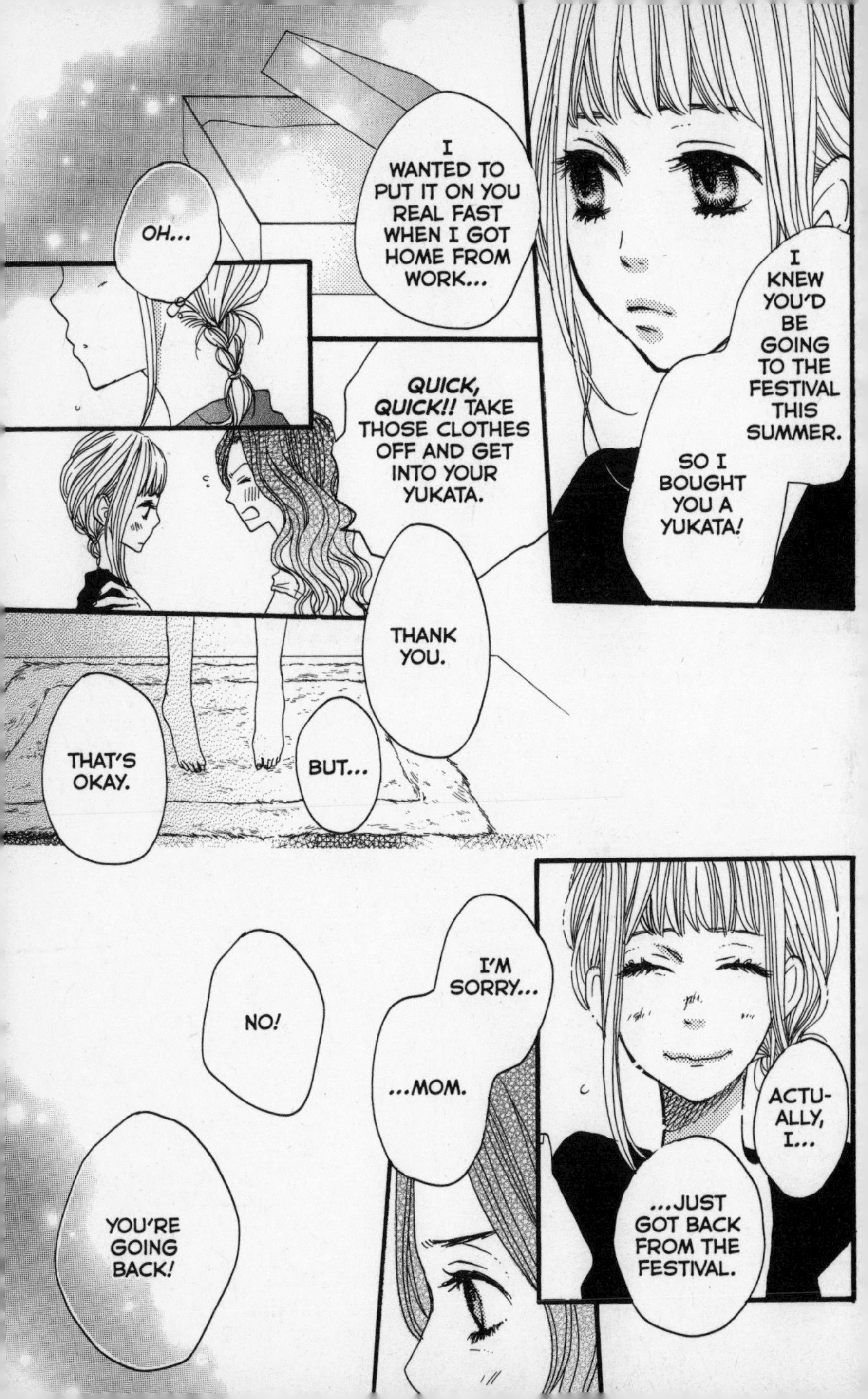

I KNEW YOU'D BE GOING TO THE FESTIVAL THIS SUMMER.
SO I BOUGHT YOU A YUKATA!
I WANTED TO PUT IT ON YOU REAL FAST WHEN I GOT HOME FROM WORK...
OH...
QUICK, QUICK!! TAKE THOSE CLOTHES OFF AND GET INTO YOUR YUKATA.
THANK YOU.
BUT...
THAT'S OKAY.
ACTU-ALLY, I...
...JUST GOT BACK FROM THE FESTIVAL.
I'M SORRY...
...MOM.
NO!
YOU'RE GOING BACK!

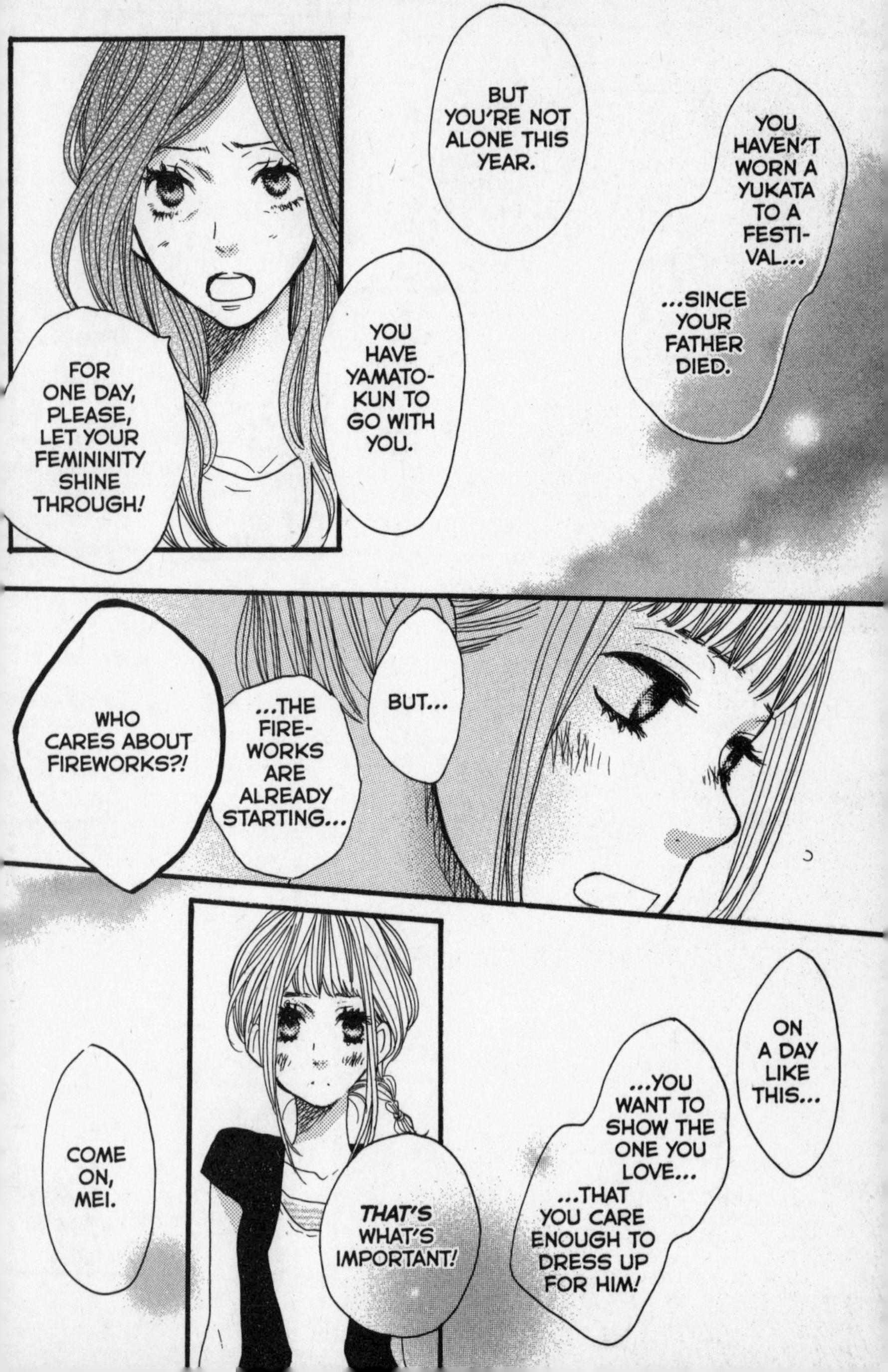
YOU HAVEN'T WORN A YUKATA TO A FESTIVAL...
...SINCE YOUR FATHER DIED.
BUT YOU'RE NOT ALONE THIS YEAR.
YOU HAVE YAMATO-KUN TO GO WITH YOU.
FOR ONE DAY, PLEASE, LET YOUR FEMININITY SHINE THROUGH!
BUT...
...THE FIREWORKS ARE ALREADY STARTING...
WHO CARES ABOUT FIREWORKS?!
ON A DAY LIKE THIS...
...YOU WANT TO SHOW THE ONE YOU LOVE...
...THAT YOU CARE ENOUGH TO DRESS UP FOR HIM!
THAT'S WHAT'S IMPORTANT!
COME ON, MEI.

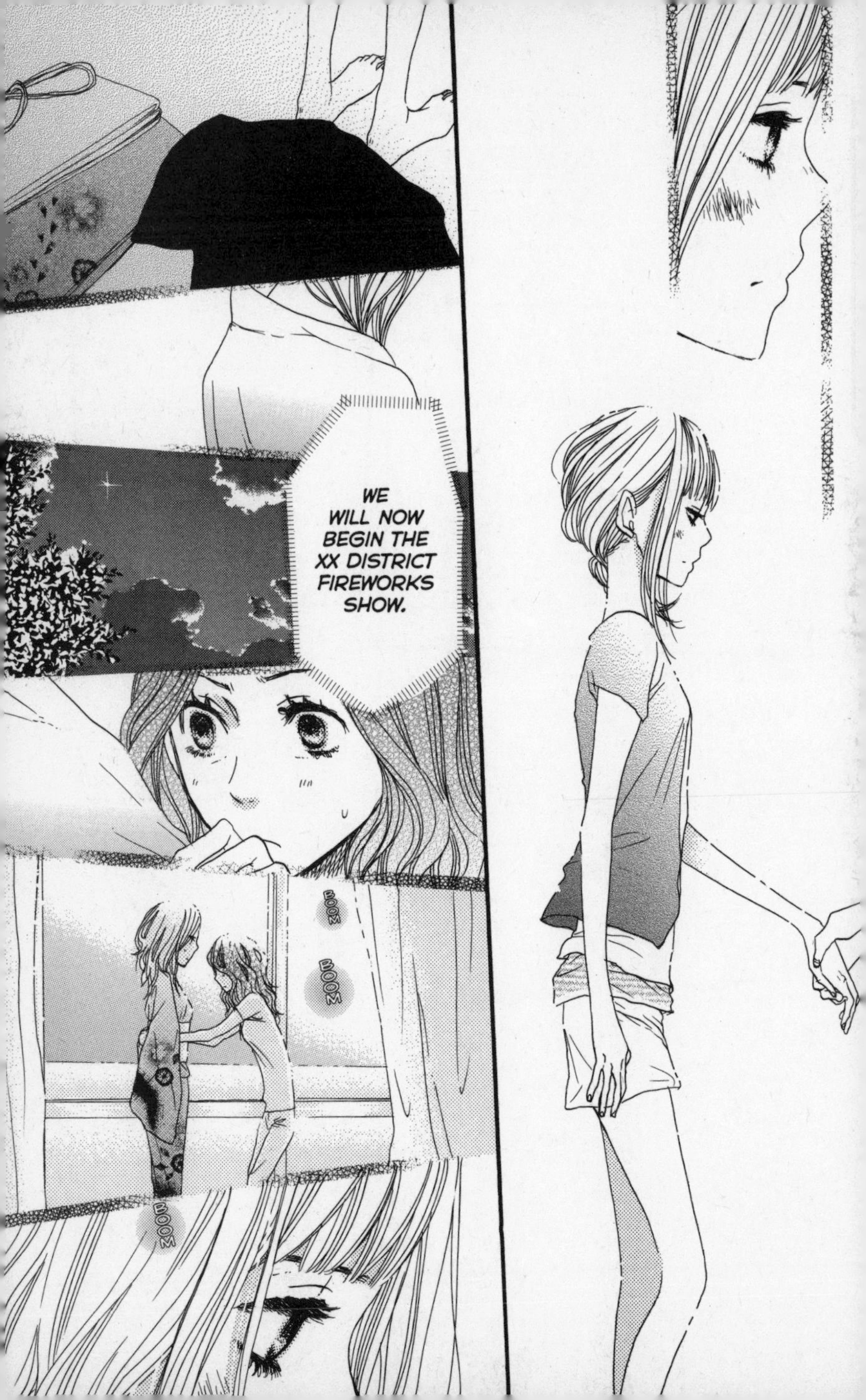
WE WILL NOW BEGIN THE XX DISTRICT FIREWORKS SHOW.
BOOM
BOOM
BOOM

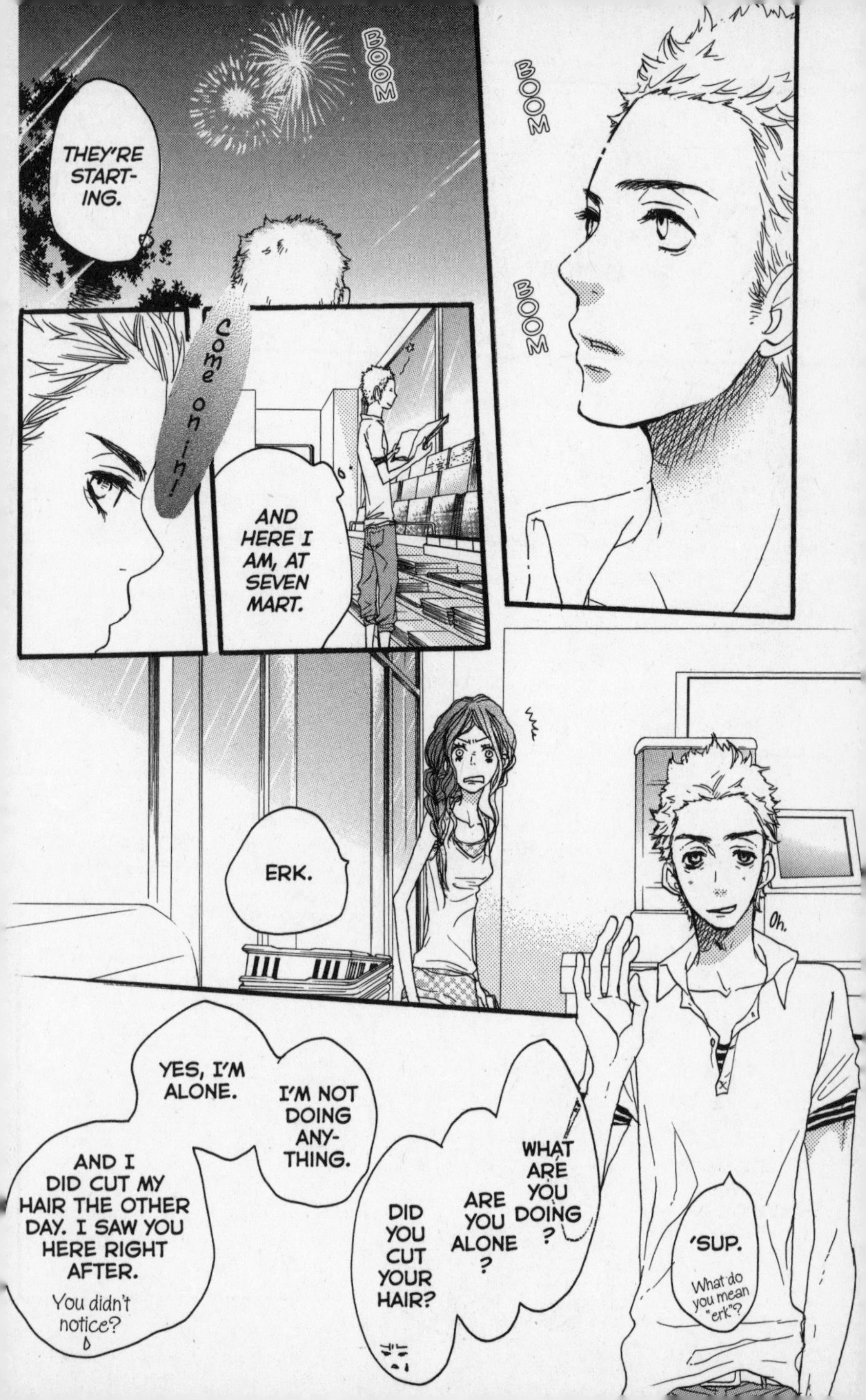
BOOM BOOM
BOOM BOOM
BOOM BOOM
THEY'RE START-ING.
Come on in!
AND HERE I AM, AT SEVEN MART.
ERK.
Oh.
'SUP.
What do you mean "erk"?
WHAT ARE YOU DOING?
ARE YOU ALONE?
DID YOU CUT YOUR HAIR?
YES, I'M ALONE.
I'M NOT DOING ANY-THING.
AND I DID CUT MY HAIR THE OTHER DAY. I SAW YOU HERE RIGHT AFTER.
You didn't notice?

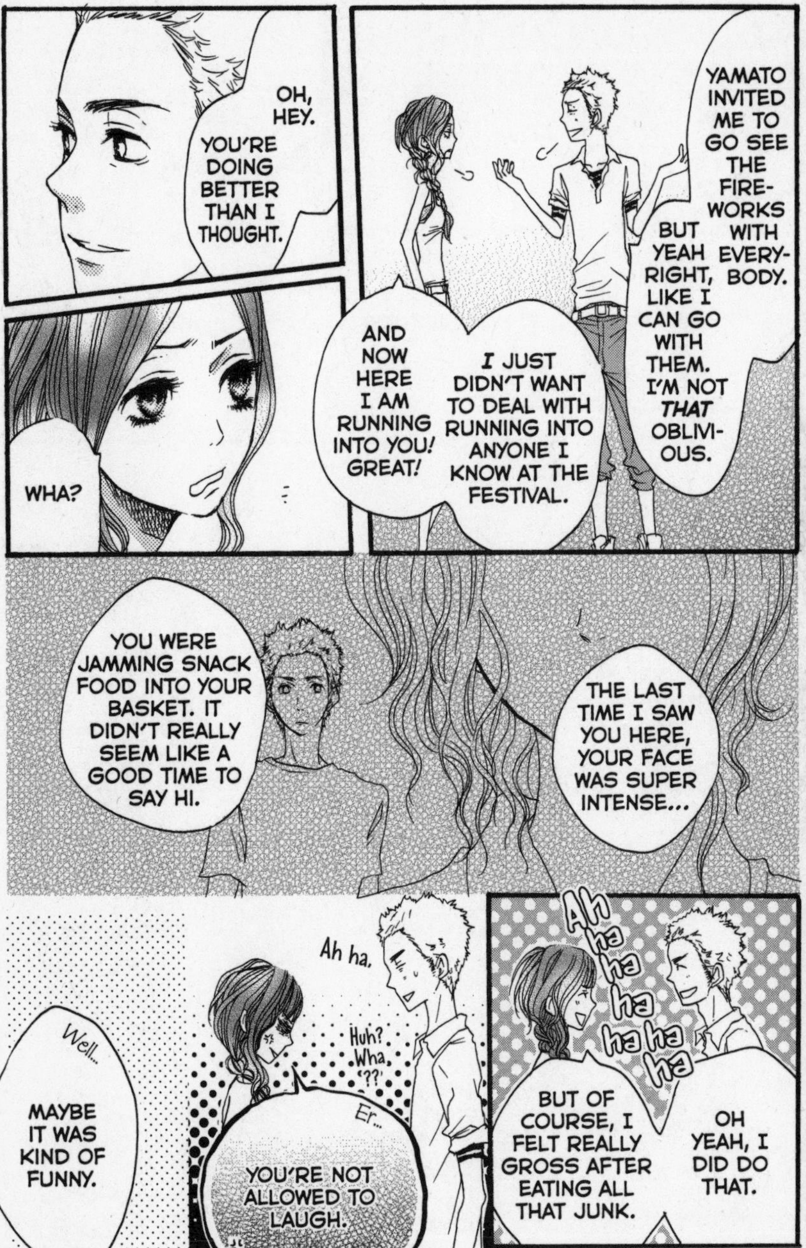
YAMATO INVITED ME TO GO SEE THE FIRE-WORKS WITH EVERY-BODY.
BUT YEAH RIGHT, LIKE I CAN GO WITH THEM. I'M NOT *THAT* OBLIVI-OUS.
I JUST DIDN'T WANT TO DEAL WITH RUNNING INTO ANYONE I KNOW AT THE FESTIVAL.
AND NOW HERE I AM RUNNING INTO YOU! GREAT!
OH, HEY. YOU'RE DOING BETTER THAN I THOUGHT.
WHA?
THE LAST TIME I SAW YOU HERE, YOUR FACE WAS SUPER INTENSE...
YOU WERE JAMMING SNACK FOOD INTO YOUR BASKET. IT DIDN'T REALLY SEEM LIKE A GOOD TIME TO SAY HI.
Ahhahahahahaha
OH YEAH, I DID DO THAT.
BUT OF COURSE, I FELT REALLY GROSS AFTER EATING ALL THAT JUNK.
Ah ha.
Huh? Wha ??
Er...
YOU'RE NOT ALLOWED TO LAUGH.
Well...
MAYBE IT WAS KIND OF FUNNY.

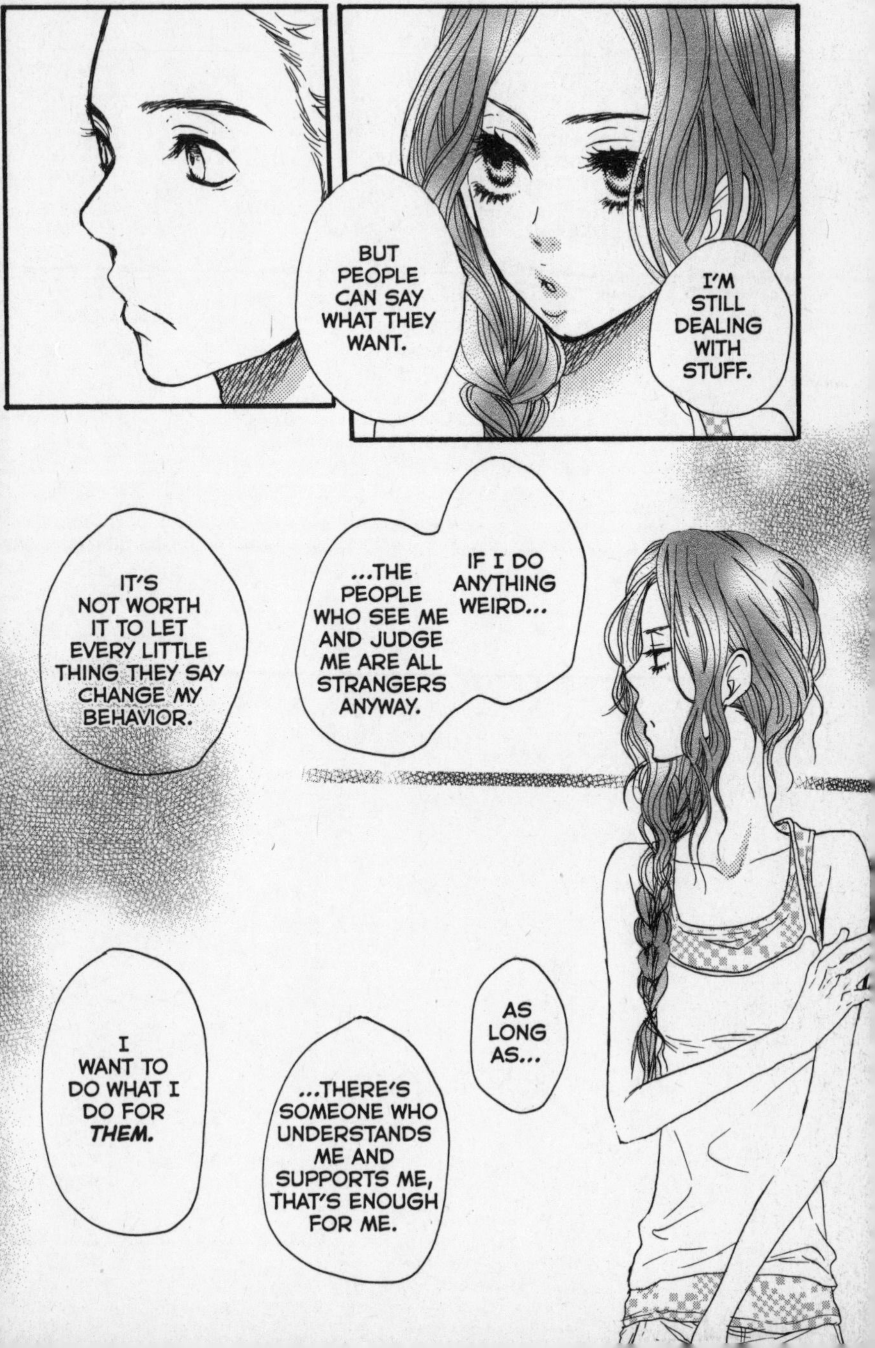
I'M STILL DEALING WITH STUFF.
BUT PEOPLE CAN SAY WHAT THEY WANT.
IF I DO ANYTHING WEIRD...
...THE PEOPLE WHO SEE ME AND JUDGE ME ARE ALL STRANGERS ANYWAY.
IT'S NOT WORTH IT TO LET EVERY LITTLE THING THEY SAY CHANGE MY BEHAVIOR.
AS LONG AS...
...THERE'S SOMEONE WHO UNDERSTANDS ME AND SUPPORTS ME, THAT'S ENOUGH FOR ME.
I WANT TO DO WHAT I DO FOR *THEM.*

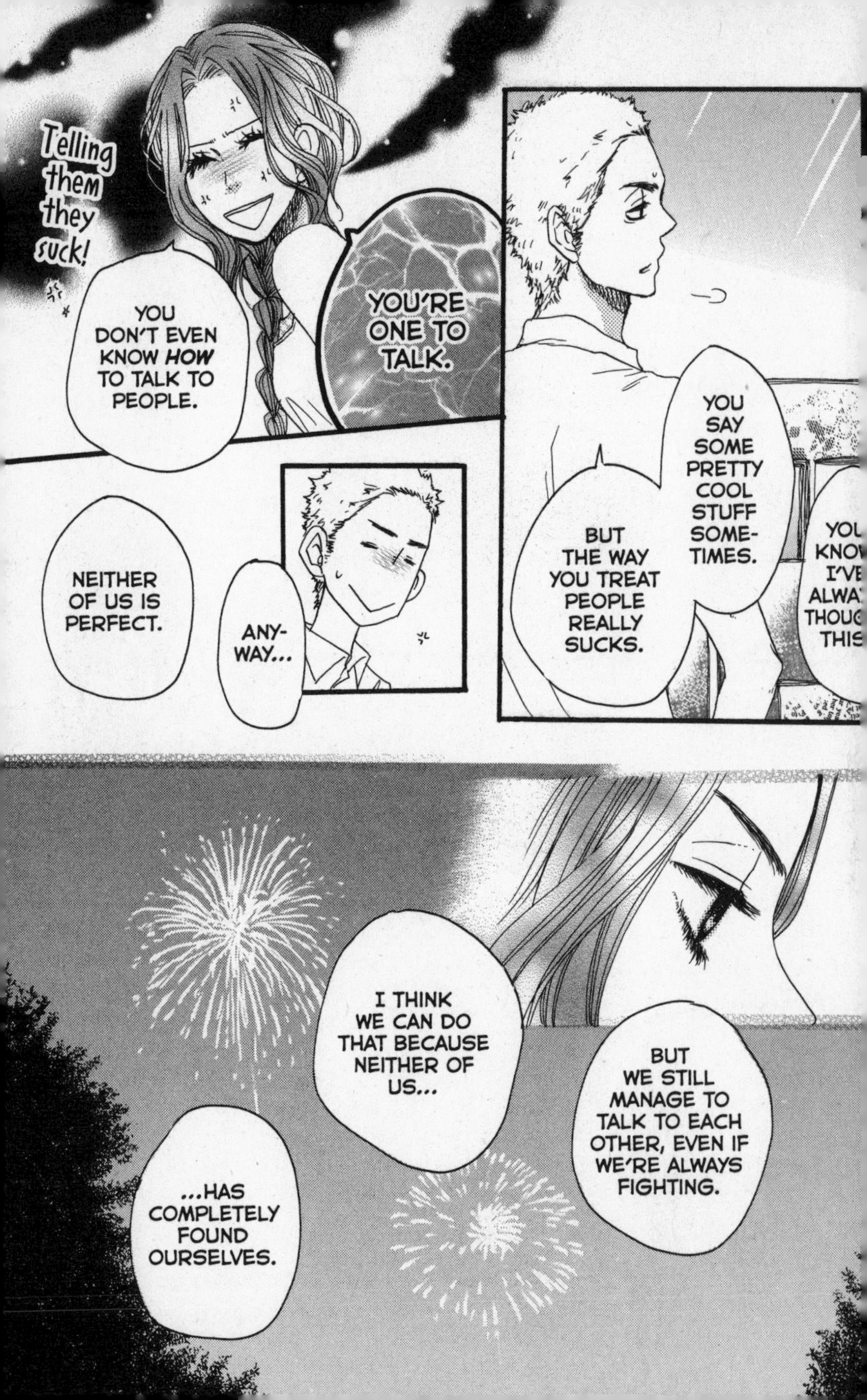
YOU KNO I'VE ALWA THOUG THIS
YOU SAY SOME PRETTY COOL STUFF SOME-TIMES.
BUT THE WAY YOU TREAT PEOPLE REALLY SUCKS.
YOU'RE ONE TO TALK.
Telling them they suck!
YOU DON'T EVEN KNOW *HOW* TO TALK TO PEOPLE.
ANY-WAY...
NEITHER OF US IS PERFECT.
BUT WE STILL MANAGE TO TALK TO EACH OTHER, EVEN IF WE'RE ALWAYS FIGHTING.
I THINK WE CAN DO THAT BECAUSE NEITHER OF US...
...HAS COMPLETELY FOUND OURSELVES.

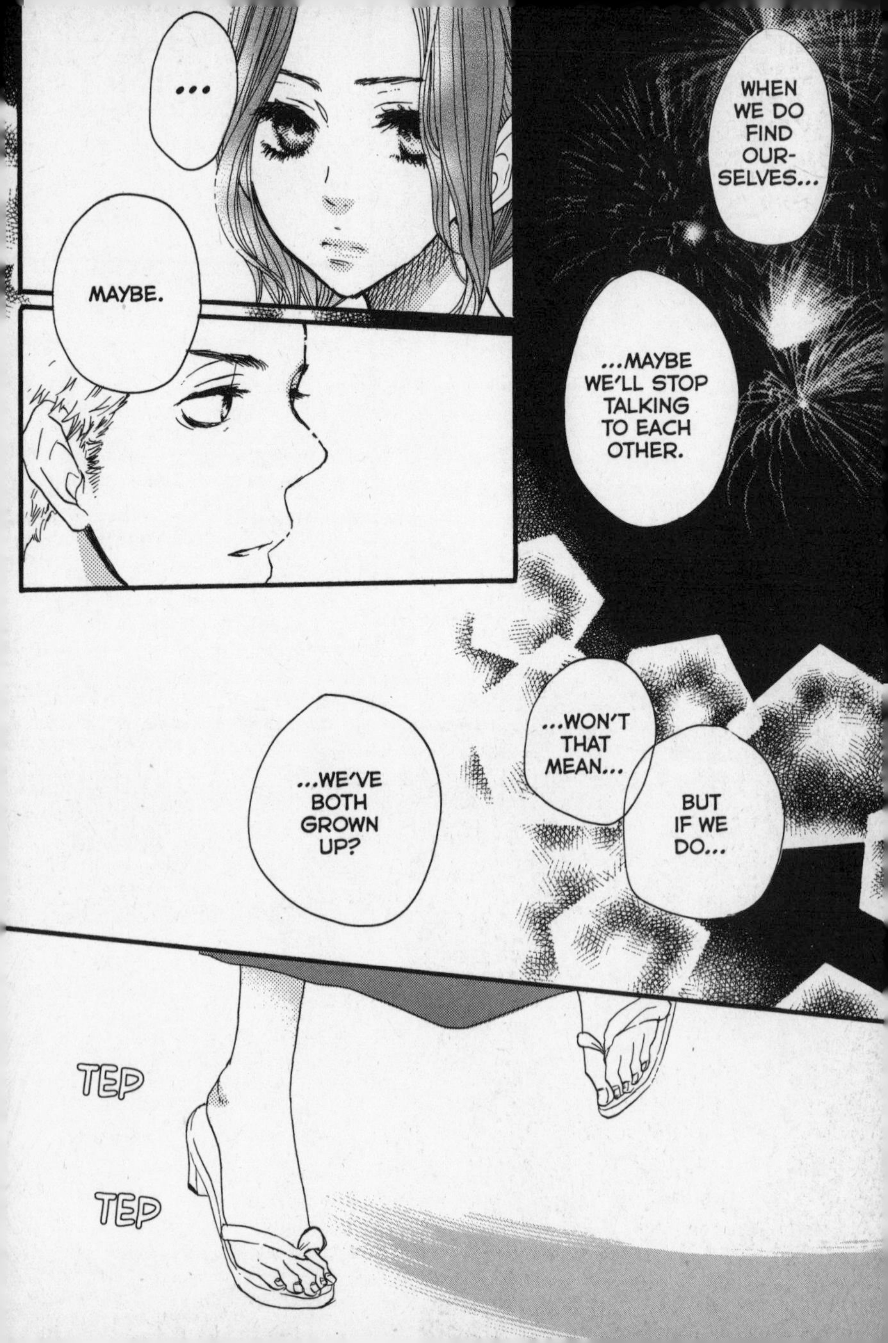
WHEN WE DO FIND OUR-SELVES...
...MAYBE WE'LL STOP TALKING TO EACH OTHER.
...
MAYBE.
BUT IF WE DO...
...WON'T THAT MEAN...
...WE'VE BOTH GROWN UP?
TEP
TEP

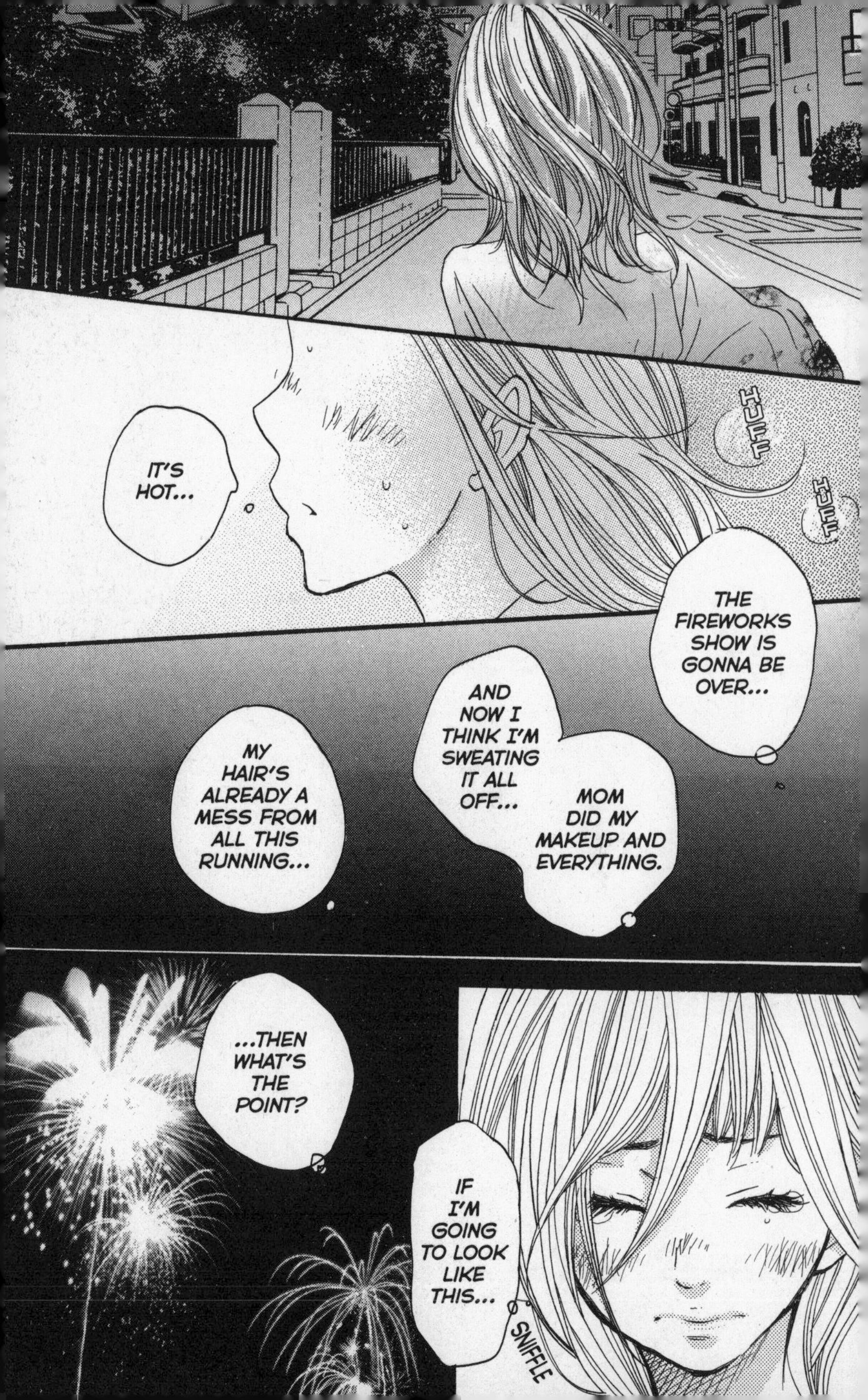
HUFF
HUFF
IT'S HOT...
THE FIREWORKS SHOW IS GONNA BE OVER...
MOM DID MY MAKEUP AND EVERYTHING.
AND NOW I THINK I'M SWEATING IT ALL OFF...
MY HAIR'S ALREADY A MESS FROM ALL THIS RUNNING...
IF I'M GOING TO LOOK LIKE THIS...
SNIFFLE
...THEN WHAT'S THE POINT?

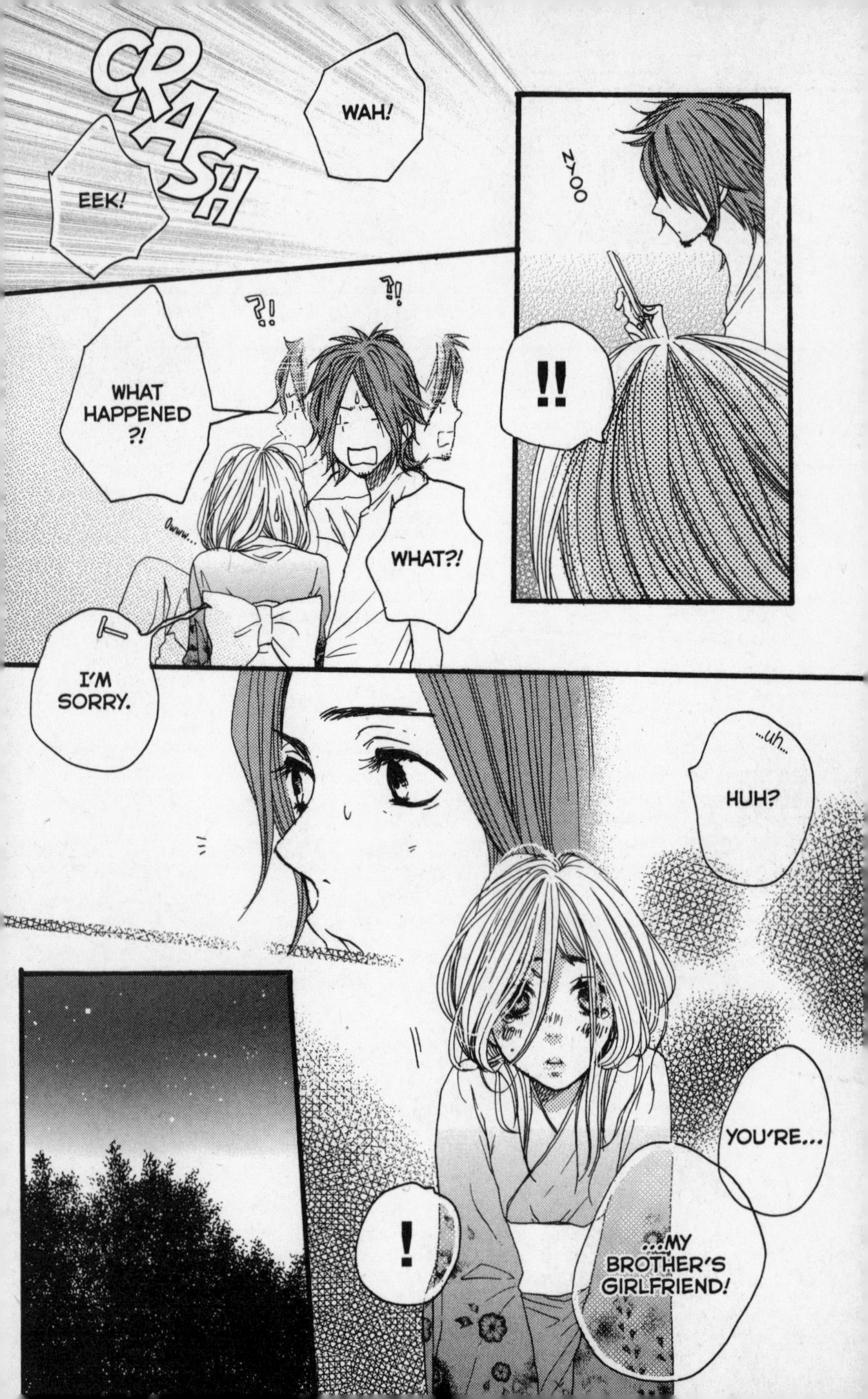
CRASH
WAH!
EEK!
NYOO
!!
?!
?!
WHAT HAPPENED ?!
WHAT?!
Owww...
I'M SORRY.
...uh...
HUH?
YOU'RE...
...MY BROTHER'S GIRLFRIEND!
!

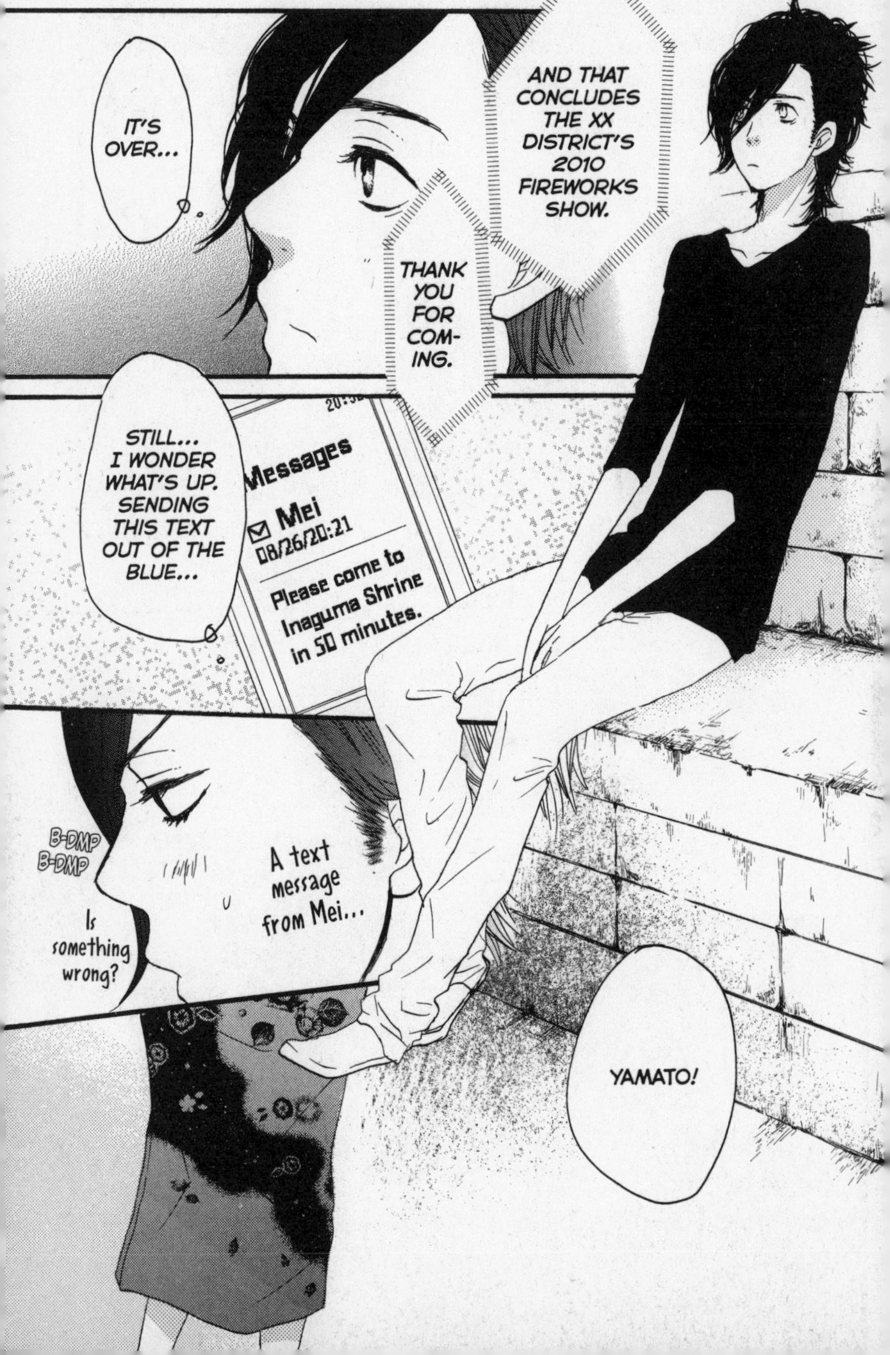
AND THAT CONCLUDES THE XX DISTRICT'S 2010 FIREWORKS SHOW.
THANK YOU FOR COM-ING.
IT'S OVER...
STILL... I WONDER WHAT'S UP. SENDING THIS TEXT OUT OF THE BLUE...
Messages
Mei
08/26/20:21
Please come to Inaguma Shrine in 50 minutes.
A text message from Mei...
B-DMP B-DMP
Is something wrong?
YAMATO!

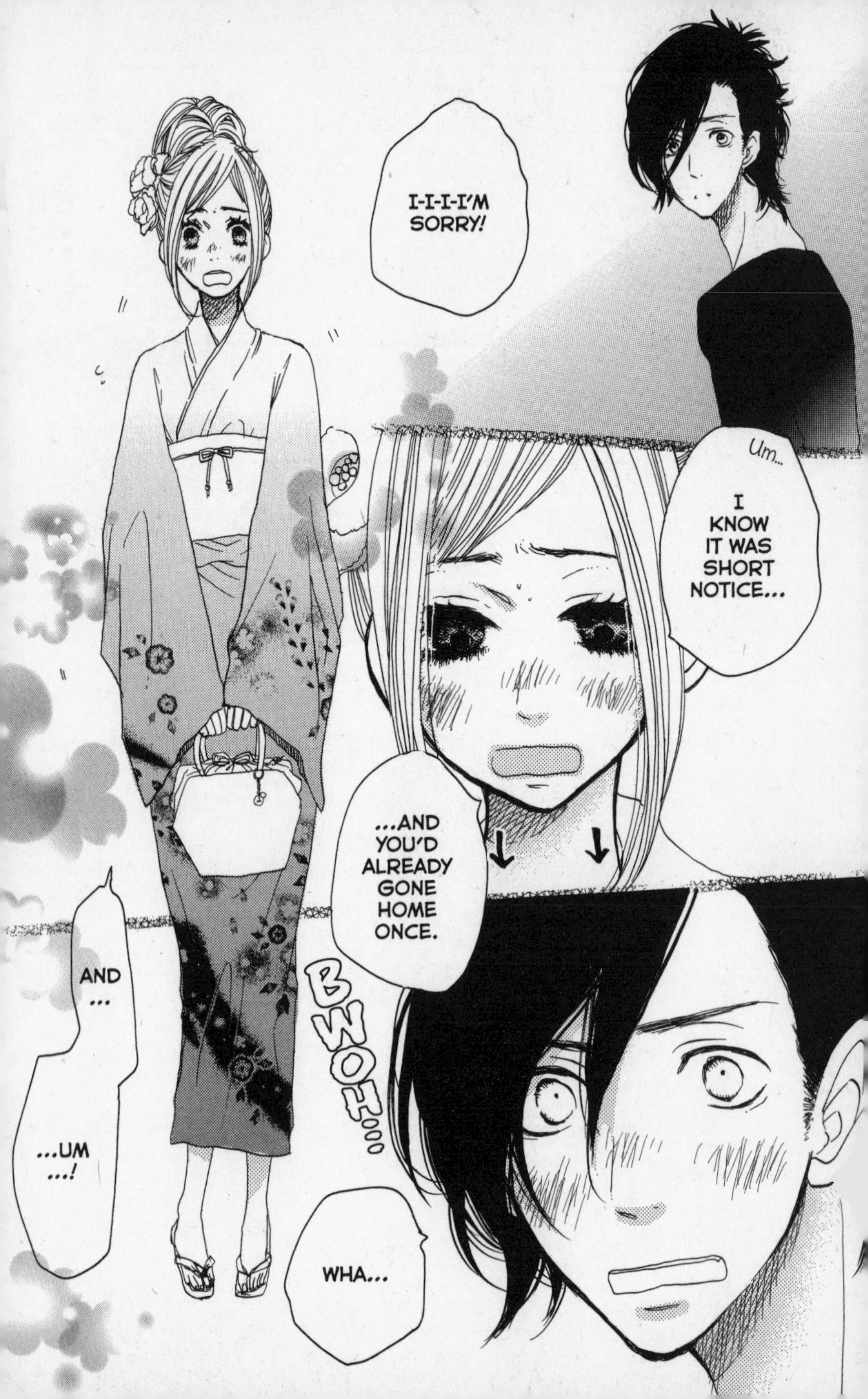
I-I-I-I'M SORRY!
Um...
I KNOW IT WAS SHORT NOTICE...
...AND YOU'D ALREADY GONE HOME ONCE.
BWOHooo
WHA...
AND ...
...UM ...!

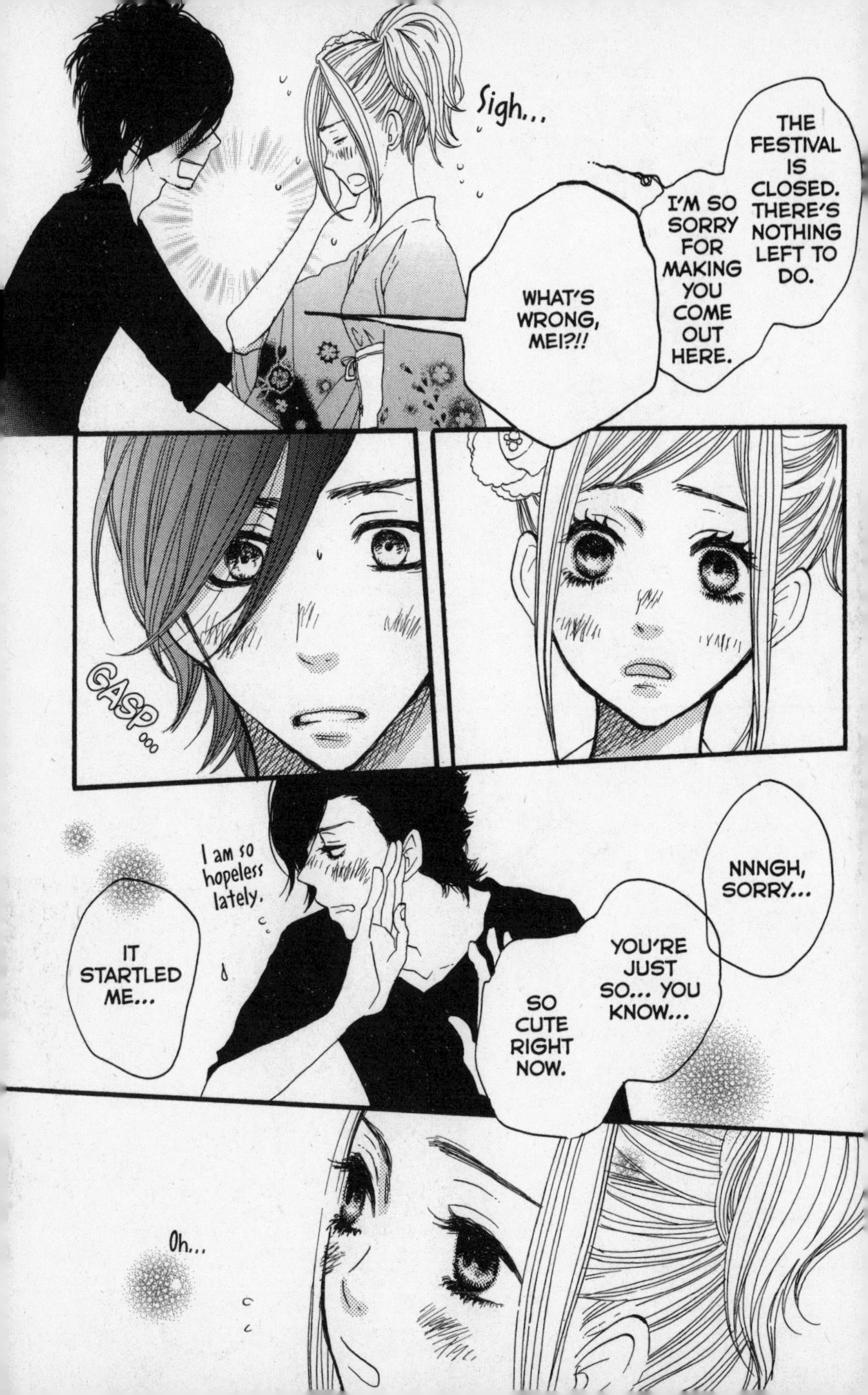
THE FESTIVAL IS CLOSED. THERE'S NOTHING LEFT TO DO.
I'M SO SORRY FOR MAKING YOU COME OUT HERE.
Sigh...
WHAT'S WRONG, MEI?!!
GASP...
NNNGH, SORRY...
YOU'RE JUST SO... YOU KNOW...
SO CUTE RIGHT NOW.
I am so hopeless lately.
IT STARTLED ME...
Oh...

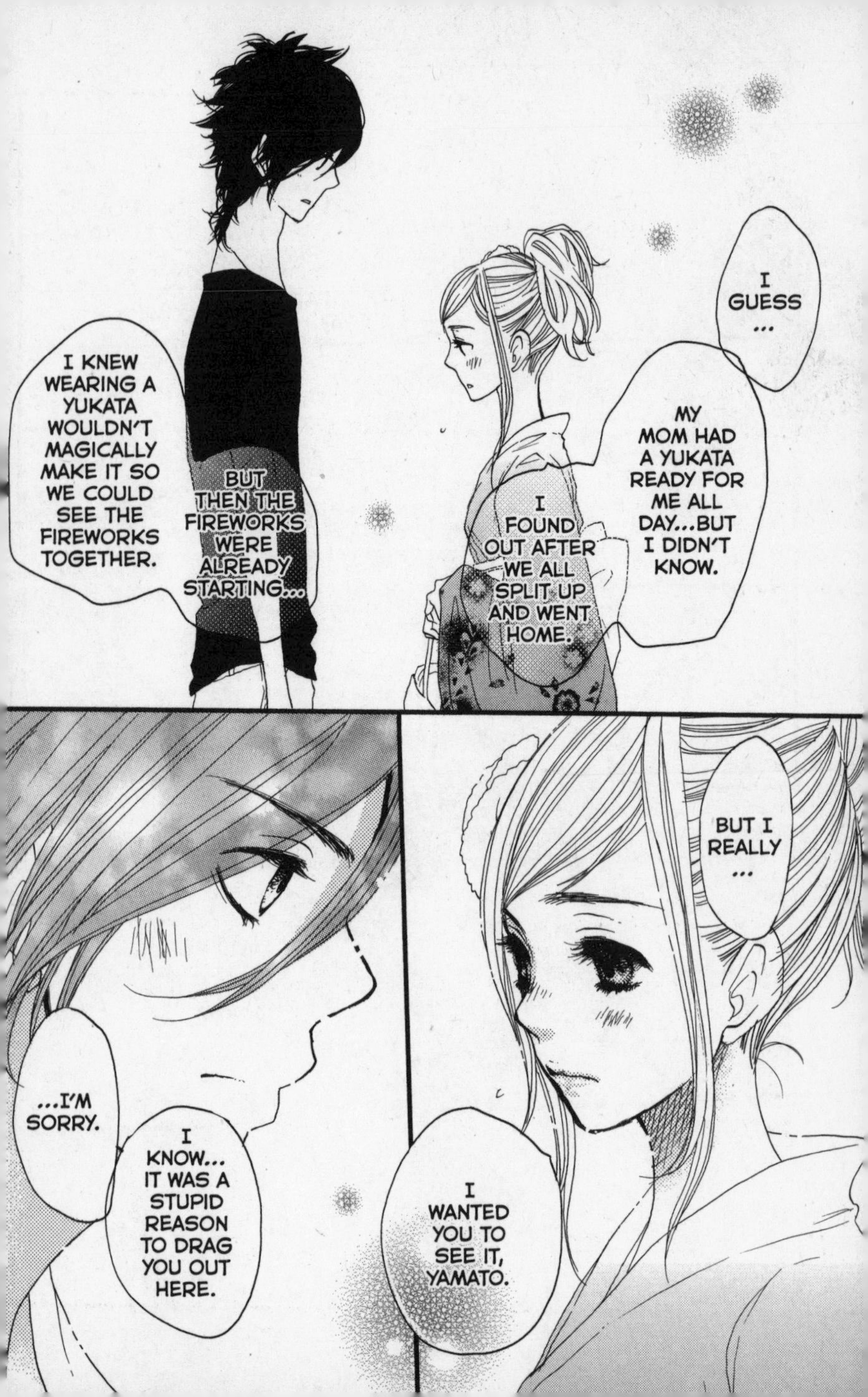
I GUESS...
MY MOM HAD A YUKATA READY FOR ME ALL DAY...BUT I DIDN'T KNOW.
I FOUND OUT AFTER WE ALL SPLIT UP AND WENT HOME.
BUT THEN THE FIREWORKS WERE ALREADY STARTING...
I KNEW WEARING A YUKATA WOULDN'T MAGICALLY MAKE IT SO WE COULD SEE THE FIREWORKS TOGETHER.
BUT I REALLY...
I WANTED YOU TO SEE IT, YAMATO.
...I'M SORRY.
I KNOW... IT WAS A STUPID REASON TO DRAG YOU OUT HERE.

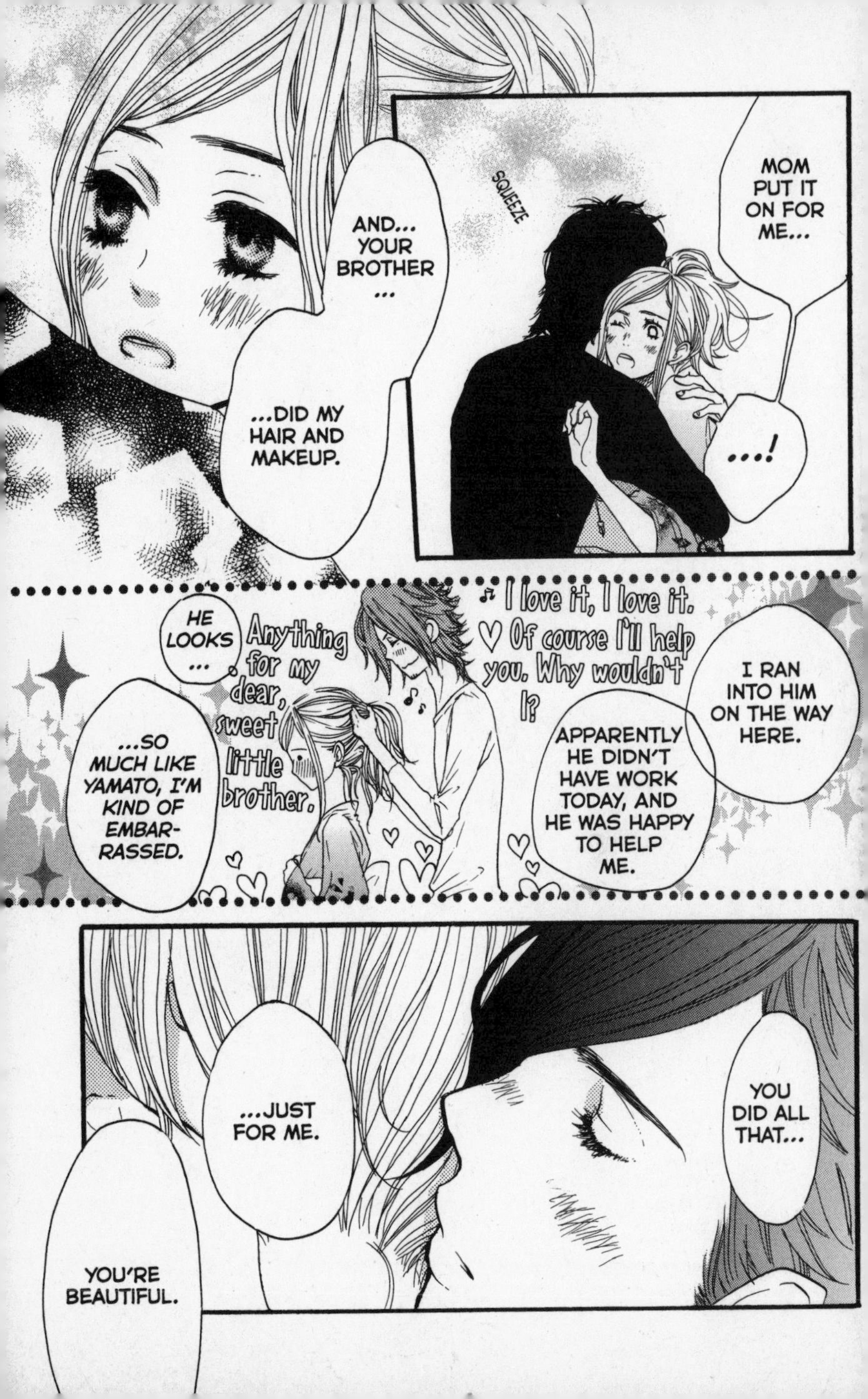
MOM PUT IT ON FOR ME...
SQUEEZE
...!
AND... YOUR BROTHER ...
...DID MY HAIR AND MAKEUP.
I RAN INTO HIM ON THE WAY HERE.
APPARENTLY HE DIDN'T HAVE WORK TODAY, AND HE WAS HAPPY TO HELP ME.
♪ I love it, I love it. ♡ Of course I'll help you. Why wouldn't I?
Anything for my dear, sweet little brother.
HE LOOKS ...
...SO MUCH LIKE YAMATO, I'M KIND OF EMBAR-RASSED.
YOU DID ALL THAT...
...JUST FOR ME.
YOU'RE BEAUTIFUL.

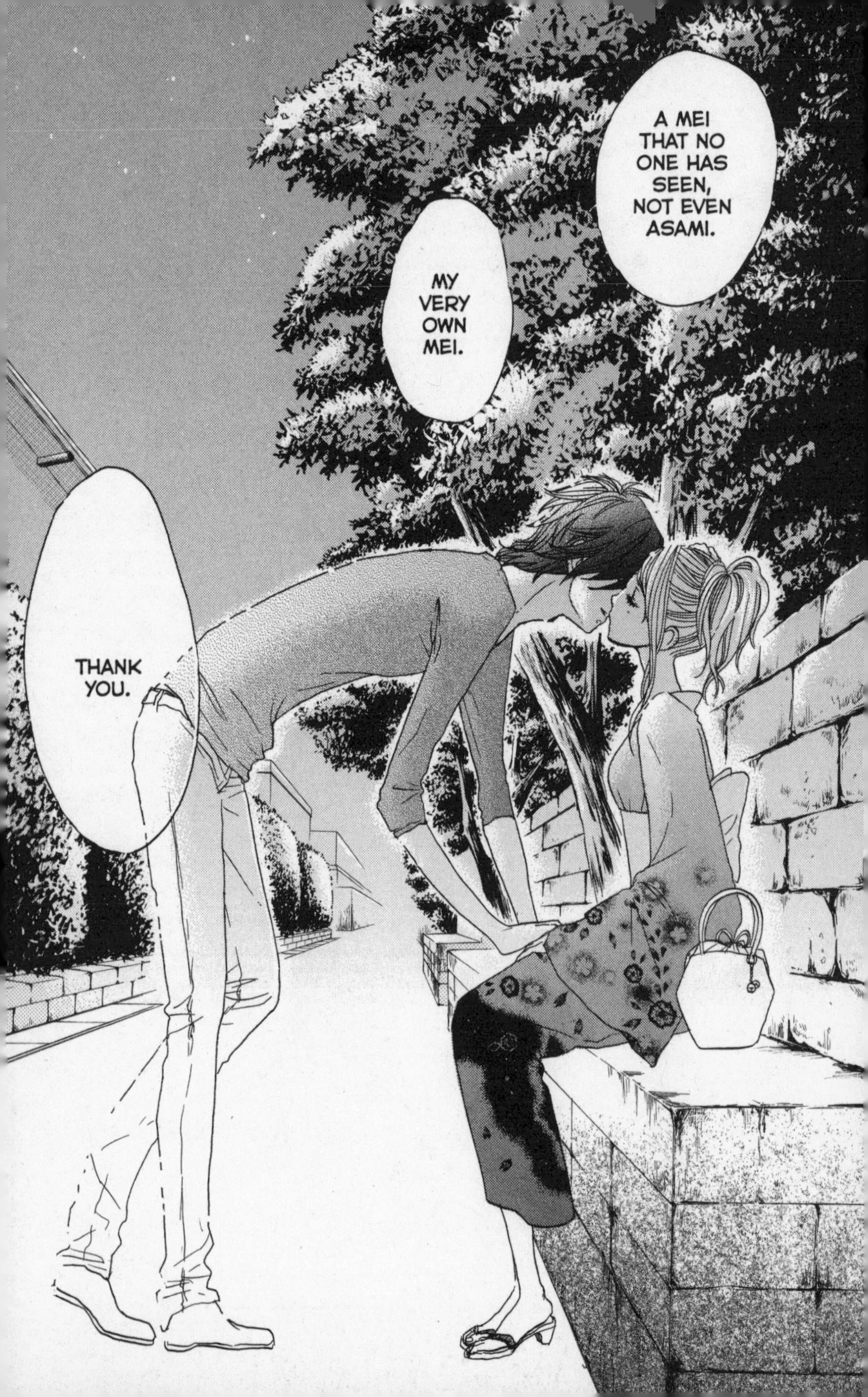
A MEI THAT NO ONE HAS SEEN, NOT EVEN ASAMI.
MY VERY OWN MEI.
THANK YOU.

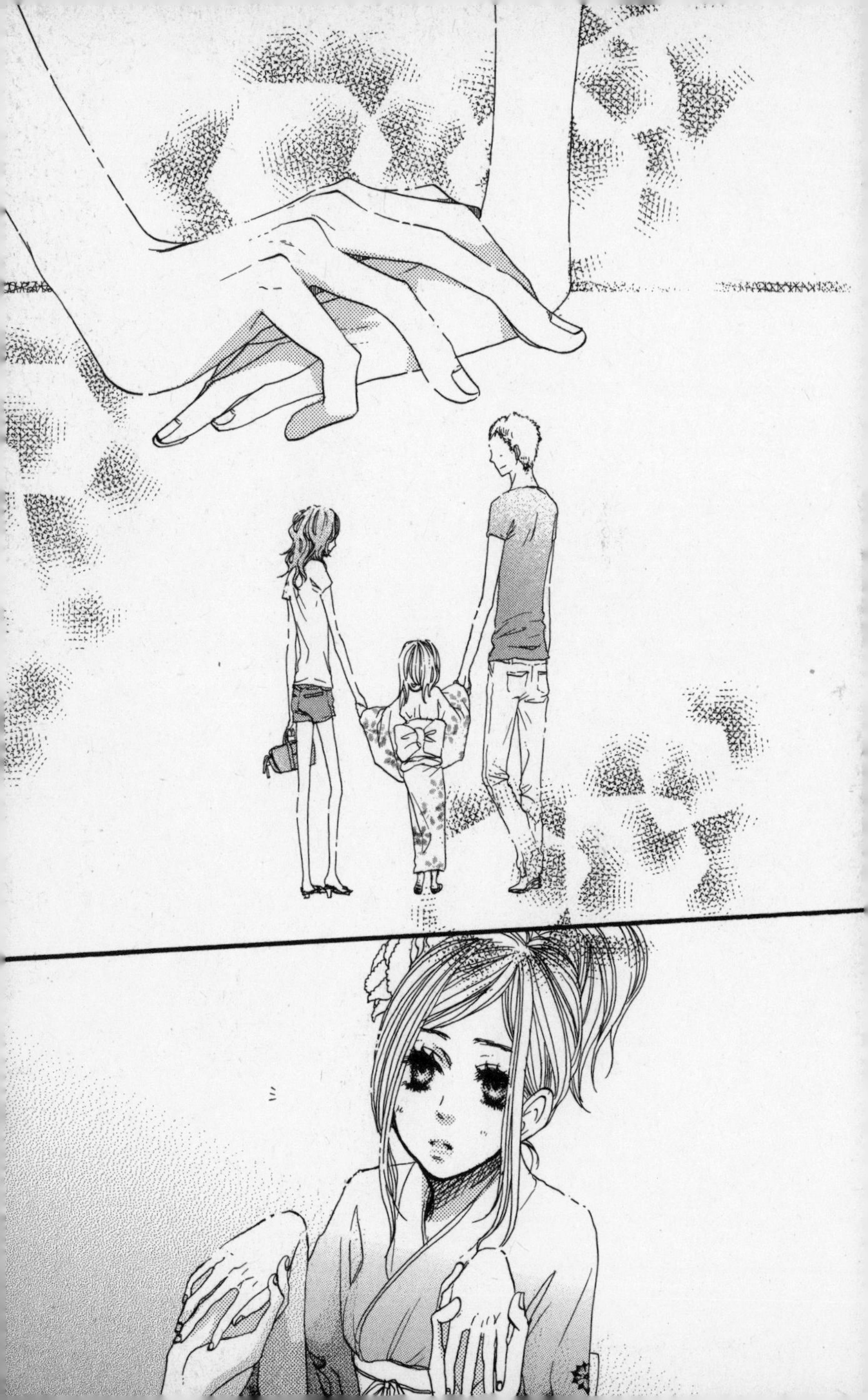

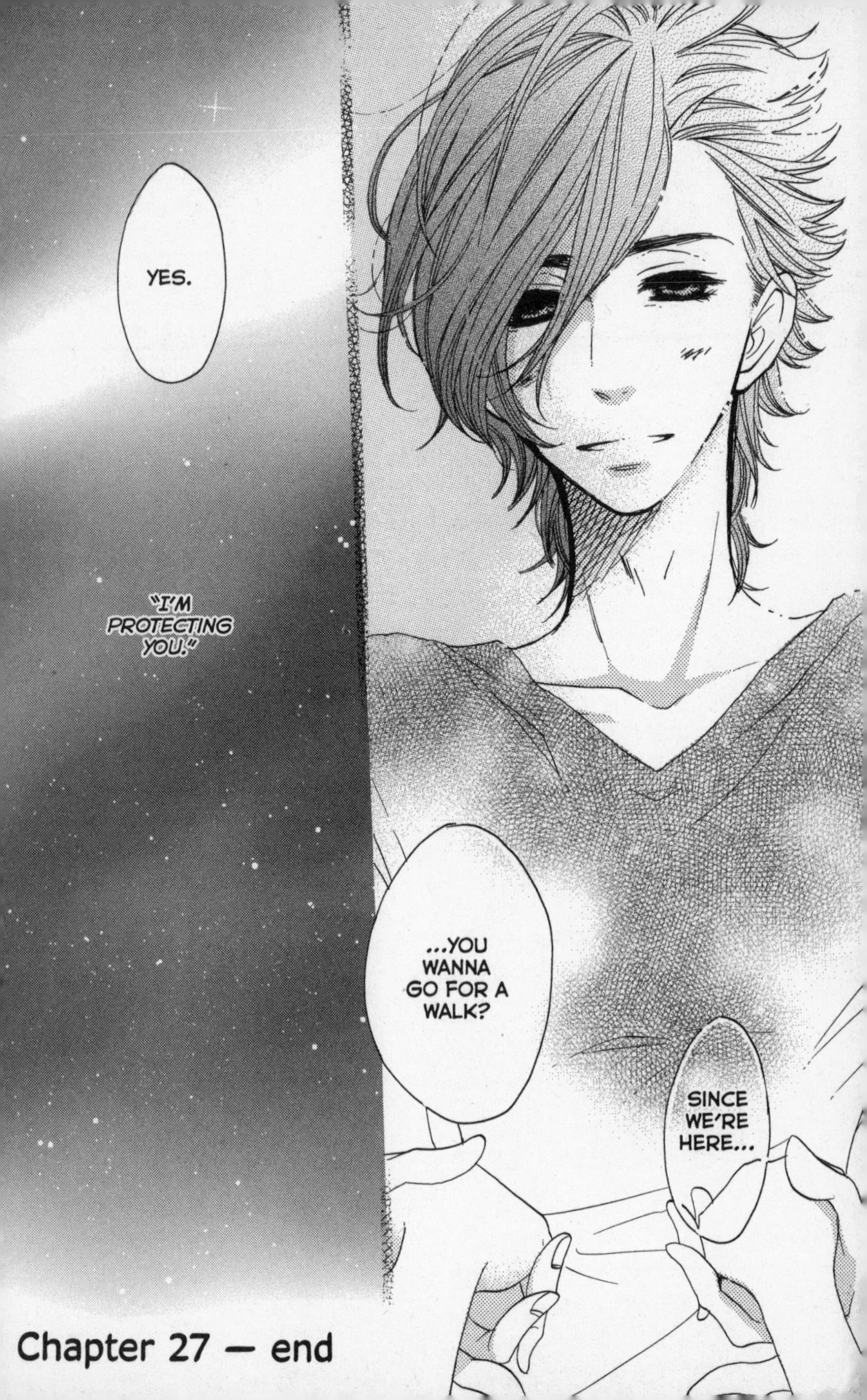
...YOU WANNA GO FOR A WALK?
SINCE WE'RE HERE...
YES.
"I'M PROTECTING YOU."

Chapter 27 — end

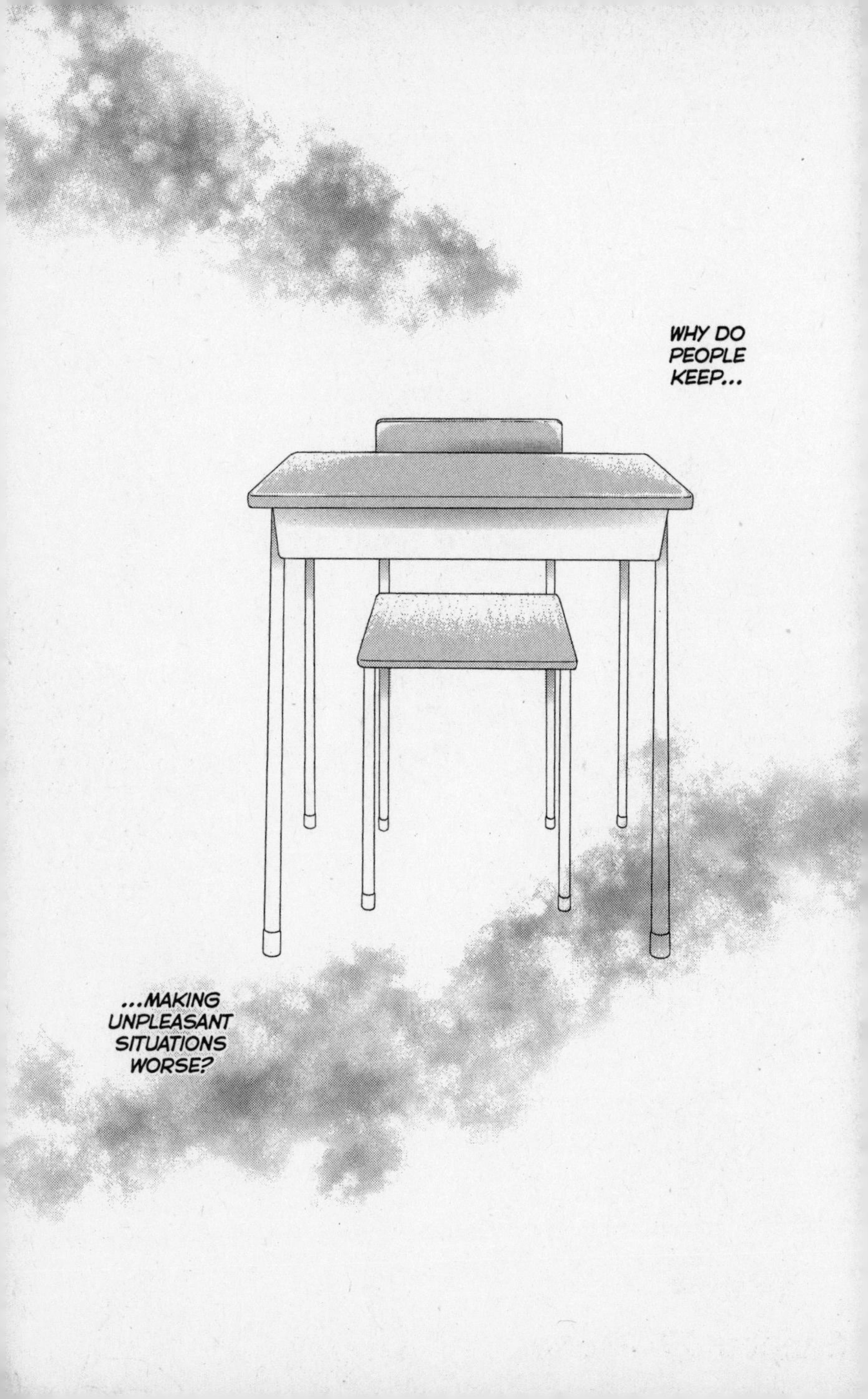
WHY DO PEOPLE KEEP...
...MAKING UNPLEASANT SITUATIONS WORSE?

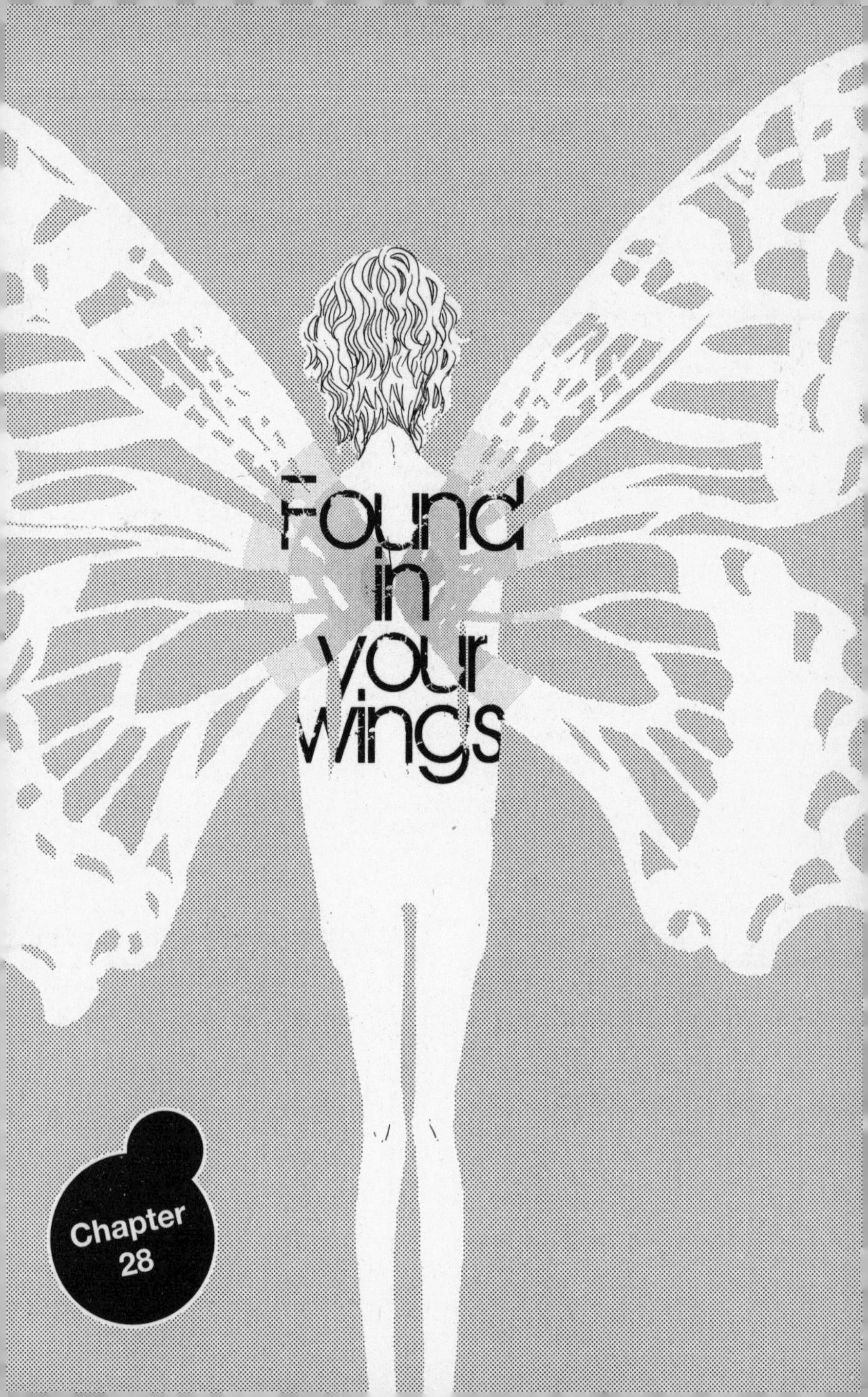
Found in your wings
Chapter 28

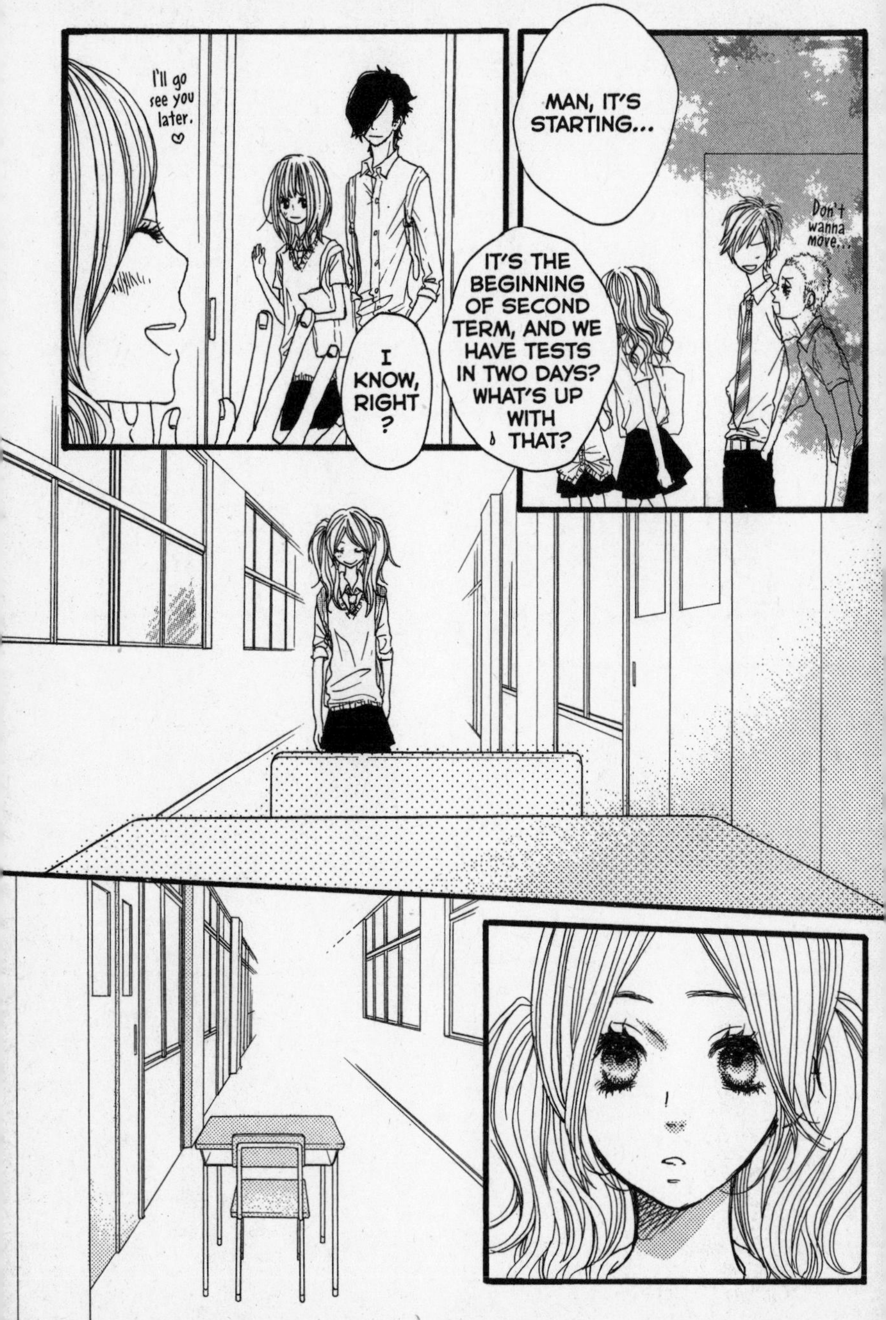
MAN, IT'S STARTING...
Don't wanna move...
IT'S THE BEGINNING OF SECOND TERM, AND WE HAVE TESTS IN TWO DAYS? WHAT'S UP WITH THAT?
I KNOW, RIGHT?
I'll go see you later. ♡

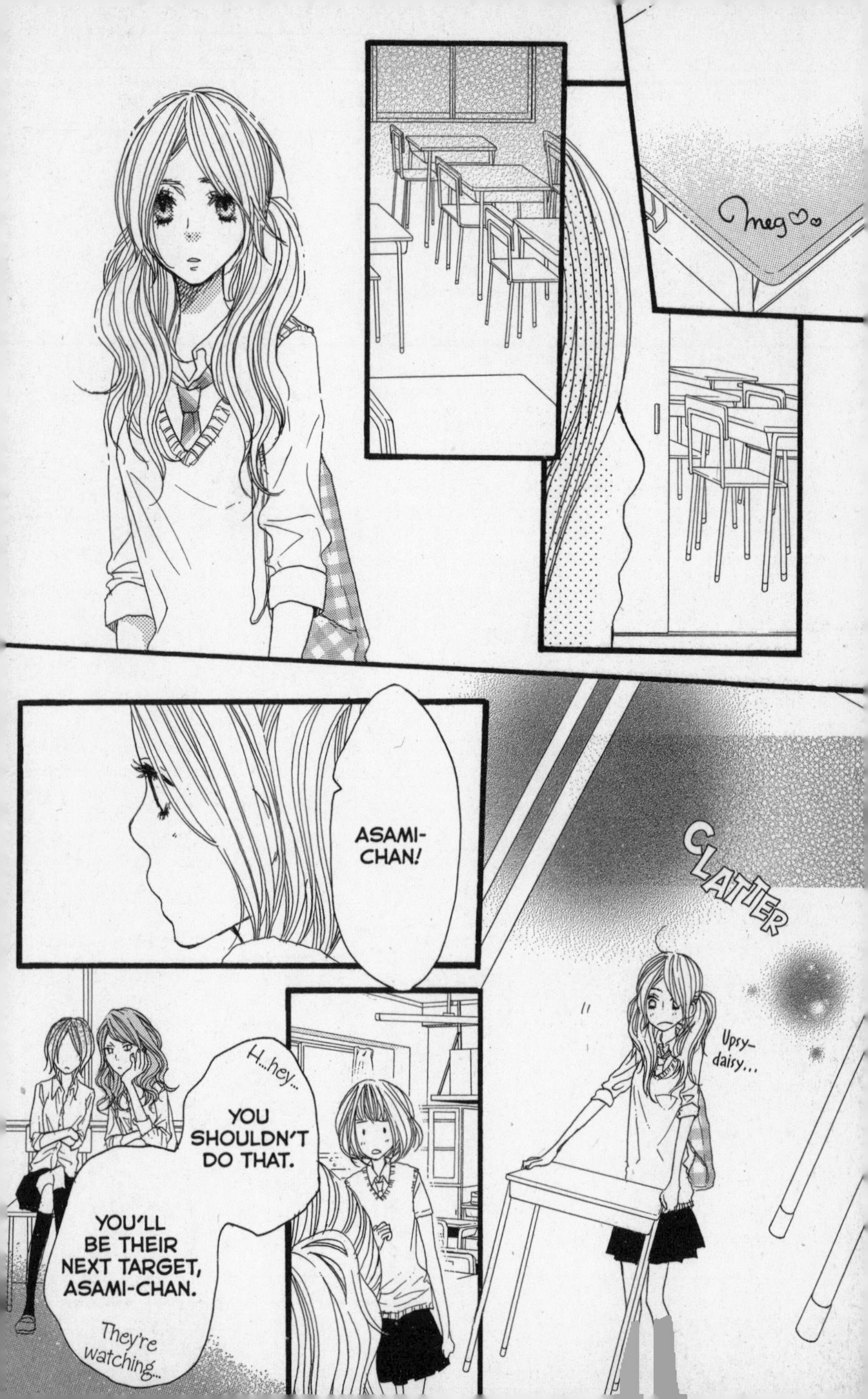
meg
CLATTER
Upsy-daisy...
ASAMI-CHAN!
H...hey...
YOU SHOULDN'T DO THAT.
YOU'LL BE THEIR NEXT TARGET, ASAMI-CHAN.
They're watching...

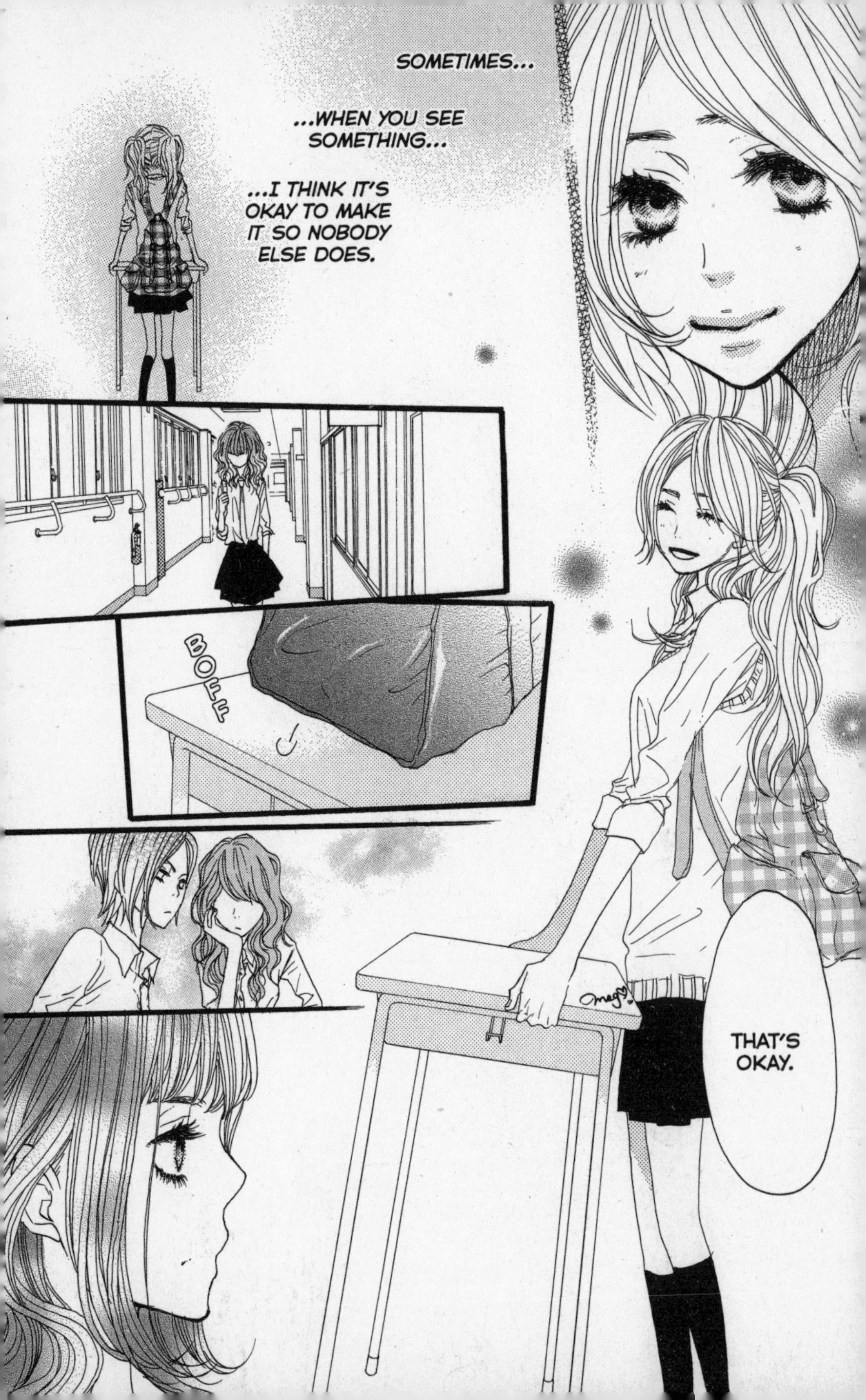
SOMETIMES...
...WHEN YOU SEE SOMETHING...
...I THINK IT'S OKAY TO MAKE IT SO NOBODY ELSE DOES.
BOFF
THAT'S OKAY.

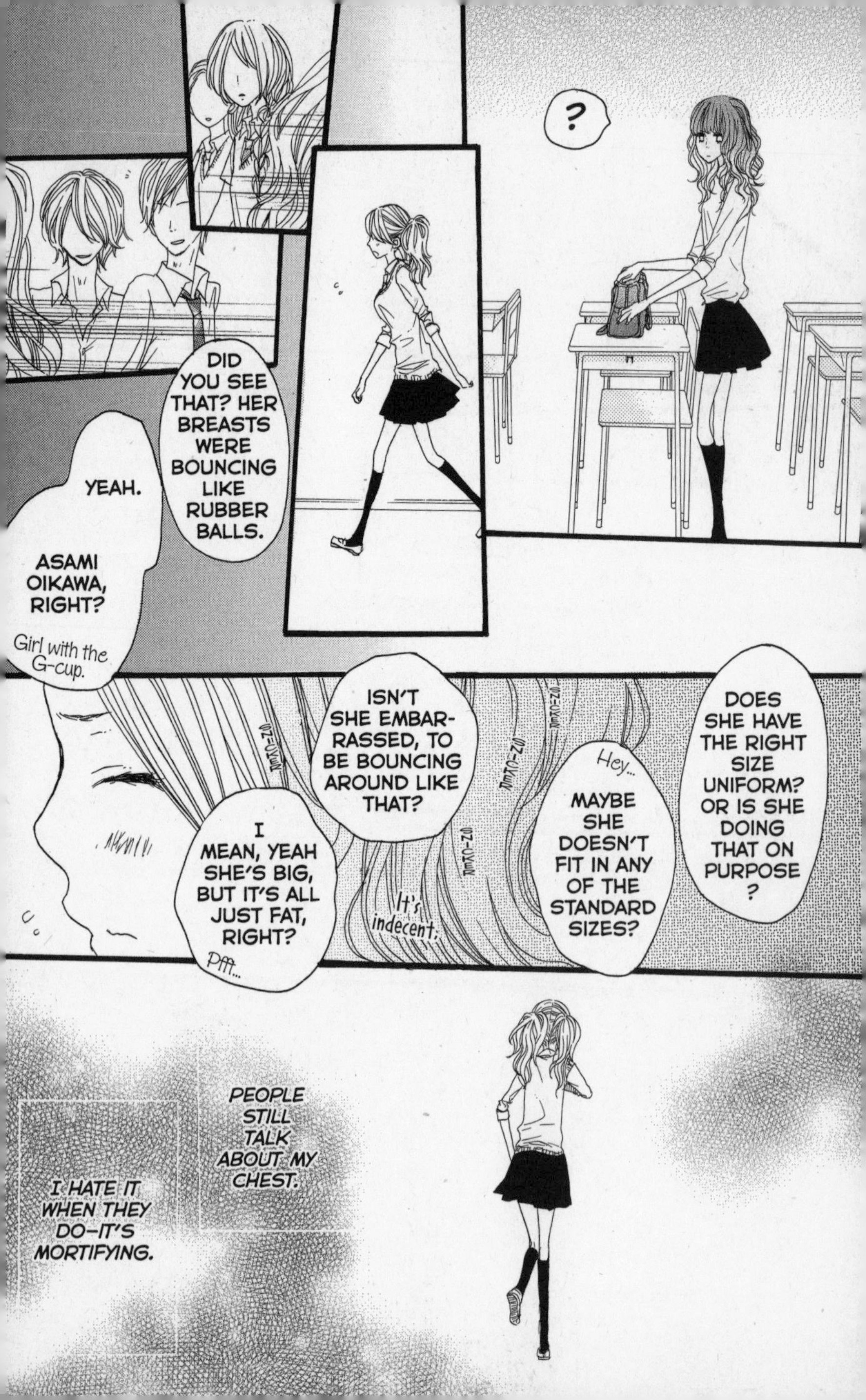
?
DID YOU SEE THAT? HER BREASTS WERE BOUNCING LIKE RUBBER BALLS.
YEAH.
ASAMI OIKAWA, RIGHT?
Girl with the G-cup.
DOES SHE HAVE THE RIGHT SIZE UNIFORM? OR IS SHE DOING THAT ON PURPOSE?
Hey...
MAYBE SHE DOESN'T FIT IN ANY OF THE STANDARD SIZES?
SNICKER
SNICKER
SNICKER
It's indecent.
ISN'T SHE EMBARRASSED, TO BE BOUNCING AROUND LIKE THAT?
SNICKER
I MEAN, YEAH SHE'S BIG, BUT IT'S ALL JUST FAT, RIGHT?
Pfft...
PEOPLE STILL TALK ABOUT MY CHEST.
I HATE IT WHEN THEY DO—IT'S MORTIFYING.

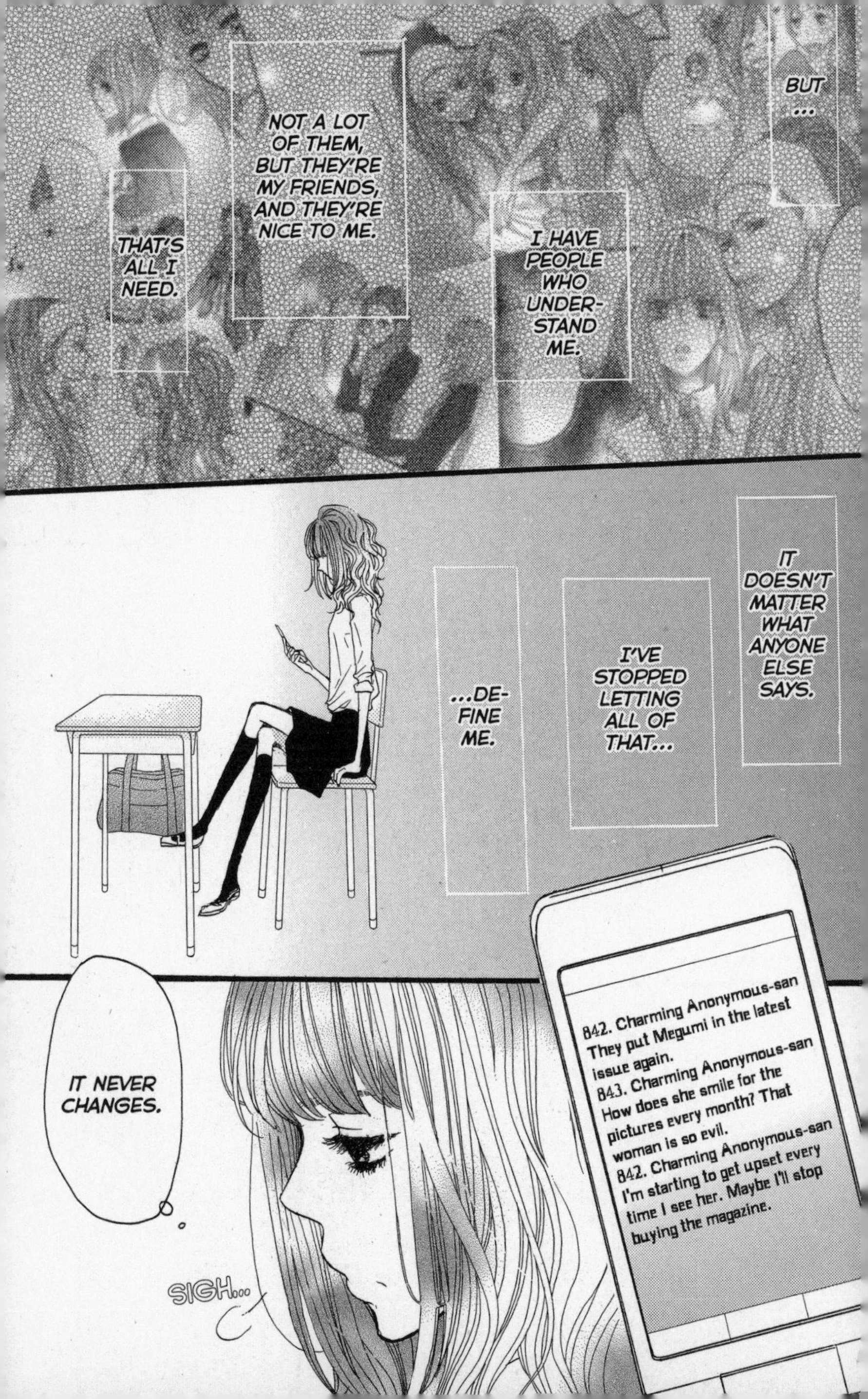
BUT ...
I HAVE PEOPLE WHO UNDER-STAND ME.
NOT A LOT OF THEM, BUT THEY'RE MY FRIENDS, AND THEY'RE NICE TO ME.
THAT'S ALL I NEED.
IT DOESN'T MATTER WHAT ANYONE ELSE SAYS.
I'VE STOPPED LETTING ALL OF THAT...
...DE-FINE ME.
842. Charming Anonymous-san
They put Megumi in the latest issue again.
843. Charming Anonymous-san
How does she smile for the pictures every month? That woman is so evil.
842. Charming Anonymous-san
I'm starting to get upset every time I see her. Maybe I'll stop buying the magazine.
IT NEVER CHANGES.
SIGH...

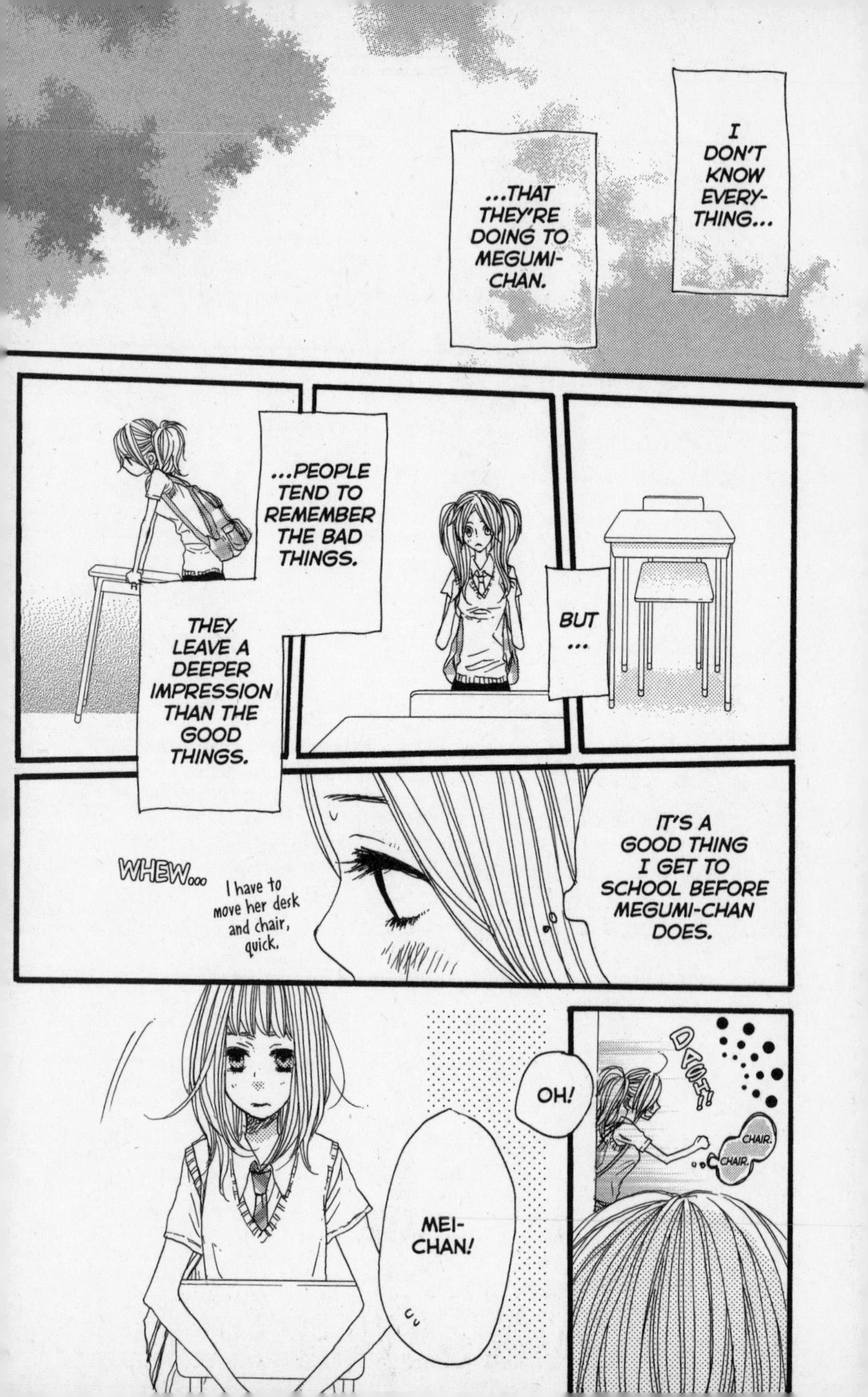
I DON'T KNOW EVERYTHING...
...THAT THEY'RE DOING TO MEGUMI-CHAN.
BUT...
...PEOPLE TEND TO REMEMBER THE BAD THINGS.
THEY LEAVE A DEEPER IMPRESSION THAN THE GOOD THINGS.
IT'S A GOOD THING I GET TO SCHOOL BEFORE MEGUMI-CHAN DOES.
WHEW...
I have to move her desk and chair, quick.
DASH!!
CHAIR.
CHAIR.
OH!
MEI-CHAN!

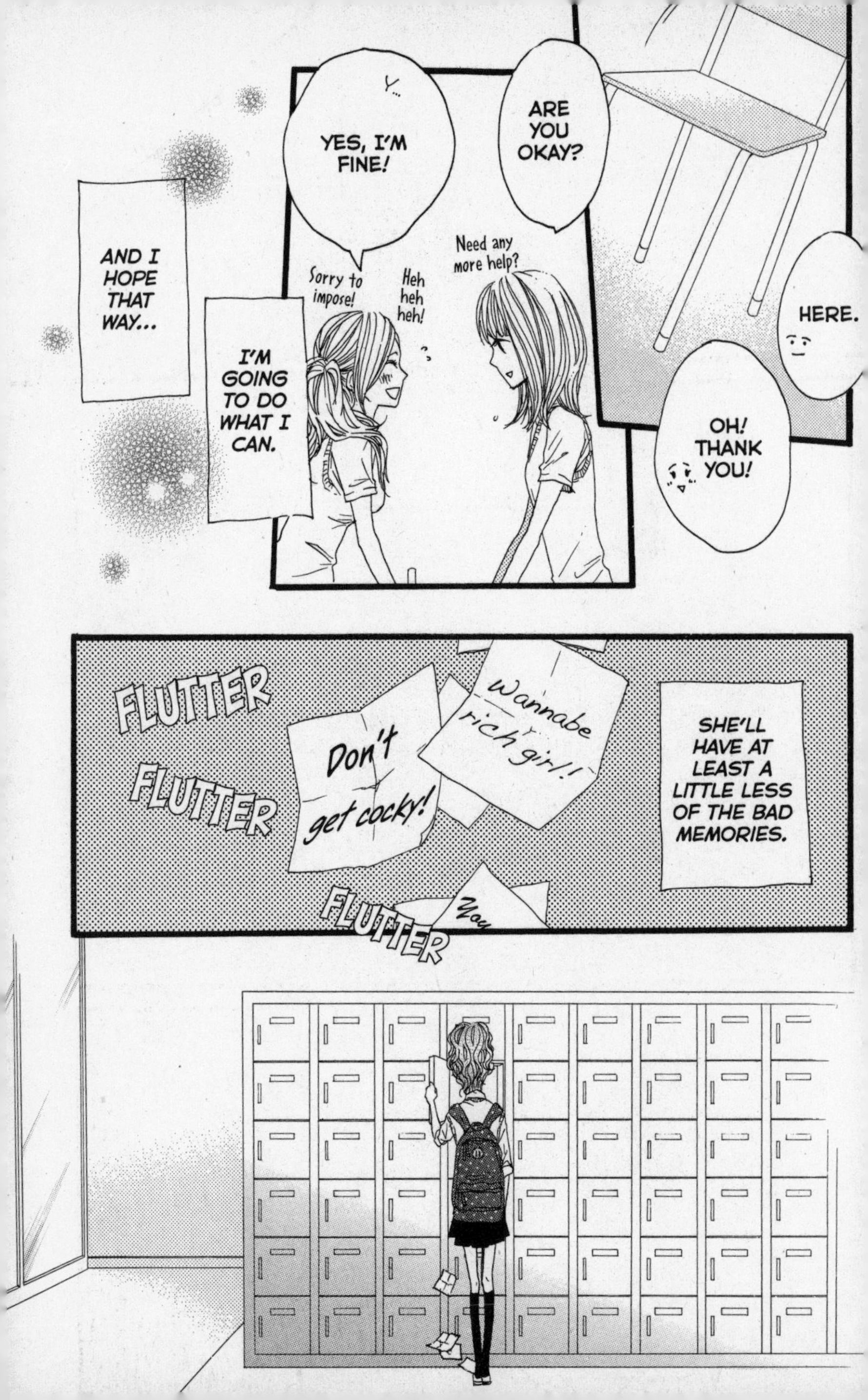
HERE.
OH! THANK YOU!
ARE YOU OKAY?
Y... YES, I'M FINE!
Need any more help?
Heh heh heh!
Sorry to impose!
I'M GOING TO DO WHAT I CAN.
AND I HOPE THAT WAY...
SHE'LL HAVE AT LEAST A LITTLE LESS OF THE BAD MEMORIES.
Wannabe rich girl!!
FLUTTER
Don't get cocky!
FLUTTER
You
FLUTTER

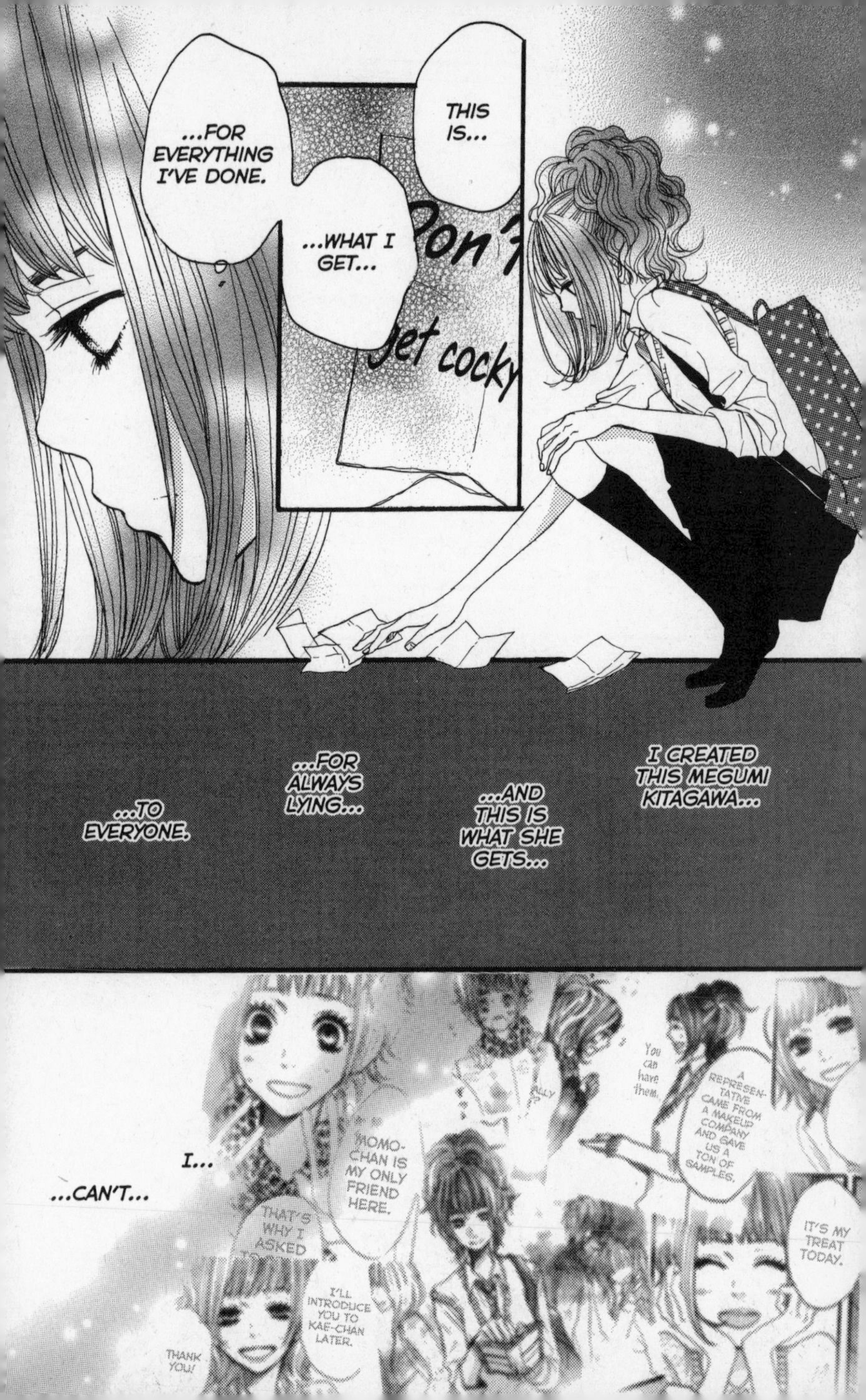
THIS IS...
...WHAT I GET...
...FOR EVERYTHING I'VE DONE.
get cocky
I CREATED THIS MEGUMI KITAGAWA...
...AND THIS IS WHAT SHE GETS...
...FOR ALWAYS LYING...
...TO EVERYONE.
A REPRESENTATIVE CAME FROM A MAKEUP COMPANY AND GAVE US A TON OF SAMPLES.
You can have them.
IT'S MY TREAT TODAY.
MOMO-CHAN IS MY ONLY FRIEND HERE.
I'LL INTRODUCE YOU TO KAE-CHAN LATER.
THAT'S WHY I ASKED
THANK YOU!
I...
...CAN'T...

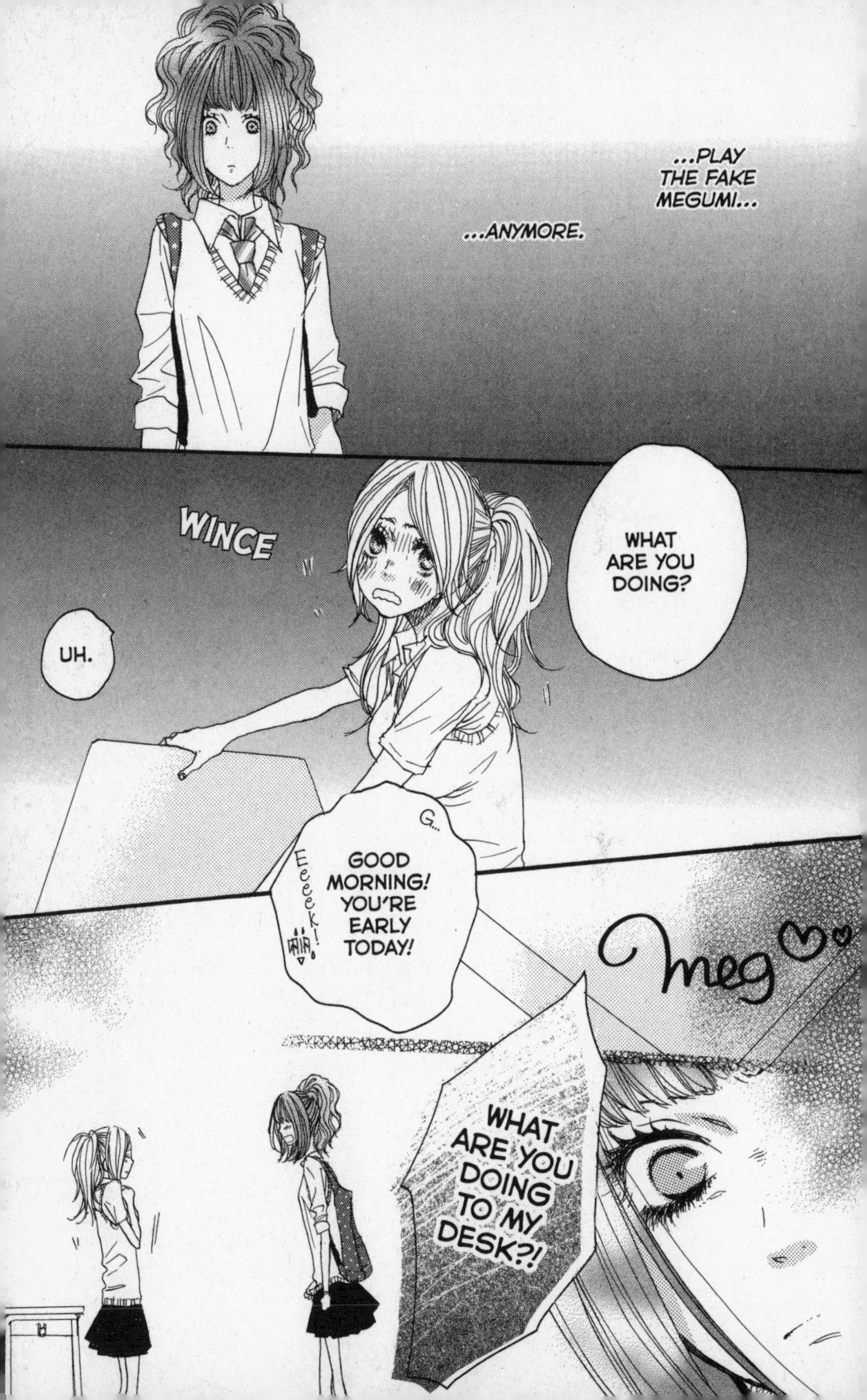
...PLAY THE FAKE MEGUMI...
...ANYMORE.
WHAT ARE YOU DOING?
WINCE
UH.
G...
GOOD MORNING! YOU'RE EARLY TODAY!
Eeeek!
Meg
WHAT ARE YOU DOING TO MY DESK?!

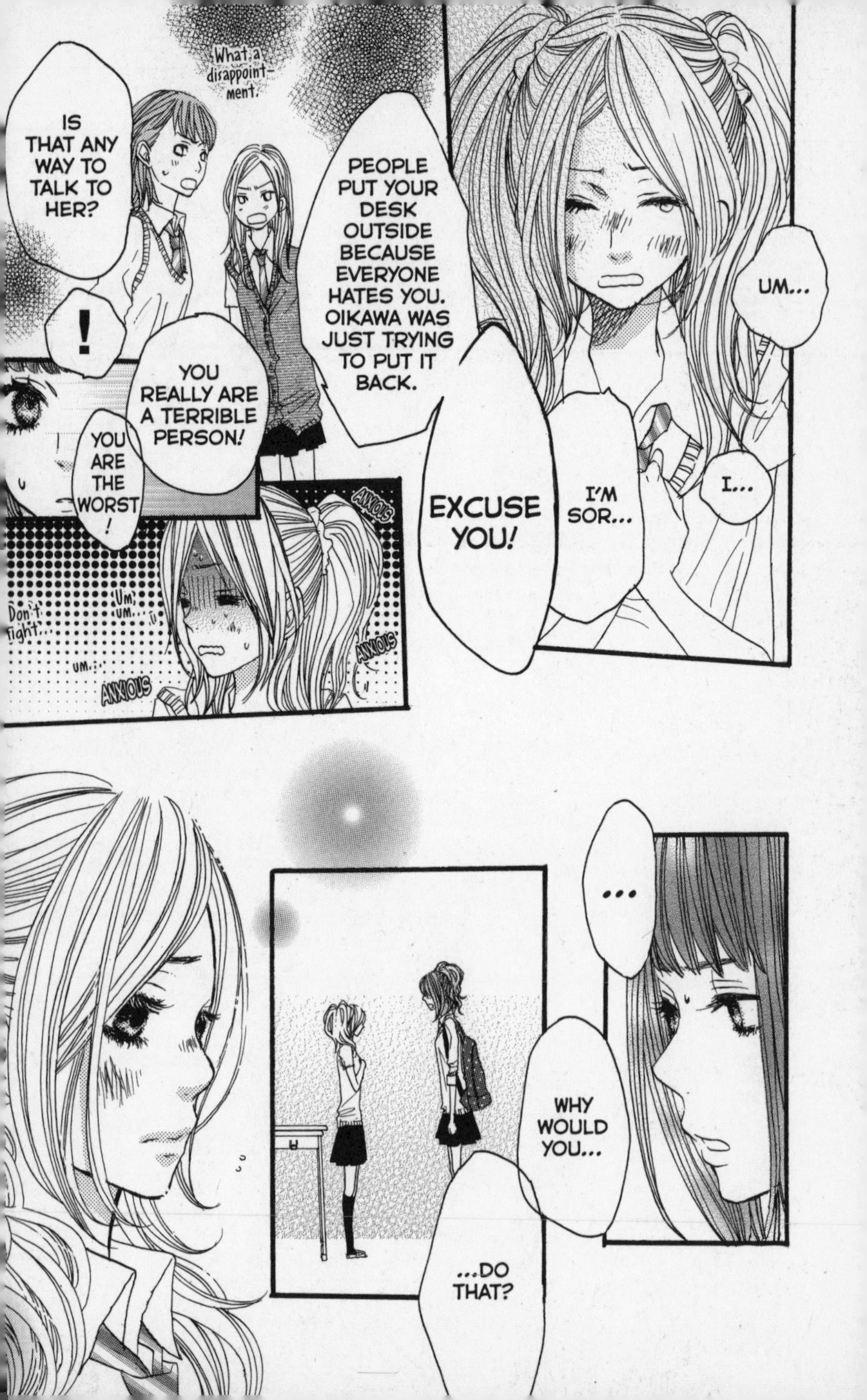
UM...
I...
I'M SOR...
EXCUSE YOU!
What a disappointment.
PEOPLE PUT YOUR DESK OUTSIDE BECAUSE EVERYONE HATES YOU. OIKAWA WAS JUST TRYING TO PUT IT BACK.
IS THAT ANY WAY TO TALK TO HER?
!
YOU REALLY ARE A TERRIBLE PERSON!
YOU ARE THE WORST!
ANXIOUS
ANXIOUS
Um, um...
Don't fight...
um..
ANXIOUS
...
WHY WOULD YOU...
...DO THAT?

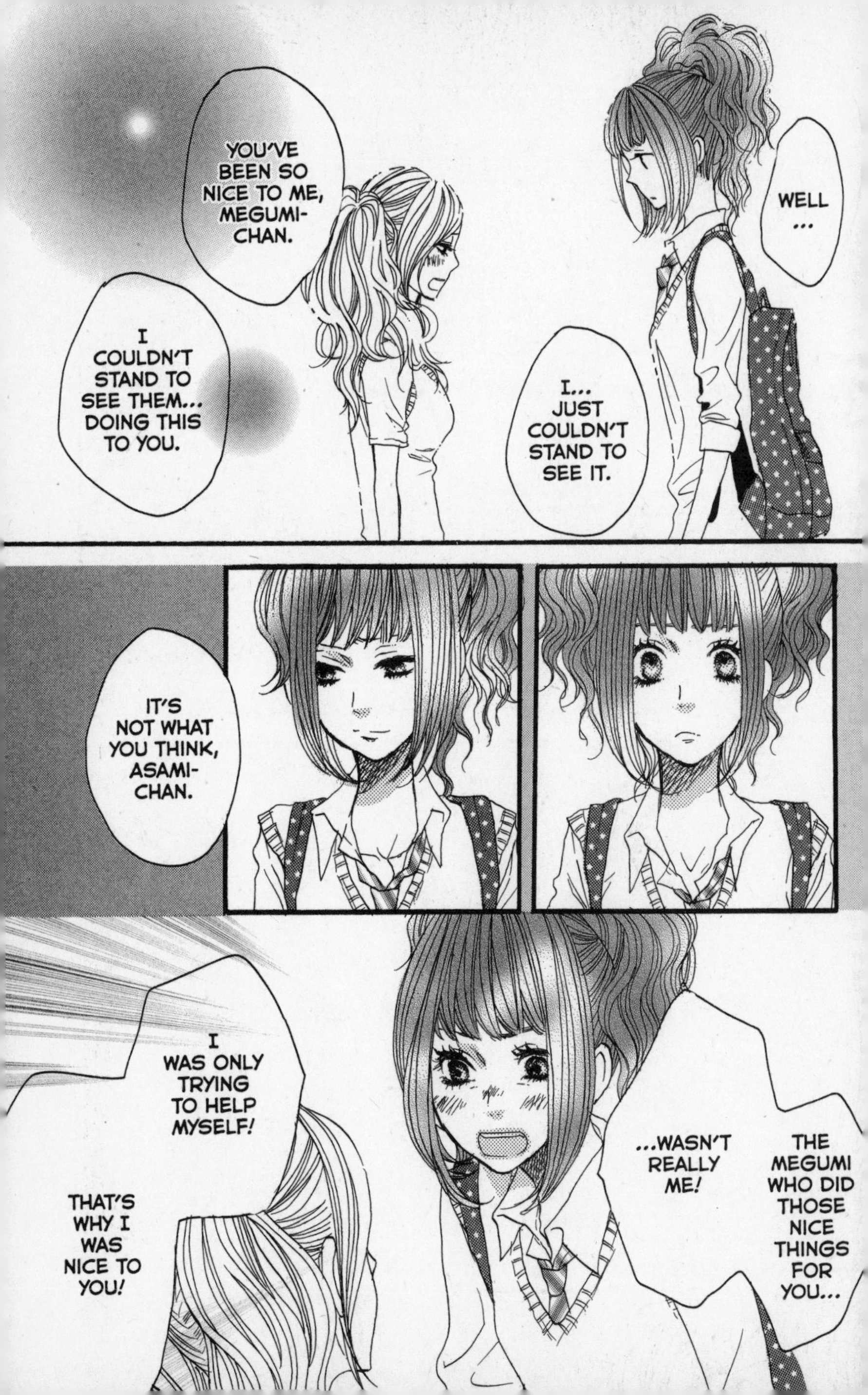
WELL ...
YOU'VE BEEN SO NICE TO ME, MEGUMI-CHAN.
I... JUST COULDN'T STAND TO SEE IT.
I COULDN'T STAND TO SEE THEM... DOING THIS TO YOU.
IT'S NOT WHAT YOU THINK, ASAMI-CHAN.
THE MEGUMI WHO DID THOSE NICE THINGS FOR YOU...
...WASN'T REALLY ME!
I WAS ONLY TRYING TO HELP MYSELF!
THAT'S WHY I WAS NICE TO YOU!

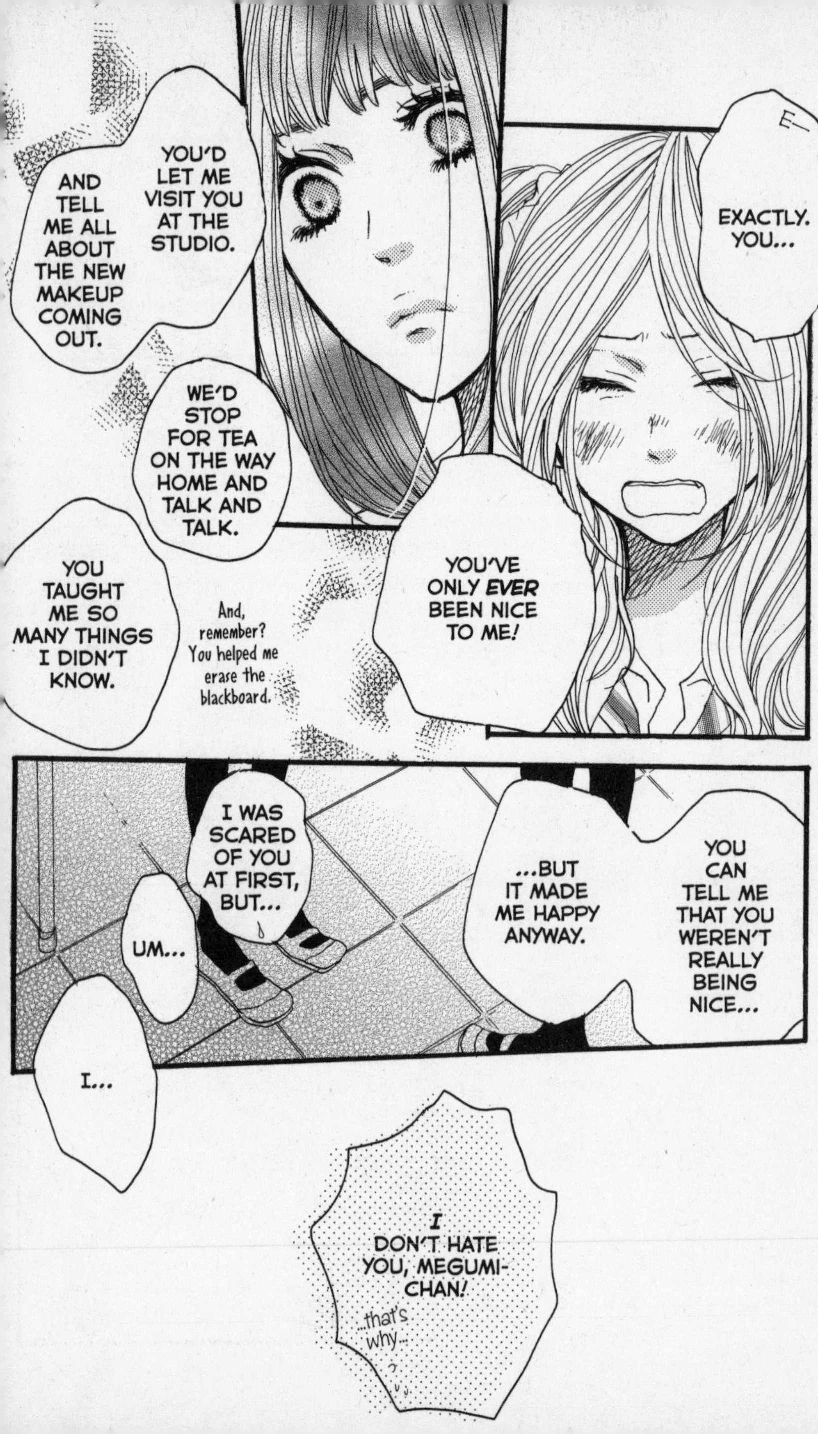
E—
EXACTLY. YOU...
YOU'VE ONLY *EVER* BEEN NICE TO ME!
YOU'D LET ME VISIT YOU AT THE STUDIO.
AND TELL ME ALL ABOUT THE NEW MAKEUP COMING OUT.
WE'D STOP FOR TEA ON THE WAY HOME AND TALK AND TALK.
And, remember? You helped me erase the blackboard.
YOU TAUGHT ME SO MANY THINGS I DIDN'T KNOW.
YOU CAN TELL ME THAT YOU WEREN'T REALLY BEING NICE...
...BUT IT MADE ME HAPPY ANYWAY.
I WAS SCARED OF YOU AT FIRST, BUT...
UM...
I...
I DON'T HATE YOU, MEGUMI-CHAN!
...that's why...

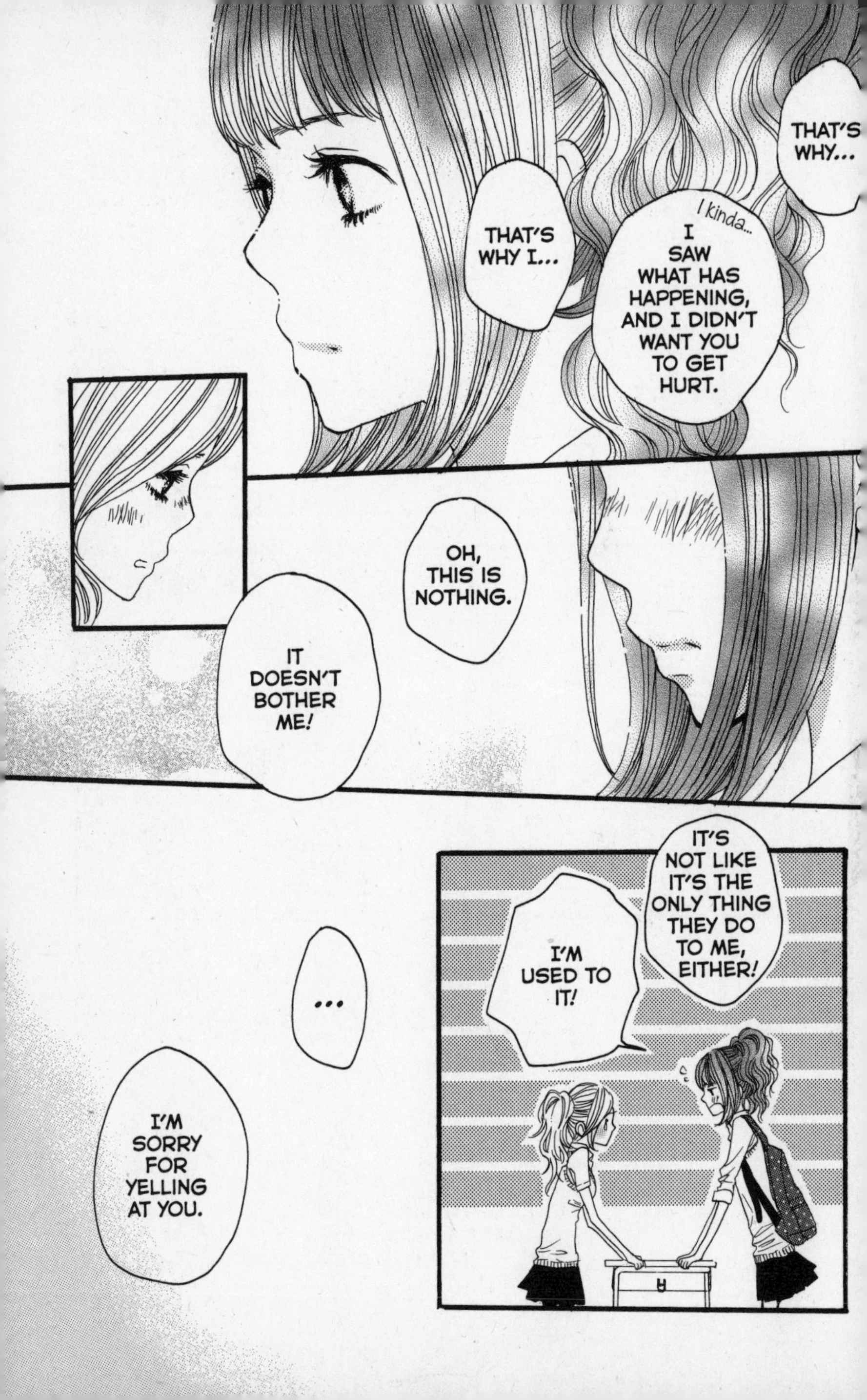
THAT'S WHY...
I kinda...
I SAW WHAT HAS HAPPENING, AND I DIDN'T WANT YOU TO GET HURT.
THAT'S WHY I...
OH, THIS IS NOTHING.
IT DOESN'T BOTHER ME!
IT'S NOT LIKE IT'S THE ONLY THING THEY DO TO ME, EITHER!
I'M USED TO IT!
...
I'M SORRY FOR YELLING AT YOU.

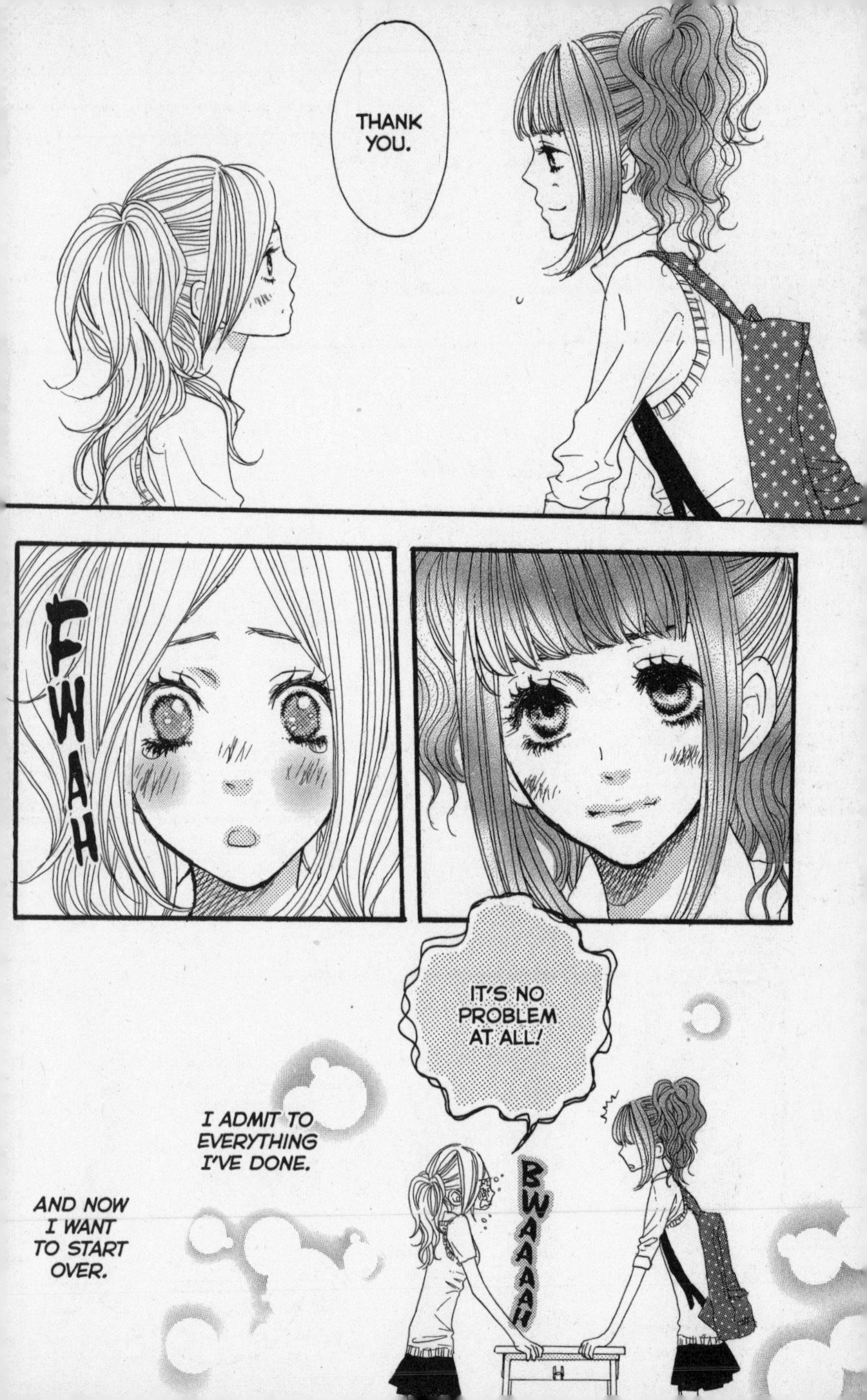
THANK YOU.
FWAH
IT'S NO PROBLEM AT ALL!
BWAAAAH
I ADMIT TO EVERYTHING I'VE DONE.
AND NOW I WANT TO START OVER.

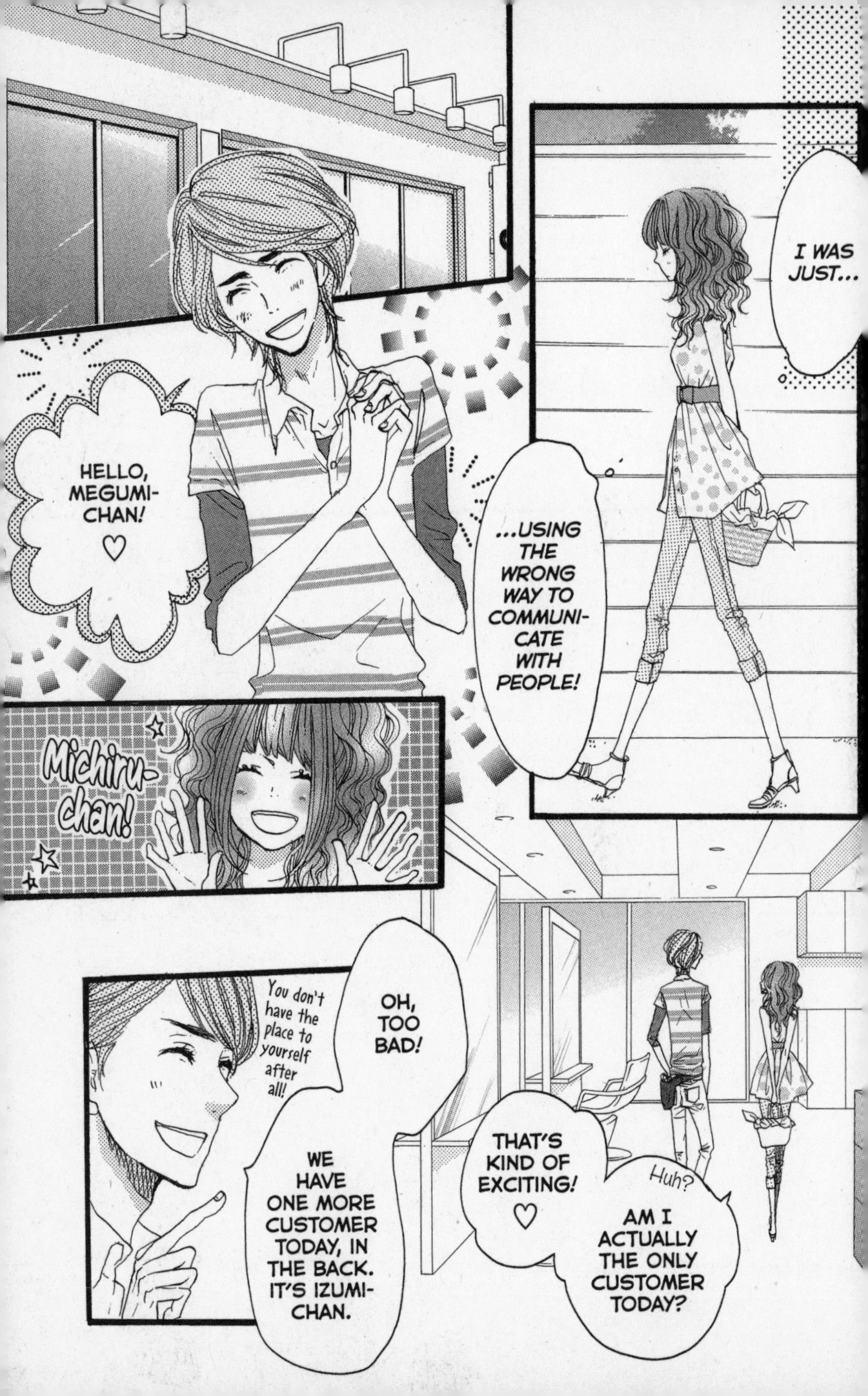
I WAS JUST...
...USING THE WRONG WAY TO COMMUNICATE WITH PEOPLE!
HELLO, MEGUMI-CHAN! ♡
Michiru-chan!
Huh?
AM I ACTUALLY THE ONLY CUSTOMER TODAY?
THAT'S KIND OF EXCITING! ♡
OH, TOO BAD!
You don't have the place to yourself after all!
WE HAVE ONE MORE CUSTOMER TODAY, IN THE BACK. IT'S IZUMI-CHAN.

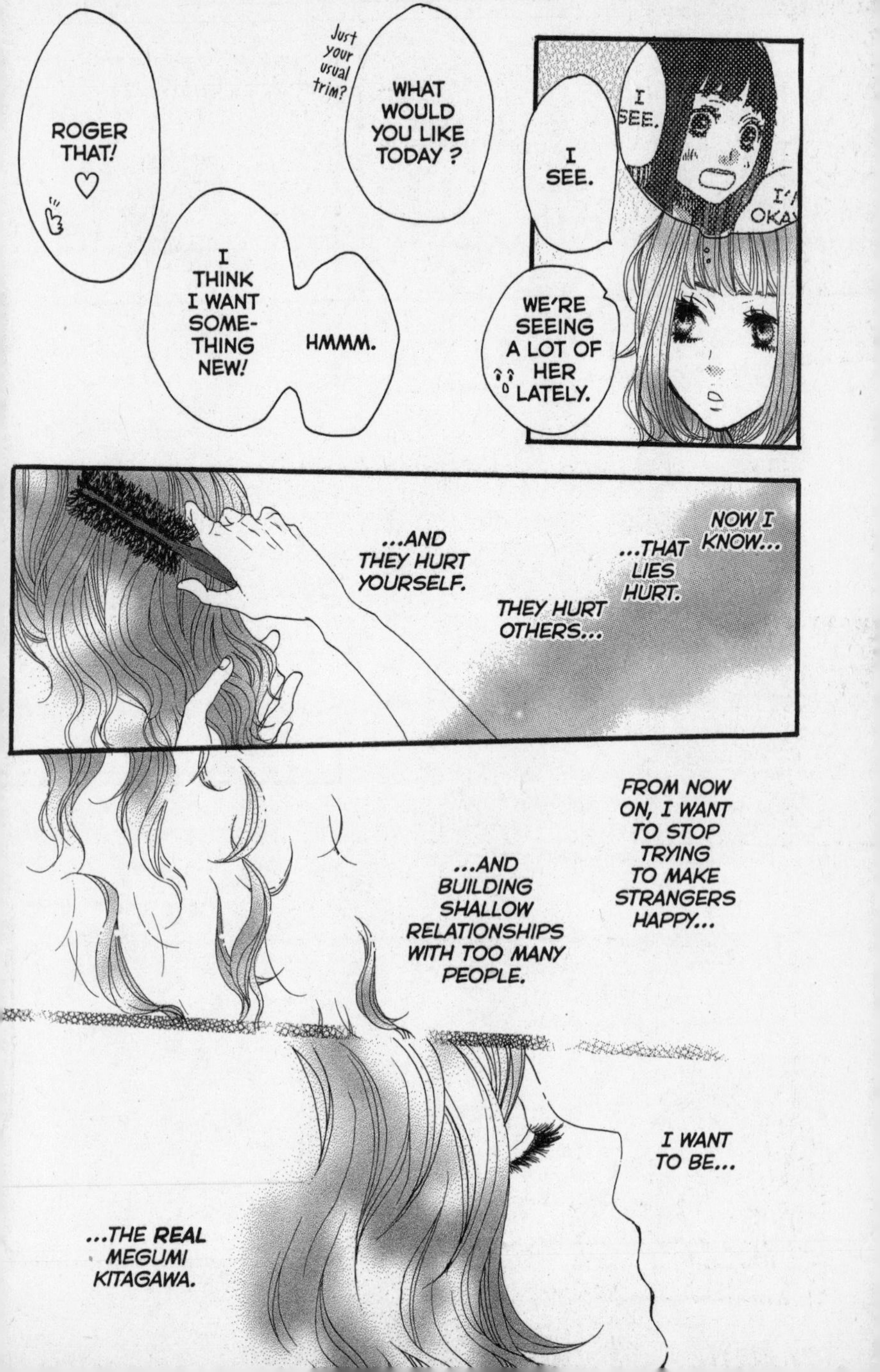

I SEE.
I SEE.
WE'RE SEEING A LOT OF HER LATELY.
WHAT WOULD YOU LIKE TODAY ?
Just your usual trim?
HMMM.
I THINK I WANT SOMETHING NEW!
ROGER THAT! ♡
NOW I KNOW...
...THAT LIES HURT.
THEY HURT OTHERS...
...AND THEY HURT YOURSELF.
FROM NOW ON, I WANT TO STOP TRYING TO MAKE STRANGERS HAPPY...
...AND BUILDING SHALLOW RELATIONSHIPS WITH TOO MANY PEOPLE.
I WANT TO BE...
...THE REAL MEGUMI KITAGAWA.

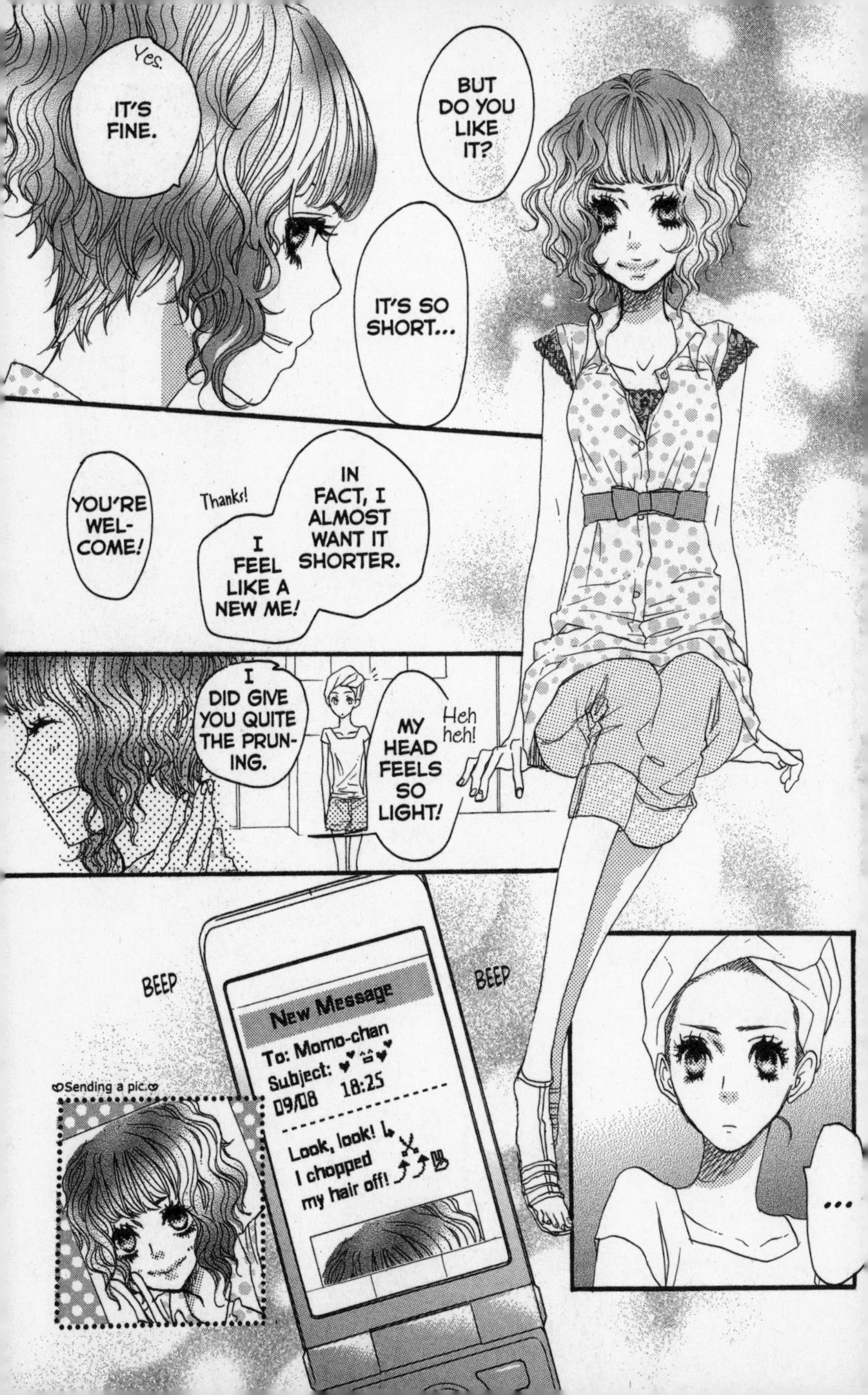
BUT DO YOU LIKE IT?
IT'S SO SHORT...
Yes.
IT'S FINE.
IN FACT, I ALMOST WANT IT SHORTER.
I FEEL LIKE A NEW ME!
Thanks!
YOU'RE WEL-COME!
MY HEAD FEELS SO LIGHT!
Heh heh!
I DID GIVE YOU QUITE THE PRUN-ING.
...
BEEP
BEEP
New Message
To: Momo-chan
Subject:
09/08 18:25
Look, look!
I chopped my hair off!
Sending a pic.

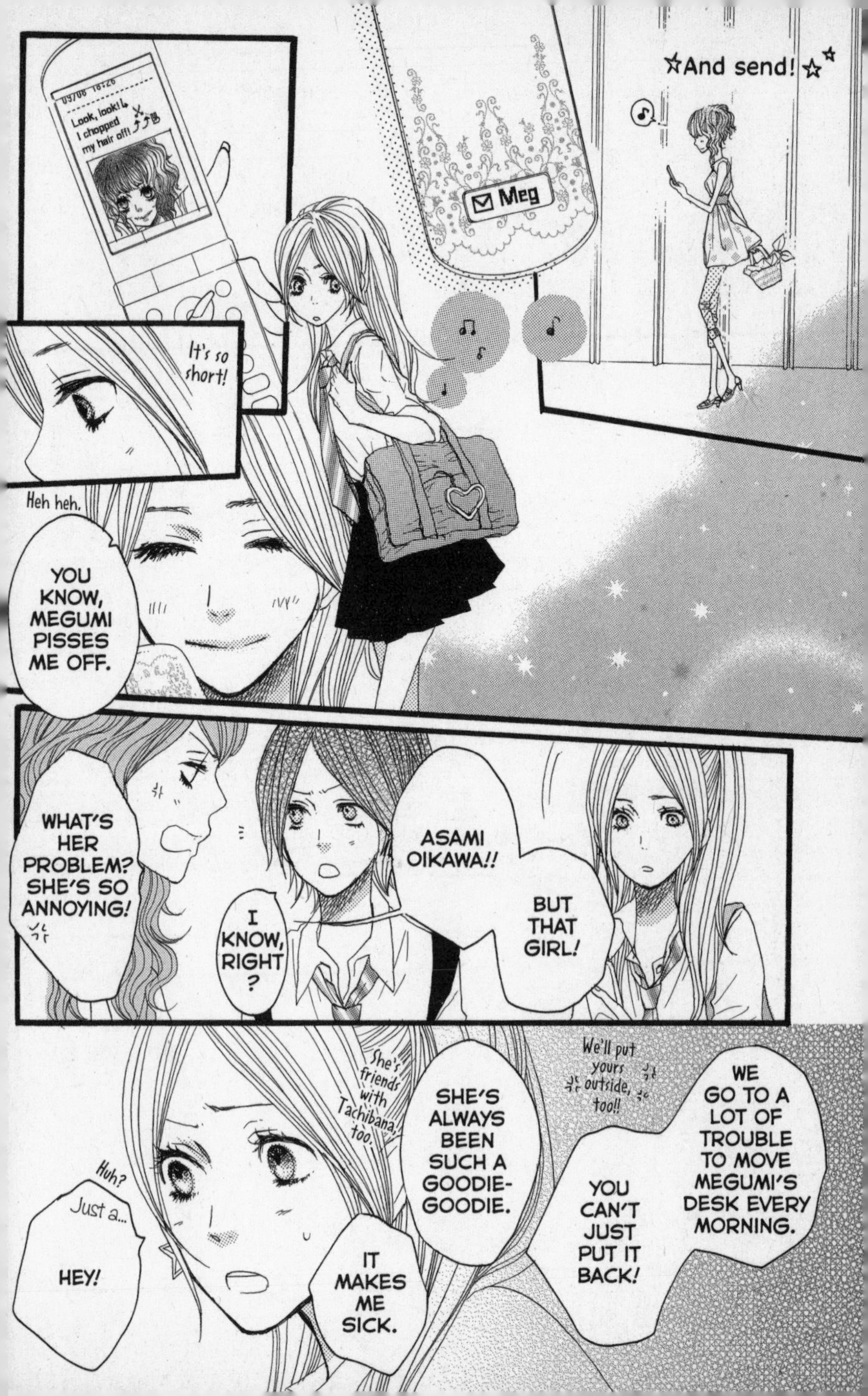
☆And send! ☆
Meg
Look, look! I chopped my hair off!
It's so short!
Heh heh.
YOU KNOW, MEGUMI PISSES ME OFF.
ASAMI OIKAWA!!
BUT THAT GIRL!
I KNOW, RIGHT?
WHAT'S HER PROBLEM? SHE'S SO ANNOYING!
WE GO TO A LOT OF TROUBLE TO MOVE MEGUMI'S DESK EVERY MORNING.
We'll put yours outside, too!!
YOU CAN'T JUST PUT IT BACK!
SHE'S ALWAYS BEEN SUCH A GOODIE-GOODIE.
She's friends with Tachibana, too.
IT MAKES ME SICK.
Huh?
Just a...
HEY!

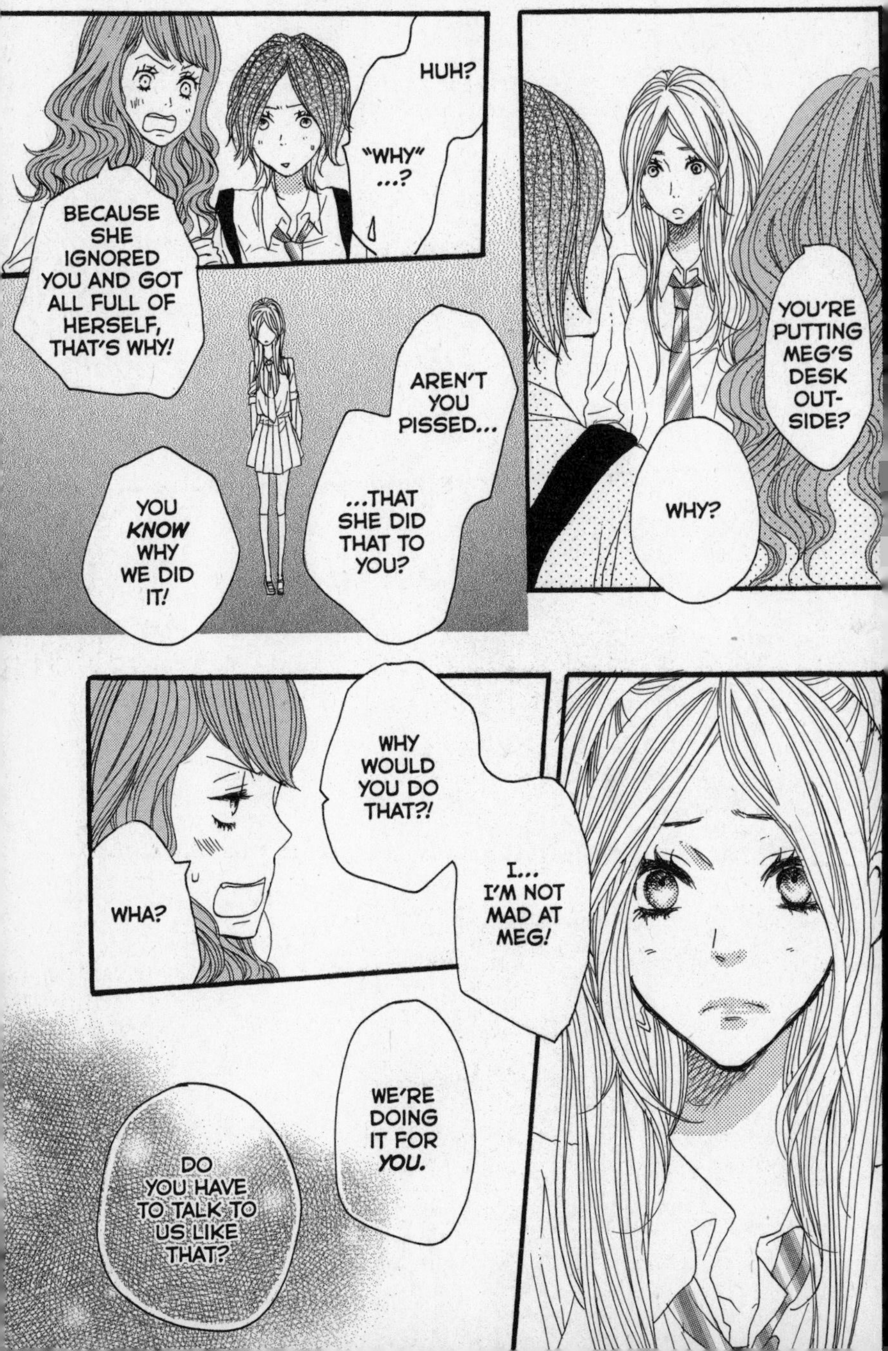
YOU'RE PUTTING MEG'S DESK OUT-SIDE?
WHY?
HUH?
"WHY" ...?
BECAUSE SHE IGNORED YOU AND GOT ALL FULL OF HERSELF, THAT'S WHY!
AREN'T YOU PISSED...
...THAT SHE DID THAT TO YOU?
YOU *KNOW* WHY WE DID IT!
WHY WOULD YOU DO THAT?!
I... I'M NOT MAD AT MEG!
WHA?
WE'RE DOING IT FOR *YOU.*
DO YOU HAVE TO TALK TO US LIKE THAT?

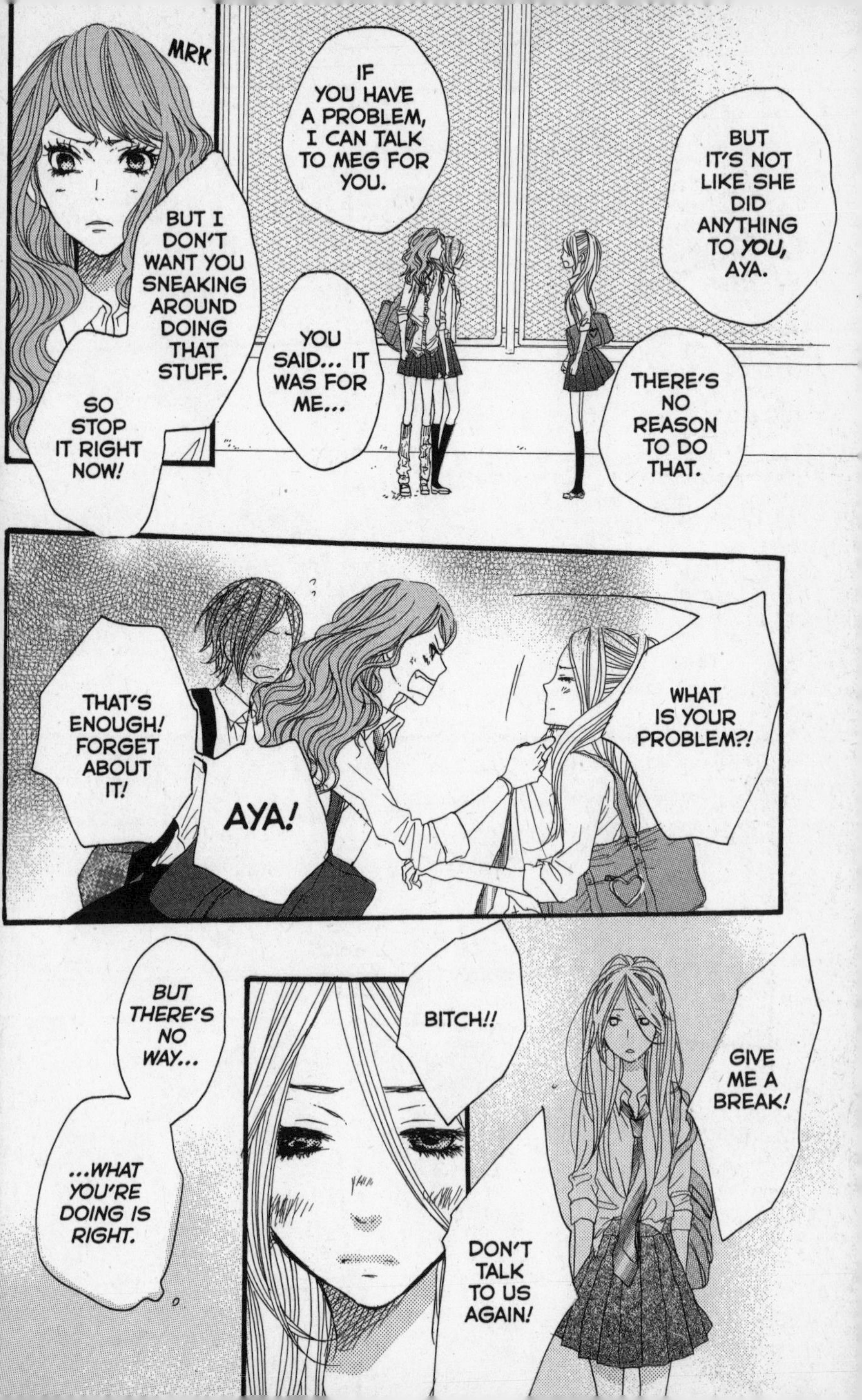
BUT IT'S NOT LIKE SHE DID ANYTHING TO *YOU*, AYA.
THERE'S NO REASON TO DO THAT.
IF YOU HAVE A PROBLEM, I CAN TALK TO MEG FOR YOU.
YOU SAID... IT WAS FOR ME...
MRK
BUT I DON'T WANT YOU SNEAKING AROUND DOING THAT STUFF.
SO STOP IT RIGHT NOW!
WHAT IS YOUR PROBLEM?!
AYA!
THAT'S ENOUGH! FORGET ABOUT IT!
GIVE ME A BREAK!
BITCH!!
DON'T TALK TO US AGAIN!
BUT THERE'S NO WAY...
...WHAT YOU'RE DOING IS RIGHT.

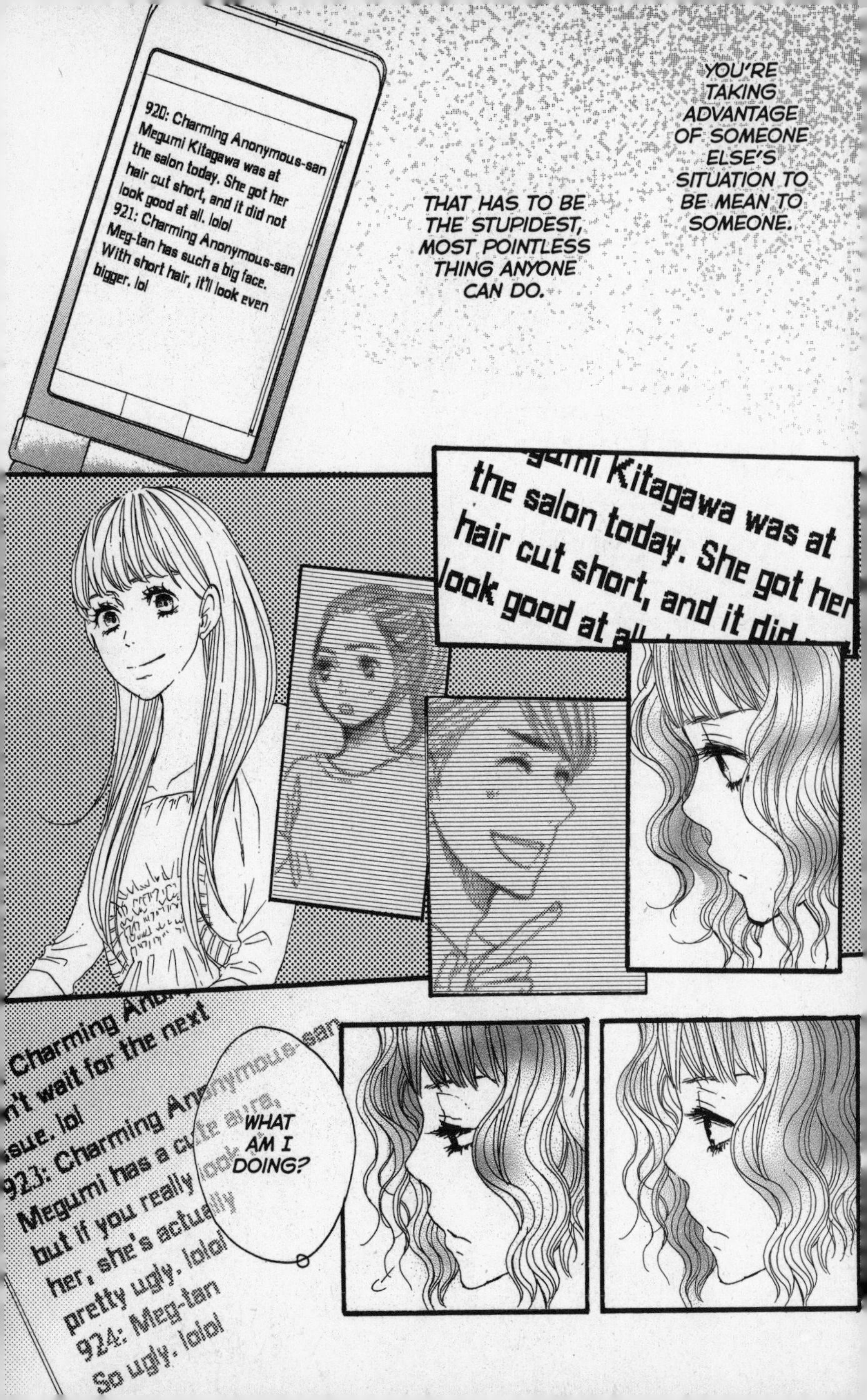

YOU'RE TAKING ADVANTAGE OF SOMEONE ELSE'S SITUATION TO BE MEAN TO SOMEONE.
THAT HAS TO BE THE STUPIDEST, MOST POINTLESS THING ANYONE CAN DO.
920: Charming Anonymous-san
Megumi Kitagawa was at the salon today. She got her hair cut short, and it did not look good at all. lolol
921: Charming Anonymous-san
Meg-tan has such a big face. With short hair, it'll look even bigger. lol
the salon today. She got her
hair cut short, and it did
look good at
WHAT AM I DOING?
Charming
n't wait for the next
sue. lol
923: Charming Anonymous-san
Megumi has a cute aura,
but if you really look
her, she's actually
pretty ugly. lolol
924: Meg-tan
So ugly. lolol

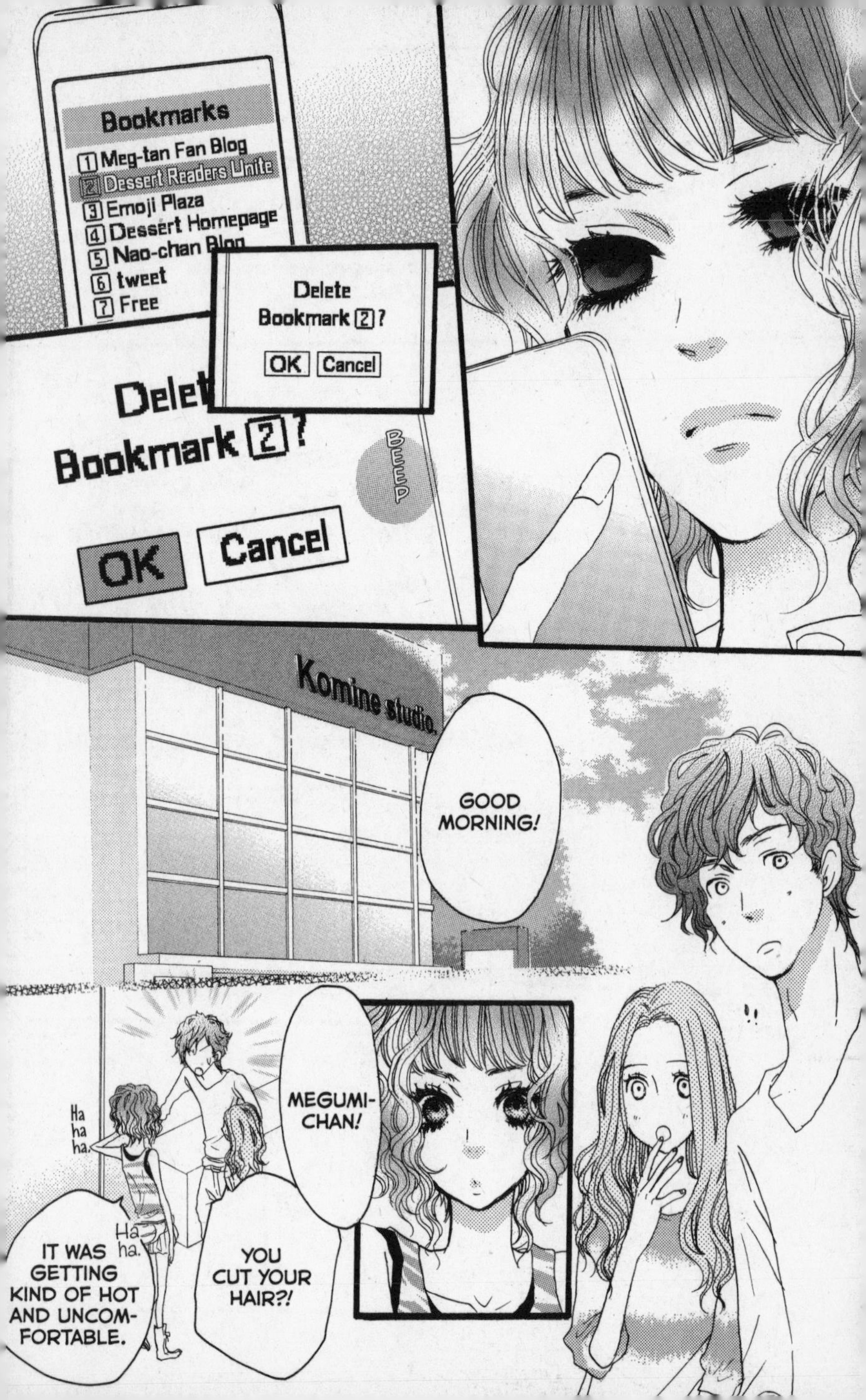
Bookmarks
1 Meg-tan Fan Blog
2 Dessert Readers Unite
3 Emoji Plaza
4 Dessert Homepage
5 Nao-chan Blog
6 tweet
7 Free
Delete Bookmark 2 ?
OK Cancel
Delet
Bookmark 2 ?
OK Cancel
BEEEP
Komine studio.
GOOD MORNING!
!!
MEGUMI-CHAN!
YOU CUT YOUR HAIR?!
Ha ha ha.
Ha ha.
IT WAS GETTING KIND OF HOT AND UNCOMFORTABLE.

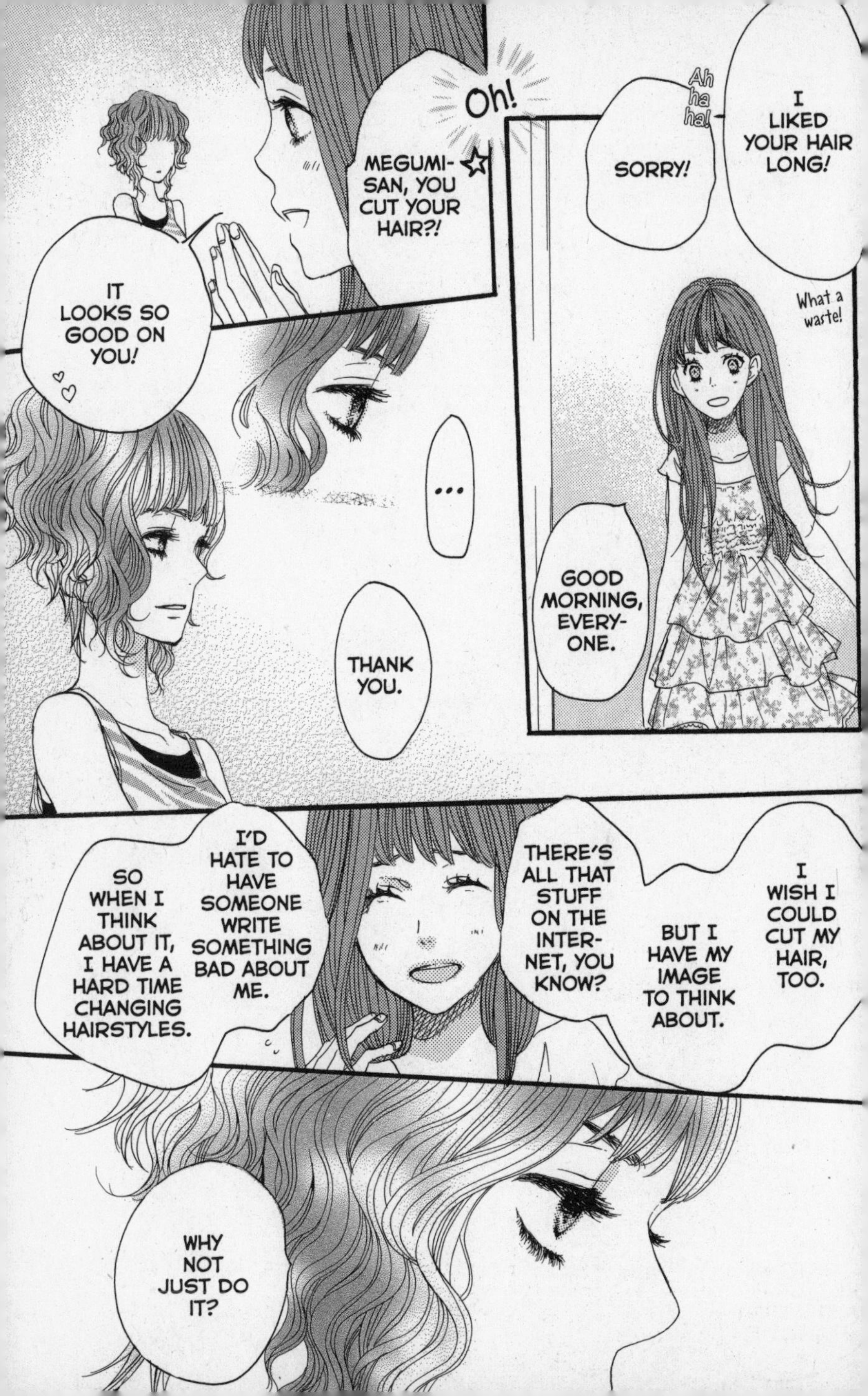
I LIKED YOUR HAIR LONG!
Ah ha ha!
SORRY!
What a waste!
GOOD MORNING, EVERYONE.
Oh!
MEGUMI-SAN, YOU CUT YOUR HAIR?!
IT LOOKS SO GOOD ON YOU!
...
THANK YOU.
I WISH I COULD CUT MY HAIR, TOO.
BUT I HAVE MY IMAGE TO THINK ABOUT.
THERE'S ALL THAT STUFF ON THE INTER-NET, YOU KNOW?
I'D HATE TO HAVE SOMEONE WRITE SOMETHING BAD ABOUT ME.
SO WHEN I THINK ABOUT IT, I HAVE A HARD TIME CHANGING HAIRSTYLES.
WHY NOT JUST DO IT?

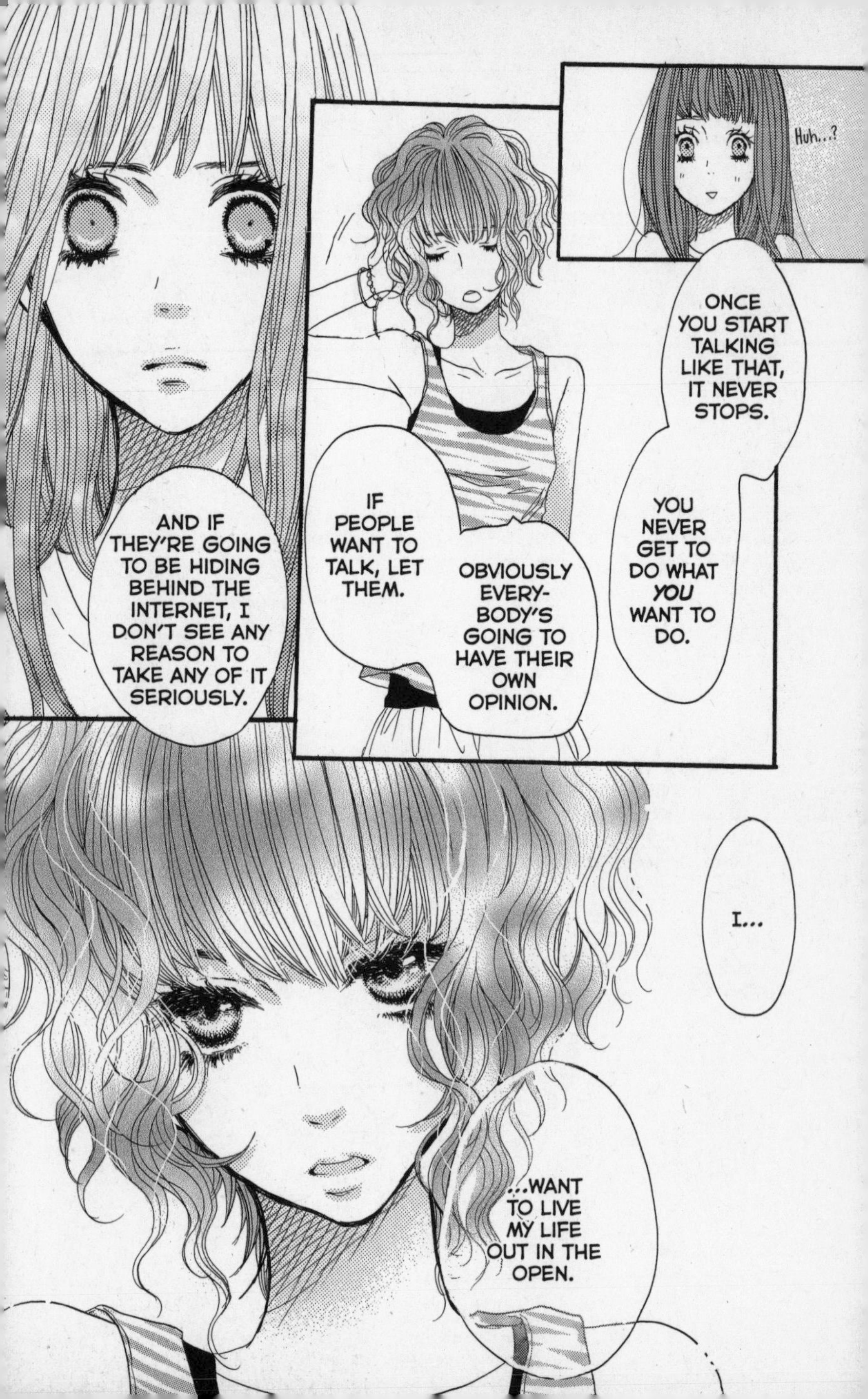
Huh...?
ONCE YOU START TALKING LIKE THAT, IT NEVER STOPS.
YOU NEVER GET TO DO WHAT *YOU* WANT TO DO.
OBVIOUSLY EVERY-BODY'S GOING TO HAVE THEIR OWN OPINION.
IF PEOPLE WANT TO TALK, LET THEM.
AND IF THEY'RE GOING TO BE HIDING BEHIND THE INTERNET, I DON'T SEE ANY REASON TO TAKE ANY OF IT SERIOUSLY.
I...
...WANT TO LIVE *MY* LIFE OUT IN THE OPEN.

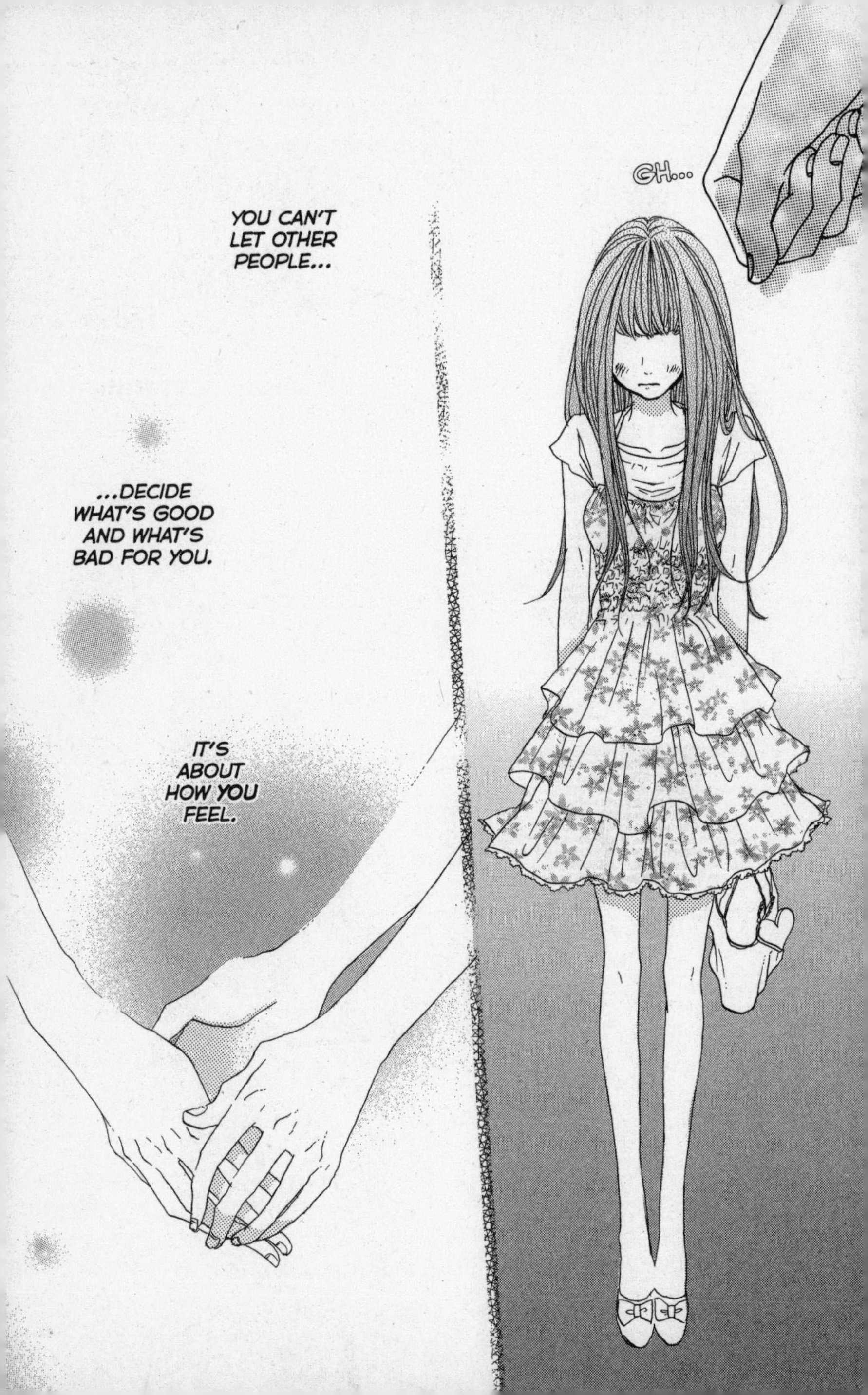
GH...
YOU CAN'T LET OTHER PEOPLE...
...DECIDE WHAT'S GOOD AND WHAT'S BAD FOR YOU.
IT'S ABOUT HOW YOU FEEL.

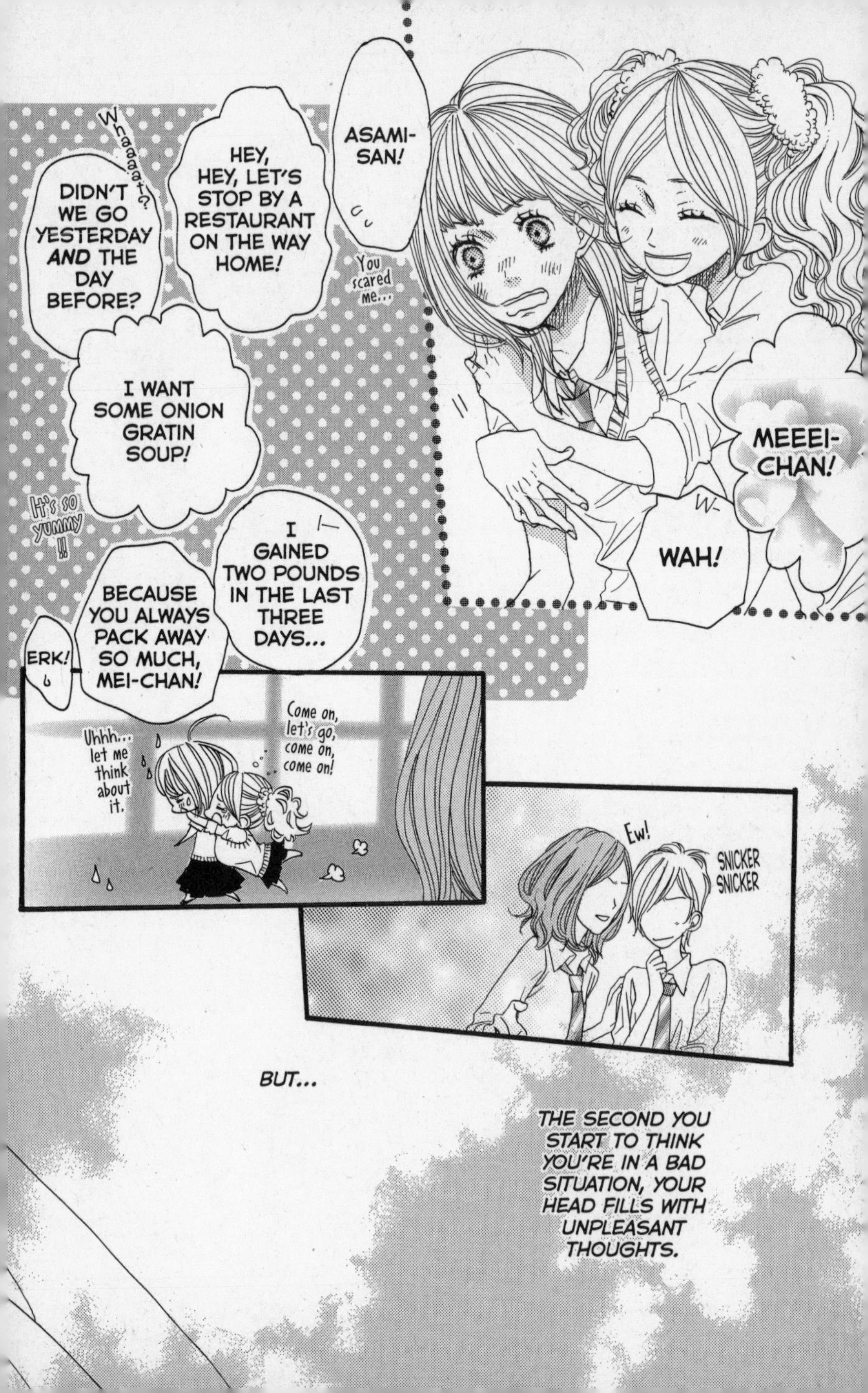
MEEEI-CHAN!
W-
WAH!
ASAMI-SAN!
You scared me...
HEY, HEY, LET'S STOP BY A RESTAURANT ON THE WAY HOME!
Whaaaat?
DIDN'T WE GO YESTERDAY AND THE DAY BEFORE?
I WANT SOME ONION GRATIN SOUP!
It's so yummy!!
I GAINED TWO POUNDS IN THE LAST THREE DAYS...
BECAUSE YOU ALWAYS PACK AWAY SO MUCH, MEI-CHAN!
ERK!
Come on, let's go, come on, come on!
Uhhh... let me think about it.
Ew!
SNICKER SNICKER
BUT...
THE SECOND YOU START TO THINK YOU'RE IN A BAD SITUATION, YOUR HEAD FILLS WITH UNPLEASANT THOUGHTS.

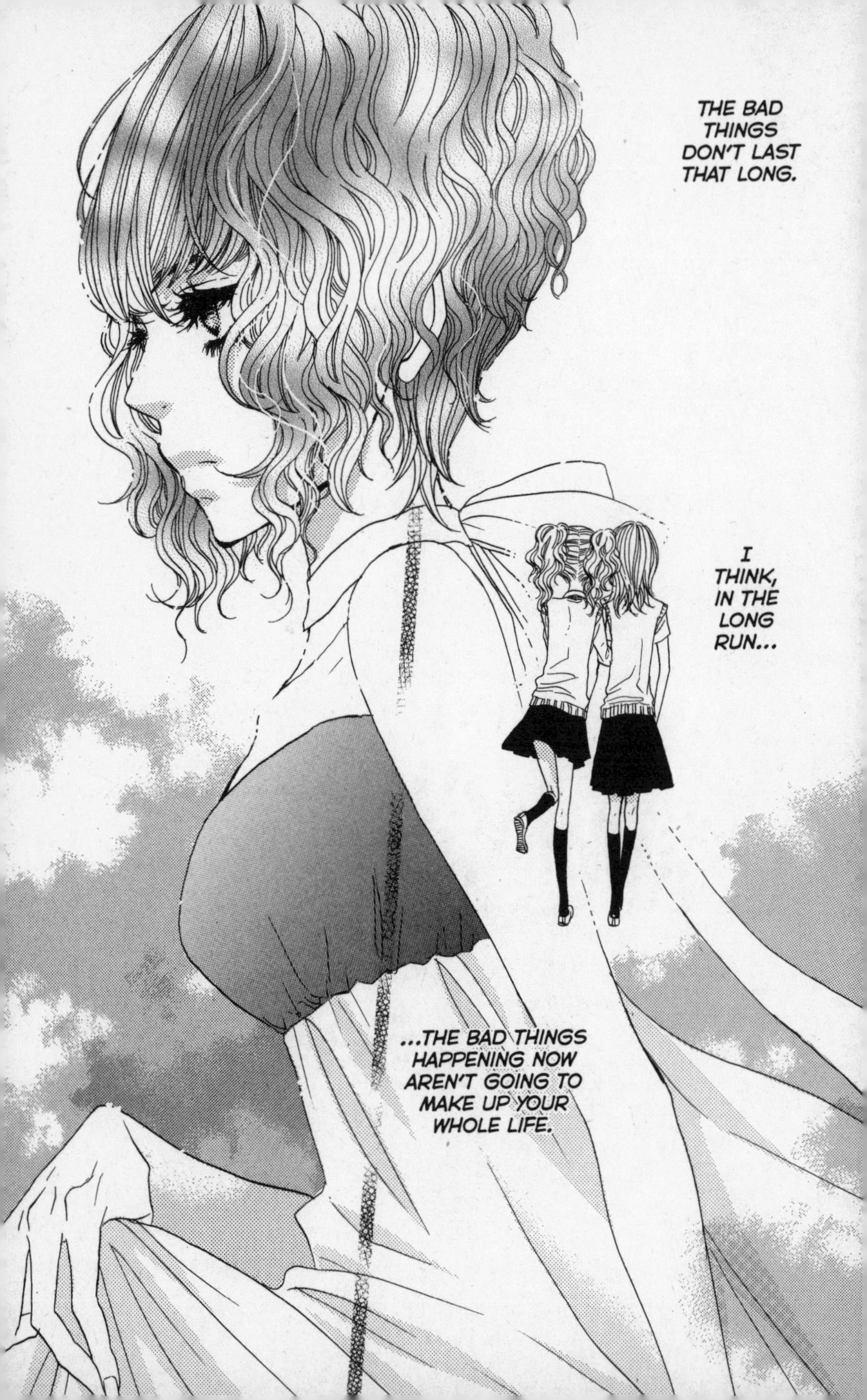
THE BAD THINGS DON'T LAST THAT LONG.
I THINK, IN THE LONG RUN...
...THE BAD THINGS HAPPENING NOW AREN'T GOING TO MAKE UP YOUR WHOLE LIFE.

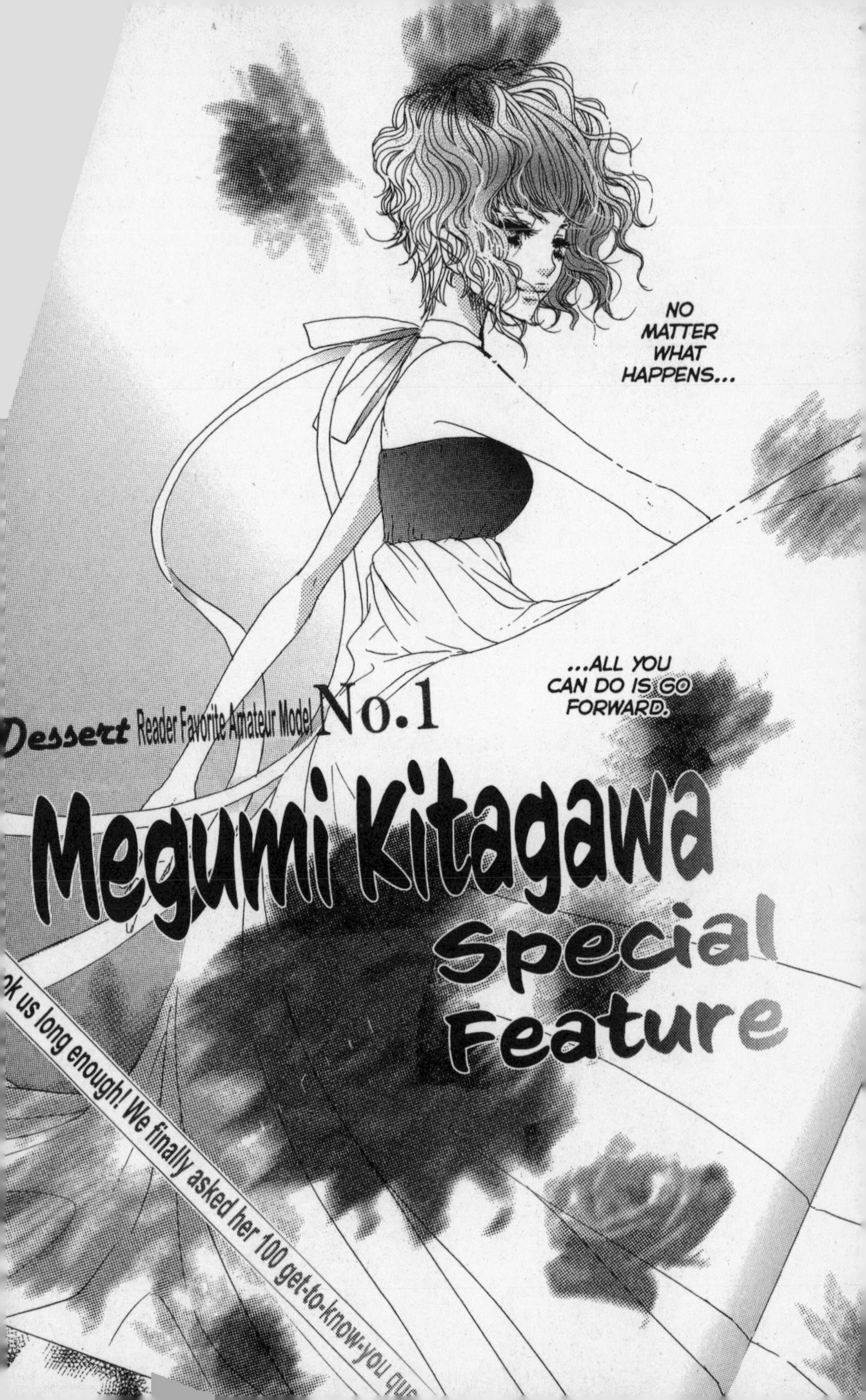
NO MATTER WHAT HAPPENS...
...ALL YOU CAN DO IS GO FORWARD.
Dessert Reader Favorite Amateur Model No.1
Megumi Kitagawa
Special Feature
ok us long enough! We finally asked her 100 get-to-know-you qu

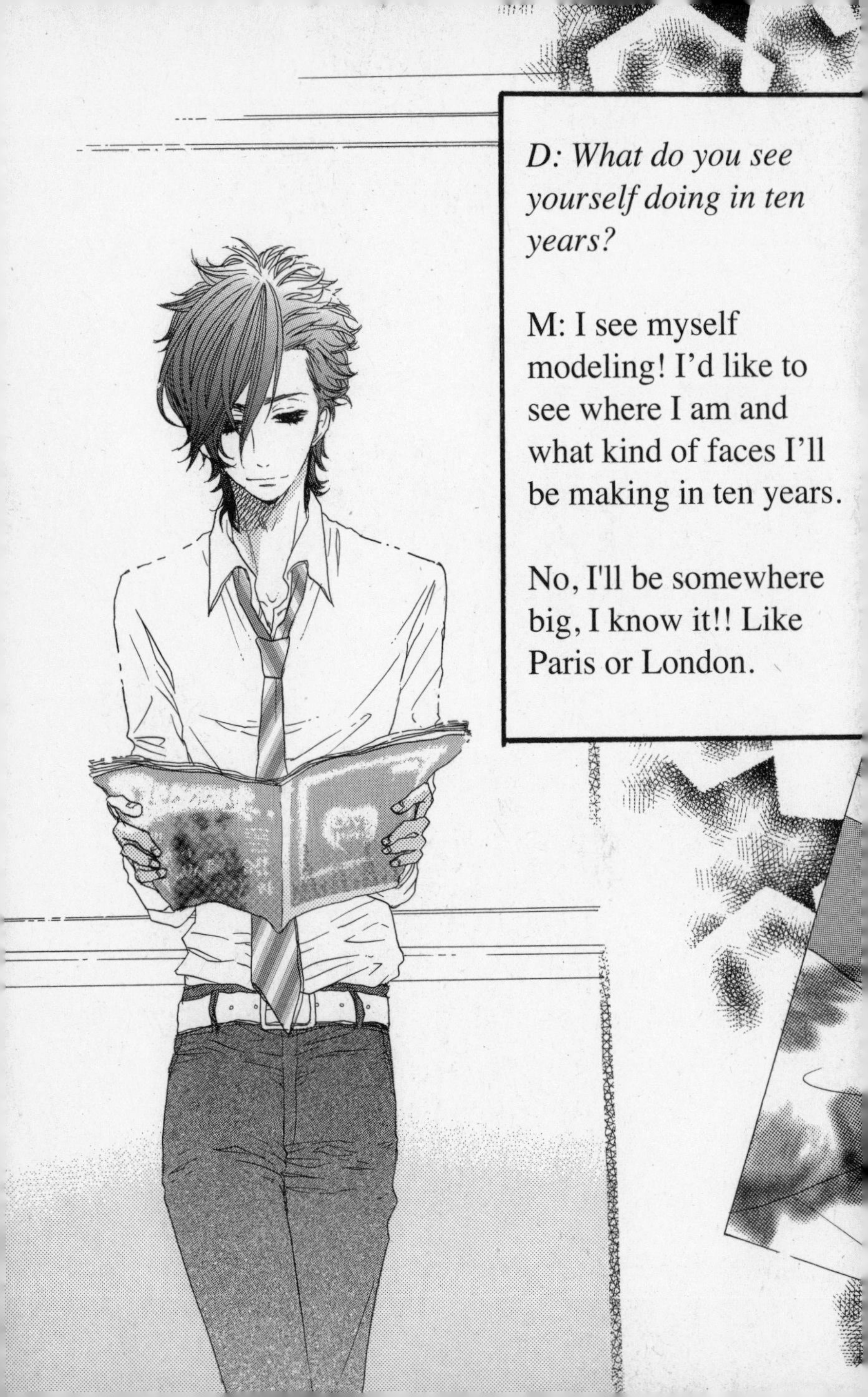

D: What do you see yourself doing in ten years?

M: I see myself modeling! I'd like to see where I am and what kind of faces I'll be making in ten years.

No, I'll be somewhere big, I know it!! Like Paris or London.

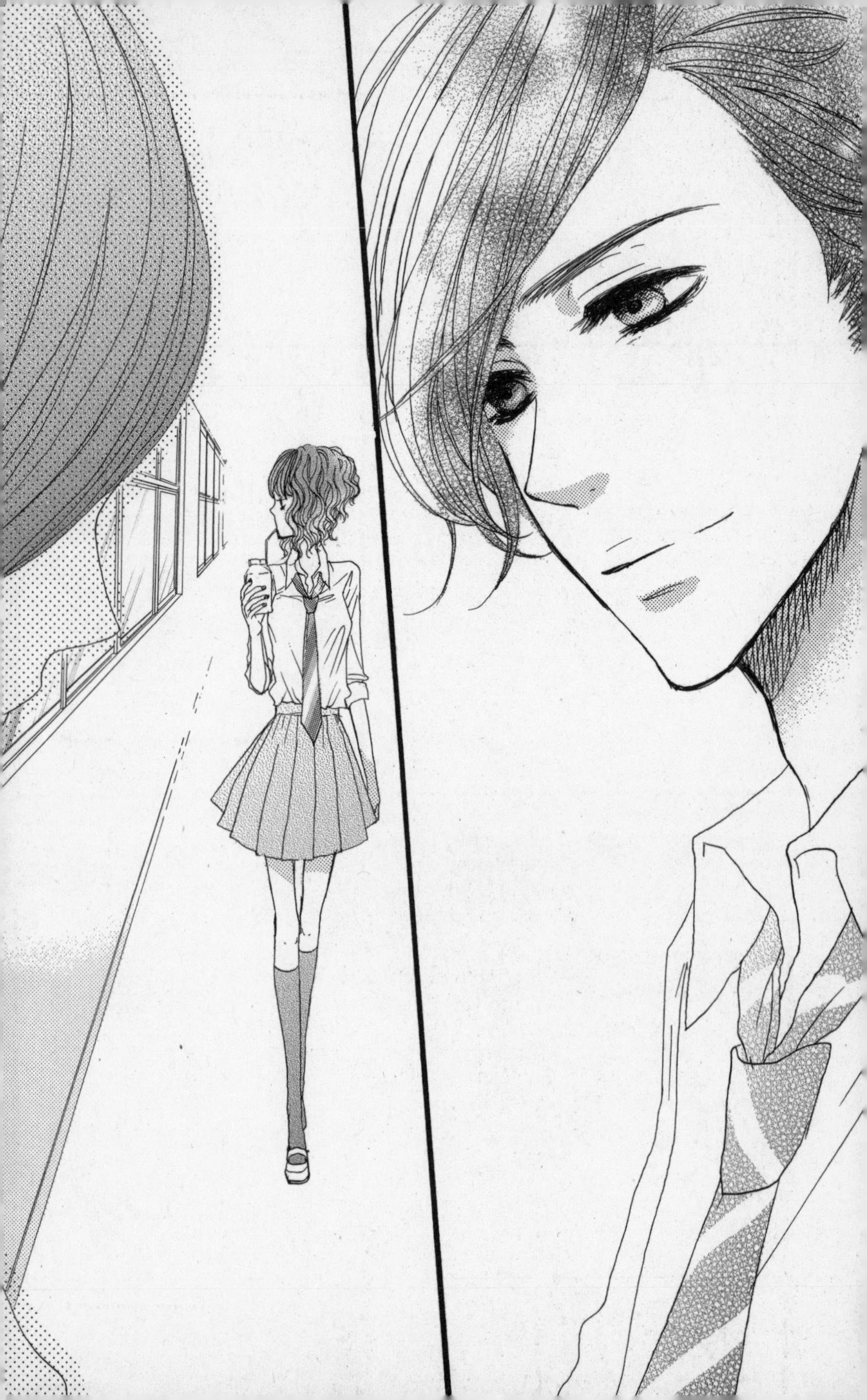

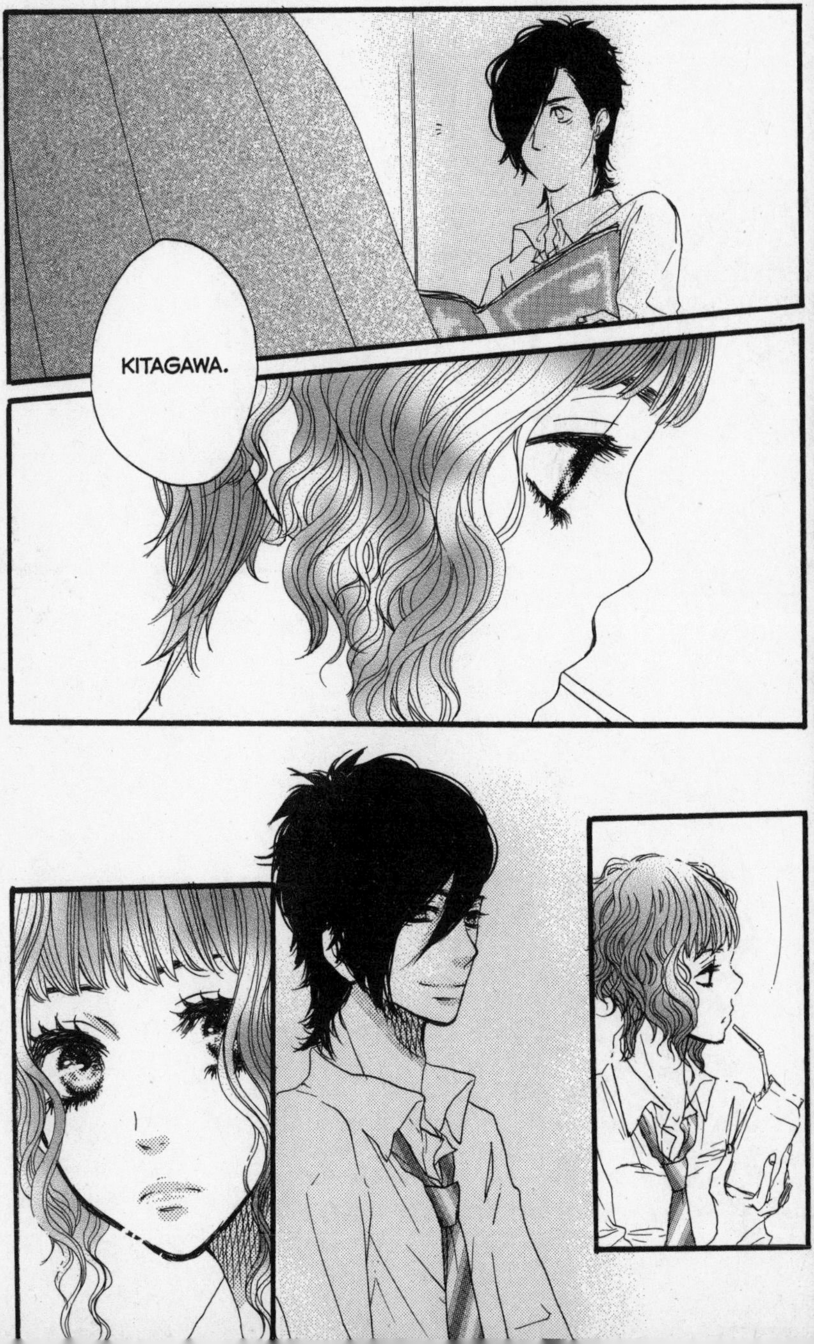
KITAGAWA.

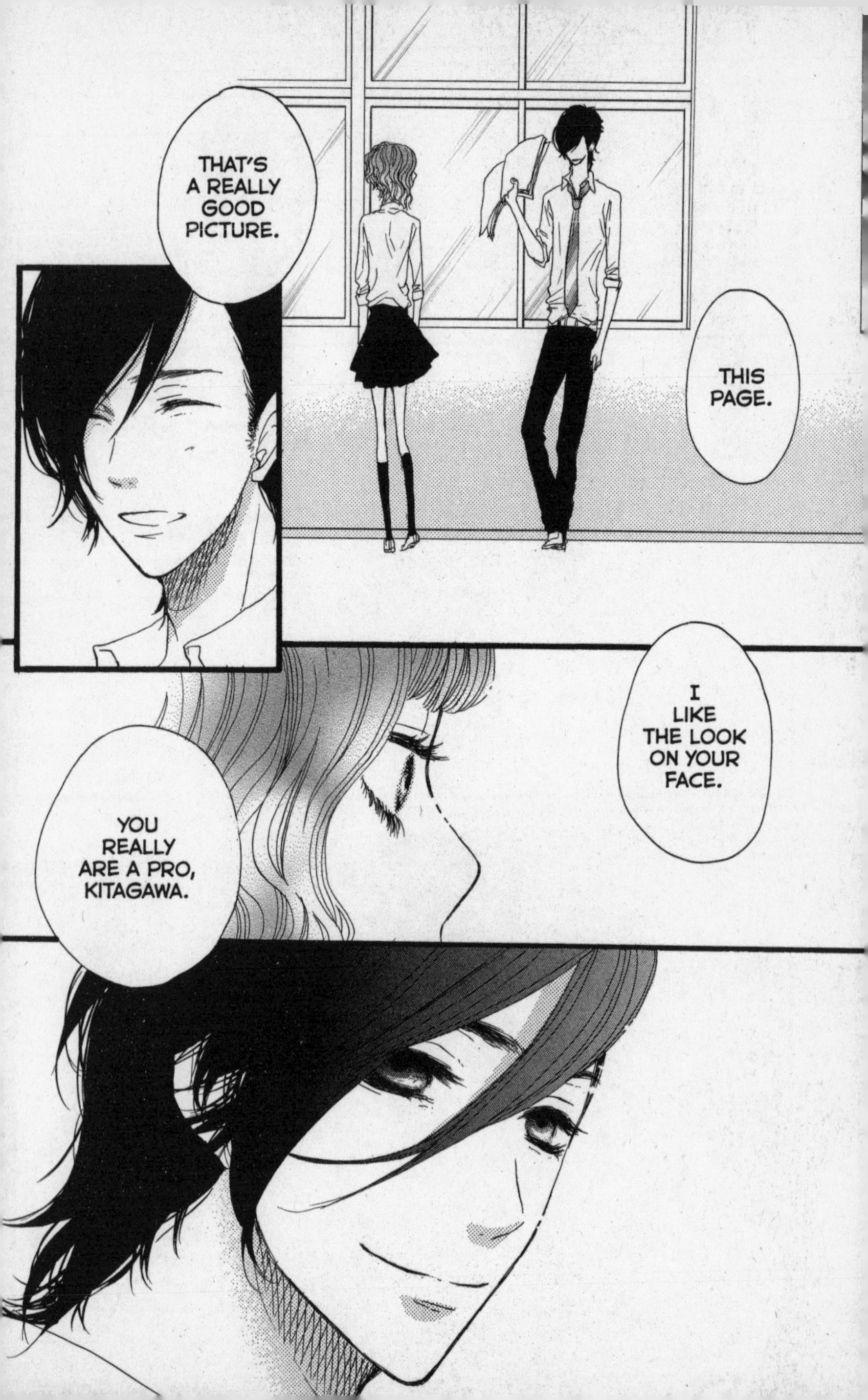
THAT'S A REALLY GOOD PICTURE.
THIS PAGE.
I LIKE THE LOOK ON YOUR FACE.
YOU REALLY ARE A PRO, KITAGAWA.

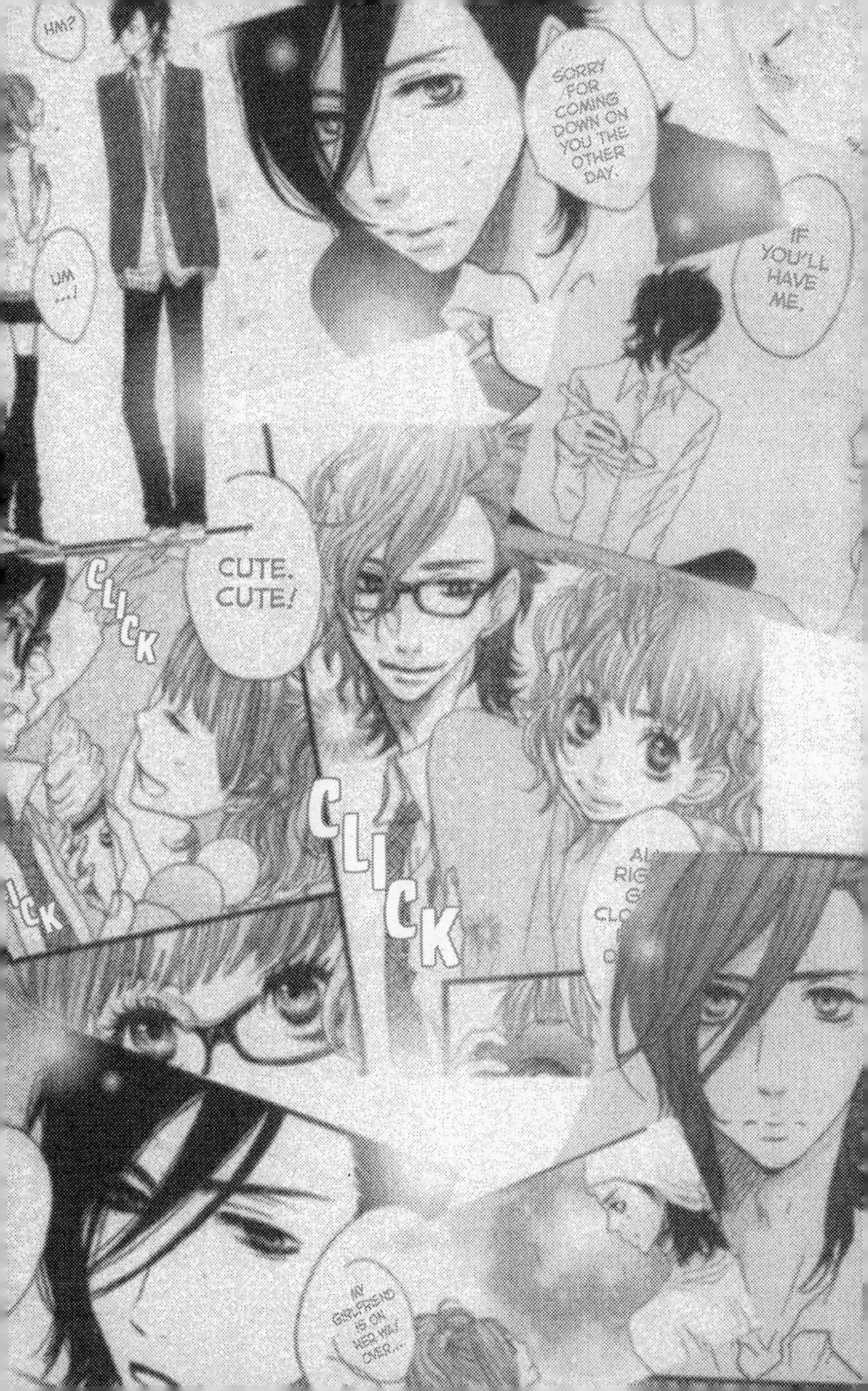
SORRY FOR COMING DOWN ON YOU THE OTHER DAY.
IF YOU'LL HAVE ME,
HM?
UM ...!
CLICK
CUTE. CUTE!
CLICK
MY GIRLFRIEND IS ON HER WAY OVER...

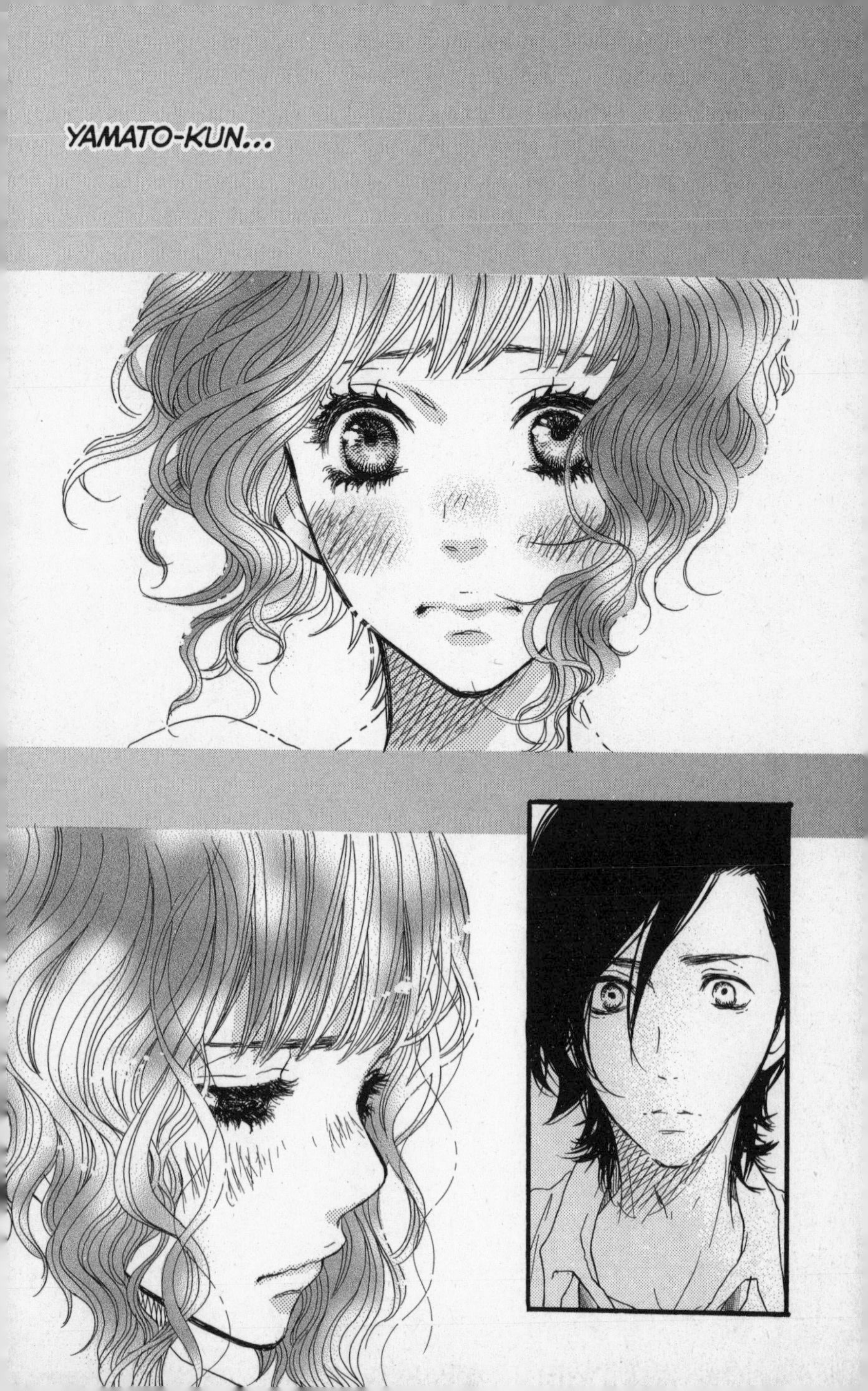
YAMATO-KUN...

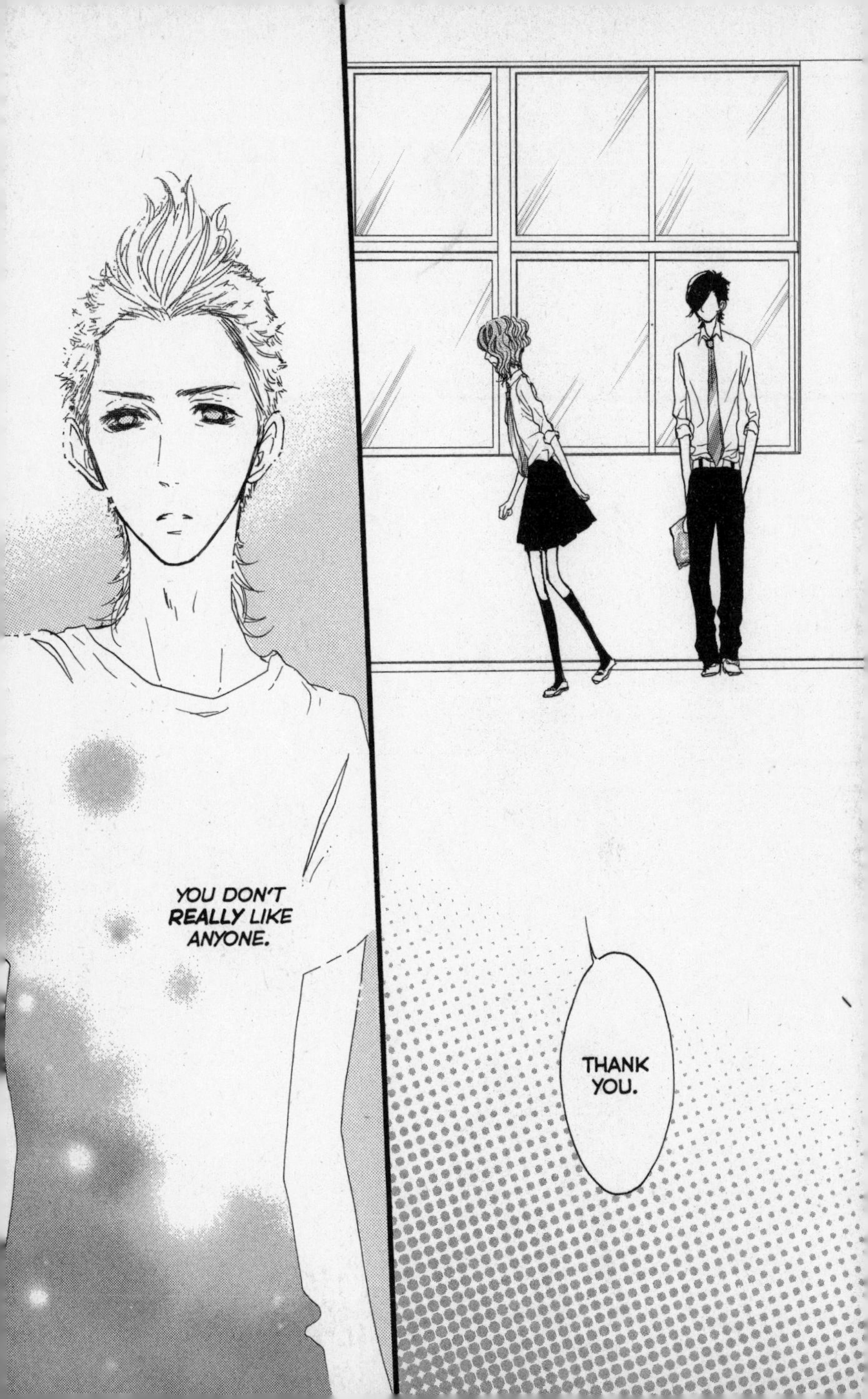
THANK YOU.
YOU DON'T REALLY LIKE ANYONE.

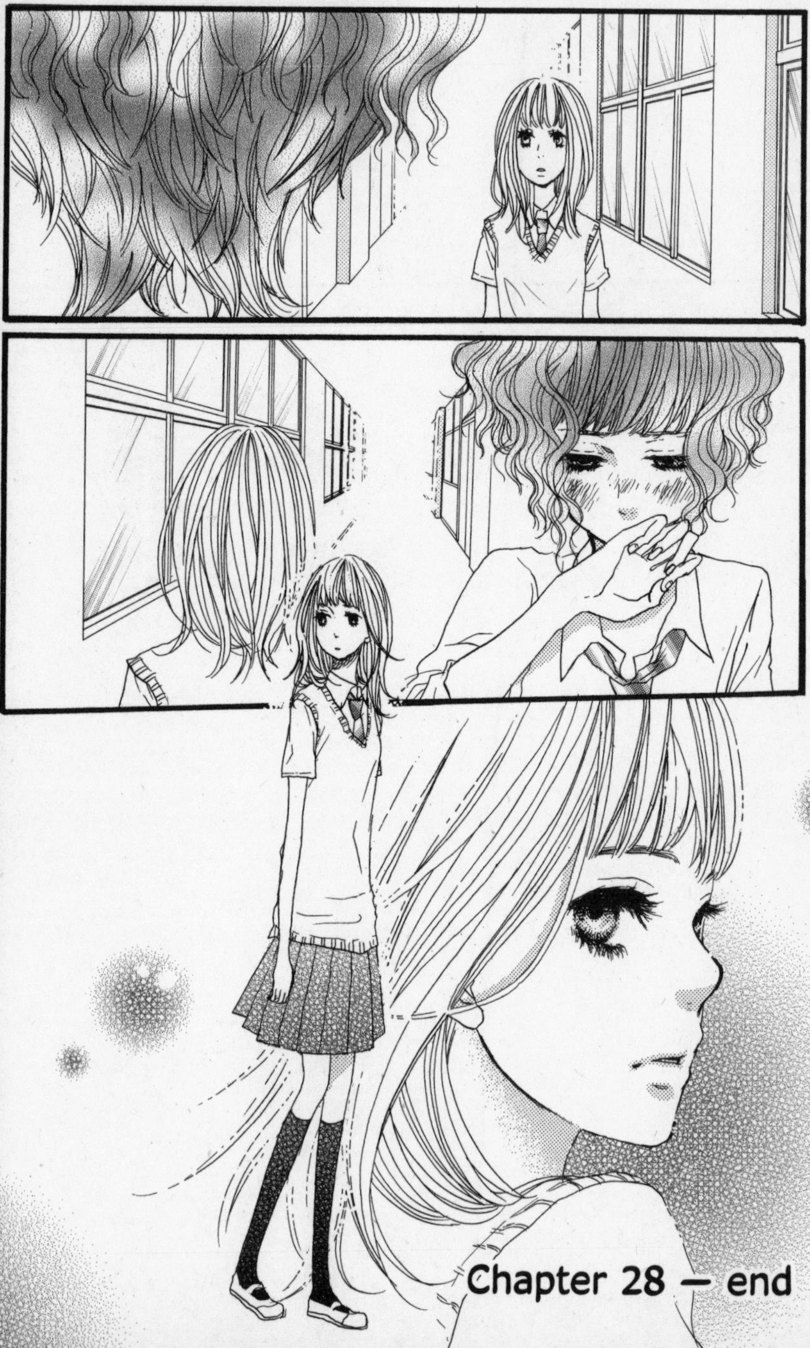
Chapter 28 — end

Say "I love you".

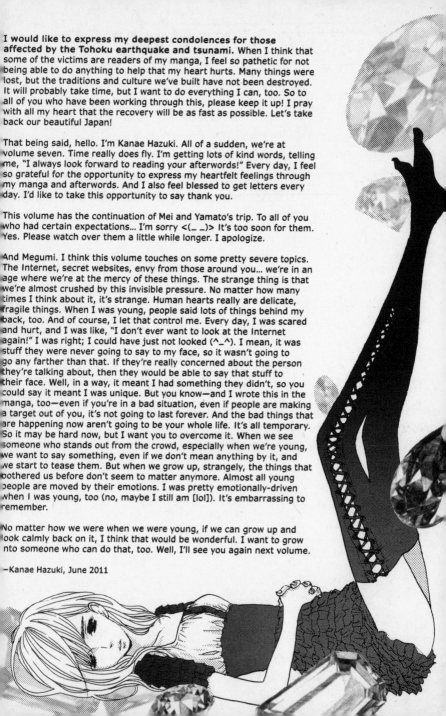

I would like to express my deepest condolences for those affected by the Tohoku earthquake and tsunami. When I think that some of the victims are readers of my manga, I feel so pathetic for not being able to do anything to help that my heart hurts. Many things were lost, but the traditions and culture we've built have not been destroyed. It will probably take time, but I want to do everything I can, too. So to all of you who have been working through this, please keep it up! I pray with all my heart that the recovery will be as fast as possible. Let's take back our beautiful Japan!

That being said, hello. I'm Kanae Hazuki. All of a sudden, we're at volume seven. Time really does fly. I'm getting lots of kind words, telling me, "I always look forward to reading your afterwords!" Every day, I feel so grateful for the opportunity to express my heartfelt feelings through my manga and afterwords. And I also feel blessed to get letters every day. I'd like to take this opportunity to say thank you.

This volume has the continuation of Mei and Yamato's trip. To all of you who had certain expectations... I'm sorry <(_ _)> It's too soon for them. Yes. Please watch over them a little while longer. I apologize.

And Megumi. I think this volume touches on some pretty severe topics. The Internet, secret websites, envy from those around you... we're in an age where we're at the mercy of these things. The strange thing is that we're almost crushed by this invisible pressure. No matter how many times I think about it, it's strange. Human hearts really are delicate, fragile things. When I was young, people said lots of things behind my back, too. And of course, I let that control me. Every day, I was scared and hurt, and I was like, "I don't ever want to look at the Internet again!" I was right; I could have just not looked (^_^). I mean, it was stuff they were never going to say to my face, so it wasn't going to go any farther than that. If they're really concerned about the person they're talking about, then they would be able to say that stuff to their face. Well, in a way, it meant I had something they didn't, so you could say it meant I was unique. But you know—and I wrote this in the manga, too—even if you're in a bad situation, even if people are making a target out of you, it's not going to last forever. And the bad things that are happening now aren't going to be your whole life. It's all temporary. So it may be hard now, but I want you to overcome it. When we see someone who stands out from the crowd, especially when we're young, we want to say something, even if we don't mean anything by it, and we start to tease them. But when we grow up, strangely, the things that bothered us before don't seem to matter anymore. Almost all young people are moved by their emotions. I was pretty emotionally-driven when I was young, too (no, maybe I still am [lol]). It's embarrassing to remember.

No matter how we were when we were young, if we can grow up and look calmly back on it, I think that would be wonderful. I want to grow into someone who can do that, too. Well, I'll see you again next volume.

—Kanae Hazuki, June 2011

TRANSLATION NOTES

Page 32: CalorieBurn

This may or may not be the *Say I Love You.* version of the Japanese energy bar CalorieMate. It's made for people with busy schedules, who don't always have time for a full meal. We suppose CalorieBurn would be the one for people who also want to stay trim. (Incidentally, a Google search for "CalorieBurn" in Japanese will bring up listings for a kind of business shoe designed to help you lose weight.)

Page 72: Eye putti

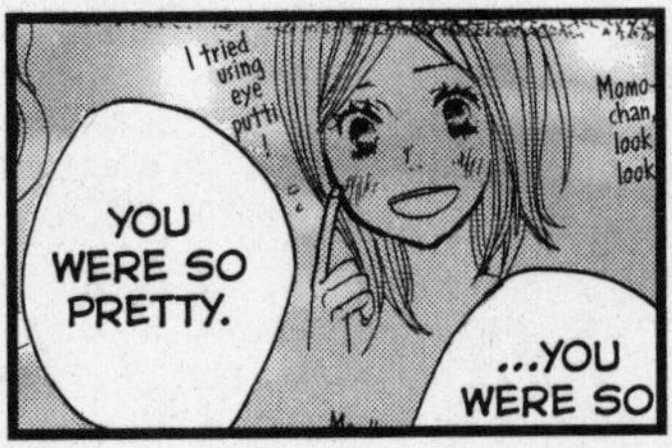
I tried using eye putti!
Momo-chan, look look
YOU WERE SO PRETTY.
...YOU WERE SO

Eye putti, or eyelid glue, is used to create a crease in the eyelid, for East Asian women who prefer the "double-lidded" look but naturally have eyelids without a crease. The glue is applied about mid-eyelid, and holds the crease in place after the eyelid is folded.

Page 94: The glare of a gangster wife

Specifically, Aiko's glare reminds Masashi of a yakuza movie, *Gokudô no Onna-tachi*, roughly translated as *Gangster Wives.* A yakuza movie is a film about the yakuza — Japanese criminal organizations. This particular film is based on a book of interviews with wives and girlfriends of yakuza members.

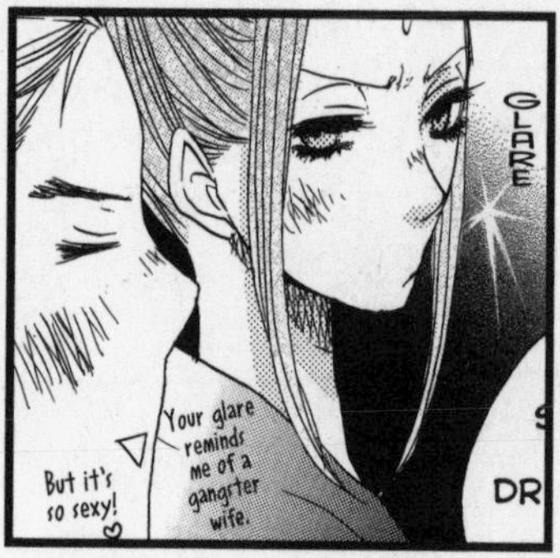
GLARE
Your glare reminds me of a gangster wife.
But it's so sexy!
DR

Page 95: Yukata

A yukata is a light summer kimono. Traditional Japanese clothing isn't as commonly worn in Japan these days, but they still bring it out for special occasions like summer festivals.

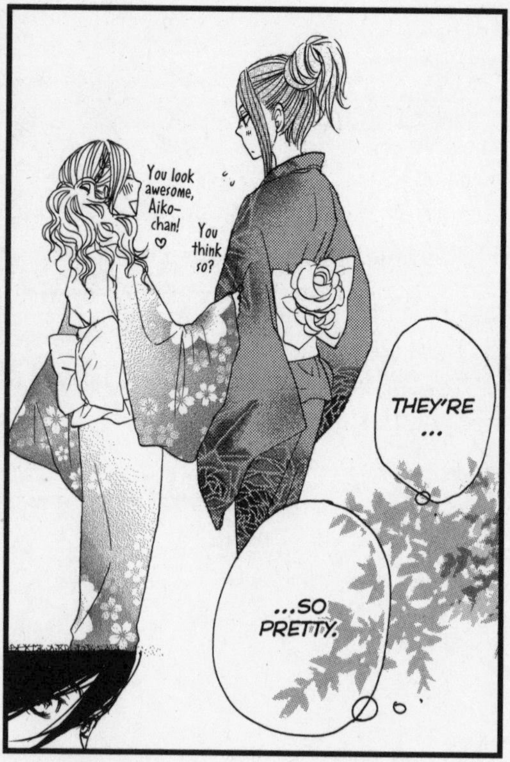
You think so?
You look awesome, Aiko-chan!
THEY'RE ...
...SO PRETTY.

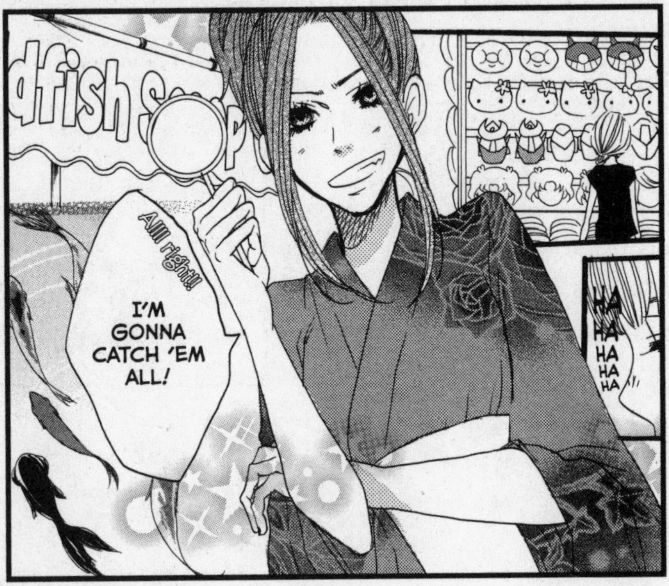
dfish Sc
Alll right!!
I'M GONNA CATCH 'EM ALL!
HA HA HA HA HA

Page 98: Goldfish scoop

Goldfish scoop is a popular carnival game in Japan that involves, as the name suggests, scooping goldfish. The most common instrument used in this endeavor, as modeled by Aiko here, is a plastic hoop with a thin sheet of tissue paper stretched across it. You're allowed to keep as many fish as you're able to catch with one of these "nets," but once the tissue tears, it's pretty much useless. Because the tissue is very easy to tear, especially after it gets wet, it takes a significant amount of skill to catch anything with such a flimsy tool.

The following pages
contain a preview of
Say I Love You. Vol. 8,
coming to print and
digital formats from
Kodansha Comics in
April 2015. Check
out our website for
more details!

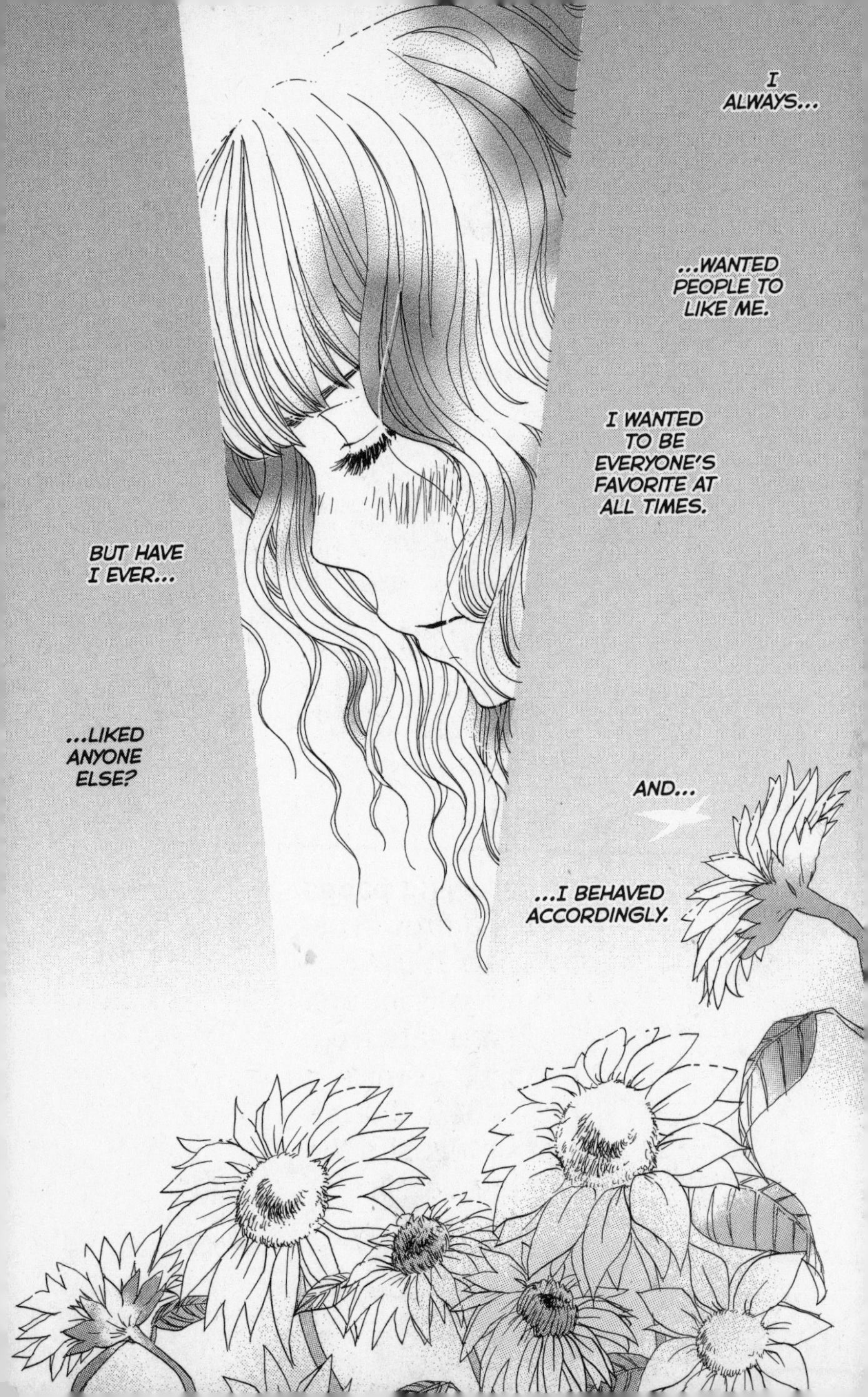
I ALWAYS...
...WANTED PEOPLE TO LIKE ME.
I WANTED TO BE EVERYONE'S FAVORITE AT ALL TIMES.
BUT HAVE I EVER...
...LIKED ANYONE ELSE?
AND...
...I BEHAVED ACCORDINGLY.

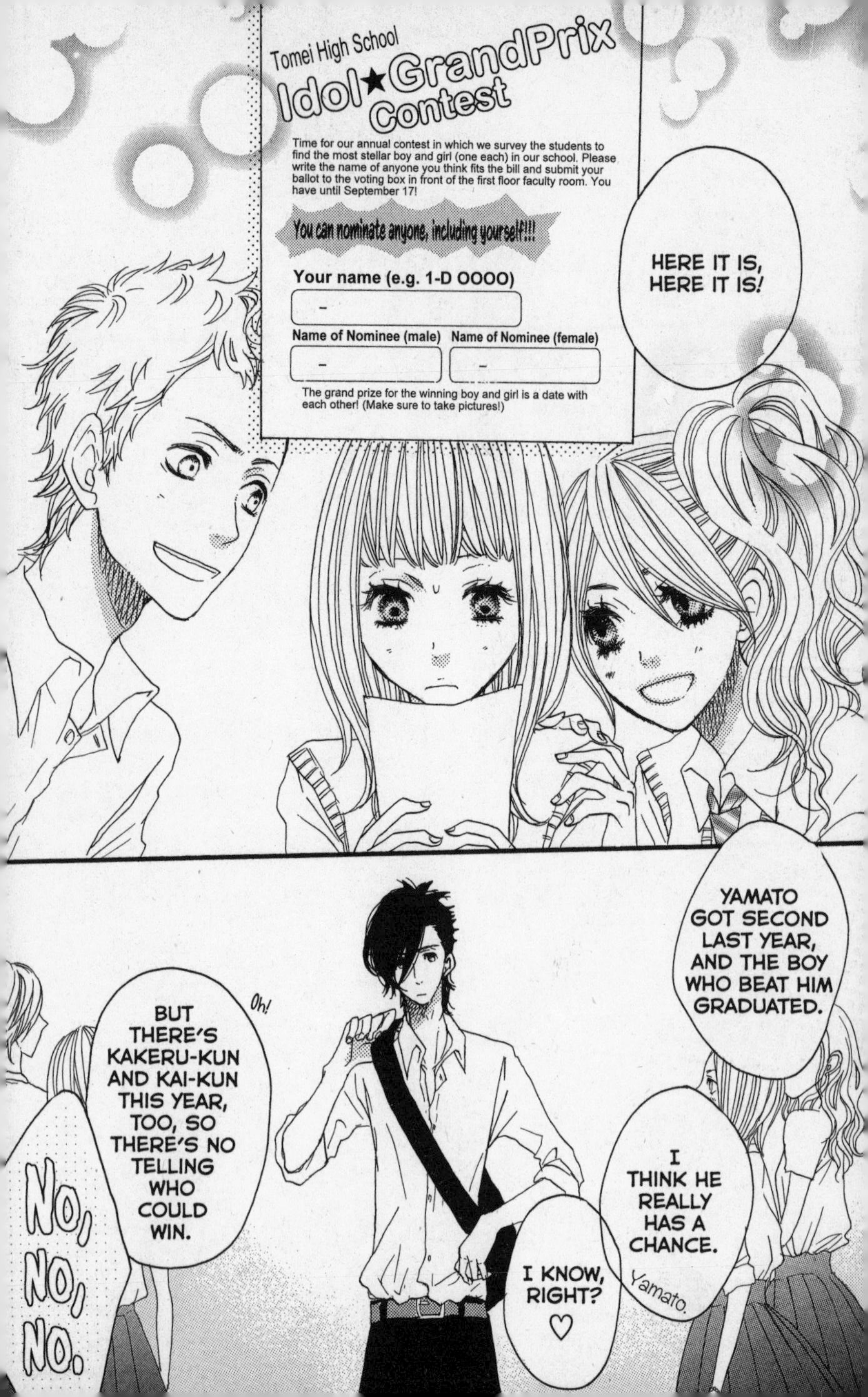
Tomei High School
Idol★GrandPrix Contest
Time for our annual contest in which we survey the students to find the most stellar boy and girl (one each) in our school. Please write the name of anyone you think fits the bill and submit your ballot to the voting box in front of the first floor faculty room. You have until September 17!
You can nominate anyone, including yourself!!!
Your name (e.g. 1-D OOOO)
Name of Nominee (male)
Name of Nominee (female)
The grand prize for the winning boy and girl is a date with each other! (Make sure to take pictures!)
HERE IT IS, HERE IT IS!
YAMATO GOT SECOND LAST YEAR, AND THE BOY WHO BEAT HIM GRADUATED.
I THINK HE REALLY HAS A CHANCE.
Yamato.
I KNOW, RIGHT? ♡
Oh!
BUT THERE'S KAKERU-KUN AND KAI-KUN THIS YEAR, TOO, SO THERE'S NO TELLING WHO COULD WIN.
NO, NO, NO.

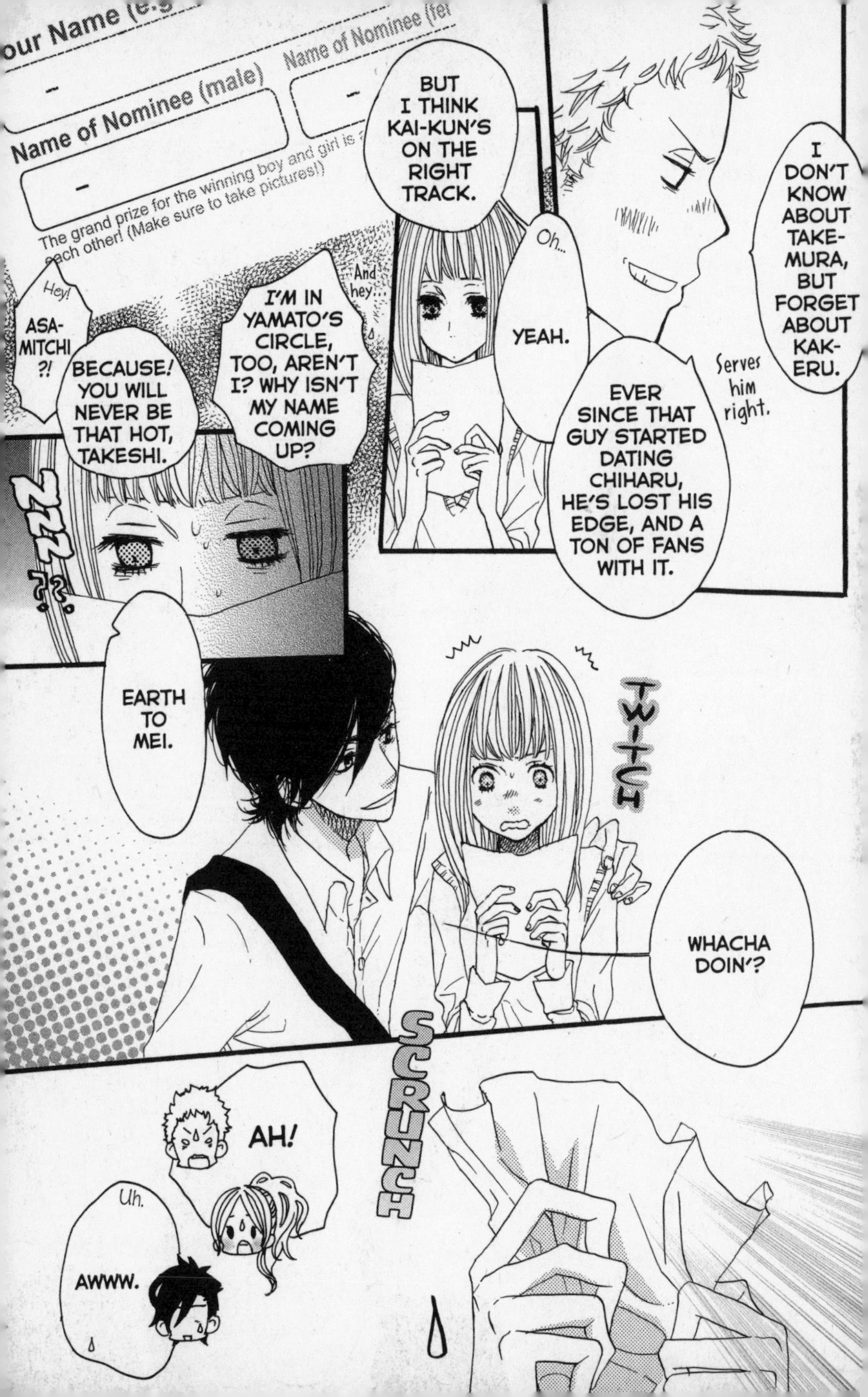
I DON'T KNOW ABOUT TAKE-MURA, BUT FORGET ABOUT KAK-ERU.
Serves him right.
EVER SINCE THAT GUY STARTED DATING CHIHARU, HE'S LOST HIS EDGE, AND A TON OF FANS WITH IT.
BUT I THINK KAI-KUN'S ON THE RIGHT TRACK.
Oh...
YEAH.
our Name (e.g
Name of Nominee (fe
Name of Nominee (male)
The grand prize for the winning boy and girl is a
each other! (Make sure to take pictures!)
And hey...
I'M IN YAMATO'S CIRCLE, TOO, AREN'T I? WHY ISN'T MY NAME COMING UP?
Hey!
ASA-MITCHI?!
BECAUSE! YOU WILL NEVER BE THAT HOT, TAKESHI.
???
EARTH TO MEI.
TWITCH
WHACHA DOIN'?
SCRUNCH
AH!
Uh.
AWWW.

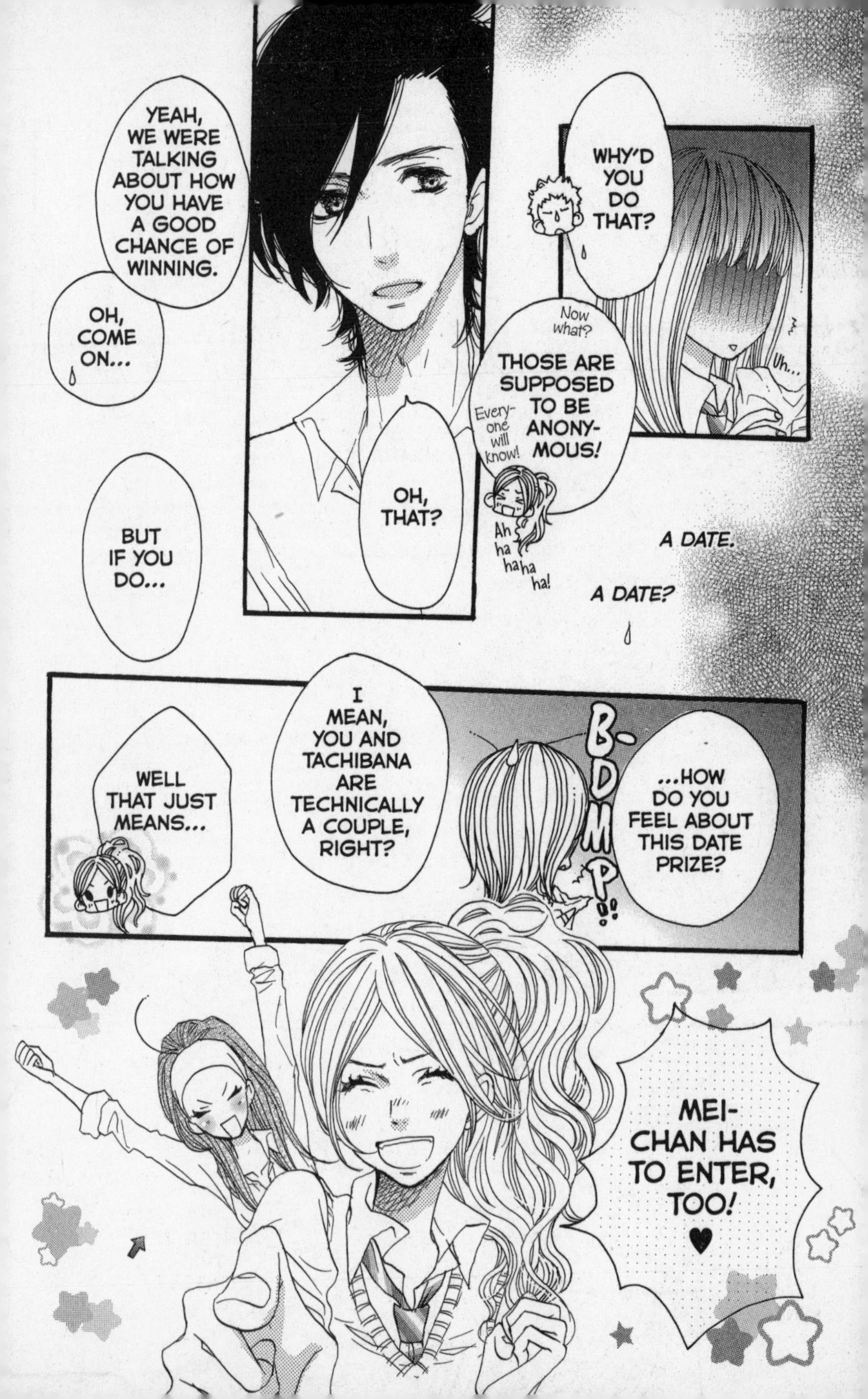
WHY'D YOU DO THAT?
Uh...
THOSE ARE SUPPOSED TO BE ANONYMOUS!
Now what?
Everyone will know!
Ah ha ha ha ha!
OH, THAT?
YEAH, WE WERE TALKING ABOUT HOW YOU HAVE A GOOD CHANCE OF WINNING.
OH, COME ON...
A DATE.
A DATE?
BUT IF YOU DO...
...HOW DO YOU FEEL ABOUT THIS DATE PRIZE?
B-DUMP!!
I MEAN, YOU AND TACHIBANA ARE TECHNICALLY A COUPLE, RIGHT?
WELL THAT JUST MEANS...
MEI-CHAN HAS TO ENTER, TOO! ♥

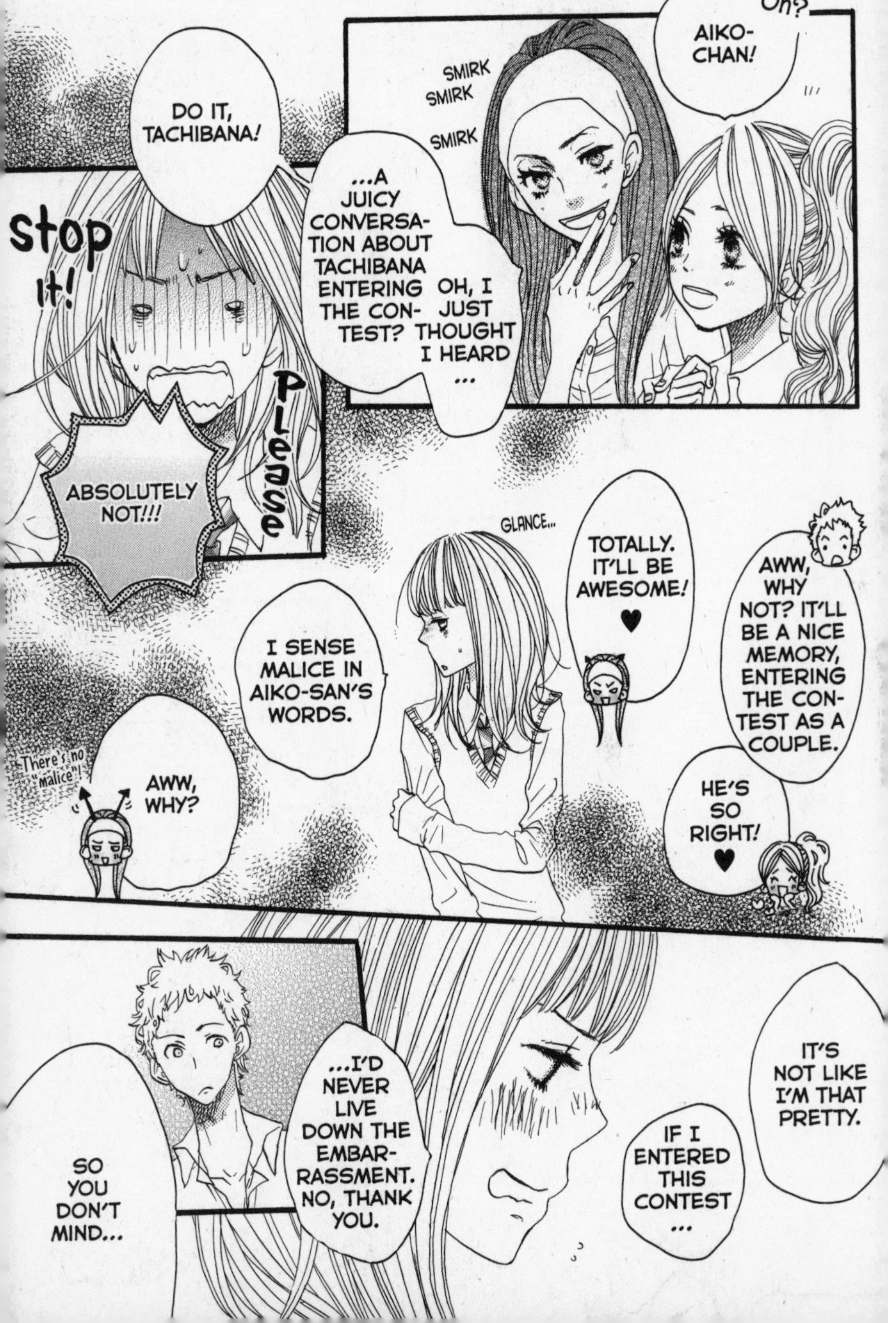
Oh?
AIKO-CHAN!
SMIRK SMIRK SMIRK
...A JUICY CONVERSATION ABOUT TACHIBANA ENTERING THE CONTEST? OH, I JUST THOUGHT I HEARD ...
DO IT, TACHIBANA!
stop it!
Please
ABSOLUTELY NOT!!!
AWW, WHY NOT? IT'LL BE A NICE MEMORY, ENTERING THE CONTEST AS A COUPLE.
HE'S SO RIGHT! ♥
TOTALLY. IT'LL BE AWESOME! ♥
GLANCE...
I SENSE MALICE IN AIKO-SAN'S WORDS.
AWW, WHY?
There's no "malice"!
IT'S NOT LIKE I'M THAT PRETTY.
IF I ENTERED THIS CONTEST ...
...I'D NEVER LIVE DOWN THE EMBARRASSMENT. NO, THANK YOU.
SO YOU DON'T MIND...

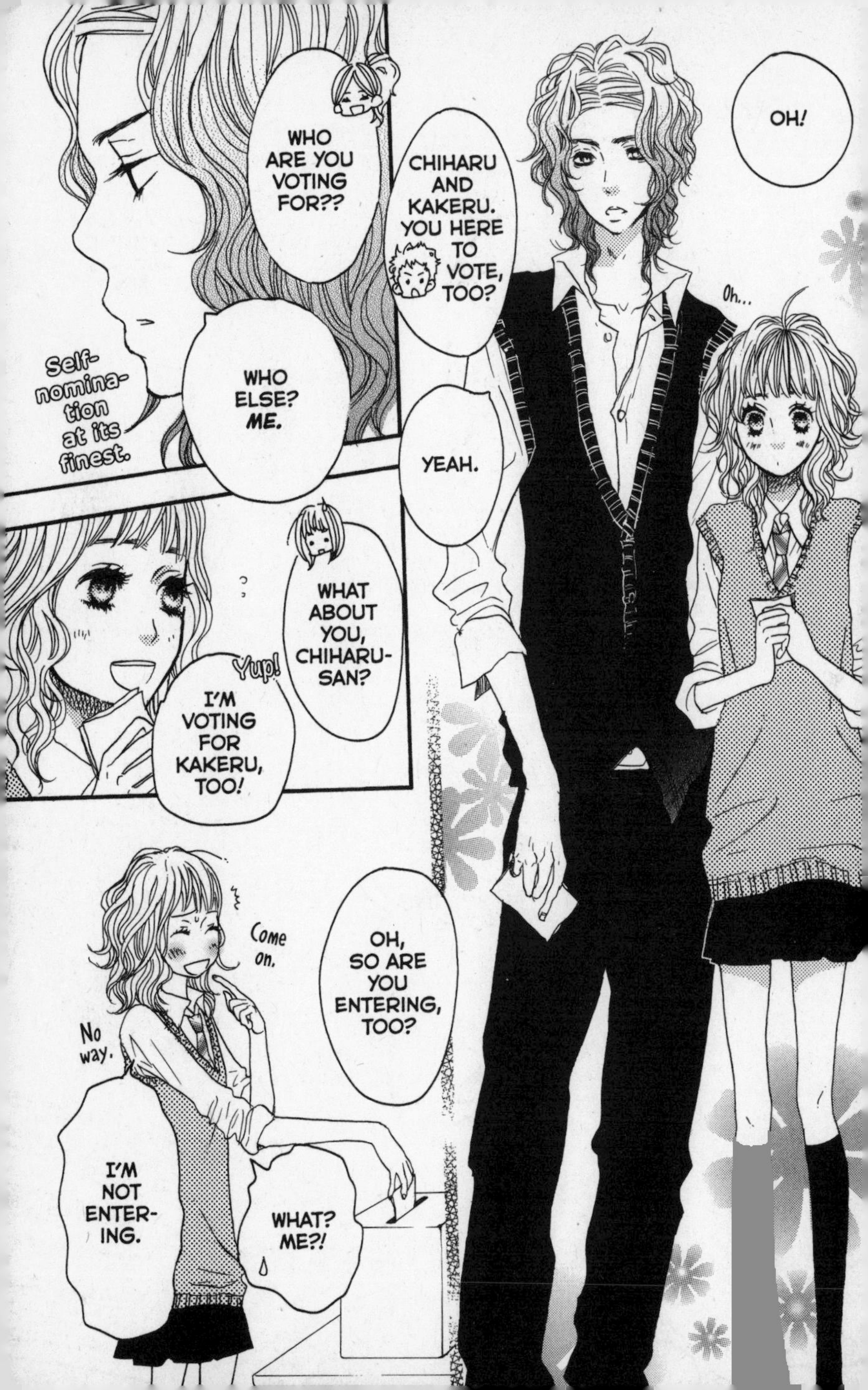
OH!
Oh...
CHIHARU AND KAKERU. YOU HERE TO VOTE, TOO?
YEAH.
WHO ARE YOU VOTING FOR??
WHO ELSE? ME.
Self-nomination at its finest.
WHAT ABOUT YOU, CHIHARU-SAN?
Yup!
I'M VOTING FOR KAKERU, TOO!
OH, SO ARE YOU ENTERING, TOO?
Come on.
WHAT? ME?!
No way.
I'M NOT ENTERING.

A Kodansha Comics Trade Paperback Original
Say I Love You. volume 7 copyright © 2011 Kanae Hazuki
English translation copyright © 2015 Kanae Hazuki

Published in the United States by Kodansha Comics, an imprint of Kodansha USA Publishing, LLC, New York.

Publication rights for this English edition arranged through Kodansha Ltd, Tokyo.

First published in Japan in 2011 by Kodansha Ltd., Tokyo as *Sukitte iinayo.* volume 7.

ISBN 978-1-61262-672-7

Printed in the United States of America.

www.kodanshacomics.com

9 8 7 6 5 4 3 2 1
Translation: Alethea and Athena Nibley
Lettering: John Clark
Editing: Ben Applegate
Kodansha Comics edition cover design by Phil Balsman